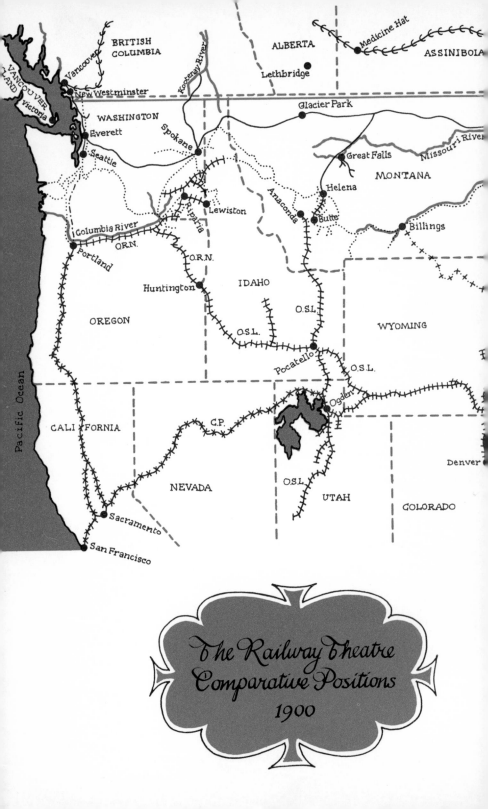

The Railway Theatre
Comparative Positions
1900

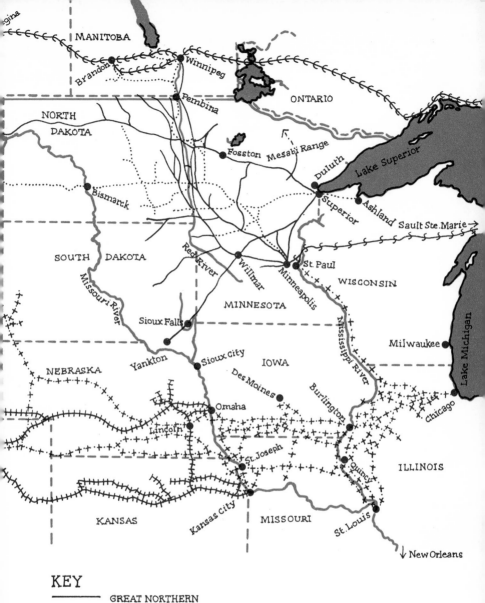

KEY

——————— GREAT NORTHERN

················ NORTHERN PACIFIC

+ · + · + · CHICAGO, BURLINGTON and QUINCY

++++++++ UNION PACIFIC including OREGON LINES (O.R.N. O.SL.)

×××××× SOUTHERN PACIFIC including CENTRAL PACIFIC (C.P.)

℮℮℮℮℮℮ CANADIAN PACIFIC

ς-ς-ς-ς-ς SOO LINE

The End of the Road

THE LIFE OF LORD MOUNT STEPHEN

Volume II: 1891–1921

Heather Gilbert

The End of the Road

THE LIFE OF LORD MOUNT STEPHEN

Volume II : 1891-1921

Aberdeen University Press

First published 1977

© Heather Gilbert 1977

ISBN 0 900015 38 1

Printed in
Great Britain at the
Aberdeen University Press

LORD MOUNT STEPHEN
(*William Notman, Montreal*)

For Ian

Preface

THE first volume of the Life of Lord Mount Stephen, *Awakening Continent*, owed much to the subject's correspondence with one man, Sir John A. Macdonald, Prime Minister of Canada during construction of the Canadian Pacific Railway. Similarly the second volume is based to a great extent on the letter books of Gaspard Farrer, merchant banker in the City of London, who over their forty years' acquaintance gradually became Mount Stephen's *alter ego*. After the latter's death in 1921 Farrer, who was his executor, could find nothing among his friend's papers which could be preserved for a 'Life': 'he so persistently destroyed letters and papers' he wrote to Mount Stephen's nephew, Frank Meighen. In the same vein he told Charles S. MacInnes of Toronto, a brother of Mount Stephen's former secretary: ' . . . I believe Beverley . . . had a great bonfire . . . After all, though Lord Mount Stephen was such a big man and so broad in his views his life was of necessity confined to business and business interests, and the history of his main work, the C.P.R., is by now a twice told tale. I am not therefore very hopeful that anyone will be able to do more than a little memoir sketch, and personally I doubt whether Lord Mount Stephen would have wished anything more should be done . . .'. Mount Stephen retired to England for roughly the last thirty years of his long life, but continued to play an influential, if less active role in transatlantic projects, these being latterly more American than Canadian. Farrer, still close to the events of these years, seemed unaware that his own correspondence with their business contacts and friends would prove so revealing.

This book does not claim to be a definitive biography. New material continues to become available, from the papers of James J. Hill, Mount Stephen's close associate in American railroading, to the handed-down oral evidence of their gardien's wife at the Stephens' Quebec fishing-lodge, which has just come to light. We may well have reached not the end of the road but only the point of departure.

I have to acknowledge the gracious permission of Her Majesty the Queen to make use of material in the Royal Archives at Windsor Castle. I should like to thank the following for their help over the years in providing, or directing me to research material, or for advice: the Directors of Baring Brothers and Company for permitting me to see Gaspard Farrer's letter books, Mr. Duncan Stirling who placed the letter books with Barings and the Barings archivist, Mr. T. L. Ingram; the Provost and Fellows of Eton for permission to use the portrait of Gaspard Farrer; Mrs. G. F. Geddes, daughter of General Frank S. Meighen, C.M.G., and her husband, the late Dr. Aubrey Geddes, for family material; the late Beatrice Hampson (Mrs. Robert Hampson), for allowing me to see letters from Lord and Lady Mount Stephen to her father, Colonel George Stephen Cantlie, D.S.O.—it was he who first told me of Gaspard Farrer's connection with Mount Stephen—and for the Notman photograph of her great-uncle; Mr. Eric Reford for his own recollections and those of his mother, Mrs. R. W. Reford, and for the use of letters and of the Countess Roberts' map of the Metis River: he also read part of the manuscript; the late Colonel the Honourable A. C. Campbell, Chapelhead, Avoch, Ross-shire, for lending me Charles Ellis's Diary of 1860; the Honourable Mr. Justice Gordon C. Hall for help in tracing Manitoba material; Professor Gerald S. Graham for his continued interest and for reading a section in draft; Professor Peter B. Waite for directing me to source material; Professor Albro Martin whose book *James J. Hill and the Opening of the Northwest* (New York 1976) had just gone to press: he kindly read at short notice part of my manuscript and permitted me to read part of his (the Hill papers were not then generally available); Stein and Day, Publishers, for permission to quote from David Farrer, *The Warburgs*; Miss C. A. Imlach, Aberchirder, the late Miss Elizabeth Grant, Dufftown, and the late Alex. Rattray, Burntreble, Lower Cabrach, for local material; my late father, the Reverend Francis Cantlie Donald, for much Banffshire lore, for information on the Church of Scotland's Mount Stephen Trust and for his own recollection of the Strathcona Banquet; Mr. Richard Storey, Historical Manuscripts Commission, who drew my attention to the Wolseley archive; Hove Area Library and the Wolseley Librarian there, Miss Judith Dale; the King's Fund Centre and London County Record Office for information and records of King Edward's Hospital Fund for London; the

James J. Hill Reference Library, St. Paul, Minnesota, for the photograph of Mr. and Mrs. Hill and for permission to publish it; the Public Archives of Canada (PAC in *notes*) and the Provincial Archives of Manitoba, who helped me make the most of brief return visits; Canadian Pacific for permission to quote from the Van Horne–Stephen letter books; Aberdeen Public Library; the Royal Commonwealth Society Library; the United States Library of the University of London; Forest Hill Library, London Borough of Lewisham, whose readers' request service produced an almost endless procession of books both old and new.

The greater part of the cost of setting up and printing this volume was met by subventions from the Northwest Area Foundation (formerly the Louis W. and Maud Hill Family Foundation) of St. Paul, Minnesota, and the Grotto Foundation of St. Paul.

Finally I must acknowledge the unfailing co-operation of my husband, Ian Grant Gilbert.

Forest Hill   HEATHER GILBERT
London, February 1977

Contents

Illustrations

I

Gathering notes

THE WOLSELEY CONNECTION: SALMON-FISHING IN
SCOTLAND

ON the twenty-fourth of May 1891 General Lord Wolseley, then
Commander-in-Chief, Ireland, wrote to his wife from Faskally
House, Pitlochry, where he was spending Whitsuntide week with
Sir George and Lady Stephen:

... A profound secret—not to be told to anyone but Frances—Can you
guess? Well—Stephen is to be made a peer! I have seen Lord Salisbury's
letter telling him of it. He has not yet chosen his title so I don't suppose
it can be in the Birthday Gazette but he means to be Lord Mount
Stephen ... Mount Stephen, called after him, is the highest point in the
Rocky Mountains through which his Rail Road runs. I think the idea is a
very good one.

Write to Lady Stephen at once and congratulate her, telling her how
much we appreciate having been told the news in confidence ...[1]

The following day he wrote again:

... I wish every peer was half as good a fellow as our good friend Stephen.
I never knew people so absolutely unchanged by richness and from my
heart I only wish they were ten times as rich as they are ...[2]

Lady Wolseley's reply was equally enthusiastic: '... I have written
to her to congratulate. One does it with good heart to those dear
nice people who deserve all the good they can get. What a pity
there are no children ...'[3]

The Stephens' friendship with the Wolseleys, which circumstances were to render very close indeed, dated back to the 1860's,
when Wolseley, after service in the Crimea and in China, was posted
to Montreal as Deputy Quartermaster General on Headquarters
Staff, Canada. The Stephens had been among the first to welcome
Garnet's bride, Louisa Erskine, on her arrival in Canada in 1867.

[1] Wolseley Papers (Hove, Sussex) W/P20.
[2] W/P 20.   [3] LW/P17.

When in 1870 Colonel Wolseley was sent west with a force of British regulars and Canadian militiamen to the scene of the first Riel rebellion at Red River, Louisa had remained with them in Montreal. Stephen became godfather to their only child, a daughter, Frances Garnet, born on 15 September 1872; he walked the seven miles from his London house in St. James's to the christening at Mortlake, his gift to the baby being a thousand pounds. From the 1890s, when the Stephens were mostly, and then permanently, resident in England, they saw a good deal of each other.

When Queen Victoria wrote to Stephen on 2 June 1891 approving of his choice of title, she added:

The Queen is glad of this opportunity to be able to thank him for his great kindness to her children and grandchildren, and has often heard her dear son Leopold and the Duchess of Albany speak of his and Lady Stephen's kindness to their little children.[1]

Stephen had rented Faskally for four years, chiefly for the salmon-fishing. The Whitsun house party consisted of General Sir Donald Stewart (known in this circle as 'the old warrior' he had been succeeded in 1885 as Commander-in-Chief, India, by General Sir Frederick Roberts) Beverley MacInnes, Stephen's Canadian secretary, and Alice, the Stephens' adopted daughter and her husband Henry Stafford Northcote, member of Parliament for Exeter. Later they were joined by Lord Elphinstone and General Sir John McNeill, an old member of the Wolseley 'Ring', the coterie of young officers who had followed Garnet into a number of military adventures. Under the Stephens' hospitable roof no account was taken of the professional jealousy between British and Indian Army: guests of both camps were subjected alike to their host's agreeable banter.

Garnet had mixed feelings about life at Faskally, writing to Louisa in characteristically facetious and inconsistent terms on 19 May:

... This is a lovely place "doon by the Toomle and banks of the Garry" ... a line in the song of "Bonnie Prince Charlie". Well I have been fishing where those two rivers join this morning and indeed last night also. The river is full of salmon they jump and play leap frog with one another all round your fly but will have nothing to do with it ... We are close to the pass of Killiecrankie where the great Battle was fought in

---

[1] A much-altered draft is in the Royal Archives, Windsor: RA A68/38; the letter sent is in the possession of Mrs. G. F. Geddes, Montreal.

1689 or 1690 (I forget which). Then Blair Athol with the Duke in it is also close at hand. This House is comfortable but absolutely uninteresting without any one pretty or even nice thing in it. The river is not more than sixty yards from the house and the fishing is all close to the house. Alice went out riding yesterday and little Harry, who does not fish, or as far as I can see do anything, moons about like a poor relation—has however grown fat. I wonder if he has any enjoyment in life and if he has what is it? Alice is looking old and very plain. Lady Stephen as nice and genial as ever: Stephen just the same good fellow he always was with plenty of fun in him and looking so much better and younger than when I saw him last in London . . .[1]

Stephen himself compared Faskally unfavourably with his Canadian fishing haunts: 'Tell Lady Macdonald', he had written to the Canadian Prime Minister on 12 April 1891, 'that salmon fishing in Scotland is not half the fun it is in Canada. The fish like the people slow and deliberate in their movements—why it should be so puzzles me. The river I have is the Tummel—a tributary of the Tay—a very pretty stream, though far behind the Matapedia, which I hope never to miss again so long as I am able to throw a fly or as the Yankees have it "sling a bug" . . .'[2] His cousin Sir Donald Smith also had a fishing lodge on the Matapedia, but so little was it frequented that over the years it fell into disrepair.[3]

On 22 May Garnet was able to tell Louisa that he had landed his first salmon, which Stephen had immediately despatched to her. He continued his observations on the house party:

. . . I can see that Alice's adopted parents bore her intensely although she is clever enough not to let them realize this fact. She plays very nicely, but I don't think she ever reads. Her mind is always on Belgravia and its uninteresting and snobbish inhabitants. I hope never again to have much to do with them. It is an unwholesome atmosphere more destructive to all that is naturally good in man or woman than living over a foul drain can be to physical health.[4]

The latter hazard was acknowledged to be a feature of life at the Royal Hospital, Dublin. One of the reasons Lady Wolseley gave (or kept to herself) for not accepting invitations to stay with friends was that she could not bear to contemplate ugliness. She declared herself to have an eighteenth century mind, and delighted in the

[1] W/P 20.
[2] Macdonald Papers 272 (Public Archives of Canada).
[3] Strathcona Papers MG29 A5 vol. 3. (PAC).
[4] W/P 20.

interior decoration of her succession of homes. Even when her husband, to whom she was devoted, had home postings she contrived to run one or more separate establishments. If not in one of these she liked to sojourn at one of Europe's fashionable spas. Marienbad was a favourite until it became unfashionable. One consequence of these constant separations was a two-way stream of somewhat trivial if frequently witty correspondence. At this particular time— 1891—Louisa was preoccupied with launching their eighteen-year-old daughter on her first London season, a campaign that vied with any of General Wolseley's as to strategy and tactics.

Already social gossip was linking the name of Frances Wolseley with that of young Hugh Morrison, grandson of George Stephen's early mentor, James Morrison, M.P. Lady Wolseley had reported early in May on Lady Chetwode's ball:

... I went in to supper with *Hugh Morrison* which had not the smallest significance, but the mothers all jumped on their chairs and thought it was the beginning of the end ...[1]

Frances herself was taking the whole operation very calmly indeed. She liked dancing and hunting but could hardly have been called frivolous. Mothers agreed that she was 'different'. She collected bookplates, and Garnet wrote to her mother from Faskally that the Stephens and Northcotes all had bookplates of which he was to send copies to Frances. He continued:

... The Stephens pay £1800 a year for this place and will see very little of it, as they go back to Canada about the end of July. The Harry Northcotes are to have *their* friends here for the grouse shooting in August. I don't think Lady Stephen likes this place, *she* misses London and the society and gossip of that vile Sodom and Gomorrah.[2]

This last remark was prompted possibly more by Garnet's often-expressed contempt for Society as the Wolseleys encountered it than by any avowal on the part of Annie Charlotte Stephen. The fragmentary evidence available as to the personality of the latter suggests that Lady Wolseley's unusually warm affection for her was entirely justified. It is significant that Louisa could write without envy of meeting 'the dear Stephens' in March 1891 at a dinner at Lord Knutsford's 'to meet' Princess Louise: '... Lady Stephen had a *magnificent* diamond necklace on. She is very, very nice',[3] and later, comparing her with Alice Northcote, whom she

[1] LW/P 17.   [2] W/P20.   [3] LW/P17.

disliked, 'Dear Lady Stephen is worth ten thousand of her. She is very genuine and kind and always the same'.[1]

Garnet wrote on 24 May that Harry Northcote, the Whitsun recess over, was returning to his parliamentary duties:

... His tummy is assuming that rounded form which the sleek, well-fed and nothing to do but prosperous citizen affects in due time. I think George Stephen is at times a little disappointed with him, that he does nothing in parliament. He can speak very well, and as you know he has plenty of natural wit and ability. Of course if he won't speak, he cannot hope to be employed. I had a very pleasant ride with Alice yesterday through lovely scenery. She has no nerve and beyond a *very* gentle trot up hill now and then we went all the time at a foot's pace. She is not witty or brilliant, but full of very worldly wisdom. No two people could be devoted more deeply and sincerely to a woman or to a child than the Stephens are to her. To all appearances her feelings towards them are as strong. She spoke a great deal about Frances and assured me she was the nicest and most natural girl she had ever known. She said she heard her praises sung in all quarters for her grace and simplicity, mingled with natural dignity. Lady Stephen showed me a number of things which had just come from a dealer whom they employ. He had bought them at Christie's at the Fitzclarence sale. She had sent for them to choose a present for Alice's birthday, now at hand. She said Alice already had more jewelry than she knew what to do with so she wished to give her a present of another kind. By my advice she selected a lovely piece of plate, and bought a delightful miniature for herself...[2]

Harry Northcote had entered the House of Commons in 1880. Born in 1846 he had been educated at Eton and Merton, and after a brief spell in the Foreign Office had accompanied Lord Salisbury as his private secretary on his 1876 mission to Constantinople. He then became private secretary to his father, Sir Stafford Northcote (later Earl of Iddesleigh, he was then Chancellor of the Exchequer and Leader of the House of Commons), until the change of Government in 1880. In the brief Conservative administration of 1885–6 he had been Financial Secretary to the War Office.

The next experience in store for Garnet was that of a Presbyterian sabbath; although in partly Gaelic-speaking country, the 'most dismal and trying service' (whether in Pitlochry or at the nearer church of Tenandry) would at least have been conducted in the English tongue. The day ended more happily for Garnet with the

[1] LW/P 17.   [2] W/P20.

unexpected discovery of just such a permanent perch as occasionally he dreamed of sharing with his inherently migratory mate:

... we all walked up the river Garry and through the pass of Killiecrankie ... We paid a visit to a Miss Stewart, such a nice old maiden lady. Her house is perched on the side of the pass, with the river running below her. Whenever I see a little house like hers, such as a few maid servants could run, situated in the country and far from other human habitation, I always think how happy you and I might be in such a home, with all our dogs and books about us, and no horrid society people to worry us ...[1]

Before the end of his stay at Faskally, he was to see Alice North-cote in a new light. The official account of her adoption, at the age of sixteen, by the Stephens—she then assumed their surname—was given in volume I. The whole truth is now unlikely to be revealed, but Wolseley's last letter to his wife from Faskally, and his next from Dublin, suggest that a version later uncovered by his own daughter Frances (that Alice was the daughter of Mrs. Stephen's charwoman and an alcoholic tradesman, adopted in childhood after the mother died)[2] had some foundation in fact:

... I went out for a four hours' ride with Alice yesterday "over the mountains and far away". She was extremely nice. I have come to like her very much and feel that I was in my mind unjust to her oftentimes in thinking her a humbug ...[3]

... Alice was I must say extremely nice and kind, and when we meet and I tell you all she told me I think you will somewhat alter your opinion of her ... During our last ride she talked a great deal about the Stephens and gave me an account of her whole life which has been until lately a very sad one and which even now has many drawbacks. She cried a good deal as she told me of her young childhood and the misery she under-went. But I must not write it. Don't tell this even to Frances.

I really believe she has the greatest admiration for you. She certainly thinks you the cleverest and wittiest woman she has ever known and thinks you a delightful picture to look at. She says she does not know any nice young men, and I can quite understand it, for until Frances wanted partners, neither did you.[4]

[1] W/P20.

[2] Papers of Frances, Viscountess Wolseley (PVW) 201, Sir Algernon Law to Lady Wolseley, 1 June 1935. Other versions were current, for example that Alice was the daughter of a clergyman from Vermont, USA, whom Mrs. Stephen rescued from a life of drudgery.

[3] W/P20.   [4] Ibid.

The subject of this last eulogy received all this with a certain amount of scepticism:

... I am longing to hear what Alice N. told you. She seems quite to have got round *you*!! I confess I find her rather oppressively patronizing *and* I find she does not do anything to help one. Why not ask us to dinner? She gives lot of parties. Tonight she is taking F. to the Opera so that is something.[1]

Louisa had already tackled Alice on the subject of 'nice young men' during a ball at Hatfield, the Marquess of Salisbury's house, in January. Alice had assured her that *the* young man to cultivate was Mr. Victor Cavendish, a future Duke of Devonshire. 'He is hideous', Louisa had reported to Garnet 'with the Cavendish underlip, but they say nice and even witty. Frances danced twice with him, but so she did with all the young men in the house ...'[2] They had in fact dined with Alice three weeks previously and occupied her box at the Opera, Lady Wolseley then complaining to her husband:

... She is a horrid little humbug. She took us on a second rate night ... In the morning she rushed here to say she could not go to the Opera *with* us, as Sir George Stephen had arrived unexpectedly and she could not leave him alone, but must go herself with him to another theatre! It was most mysterious, for I don't believe sensible Sir George would arrive "sans crier gare" and upset her arrangements ... She was really, I may say, *vulgar* ... treating us quite like country cousins ...[3]

Alice might well have been tempted to grasp an opportunity to be seen at the theatre alone with her 'adopted parent'. The editor of the Montreal *Gazette*, recording some reminiscences by Stephen's niece, Mrs. Reford, wrote:

Lord Mount Stephen is remembered as a man of imposing appearance; a presence that was felt at once. He had a finely shaped head and finely shaped hands. In a theatre cloak and opera hat, he was so commanding a figure that people would turn round and stare ...[4]

In March Louisa had told Garnet that Sir George Stephen seemed angry with Alice for 'wearing herself out with society dinners, luncheons, teas, all day long ... she is quite exhausted and hysterical ... I don't think they see her as much as they used to ...'[5]

[1] LW/P17.   [2] Ibid.   [3] Ibid.
[4] From recollections of Mrs. R. W. Reford, told to E. A. Collard of the Montreal *Gazette*.   [5] LW/P17.

At all events she was obliged to report on 29 May that at the Opera the previous evening Alice had 'comblée'd' Frances with attentions, afterwards taking her on to a party at Chesterfield House and to another at 'Bisch's' (Mrs Bischoffsheim's). Again on 4 June Frances was dining with the Northcotes and going on to the Opera.

In addition to their preoccupation with their daughter at this time the Wolseleys were much concerned with the question of their own future. In February 1891 Garnet had written from Dublin to Louisa at Ranger's House, Richmond Park, which had for some time been their permanent base:

> ... I miss you very very much, even although you do bully me. Whenever I have been away from you before, it was because I was doing something: but now I am doing nothing beyond getting old. My hopes are gone and very soon I shall take no interest whatever in life ...[1]

At the age of fifty-eight the man who had been known as 'our only General' was beginning to find life an anticlimax. Desk work did not appeal to him; his efforts to modernize the army had met with only limited success under the regime of the Duke of Cambridge, Commander-in-Chief now for thirty-five years. Even Wolseley's military talents had never been fully exploited; all his wars had been 'little' wars. What was perhaps his most genuine ambition—to die gloriously in battle—was unlikely now to be achieved. What was he to do? He turned instinctively to the man to whom, some twelve years later, he was to dedicate his memoirs: to George Stephen.

In her letter of 7 January 1891 Louisa had written:

> ... Alice Northcote tells me—which is rather dreadful—that the Stephens won't go to Canada till August this year as they have taken this place in Scotland, *but* they would like you *there* ...

What was 'dreadful' to Louisa was that she and Garnet had been cherishing the hope that Wolseley might be appointed Governor-General of Canada in succession to Lord Stanley. With Stephen on the spot some influence might, they thought, have been brought to bear, either with the retiring Governor-General or with the Prime Minister, Sir John A. Macdonald. But only eight days later Garnet learned from General Sir Redvers Buller, his late colleague at the War Office and another 'Ring' member, that he was not to go to

[1] W/P20.

Canada. To Louisa he commented wryly: 'I thought little Stanhope [Secretary of State for the Colonies, formerly at the War Office] would have been only too glad to have put the Atlantic between me and him'.[1] Wolseley was by no means universally popular, despite his place in public esteem.

Although Stephen deserved in full the credit for 'unvarying friendship' attributed to him in the dedication of Wolseley's memoirs, and regarded his friend with undoubted affection, he did not necessarily act in accordance with the Wolseleys' every passing whim. He certainly made no mention of the Governor-Generalship in his letters to Macdonald, and would probably much have preferred to broach such a subject personally if at all. It is with some surprise that one finds him, in a letter to Macdonald in May 1889, setting out the reasons why Sir Adolphe Caron should not be made Minister of Railways in succession to the late John Henry Pope, albeit adding 'Pardon my venturing to trouble you thus'.[2] In the event Macdonald became his own Railways Minister.

CANADIAN PACIFIC: AFTERMATH AND FUTURE PROSPECTS

Stephen was looking forward to his visit to Canada, to spending the Fall at his new fishing lodge at Grand Metis and to seeing the Macdonalds before they left their country home at St. Patrick, near Rivière du Loup.[3] The previous year, full of the grievances and frustrations which had attended his efforts to tidy up the affairs of the Canadian Pacific and its relations with the Department of Railways, he had finally left Canada in August without paying a farewell visit to Macdonald's Quebec home. Writing to Macdonald on 29 July 1890 about the railway matters still outstanding, he had concluded: 'We go up to Metis tomorrow. I feel sure under the circumstances you will agree with me that it is better I should not go up to Rivière du Loup'.[4] Stephen wrote again on 7 August, after the ' "short line" source of irritation' had been disposed of, leaving the British Columbia arbitration as the chief bone of contention. He could not resist enclosing a letter which he had written to Macdonald on 3 September 1889 but which had not at the time been sent as it seemed that the short line and land matters were about to be settled. His successor in the presidency of the C.P.R.,

[1] W/P20.
[2] Macdonald Papers 271.
[3] Macdonald Papers 272.
[4] Ibid.

William C. Van Horne, was preparing, too, a narrative with 'chapter and verse of all our complaints'. 'We sail on the 20th from New York', he concluded, 'I have some heavy financial operations on hand for the C.P.R. . . . Once I get these out of hand I shall then be free and better able to keep calm about C.P.R. matters . . .'[1]

This called forth from Macdonald the placid response:

. . . I regret very much that we are not to have a quiet talk on the past and future of the C.P.R., and the various questions which seem to cause you annoyance. I really think you have allowed your mind to dwell too much on these irritating matters instead of considering them as naturally arising out of every great work. If we only knew all Villard's troubles on the progress of the Northern Pacific, we I think would find them to exceed yours infinitely both in quality and quantity. The point of view to take is that the C.P.R. is prosperous and likely to be more prosperous, and that all past annoyances should be forgotten.

As we are not to have a meeting and a quiet chat I think it would answer no good purpose to enter upon a correspondence in writing as to your real or supposed grievances. It would be never ending and would make matters worse. All I can say is of the causes which prevent our acting with complete cordiality—you don't, I think, give sufficient thought to the troubles and difficulties which beset the Government and you have exaggerated our power—forgetting that we have a strong opposition and a watchful press which charge us with being mere tools of the C.P.R.—and not knowing that more than once we were deserted by our own Parliamentary friends in Caucus and that it was only my individual power over them that enabled us on more than one occasion to come to your relief. I trust that . . . when you return (you) will find the C.P.R. as flourishing as both you and I wish it. I hope that the next fortnight will give us assurance of a bountiful harvest in the North West and then everything will blossom like the rose.[2]

Stephen received Macdonald's letter at his Montreal house en route from Metis to New York and the steamer. He had no premonitions himself that he would never again see his friend at Rivière du Loup, but he paused to scribble a last farewell:

I must send you a line before leaving to say goodbye to you and Lady Macdonald and tell you how pleased I was to get your letter of 13th this morning only. I *know* you do not *mean* to be either unfriendly or unfair to the C.P.R. But that has not saved the Company from much that cannot be said to be either fair or friendly on the part of the Government . . .

[1] Ibid. The enclosed letter of 3 September 1889 was quoted at length in *Awakening Continent*: The Life of Lord Mount Stephen, vol. 1, p. 242.
[2] Macdonald Letter Book 27. 124.

To the last minute he reiterated what was in his mind until 'The cab is at the door. Goodbye—Love to Lady Macdonald and to Mary. Always yours, Geo. Stephen'.[1]

For the next six months Stephen's letters to Macdonald dealt with every topic of current interest except that of the British Columbia arbitration: relations between Canada and the United States; the prospect of a new Atlantic steamship service from Canada; improvement of communications between Canada and the Far East and Australia; the Barings crisis; the latest manifestation of unfriendliness to the C.P.R. by the Manitoba government; the Canadian General Election of 1891. On 21 October 1890 Stephen wrote from his London home, 25 St. James's Place:

Today being the Tenth anniversary of the signing of the C.P.R. contract I must send you a line, if only to remind you of the fact and to offer my sincere congratulations that you are today in infinitely better health and with a far better prospect of its continuance for many years to come than could with truth be claimed in 1880. I am thankful that we are both here and able to point to the completed contract, when occasion calls up the hostility with which the enterprise was assailed during the years 1880/86. You doubtless have forgotten long ago Tyler's attack on the Company in 1883 when we were trying to make a market for the C.P.R. shares in New York and Amsterdam. He was powerful enough then to make it impossible for us to attempt to offer any shares in London. No one in London would have taken a share at 10¢ on $. I have not a report of Tyler's speech, but you can gather what its drift must have been from my reply inclosed, on which I stumbled the other day among some old papers. The G.T.R. people were "riled" in the highest degree especially Hickson, because of my audacity in venturing to address the shareholders of the G.T.R. Company direct by a circular letter[2] but in those days there was not a newspaper in London who would print anything coming from the C.P.R., or anything from any source, in its favor, so that I had no other way open to me by which I could reach the people Tyler had filled with his rubbish. The publication of the letter had the effect of gaining us a few friends here and of making more steadfast those we had already made, in Holland, &c. At that time, G.T.R. 1st Preference shares were selling here at 109. Last week they were selling at 61. The common shares were 27 they are now about 9½. C.P.R. shares were selling in a small way in New York and Amsterdam about 60/62. They are now about 80, which though nothing to brag about are in marked contrast to G.T.R. experience. If we have thus avoided the failure

[1] Macdonald Papers 272.
[2] Reproduced Gilbert, vol. 1. App. III.

and collapse that have overtaken our overloaded and would-be rival, we are far from having achieved the success which ten years ago both friends and enemies alike predicted. Success—commercially—is still in the future, but with reasonably fair treatment at the hands of the Government and people of Canada it is certain to come, to the extent at least, indicated in the last annual report, viz. that by 1893 the earnings of the Company will be more than sufficient to pay its shareholders a 5% dividend annually. I feel certain it will do this and maybe 6%. But there is nothing in that that can be called a great success. So far, as you know, the net earnings of the railway have yielded the shareholders just two dividends of 1% each, that is, 2% in 10 years out of net earnings. The 3% dividend is nothing but a return of the shareholders' own capital, though the scheme of providing a guaranteed dividend really saved the Company.

Now suppose in 1893 when the guaranteed dividend expires, the Company is able to pay 6% out of earnings instead of 5% as indicated in the last annual report, do you think any man in Canada, or elsewhere, would have invested one shilling in the enterprise in 1880 even if he had had an assurance that after 13 years he would be getting 6% upon his investment from net earnings? It was a merciful thing that the future was hidden from us.

I have been led into this train of thought by the concluding paragraph of Van Horne's letter to you of 26 September to the effect that when "the C.P.R. has received from the Government all it is entitled to under the contract it will still be far from overpaid". It is quite true, what I have more than once said to you that the C.P.R. cannot as yet and judged by results, claim to have achieved a success. It has avoided a collapse and a failure and that is about all, speaking of course in a financial sense. Yet Canada is full of people who ought to know better, who believe it to have been a great "bonanza" to all connected with it, quite ignoring the fact that there is about 150 million $ of private capital that has been "poured" into the concern . . .[1]

Macdonald penned a cordial reply from Ottawa on 10 November:

Many thanks for your reminder of the *birthday* of the C.P.R. What a change that event has made in this Canada of ours! And to think that not until next year was it expected that the infant prodigy would arrive at maturity.

Your health is now fully recovered from the strain that the vast responsibility thrown upon you in nursing the railway entailed. Mine is very fair, but I feel the weight of 76 years greatly. We can both console ourselves for all the worry we have gone through by the reflection that we have done great good to our adopted country, and to the great Empire

[1] Macdonald Papers 272.

of which it forms a part. I have read over again your admirable letter of 1883 to the G.T.R. shareholders.

I think you have great cause for thankfulness at the success of the line, instead of feeling disappointed. Its pecuniary returns within such a short period after construction are almost as remarkable as the unprecedented speed of construction. You, personally, have had an enormous amount of strain, responsibility and worry, but the enterprize has been a success from the beginning.

The Government and Parliament will do what they can to sustain and help the line, but it must be remembered that in 1891 we are to go to the electors, and one cannot foresee the result . . .

After discoursing on some other topics, Macdonald ended by saying: 'I return you the 83 letter', but added a postscript: 'I shall keep the 83 letter after all'.[1] Inevitably the moratorium on discussion of the British Columbia arbitration was lifted by Stephen: the gist of their final exchanges is given in chapter IX of volume I, ending with Stephen's undertaking of 1 May 1891 not to allude to the matter again. In March the General Election had left Macdonald victorious but completely exhausted; he died on 6 June.

Curiously enough, the most moving account of what might be termed Macdonald's last public appearance came from the pen of a Manitoban Senator, Marc Girard, to the Lieutenant-Governor, Dr. Schultz, whom he represented. The letter was headed 'Senate, 10th June 1891' and began: 'I am just coming from the Great Chief's Funeral . . .' Macdonald's biographer, Donald G. Creighton, has described how on that June day in Ottawa 'the tropical atmosphere seemed to grow ominously heavier . . . A curious yellow haze hung in the air. To the west, a great black cloud soared menacingly over Parliament Hill. There came a sudden fierce gust of wind—a violent scattering of huge raindrops. And then, in an overwhelming deluge, the storm broke upon the city . . .'[2] Wrote Senator Girard:

. . . we had just left the Church when a storm, a true storm of thunder and rain, fell on the people: it was a great surprize for many in their ceremony attires although it was a very much needed rains and the first one this season: it gave occasion for some people to remark that Sir John was to make good to the people even in his death, and that during life, he faces big storms, and always in the interest of the people . . .[3]

[1] Macdonald Letter Book 27.223.
[2] Donald G. Creighton: *John A. Macdonald, The Old Chieftain*, Toronto, 1955, pp. 577–8.
[3] John C. Schultz Papers 1880–95/342. Provincial Archives of Manitoba. These papers became available only in 1972.

On his visit to Canada that year Mount Stephen travelled over the entire main line of the C.P.R. by daylight and over most of the important branches. The *Railway Times* of 26 September 1891 reported that he had 'found the line in splendid condition throughout and expresses himself as much impressed by the great changes in the character of the line and the facilities for handling traffic, the result of expenditure and improvements during the past few years. If these are continued, Lord Mount Stephen believes that in two or three years the earnings of the Canadian Pacific will exceed all anticipations. The country along the line is developing wonderfully and the crops this year are exceptionally abundant. The mineral and timber resources of British Columbia are attracting outside capital, and new mines and saw mills are appearing everywhere'.

Mount Stephen had written in the same sense to his young friend Gaspard Farrer in London, who replied on 9 September:

... however great the prosperity in store for the C.P.R. it cannot be too great to recompense your and Van Horne's faith and devotion, and I trust sincerely that it will never give you another moment's anxiety. As you may imagine the market are all talking of par before 1892, and speculating on increased dividends. I am hoping—the narrow banker's view, you will say—for a fixed 5% distribution ensured by the accumulation of a dividend reserve fund, and when that is a goodly sum all surplus put back in the road. That would take and keep the stock well over par so that no present shareholder could complain, and would shift the stock from the market to the permanent investor, after all the best of bankers who will always have money to spare for the Company in bad times as well as in good.[1]

In Montreal the Stephen family had their own late 'clyack' that year, although Lord and Lady Mount Stephen could not be present at this family harvest home. The latter had written from Faskally on 6 May 1891 to their young nephew in Montreal, George Stephen Cantlie:

... I received a few lines from your mother [Eleonora Stephen] last week, in which she said that poor Granpa was failing fast, but not having had a telegram we hope that he has rallied, though it seems almost selfish to wish it. Still I would like to see him once more. He has been such a good man, and lived such a good life, that one knows eternal happiness awaits him ...[2]

[1] The Letter Books of Gaspard Farrer, in the possession of Baring Brothers and Company, have not been catalogued in detail and will not as a rule be footnoted.
[2] Letter in the possession of the Hampson family, Ottawa. William Stephen was aged 91 and his wife 90.

Just at the turn of the year 1891–2, at a time when in northern Scotland in a late harvest the stooks might still be lying out in the fields crusted with snow, William Stephen and his wife Elspet Smith were both gathered in.

'STILL ACHIEVING, STILL PURSUING': NEW PARTNERSHIP WITH HILL

The Mount Stephens had sailed from New York on 7 October. Writing on that day to the Montreal manager of the British Bank of North America, Gaspard Farrer promised to sound Mount Stephen on his return as to future banking possibilities in the developing areas; it looked as though British Columbia and the Pacific coast, rather than the North West, were the most obvious growth areas:

... I know Mr. Jim Hill—of the Great Northern—is crazy on the possibilities of Washington Territory and Puget Sound points compared to the prairies of Minnesota and Dakota of which he has had much experience, and I am told by Northern Pacific people that the extraordinary increases in their earnings during the last few years have arisen entirely from traffic originating on, or destined to, points west of Helena [Montana] ...

Stephen's affection for Canada, and his concern for her interests, were undiminished by the fact that he was gradually easing himself out of his Canadian Pacific responsibilities. But during the last thirty years of his life his transatlantic dealings were undoubtedly more American- than Canadian-orientated. Macdonald's death loosened one tie: continuous contact with James Jerome Hill of St. Paul, Minnesota, strengthened the other. One remarkable fact emerges from the fairly comprehensive and often wide-ranging correspondence between Stephen and Sir John A. Macdonald. While it is now obvious that Macdonald was not always entirely open with Stephen—ignoring the latter's sustained miserere on the subject of the railroad whose interests he imagined he had betrayed, the Prime Minister would go his own way, bowing to political necessity, maintaining his relations with useful individuals whose actions Stephen decried—what is perhaps more surprising is that latterly Stephen was completely silent upon a matter that must certainly at times have been uppermost in his mind: the emergence of the Great Northern Railroad of America. They may have discussed it in conversation, for they met at intervals either at Ottawa or in Quebec.

By 1890 there was no secret about Hill's intentions to build to the Pacific. But except in connection with the relations between the Soo Line, acquired by Stephen and Donald A. Smith for the benefit of the C.P.R., and the St. Paul, Minneapolis and Manitoba, Hill is mentioned only once in the later Macdonald correspondence, as having been at Metis in July 1889. This was during the crucial period in the incubation of their Pacific plans. If the American Northern Pacific Railroad is mentioned, it is in connection with its designs on Manitoba, not as a possible alternative by which the St. Paul, Minneapolis and Manitoba might reach the Pacific. This would of course be quite in accordance with Stephen's policy of confidentiality as regards business affairs; the Great Northern, like the 'Manitoba', was very much Hill's project. Stephen had no inhibitions about showing Van Horne's letters to the Prime Minister (indeed, the new C.P.R. President wrote on occasion with this in mind) but his instinct would have been to keep Hill's business entirely private. After all, the American railway was not in partnership with the Dominion Government, as Stephen liked to think was the case with the Canadian Pacific. Stephen's position *vis-à-vis* the C.P.R. and the 'Manitoba' had long been established, and while the Great Northern was a new factor in the equation, the result, in Stephen's calculation, was the same. To mix mathematical metaphors, the proposition that Stephen would ever work against the interest of the Canadian Pacific was absurd. One might have expected some written reiteration of this, particularly at a time when the weaknesses of the Onderdonk section of the C.P.R. in British Columbia were casting doubts on the reliability of the through line as Canada's outlet to the Pacific.

GREAT NORTHERN: THE ANTECEDENTS

Stephen's very occasional references to Montana in letters to Macdonald may be significant. In October 1887 Colonel James Baker, brother of Sir Samuel White Baker of the Nile, had asked Macdonald for an introduction to the C.P.R. directors in the hope of supplying coal from his Kootenay (British Columbia) mine to the railway. Stephen wrote to Macdonald:

MR. AND MRS. JAMES J. HILL
(by permission of the James J. Hill Reference Library)

I have seen Col. Baker and have convinced him that his coal mine is beyond the reach of the C.P.R. If the coal be all that he thinks it is he ought to be able to sell it to some of the great mining companies in Montana just south of it who use enormous quantities of coal for smelting purposes. I tried to be as kind as I could in giving Col. Baker my views so that he could not think I had not given him a full hearing. I wish he or someone would find a workable deposit near the coast. This Kootenay deposit is only 80 miles from Galt's mine and over 700 from the coast. How like his brother Baker Pasha he is.[1]

Faced with a replica of Baker of the Nile, the man—impressive of stature and with the glittering eye of the Ancient Mariner—who had finally stirred Mr. Gladstone, against his better judgment, to send General Gordon to the Sudan in 1884, Stephen might well have summoned to his aid his own special knowledge of developments in Montana. Immediately west of the prairie lands of the Dakotas, rapidly being settled in the wake of the railway-builders, Montana's growing mining industry held out the promise of a profitable future in terms of freight traffic. In January 1886 the Montana Central Railroad Company had been incorporated with $5 million of stock, 'ostensibly', writes Hill's biographer Pyle, 'to connect the new town of Great Falls with Helena, Butte and other points'. In May 1887, when an issue of $10 million of Montana Central bonds was made, a hitherto verbal contract 'long since made and partly executed' between the directors and James J. Hill was superseded by an agreement whereby Hill was to furnish 'in addition to past advances' the money necessary to construct and equip the line, receiving in exchange the stock and bonds of the Company. To quote Pyle again: 'The Montana Central was, to all intents and purposes, James J. Hill'.[2] The 'Manitoba' had staked its claim. By August of that year the St. Paul, Minneapolis and Manitoba Company had officially assumed the agreement entered into by its president; the following year it acquired the entire capital stock of the Montana Central Railroad Company and $2.5 million of its first mortgage bonds for a sum equivalent to the actual cost of the property.

John S. Kennedy, the New York banker who had joined the original 'Manitoba' enterprise in the late 1870s, told Hill that people there 'all seem to be waking up to the idea that sooner or later we will

[1] Macdonald Papers 270.
[2] Joseph G. Pyle, *The Life of James J. Hill*, New York 1917, 2 vols., vol. I, p. 388 ff.

2

become a transcontinental line'.[1] In the west, the full significance of Hill's recent moves had not yet been discerned, nor was it entirely appreciated in London financial circles familiar with American railroading. On 13 March 1888 Gaspard Farrer, of the accepting house of H. S. Lefevre and Company, the man who was gradually to become George Stephen's *alter ego*, wrote to Oliver Northcote, of the firm of J. Kennedy Tod and Company in New York:

... thank goodness we had no interest in Montana Central or Eastern Minnesota issues; buyers of those Roads won't forget Mr. Hill for some time I fancy.

The word 'transcontinental' implied also connection with the Atlantic coast, and as it happened this was achieved first. In 1887 the 'Manitoba' effected a connection with the Great Lakes head of navigation at Duluth through the Eastern Railway of Minnesota, and the following year the Northern Steamship Company, a subsidiary of the 'Manitoba', had its own vessels on the Lakes. At the same time Hill was establishing friendly relations with the Chicago, Burlington and Quincy Railroad, whose useful ramifications made it the strongest railroad system in the middle west, and with the Chicago, Burlington and Northern, to which Hill could offer terminal facilities at St. Paul and Minneapolis in exchange for entry into Chicago.

The further education of Gaspard Farrer was soon to be set in train. In May 1888 he arrived in America on one of his regular trips, mixing business with pleasure. He visited St. Paul, and after his return to London wrote to Hill on 20 July that he had been with George Stephen at Metis for a couple of days and 'tried to give him a glimmering of what I had seen; he is keen about seeing your new country and will I think be sure to go there on his next visit to the North West . . .' He added in a postscript that he had just been meeting the owner of one of the richest mines in Butte and had been 'staggered' at current freight traffic figures; the future seemed extremely promising, the more so that the Union Pacific was so unpopular.

Pyle writes of Hill's hurried visits to Europe during these years, where he made himself and his plans known both to financial houses and personal investors.[2] Hill's 'powerful personality drew and held men . . . This man, with his big brain, his prophetic gift,

---

[1] Ibid. p. 401. [2] Ibid. p. 407.

his Napoleonic eye, inspired at the same time business confidence and personal attachment'. Supplying the introductions was Stephen, already spending part of the year at his London house in St. James's Place and becoming well-known both in the City and socially. As regards eventually reaching the Pacific, the main question at first was whether this should be achieved by construction of an entirely new line or by purchase of an existing one—in effect, of the Northern Pacific, whose uncertain state financially brought this alternative within the realm of possibility. Even had the Union Pacific been in this category, the unsatisfactory nature of its Pacific connection at this time quite apart from its more southerly location would have lessened its attraction. It was not until it got control of the Central Pacific and Southern Pacific systems that the Pacific railroad which had been first in the field really won its race.[1]

It may be well at this point, before adverting to the 1889 discussion on the subject between Hill and Stephen, to review briefly the history of the Northern Pacific since their earlier contact with it as a competitor of the St. Paul, Minneapolis and Manitoba. An interesting slant is given in the memoirs of Henry Villard, president of the Northern Pacific during this intervening period. Pyle describes him as both a dreamer and a man of action: endowed with both vision and daring, he had been one of the first to see the possibilities of combination among the railroad systems of the United States.[2] Born Ferdinand Heinrich Gustav Hilgard (1835–1900), Villard had emigrated at the age of eighteen not knowing a word of English. The memoirs were first written in German.[3] He had, nevertheless, a career in American journalism before coming into railroading in 1870 through his involvement in Germany with dissatisfied bondholders of the Oregon and California and Kansas and Pacific railroads. Five years later he found himself president of the Oregon and California and the Oregon Steamship Company (merged in 1879 into the Oregon Railway and Navigation Company) and was appointed receiver of the bankrupt Kansas Pacific. His first connection with the Northern Pacific was in 1880 when the latter, building towards the Pacific coast, found the Oregon road already in possession of the left bank of the Columbia River. From a position of strength Villard came to terms with the Northern

[1] Robert E. Riegel, *The Story of the Western Railroads*, New York, 1926, p. 312.
[2] Pyle, op. cit. vol. I, pp. 332-4.
[3] Henry Villard: *Memoirs of Henry Villard, Journalist and Financier*, London, 1904, 2 vols.

Pacific, although the latter subsequently had a striking success with
the sale to a powerful syndicate of $40 million worth of first mort-
gage bonds.

With the financial support of friends Villard presently formed a
new proprietary company, the Oregon and Transcontinental,
owning a majority of both Oregon and Northern Pacific stock.
Peace on the Columbia River was assured in addition to access to
Portland on the Pacific coast, and by 1881 Villard had been elected
president of the Northern Pacific, with Oregon representatives
having a controlling voice on the board. Villard called this move on
his part the boldest resolution of his whole business career.[1]
Unfortunately, according to Pyle, 'The fluctuations that marked
his brilliant career indicated a possible indifference to the less
conspicuous but no less necessary qualities of conservative administration and circumstantial knowledge of how to operate at a profit.
Big outlines inspired him; before details he was embarrassed, cold,
sometimes impatient . . . He found $34 million of proceeds of bond
sales in the railroad's treasury, and proceeded to spend it royally
. . .'[2] This bond issue was aimed at completing and equipping the
main line to the Pacific. From Villard's account his experience in
the next two worrying years were indeed very similar to that of
George Stephen during construction of the Canadian Pacific, with
the Oregon subsidising the Northern Pacific in the same way as the
'Manitoba's' earnings had contributed towards sustaining the
credit of the C.P.R. There was a short-lived moment of triumph
when in August 1883 the opening of the Northern Pacific as a
through line was celebrated—the last spike being driven in western
Montana—in the presence of an impressive company of not only
American but also European guests including President Arthur,
General Ulysses Grant and the young St. John Brodrick, member
of Parliament for West Surrey.[3]

Before long the strain on the Oregon company was proving too
great while the creation of a second mortgage on the Northern
Pacific was followed by a slump in its shares. Villard's hopes that
earnings on the through line would restore the balance were to be
frustrated: it was actually running at a loss. The almost inevitable
chain reaction set in: friends sold their holdings and a hostile

[1] Villard, op. cit. vol. I, pp. 291–8.
[2] Pyle, op. cit. vol. I, pp. 332–4.
[3] Villard, op. cit. vol. I, pp. 300–10.

Press made the most of the situation, even attacking Villard personally—as Stephen was to be attacked in 1884—for moving just then into a splendid new home. By December 1883 Villard was bankrupt and the Oregon and Transcontinental very nearly so. A group of friends offered help on condition that he resign the presidency of both the Oregon and Transcontinental and the Oregon Railway and Navigation Companies. Although by then a good deal of sympathy was being accorded the defeated giant, Villard gradually withdrew from all his posts and by 1885 was again living in Germany, having refused offers from railroads in Turkey and in East Africa. The Northern Pacific, however, were reluctant to dispense altogether with a man of his experience, and after Villard had returned to New York as a representative of the Deutsche Bank he was persuaded in 1888 to become a director again, mainly because of his concern for the Company's German investors. The Northern Pacific was still financially embarrassed— Hill would have said because of its policy of financing by bond issues instead of relying on earnings. As with the C.P.R., construction costs had exceeded estimates, branch lines were urgently needed and, moreover, the preferred stock was approaching maturity. Having secured their giant again, however, the board declined to follow his ambitious advice. Villard could see that Hill, whose Montana Central was already a threatening competitor, had every intention of building westward to Spokane in Washington Territory, and thence to Puget Sound, and advised bold action either to prevent completion of a rival line to the Pacific or to meet such competition as would thus be offered. In his opinion, when an issue of third mortgage bonds was decided upon, at $12 million it was too small. At this point there was some question of the company being taken over by the Union Pacific; the latter then backed out and the two Pacific lines stepped up their competition. Meanwhile in 1888, in the interests of his German investors, Villard resumed the presidency of the Oregon and Transcontinental Company. He was warned that the forces apparently closing in upon the Northern Pacific included, as well as the Union Pacific, James J. Hill and his 'Manitoba' followers, each party backed by its own formidable phalanx of New York financiers and brokers, all busily arming themselves with Oregon and Transcontinental shares.[1]

[1] Ibid. pp. 313–31.

Hill had indeed written late in 1888 to John Murray Forbes, president of the Chicago, Burlington and Quincy, concerning the latest developments in Montana and westward:

... We have just put on through passenger trains to Butte, and have arranged with the Union Pacific for direct connection, both freight and passenger, with their lines, by way of Ogden [Utah] to San Francisco and by way of Pocatello [Idaho] and the Oregon Short Line to all points in Oregon.[1]

Villard claims to have come victorious out of this situation in that the Union Pacific, while shrinking from taking over the Northern Pacific, had bought at a satisfactory price all the stockholdings in the Oregon and Transcontinental Company of the Oregon Railroad and Navigation Company, no longer now in a position to subsidise the Northern Pacific and therefore of no value to the proprietary company. (The Union Pacific had then built the Oregon Short Line mentioned in Hill's letter to Forbes, connecting Butte via Pocatello with Huntington in Oregon, giving access there to the Oregon Railroad proper.) In 1889 Villard was elevated to the new office of chairman of the Northern Pacific, severing all links with the Oregon, and proceeded to devote himself to devising a comprehensive financial scheme that would provide for the road's current needs and plans as well as for the repayment when due of outstanding mortgage bonds. This was quite favourably received and until early 1890 all went well.[2]

In May 1889 James J. Hill, still thinking in terms of a merger with the Northern Pacific, wrote to Stephen in Montreal:

The Northern Pacific and the Oregon and Transcontinental have given me much concern, as through the latter the first can be controlled for a very little money comparatively ...

Referring to their 'proposed new company', he foresaw that ultimate control of the Northern Pacific, and with it the removal of 'building contests, rate wars etc', would be very attractive to investors. Stephen might think that he was 'going pretty fast in Northern Pacific matters', but the possible results were certainly attractive: 'the entire property controlled by the new company would have an earning capacity of about $3 million a month. And this, with the advantage of removing all expensive rivalry and competition, would alone save 5 per cent., which is $1 million per

[1] Pyle, op. cit. vol. 1, p. 436.   [2] Villard, op. cit. vol. 1, p. 321.

annum'.[1] Stephen spent the last week of May at St. Paul and the following month Hill wrote to him again:

The more I think it over the more I am convinced that the thing for us to do is to "take the bull by the horns" and get control of the Northern Pacific, and by one stroke settle all questions at once. This will cost less money and will bring the best results in the least time. Looking over the ground we find the Northern Pacific is the only interest of any magnitude in the entire territory we want to control. It is pursuing a very aggressive course, almost regardless of permanent cost and business judgment, at the same time it is doing both the "Manitoba" and the Canadian Pacific Railroad great damage and in such a way as to compel both to spend large sums of money to no good end. They are cutting rates in Manitoba to an extent that cannot fail to greatly reduce the revenues of all concerned from that province, and the facts as stated in your letter that their lines in Manitoba will not pay anything for six years (and I think it will be ten) is a permanent reason why they cannot hold to any agreement. A starving man will usually get bread if it is to be had, and a starving railway will not maintain rates. Whenever I take up this question, I want to go right at the work of getting control of that company, and when we look at both sides and the large sums at stake all around, on the one side, and at the strong, peaceful solution of the questions on the other, I am more anxious than ever to carry out the plan . . .[2]

Ten days later Stephen, in Pyle's words 'careful and perhaps less convinced', gave his considered reply:

I am not clear in my own mind as to our ability to capture the control of the Northern Pacific. That is, I do not see so clearly how it is to be done as I do our ability to build a new line of our own. Of that I have no doubt, and think I can see my way to finance an extension to the Coast on very economical terms so far as the finding of the money is concerned. It may be, when I see you, that the difficulties in the way of capturing the Northern Pacific may disappear. I am very much impressed by what you say as to the advantages of our getting to the Coast by a control of the Northern Pacific rather than by building a new line if it can be done. I have so much confidence in the soundness of your judgment in such matters that my inclination is always to accept your views, largely because they are your views. The advantages to the St. Paul, Minneapolis and Manitoba and the Canadian Pacific Railroad as well, of our getting control of the Northern Pacific are very clear, and I think when you

[1] Pyle, op. cit. vol. I, pp. 450-1. Stephen's visit to St. Paul is referred to in Stephen to Macdonald, 23 May 1889, Macdonald Papers 271.
[2] Pyle, op. cit. vol. I, p. 451.

come down we must try to come to some definite conclusion as to the course to be pursued and follow it up vigorously. If we decide that a control of the Northern Pacific is out of reach, then I suppose we ought to go vigorously and promptly to work on a new line.[1]

Stephen was keeping a particularly wary eye on the Northern Pacific's renewed activity in the Canadian West. Only temporarily deterred by the debacle of the Red River Valley Railroad at the end of 1888, the American road seemed once again determined to get a foothold there, whether by new construction of branch lines or by purchase. From Metis Stephen wrote to Sir John A. Macdonald on 7 July 1889, enclosing Van Horne's latest letter:

... You will not fail to notice what he says about the Northern Pacific's operations in the direction of the Kootenay and will appreciate his anxiety as to keeping up the credit of the C.P.R. Company so that it may be in a position to head them off—"mop the floor" as he expresses it, and I am certain he is right when he says that it is just as important to the Government of Canada as to the Company that the latter should be in that position ...[2]

Despite the fact that Stephen had latterly favoured the cancellation of the C.P.R. contract's Clause 15, which had given them a monopoly of branch-line building between their main line and the American boundary, it still seemed to him preposterous that the Government should be pressing the company for more branches in the north west, financed by already limited resources, while the Northern Pacific was then liable to duplicate such lines, subsidised, moreover, by provincial governments. A week later he reported that Mr. Hill had been with him at Metis for a few days:

... He is posted fully on Northern Pacific plans and confirms my views as to them. They are at the end of their tether in the U.S. They cannot sell any more bonds there and their scheme now is to take advantage of the credit the C.P.R. has created in England and to float bonds there secured on a land grant for an amount far in excess of any money they mean to spend in building any roads in the Nor West and with the surplus aid to help the Northern Pacific proper. I have no doubt Hill is right in his views ...

It is hard to believe it possible that either the Dominion Government or the Manitoba Government can really desire to see the Nor West Americanised, though that is the inevitable effect of the policy of aiding and bonusing the Nor Pacific in building lines in Manitoba and the Nor West.[3]

[1] Ibid. p. 452. [2] Macdonald Papers 271. [3] Ibid.

Towards the end of July 1889 Macdonald forwarded to Stephen a telegram just received from Winnipeg to the effect that the Northern Pacific were completing negotiations in Montreal for the purchase of the Manitoba North Western Railroad. It was suggested that Macdonald get the Canadian Pacific to block the deal. Stephen's reply was unusually calm and philosophic; loafing at Metis—the fishing season over—he was getting the whole thing into perspective:

... I know nothing of the deal said to be going on between the Northern Pacific and the Manitoba and North Western except what I have seen in the papers. The Canadian Pacific Company could have bought the Manitoba and North Western anytime these two years past but not on terms that we could justify to our shareholders. The trouble is that Manitoba and North Western has cost the present owners one way and another far more money than the property is worth or is likely to be worth, in our day. It never has earned one cent of interest on its capital cost, and it will be many years before it can pay any reasonable return on the price the N.P. may pay for it. It was a cruel thing of poor old Pope to compel them to accept C.P.R. rates and to that briefly, if not entirely, must be attributed the cause of the Company having to sell to anyone. If the N.P. people conclude to buy it, the only thing we can do that I can see is to help the Manitoba and North Western Company to get as good a price out (of) them as possible. This on the principle of "Beggar my neighbour". It would be more than our credit could stand to undertake the additional load of unproductive road, and whatever we do we must do nothing to impair the credit of the C.P.R. Company. If we lose our credit, we lose everything and become powerless for the many things standing ahead of the Company yet to be done in the N.W. as well as elsewhere.

It is far better, if the N.P. must have more roads in our country, that they should buy existing ones, than to build parallel useless lines. They are in the country now, and nothing we can do can stop their extending. The great mistake was made when Tom White practically told the Winnipeg agitators that the time had come for the Government to allow the American lines to build across the Frontier. But that is all spilt milk now and we must—I say we, I mean the Government and the C.P.R. Company, must try to circumscribe the scope of their operations as much as possible.[1]

Stephen's rational approach dissolved as he added a light-hearted postscript regarding the daughter of a former Governor-General: 'Tell Lady Macdonald that Dufferin's eldest girl is engaged to (?)

[1] Ibid. John Henry Pope was the late Minister of Railways, Thomas White the late Minister of the Interior.

Ferguson, a well to do young Scotchman who *fancies* he is an Irish Home Ruler'.

That summer it was agreed that the 'Manitoba' should proceed with independent construction from Montana west to Spokane, Washington Territory, and Puget Sound on the Pacific. Hill secured an agreement with the president of the Union Pacific, Charles Francis Adams, for the use of his tracks from Spokane south-west to Portland, Oregon; in 1891 by another agreement he acquired joint ownership with the U.P. of a line building from Seattle to Portland.[1] Villard of the Northern Pacific, meanwhile, had been keeping a close watch on Hill's movements, although the latter was careful to maintain good relations between them. Villard, hearing of financial plans for the 'Manitoba's' new construction, and of the agreement with Adams, conceived the bold idea of forestalling competition from that quarter by making a bid for a majority interest in the 'Manitoba'. In his memoirs he relates that he heard through friends that Hill was disposed to sell his holdings and those of his friends at a reasonable figure. Having arranged to raise $20 million, he made, he says, an appointment with Hill which only Villard kept.[2] Pyle's version is that Hill, resenting the implication that such a thing was possible, merely gave a non-committal reply.[3]

By the autumn of 1889 it was becoming generally known in railroading circles that the 'Manitoba' had decided to build to the Pacific. In September the Great Northern came into being, the product of an elaborate quadrille directed by the circumstance that, under the 'Manitoba's' charter, the latter's maximum stock holding was only $20 million. The catalyst was the Minneapolis and St. Cloud Company, whose capital stock the 'Manitoba' had held for some time. At a meeting of its stockholders its name was changed to the Great Northern Railway Company. Then in November the new company formally accepted the proposal of the 'Manitoba' for the transfer of its property. This made a total of $40 million worth, half common stock, half preferred. The Great Northern then leased for 999 years the property of the St. Paul, Minneapolis and Manitoba, assuming its financial obligations as from midnight on 31 January 1890. On 9 June 1890 the Great

[1] Pyle, op. cit. vol. I, p. 458.
[2] Villard, op. cit. vol. I, pp. 335–6.
[3] Pyle, op. cit. vol. I, p. 336.

Northern, with more 'setting to partners', 'requested' the 'Manitoba' to extend westward from Pacific Junction, Montana, to Everett on Puget Sound. This was granted after two weeks, and in August 1890 the work began which was to take the Great Northern through line to the Pacific by January 1893.[1]

CANADIAN PACIFIC: GLEANINGS

Stephen's letter to Sir John A. Macdonald of 4 September 1889 spoke of 'my return from Montana on Saturday morning'.[2] At once he was plunged into the tangled problem of the Canadian Pacific's land grant which had never been finally settled after completion of the line and repayment by the Company of its debt to the Government. This was no doubt partly because of misunderstandings following the death in 1888 of the then Minister of the Interior, Thomas White. At all events the last stages of the controversy, added to the other bones of contention between the Government and the Company, kept Stephen's letters at a querulous pitch once more. He blamed himself for not having insisted on the matter being dealt with immediately the lands had been earned, four or five years earlier.[3] The delay in their location, apart from anything else, hampered the Company in its efforts to prevent the Northern Pacific occupying the territory ahead of it in Manitoba and elsewhere.[4] On 19 September Stephen was off to New York, but on the 23rd was back in Montreal, telegraphing for an appointment with the Prime Minister that week, before leaving for England. Macdonald, himself, would have liked to be going with him, but had an equally large helping of unfinished business on his plate which he could less easily escape from.[5] After his last interview with Stephen on 25 September it looked as if the land question at least was nearly disposed of.[6]

But not quite. On 18 November Stephen's cousin and ally in many enterprises, Donald Alexander Smith, wrote to Macdonald from his house on Dorchester Street, Montreal (Smith had already apparently been involved in discussions with Macdonald over the Short Line question and the C.P.R.'s access to Halifax):

[1] Pyle, op. cit. vol. I, pp. 460-1.
[2] Macdonald Papers 271.
[3] Ibid.   [4] Ibid.
[5] Macdonald Letter Book 26.234. Creighton, op. cit. ch. 15.
[6] Macdonald Papers 271.

A cable message from Sir George Stephen to Mr. Van Horne, copy of which Van Horne told me he was to send you, would indicate that he, Stephen, is anything but in a pleasant or comfortable frame of mind regarding the unsettled matters between your Government and the C.P.R. Company. Why should we not have all these things disposed of without further delay? In this I do not refer to the arbitration on the British Columbia portion of the Road, but to the facilities for traffic with Halifax about which we spoke last weekend and the selection to be made of lands in the North West. Surely there ought to be no difficulty in coming to a definite understanding on this latter head and although I am much pressed with business here in view of leaving for England on Thursday of this week, I would make an effort to be in Ottawa on Wednesday to endeavour to effect a settlement, if you would kindly arrange an interview for the forenoon of that day.[1]

This was not the first such cable that Stephen in London had despatched to the C.P.R. president. On October 15, immersed in his difficult negotiations with the Andersons over a fast Atlantic steamship service to Canada,[2] he had wired: 'Anxious to hear how you settle land and Short Line matters. Important dispose of both promptly. Delay doing harm here',[3] achieving the reply 'No progress land and Short Line. Expect something during the week'. The Short Line question was resolved the following July[4]; as there appears to have been no further transatlantic correspondence on the subject of the land grant it may be supposed that Smith's intervention had been successful, at least in quieting the apprehensions of his cousin. According to the C.P.R. Company's Annual Report for 1890, a final settlement was reached only in October of that year.

Before leaving for England in September 1889 Stephen had begged the Canadian Prime Minister to be perfectly open with Van Horne on all matters that concerned them both:

... You may be sure of one thing that Van Horne wants nothing from the Government that he is not on every ground justified in asking. You are *quite safe* in giving him your whole confidence. I know him better, perhaps, than anyone here and I am satisfied that I make no mistake when I ask you to trust him and to dismiss from your mind all suspicion that would lead you to look upon him as a sharper bound to take advantage of the Government every time he gets the chance. I will guarantee that he *never* will be guilty of anything of that kind and when anything turns

[1] Macdonald Papers 265.
[2] See Gilbert, vol. 1, index references: Atlantic steamship service(s).
[3] Macdonald Papers 288.   [4] Gilbert, vol. 1, pp. 238–43.

up that seems to you to need explanation pray do not hesitate to ask *himself* for one. He will always tell you the truth ... let me beg of you to give your whole confidence to Van Horne and everything will be easy and come right ...[1]

Macdonald did not take this recommendation too seriously. The following year, for example, he wrote to Stephen on 3 June, after a meeting at which they had both witnessed a discussion between Van Horne and the Government Engineer, Collingwood Schreiber: '... V.H. is a first rate man for his position and never misses a point on his case ...'[2] He referred particularly to Van Horne's perhaps oblique mention of a proposed line from Edmunston, New Brunswick, near Lake Temiscouata (already connected by rail to Rivière du Loup), to Moncton, which it was believed the Government were to subsidize the C.P.R.'s old rival the Grand Trunk Railroad to build. Sir Donald Smith had on 6 May 1890 telegraphed Macdonald from Montreal:

Rumour speaks of a possible subsidy to a line from Edmunston to Moncton. Cannot believe that knowing the circumstances under which the Short Line was taken up at the urgent request of the Government and that the C.P.R. Company stands ready to fulfil the agreement made last year in respect of the Harvey Moncton cut off you and your colleagues will permit any such injustice which you will agree with me would amount to breach of faith with the C.P. Company.[3]

Stephen replied to Macdonald's allegation that Van Horne had entirely changed his ground (he agreed that the latter's verbal battle with the Government Engineer had not been devoid of amusement for the onlookers) by asserting that the Pacific president had merely been upholding the Company's rights as contained in recent agreements with the Government; he could see no change of front: 'I understood his reference to Temiscouata was only by way of illustration and to show the need of protection against all other lines than that by way of Chaudière to which Schreiber as I took it was trying to limit it'. He went on:

I know Van Horne perhaps better than he does himself, and I am *certain* he is asking for nothing but what is dead fair and does not *mean* to ask for anything more. You may be sure this is the case. As to the Temiscouata neither he nor I can bring ourselves to believe it possible the

[1] Macdonald Papers 271.   [2] Macdonald Letter Book 26.486.
[3] Macdonald Papers 265.

Government will throw away public money on such an utterly useless and mischievous scheme. It could not help Halifax ... while it would do irreparable injury to the Intercolonial Railway and in a lesser degree hurt the Short Line. I do not believe the GTR shareholders would invest one dollar in *any* line to Halifax. Halifax has already two lines to the west, either of which could do five times the business to be done or ever likely to be done. Why then should the Government aid in building a third one?

Pardon this long story. I am off tomorrow with our Royalties to Causapscal but will be back here next week. I am very anxious to get all these outstanding matters closed. You have no idea how they interfere with the proper work of Van Horne which is looking after the operation of the Railway.[1]

Macdonald, with his elder statesman's long experience of human nature, strove to maintain an impartiality not altogether divorced from political opportunism; Stephen contributed to Conservative Party funds: Joseph Hickson, General Manager of the Grand Trunk, virtually controlled the votes of his employees. In April 1889, on receiving from Stephen a plaintive end-of-session appeal: 'I am feeling rather sore at seeing among your subsidies one to the G.T.R. (practically) for a competing line from Perth to Montreal by way of Cornwall, to the C.P.R. short line from Perth to Montreal which was built without one cent of subsidy from either the Dominion or Provincial Governments. I also see $375,000 to the G.T.R. to enable it to cross the Detroit river by a Tunnel at Port Huron while the C.P.R. has to make its own crossing without aid, at Windsor ...'[2]—Macdonald wrote in reply:

It is rather an amusing coincidence that the messenger who brought me your note of the 26th brought me also one from Hickson. In this he followed up a conversation of the night before and complains bitterly of the treatment of the G.T.R. by us. After his letter I saw him and he *with much sorrow* informed me that his Company must assume a hostile attitude towards the Government.

He complains of the Short Line business and of the construction of the road from Hamilton to Woodstock, of the Niagara Falls road to Hamilton and some others all calculated to bring the C.P.R. into active rivalry with the G.T.R.

Then again only yesterday I quarrelled with two of my Western supporters by refusing a land grant to a line from Winnipeg to Lake of the Woods and thence to Duluth on the ground that although the C.P.R. had surrendered the monopoly the Government having aided your Road

[1] Macdonald Papers 272.   [2] Macdonald Papers 271.

to be built on Canadian soil should not subsidize another line to take away the trade from it . . . [1]

The picture of Macdonald delicately balancing the scales might well have been the subject of a Bengough cartoon. It would be tedious to go on too long citing the placatory epistles, first to one side, then to the other.[2] In July 1889 Macdonald was corresponding with the Colonial Secretary in London, Lord Knutsford, regarding a knighthood for Hickson:

I am most interested in this matter not so much on his account as on the ground that it is important that the G.T.R. should not be "left out in the cold" altogether when the rival system has had honours showered upon it. It has so happened that all the burden of attending to the transport of any of the Royal family visiting us has fallen upon the G.T.R. people and principally on Mr. Hickson . . .[3]

It so happened that the 'Royalties' whom Stephen was taking to La Fourche, Causapscal, the fishing lodge on the Matapedia which at the time he still retained, in June 1890—they were, in fact, the Duke of Connaught and his suite, marshalled by Stephen's friend Major General Sir John McNeill, Equerry to the Duke,—travelled from Vancouver on the Canadian Pacific, following for the most part an itinerary made out by Van Horne.[4] Stephen could not resist suggesting that Hickson got his knighthood for patriotically ruining the Grand Trunk, but told Macdonald 'Apart from his vanity and wrong-headedness he is a good kindhearted fellow, though I cannot forget senseless hostility to the C.P.R. even if I forgive it'.[5] Acknowledging Macdonald's reply of 15 January 1891, Stephen, to tease his friend further, chalked up another point against the G.T.R.'s former manager (for Sir Joseph had just resigned):

If Hickson's knighthood was really his reward for civilities to H.R.H.'s &c. he very soon showed the usual want of gratitude for favors granted. You may not know that when the Duke of Connaught was in Canada last spring, Hickson after writing an effusive letter to McNeill offering to do anything and everything he could for their H.R.H.'s, because they changed the arrangements made for them and came down from Toronto to Montreal by the C.P.R. he was goose enough to take offence, and sent

[1] Macdonald Letter Book 25.403.
[2] See, for example, Gilbert, vol. I, p. 243.
[3] Macdonald Letter Book 26.94.
[4] Macdonald Papers 272. [5] Ibid.

in a bill to McNeill charging the Duke some $300 for hauling his car from North Bay to Toronto &c.&c, McNeill at the request of the Duke sent the bill to Van Horne asking him to say whether he should pay the amount. Van Horne kept the bill and paid the amount to the G.T.R. out of his own pocket . . .[1]

The Grand Trunk's electoral support of the Conservative Party, already weakening, did not survive Hickson's departure, but the rivalry went on. At the height of the 1891 election campaign Macdonald cabled to Stephen in London: 'Grand Trunk out in favour of opposition whose policy is discrimination against England. Act promptly—if necessary denounce course in Press. Danger great'.[2] A further cable reported that G.T.R. men were being instructed, on pain of dismissal, to vote for the "discrimination against England" party. (In his draft cable, the Prime Minister's secretary, Joseph Pope, had adopted Stephen's word "annexation" but was instructed to alter this, for lack of proof.)[3] Stephen's reaction had been in favour of a vigorous Press campaign in London, where the G.T.R. was based. This course was apparently not pursued—mercifully, as it turned out; on 28 February Stephen wrote to Macdonald:

It was fortunate that we did not try to inspire attacks by the Press here on the G.T.R. for meddling with the Elections on the side of the Grits, in view of Van Horne's bold and outspoken manifesto on the side of the national policy and antireciprocity, limited or unlimited. I believe Van Horne really believes that the best thing for Canada is a high wall between it and the U:S—no reciprocity of any kind—though people here with their Free Trade notions say he only meant "to help his friend Sir John Macdonald", and will not believe that he believes free trade with the U:S would be an injury to Canada.

Van Horne's courage is greater than mine. Had I been President of the C.P.R. I should have hesitated a long time before I came out openly in my official capacity . . .[4]

Hickson's successor was quick to pick up the gauntlet. Wrote Stephen on 7 March:

. . . Mr. Sargeant's counterblast to Van Horne's manifesto was amusing especially to me. You have of course forgotten how I used to try to persuade you that the G.T.R. was by its geographical position—by the

---

[1] Ibid. [2] Ibid.
[3] Ibid. (Implied was 'annexation of Canada by the United States').
[4] Ibid.

necessity of its existence—antinational, that it was and must ever be essentially an American Railway, with its western end in Chicago and its eastern in Portland—its local Canadian business being only incidental and secondary in importance . . .[1]

By this time Macdonald was safely reinstalled, even if both his health and his majority in Parliament left much to be desired. In a later letter Stephen attributed the continuation of the Grand Trunk's wasteful policies in Canada throughout Hickson's regime— resulting in an absence of dividends even on its preference shares —to the fact that the management was based in London. 'A pole 3000 miles long is too long to be workable'.[2] There was another company which shared this disadvantage: the Canada North West Land Company.[3]

CANADA NORTH WEST LAND COMPANY

By 1888 it was quite clear that the Land Company had not been a success. The Board sat in London under the chairmanship of the capable Thomas Skinner, but the Canadian manager, W. B. Scarth, Conservative member of Parliament for Winnipeg, went his own way, giving but scant attention to Company affairs and seldom communicating with the Board. He obviously preferred the political to the business sphere, and even his intervention on behalf of the C.P.R. in the Manitoba agitation only roused Stephen's contempt: 'That well-meaning fool Scarth', he wrote to Macdonald on 15 February 1888 after one incident, 'by his clumsy and mala-droit efforts has been the cause of this new trouble . . .'[4] The London Board also had its internal difficulties: ten days later Gaspard Farrer was writing to Stephen listing the reasons why he should not become a director, as Skinner wished: ' . . . Lastly but not least I will not supplant Lord Elphinstone, your friend, as regards the Company as disinterested and honest a man as any of its directors or shareholders . . .' Only the consideration that it would seem like desertion prevented Skinner himself from resigning.

Following his resignation from the presidency of the C.P.R. that August, Stephen had gone over to England, leasing for a time the Buckinghamshire home of Lord Chesham. From Latimer he wrote

[1] Ibid. [2] Ibid.
[3] See Gilbert, vol. 1, index references: (Canada) North West Land Company.
[4] Macdonald Papers 271.

to his parents still living in Montreal, on 14 September, giving an account of the visit which he and his old schoolfriend, General Sir Donald Stewart, had paid to Dufftown, scene of their Scottish boyhood.[1] Back in the south he was immersed in schemes for state-aided colonization,[2] and wrote to Macdonald on 28 September, wishing the Canadian Prime Minister were there to discuss emigration policy with the British Government. Stephen was satisfied that success could be achieved only by the two governments getting together over the business 'and *alone*. The intervention of the North West Land Company and Scarth can only do harm to the success of the scheme and to the interests of the Land Company as well. I hear Scarth has again got himself and his Company into a scrape . . .'[3] He enlarged on this in a letter of 7 October:

. . . Scarth has again got himself and his Company into trouble by the foolish way he disposed of the crofters sent out last season and what the result will be to Scarth remains to be seen, but it looks ominous for him just now. He seems to be utterly wanting in sense . . . Scarth reported to his Company that out of some 160 sections of land set apart by the Department of the Interior for the crofters, there were only 5 sections fit for settlement, which I cannot but think absurd. If that be true, there is no use talking any more about settling the Nor' West . . .[4]

By this time the London Board were coming to the conclusion that Scarth must choose between his parliamentary seat and his office with the Company. To Macdonald this spelt political disaster. Already in January 1888 the provincial government of Manitoba had fallen from the hands of the recalcitrant Conservative Norquay into those of the Liberal Greenway; a by-election at Winnipeg would be fatal. He appealed to the erstwhile member for Selkirk Donald A. Smith, who replied from Montreal on 4 October:

You already know both from Stephen and myself that the members of the Canada North West Land Company Board in England have complained much that Mr. Scarth has not given the requisite attention to the Company's business and urge that he will either apply the whole of his time to their work or resign. He has certainly been away too long from Manitoba and that when his services were most needed in course of the last twelve

---

[1] Gilbert, vol. I, pp. 186–8. (The letter is published in full in Heather Gilbert, *Mount Stephen* : *A study in environments* in *Northern Scotland*, vol. I, no. 2, 1973 (Centre for Scottish Studies, University of Aberdeen).
[2] See Gilbert, vol. I, pp. 223 ff.
[3] Macdonald Papers 271.   [4] Ibid.

months and it would never do to have this repeated. I entirely recognise and agree with what you say in your letter to me of the 2nd. received yesterday about the effect of opening his constituency at present and although in view of the feeling of the C.N.W. Ld. Board largely shared, I must say, both by Mr. Osler and myself, it will be an awkward task to undertake, I will do my best to have the matter lie over until after the next session provided Scarth will undertake to be no more than ten days in Ottawa during the sitting of Parliament and away from Manitoba and the North West not longer than a fortnight . . .[1]

Smith was planning to sail for England on the 13th, but was prepared to spare some time on a brief visit to Ottawa first to discuss this delicate situation with the Prime Minister.

This offer was apparently not accepted, but Macdonald reported the correspondence with Smith in a letter to Stephen on 11 October, written while Stephen's of the 7th was still on the way. Scarth had told the Prime Minister that he was called on to resign his seat and that a successor must be found. Macdonald outlined to Stephen the dangers he foresaw in Manitoba, where Greenway's position, although shaky, was not yet sufficiently precarious to ensure the safety of the Conservative seat at Winnipeg. Then, craftily using the sort of argument Stephen employed when discussing the C.P.R.'s relations with the Government, he continued:

Now the N.W. Land Co. is not a political body but it has nearly identical interests with the C.P.R. Now at the instance of your Company the Government instead of letting it fight out the legal question with Greenway and the Northern Pacific for the next two years has agreed to ask the Supreme Court to give an immediate opinion of the legality of the Provincial Acts. This has renewed the storm against our Government and Winnipeg is threatening resistance. Now it would have been easy for us to wash our hands of the whole matter, but Judge Clark is confident of success, and if a favourable decision (for the C.P.R.) is obtained, the N. Pacific will drop the thing like a hot potato, and you will have the control of the position again.

But if we help you, you must help us. Let Scarth remain in Parlt. till after next session and I won't ask a longer delay. I wrote Sir Donald and he sees the position but writes that Scarth must not be absent from Winnipeg but for some ten days. I have written him (Scarth) but I don't see how he can in justice to himself accept such terms. He had better resign at once whatever the consequences.

I have been corresponding with Lt. Governor Schultz on the situation

[1] Macdonald Papers 265.

and he says that opening Winnipeg "would mean the election of a Grit with a howl of triumph all through the Dominion while a few months' forbearance might change the face of political matters". He goes on to say "The Red River Valley Railway cannot be conveyed by the Act and agreement till a number of conditions are complied with and through Trains come to a Rifle Shot of old Fort Garry across the Assinniboine (sic) . . ." . . .'[1]

The Prime Minister's letter was written ten days before the battle of Fort Whyte, described in volume I.

On 22 October 1888 cables passed between Macdonald and Stephen. The latter's read: 'Strongly advise Scarth in his own interest to retain seat and resign connection with Company. Fear resignation seat will not secure him in service Company'. Macdonald cabled 'Pray save Scarth. Honest industrious popular. Crofters apparently happy'. To this Stephen replied next day: 'Gladly do anything for Scarth. Meantime he should act on Smith's suggestion which is utmost possible now. Own view is eventual severance his connection being only question of time, his services not being required'.[2] Meanwhile Macdonald had reported to Scarth the contents of Stephen's letter of 7 October and of the first cable, saying that he did not know whether Stephen had got his letter of 11 October before cabling. He added: 'I suppose you have been writing your friends on the Board, and know all about this Crofter business. If you are relieved of your connection with the Company I need not say that I shall lose no opportunity of forwarding your interests.'[3] On the same day he wrote to Stephen:

---

[1] Macd.LB 25.181, Macdonald to Stephen 11 October 1888. Judge George M. Clark was Chief Solicitor to the C.P.R. (see vol. I, p. 220). What Schultz actually wrote on 8 October 1888 was: 'Scarth saw me today to ask what I thought of Winnipeg were it opened and I told him that it would mean the election of a Grit with a howl of triumph all through the Dominion while a few months' forbearance might change the face of political matters. It is bad enough to have Provencher open and it should be left open till the last moment . . .' (Macdonald Papers MG 26A, vol. 264, Public Archives of Canada). The papers of Dr. John C. Schultz, 1880–95 and 1887–91 in the Provincial Archives of Manitoba, provide further evidence of the precarious position of the Conservative Party in Manitoba at this period, and give further evidence of the characteristics displayed by Scarth of which those interested in the Canada North West Land Company despaired. Wrote the Hon. Joseph Royal to Schultz on 9 February 1888: ' . . . Zeal in politics is a most dangerous factor, and indiscreet friends are sometimes worse than foes. However that may be, Scarth is a good fellow and paved with the best of intentions . . .' (322, Schultz Papers 1880–95) and on 16 February 1888, C. S. Drummond of Drummond Bros. and Moffat, Winnipeg, to Schultz: ' . . . Surely (Scarth) has made a mess of a sufficient number of things to have taught them a lesson at Ottawa—he is a right good fellow but as a diplomat is a serious failure' (324, Schultz Papers 1887–91).   [2] Macdonald Papers 271.
[3] Macdonald Letter Book 25.197.

. . . I was greatly grieved to get your letter and cable about Scarth. He is such a good fellow and so perfectly honest and reliable that I have a great regard for him. I wired you today to save him—as a matter of policy he should be kept as a friend of the C.P.R. just now. Greenway and his Attorney General Martin are behaving so outrageously that we are "laying pipe" to upset their Government and the Lt. Governor Schultz won't stand them long. Then we must have a new Ministry and a General Election. Van Horne and Clark both see the overwhelming importance of upsetting these fellows . . . Now there will be a good deal of sympathy for Scarth—and he will feel very bitter and might do some mischief. I want him and every Conservative to work like Trojans at the Election. I don't want any "*Sore Heads*". A word to the wise. I think this of such importance that I am writing heaps of letters to the N.W. and sometimes think of going up myself. If I were ten years younger I should be there now . . .[1]

Where Macdonald really wanted to be was in England, accepting Stephen's pressing invitation to Latimer, this 'very nice quiet place, trains to and from London every half hour and so quiet that it might be a thousand miles from London', instead of at Ottawa, one eye on Manitoba and the other on Washington, waiting for repercussions on Canada of the imminent presidential election.

Stephen was equally anxious to have Macdonald with him and not only on account of the emigration question. Acknowledging the latter's letters of 10 and 11 October on the 26th, he expressed his disappointment that Macdonald was to be deprived of the benefit of the sea voyage and the break before the beginning of another arduous session. For himself, thinking chiefly of the Manitoba troubles and full of foreboding about the future of Canada, he would have welcomed a talk with the Prime Minister: ' . . . There is no one I can make a confidant of but you hence my craving to see you'. He concluded:

. . . As to poor Scarth he has been such a fool for his own interests that it is now beyond the power of anybody to save him. The most that can be done is to delay the end. The N.W.L. Co. have become convinced that their business can be *better* done by a cheaper and less important man, in short, that they have no use for him. The Company as you know has so far been a disastrous affair for its shareholders who have never received a cent of return on their investment, and it has further failed as an effective instrument for promoting the settlement of the country

---

[1] Macdonald Letter Book 25.204.

so that there is nothing left for the Company to do, but so to husband its resources and to economise in every possible way that the principal of the capital invested in it may eventually be saved and returned to its owners. The business has been a huge failure and a disappointment to every one connected with it and the result is that Scarth's occupation has gone beyond recovery. This is the plain truth of the position as it appears to me and I need not say how sorry I am it should be so. I know how very serious a thing it is for Scarth, who, I quite agree with you in all you say, but we have all to succumb to the inevitable. All this you understand is my own personal view—I am not a Director of the N.W. Land Company but I know pretty well what the real views of the Directors are . . . Scarth should at once set about looking out for some other occupation. Everybody connected with the Land Company likes him personally, and will be glad to do anything they can to help him . . .[1]

Sir Donald Smith, who was a director, had arrived in London to find Scarth's tenure of office, as he wrote to Macdonald, 'hung on the most slender thread'. The Board were unanimous that he ought to go, and 'even our friend Stephen, with all his goodwill personally towards Scarth, has evidently adopted the same view'. The situation was much more critical than the Prime Minister seemed to think; Smith was doing his best, and should he succeed in keeping Scarth in his position with the Company Macdonald must see to it that Scarth spent less time at Ottawa.[2]

In January 1889 Stephen, still at Latimer, was 'still doing my best to keep Scarth where he is, but it is not easy'. Scarth seemed to attend to everything but his work; he scarcely ever wrote to the Board.[3] Stephen was watching enviously the current rush of emigrants to South America, with the consequent 'marvellous' development in these countries. In comparison, the task of filling up the Canadian North West was an uphill one; yet according to Scarth, the Government had no good free lands left east of Medicine Hat. It looked rather as though the proportion of lands taken up greatly exceeded that of lands actually settled: 'one of the worst things that can happen to a country'.[4]

---

[1] Macdonald Papers 271.   [2] Macdonald Papers 265.   [3] Macdonald Papers 271.
[4] Ibid. (In a letter of 8 August 1911, Farrer told a correspondent that in 1882 the Canada North West Land Company was advised to choose land east of Moose Jaw; now immigration was mostly west of Moose Jaw).

Stephen added a postscript to his letter of 25 January 1889: 'What does that crank Goldwin mean by trying to persuade the crofters that Canada is not a suitable place for them. He ought to be "tarred" '. He referred to Goldwin Smith; the two corresponded on a wide range of subjects, although Smith regarded Stephen as an imperialist. The preface to Elisabeth Wallace: *Goldwin Smith*—Victorian Liberal (Toronto, 1957) contains a useful assessment of Smith.

Scarth was still *in situ*, both politically and with the Land Company, when the Prime Minister wrote to him in May that the C.P.R. had finally been persuaded to undertake further extensions in south-western Manitoba which they had until then rejected as being uneconomic. This would attract the usual land grant but no money subsidy. Macdonald suggested that some political capital might be made out of this bonus to the area if Scarth were to inspire a paragraph in the local Press stating that this had been done at the urgent request of Scarth and of Thomas Mayne Daly, who represented Selkirk at Ottawa.[1] That this—and in fact all Macdonald's pleading on behalf of Scarth—was in the current climate of Manitoba a vain effort, was indicated the following year on the passing of the provincial Legislature's land confiscation act. Greenway himself admitted to Thomas Skinner that the object of the Act was to reach the lands of the Canada North West Land Company, and tacitly conveyed to the chairman of the Board that the real target was Scarth, because of his hostility to the Greenway government politically.[2] Nevertheless Macdonald agreed with Scarth that he should not 'play Mr. Greenway's game' by resigning his office, offering to write to the Canadian High Commissioner in London, Sir Charles Tupper, 'or to Sir George Stephen, or to both, pointing out the advantages the Company has hitherto gained by your being in Parliament and the folly of supposing that they can do anything with Greenway . . .'[3]

As regards the advantages mentioned, there was later a suggestion that Scarth's influence had enabled the Land Company to evade taxation. A letter from Gaspard Farrer to Sir Donald Smith on 12 March 1892 quoted Greenway as saying that the Manitoba and North Western had never paid tax on its land grant. On the other hand, the C.P.R. had been granted exemption from taxation for twenty years from completion of the line and in 1902 Farrer was still in some doubt as to whether this also applied to the Land Company.[4] When the 1891 General Election loomed ahead the question again arose as to whether Scarth should not choose between his parliamentary seat and the Company. Donald Smith was confident the Board would not consent to his having both. 'That he has retained his seat so long is entirely owing to the support

[1] Macdonald Letter Book 25.426.
[2] Macdonald Papers 272.
[3] Macdonald Letter Book 27.350.
[4] Gaspard Farrer Letter Books, Farrer to Robert Meighen, 4 June 1902.

Osler and I have extended to him,' he wrote to Macdonald,' and it would not be possible for us to repeat this under present circumstances . . .'[1] Stephen also strongly agreed with this. In the event Scarth was displaced at Winnipeg by Sir John A.'s son, Hugh John Macdonald.[2]

On 9 September 1891 Gaspard Farrer, writing to Mount Stephen, was agreeing that there had been 'too much scolding of Scarth about trifles'. By the following year, however, the London Board were again getting restive, and on 12 March 1892 Farrer wrote to Donald Smith that despite their friendly feelings towards Scarth personally, they had come to the conclusion that he was impossible. For himself, Farrer regarded him, in characteristic terms, as 'straight as a die and zealous as can be' but his business management had been 'a continual bungle' and an 'accumulation of muddling'. He hoped that whatever changes were made might be brought about with good feeling, and in the best interests of the Company. A quite radical change was in fact being discussed: the transfer of the Canada North West Land Company to Canada.

[1] Macdonald Papers 265.
[2] Scarth was to remain prominent in public life; in 1895 he was appointed Deputy Minister of Agriculture of Canada and in addition in 1897 Deputy Commissioner of Patents (administrative, not political posts).

II

Transatlantic circuit: the Great Northern

GRAND METIS

... Every morning on my way to the city I pass close by my house one
of the big fishing-tackle shops, and never fail to think of you or to hear
the running waters of Metis in my ears ...

When Stephen acquired the property at Grand Metis in County
Matane, Quebec, in 1887 he little guessed what the future was to
be for it or for the two friends who were to become so attached to it.
At the time his ties with Canada were still strong; in February of
that year he had written to Macdonald: '... I dare say I may
always remain a Director of the C.P.R. having so much at stake in
it, but I must be rid of all responsibility ...'[1] But his worries were
not to be so easily shaken off and very soon he was to be making
the most strenuous efforts to cut himself off from what promised
never to be a sinecure. The fact that he chose to begin afresh with
a new salmon river at this stage surely indicates that he hoped to go
there regularly for some time. This gains further emphasis from the
circumstances obtaining at Metis; he must have been very much
attracted to the place to take the trouble he did to make it a worth-
while fishing resort.

When Stephen first went to Metis there was hardly any fishing
at all because of the greatly restricted waters below the dam belonging to the Price Brothers' sawmill and above tidal water. He
apparently made up his mind, however, that if the mill dam could
be blown up and access given the fish to about two miles of water
above, he might get very good sport. The opportunity came to do
just this when Price Brothers decided to move their sawmill above
the Metis Falls, both to avoid breakage and damage to their logs
and to facilitate rail shipments. At the risk of spoiling the river
forever, Stephen went ahead with dynamiting the dam, achieving
in the end the result he had hoped for, although the river would

[1] Macdonald Papers 270.

have taken one or two seasons at least to settle down. For this reason he kept on his other fishing lodge at Causapscal until 1891, meanwhile building a new house at Metis, to be known as Estevan Lodge.[1]

The name itself presaged something of the activity that was to become characteristic of Metis; it was the telegraphic code-name which Stephen latterly adopted. Circumstances were to cause him to close very firmly this chapter of his life, but for many years the life of Metis went on for his business friends who could meet there in relaxing surroundings to discuss plans and make decisions, and for his young relatives. The latter were without doubt the more serious fishers. The friend who found the London fishing-tackle shop so evocative was Gaspard Farrer, and he was writing in the spring of 1917 to John W. Sterling, Stephen's lawyer in New York.

GASPARD FARRER

Farrer had written to Stephen on 28 May 1887: '. . . It is too amazing to be away the first year of Metis . . .' In the years that followed he was always disappointed if business kept him in London when he might have been at the fishing, either with Stephen or with Sterling and other friends. His association with Stephen dated from 1880 when Gaspard was twenty years old; his aunt Cecilia was married to Sir Stafford Northcote, later Earl of Iddesleigh, so that their first meeting may have been in the family circle, Alice Stephen having married the Northcotes' second son. Gaspard's first American visit was to his cousin Hugh Oliver Northcote in New York. Stephen had business connections, too, with Farrer's family firm of H. S. Lefevre; beyond that, all had links with Baring Brothers, Farrer becoming a partner there in 1902 after years of working fairly closely with them. Gaspard's first recorded recollection of the association is of sitting in on the early talks about the Canadian Pacific project. He was soon filling the role of the son Stephen was never to have, writing to the latter in terms of affection not used in the letters to his own father, Sir William J. Farrer, which survive in Gaspard's letter books.

Educated at Eton and Balliol, Gaspard Farrer was very much a man of his time, conformist, retaining something of schoolboy enthusiasm well into middle age. He very quickly absorbed the lore of the

---

[1] Mr. Eric Reford to the author, 19 March 1975.

North American industrial and banking world, and became acquainted with its prominent personalities, some of them rather more picturesque than would be found in the City of London. He attached great importance to personal contacts, to making and keeping friends—sometimes through thick and thin—and also to making money, which was, after all, his profession. Too ready, on occasion, to accept people—especially Americans—at their face value, he was less aware than he might have been of the effect that the environment which he took for granted might have on transatlantic visitors. He would find people easy to deal with and 'perfectly straightforward' who on their home ground were nothing short of machiavellian. On the other hand he shared with Stephen to some degree the unreasoning antisemitism of the age. He was himself not always perfectly straightforward, and could with some people be extremely guarded. With Stephen and with Sterling he was frankness personified; he had the greatest admiration for James J. Hill and his achievements, but from an early date watched him also with a critical eye. He had a passion for statistics and would spend leisure hours reshaping balance sheets and company reports with an eye to the ordinary investor, of whom he tended to have a poor opinion. He realized that these reports were to some extent purposely obscure, but also that the compilers had inhibitions about proclaiming accomplishments that had cost too dear to be lightly advertised. Business was his main interest in life; he never married but eventually set up house with his elder and younger brothers Frank and Harry—of the other family firm of solicitors in Lincoln's Inn Fields—in St. James's Square, with a weekend house at Sandwich where he played golf.

JOHN W. STERLING: JAMES STILLMAN

The occasional gaiety and wit of Gaspard's earlier letters could still be evoked in later years when writing to John W. Sterling of New York, a man—some five years younger than Stephen—who inspired in his friends the most paradoxical feelings of respect, affection and, as often in Gaspard's case, the irrepressible desire to tease. A member of the law firm of Shearman and Sterling, he was possibly the safest man in New York, the quintessential trustee. With a well-to-do background, Sterling was a product of Yale and the Columbia Law School. Stephen's first mention of him is in a letter to Macdonald of April 1888; Farrer first writes to him on 8 August 1890, but as to an established friend. On 24 June 1891 Farrer is writing to the Montreal manager of the British Bank of North America who has just turned down a proposition of Sterling's firm:

... I think Mr. Sterling is a man well worth taking trouble to cultivate both on account of his intimate relations with Canadian Pacific friends as well as for a marvelous [sic] knowledge of New York business men and their ways; he is charming personally and as straight as a die and I hope you will get the chance of coming across him again as you would like him and would find him most satisfactory in business dealings. I feel some hesitation in writing you about anyone in New York but I have seen something of the man and a great deal of his work: and this must be my excuse ...

Possibly the greatest test of confidentiality as it was practised between Sterling and his other friends was in his close friendship with James Stillman of the National City Bank.[1] Stillman's interests lay in other, and sometimes opposing directions, yet Hill, Stephen and Farrer could discuss anything and everything with Sterling, secure in the knowledge that it would go no further, or at least not outside their own circle. To Stillman, Sterling was sometimes 'Lord John' because of his connection with Lords Mount Stephen and Strathcona. The banker would occasionally go with Sterling to Metis, along with the man who had first introduced them, J. O. Bloss, the stout, smiling cotton merchant, known to Farrer as 'Blossie'.

According to Stillman's biographer, Anna Robeson Burr, 'Throughout James Stillman's career, the presence of John Sterling in daily contact must be taken for granted as a constant factor'. Sterling, a bachelor, lived 'around the corner' from Stillman, parted from his wife and equally lonely. Burr devotes some paragraphs to the 'picturesque figure' that was Sterling: 'He was an astute mind, ingenious and resourceful, a schemer whose loyalty was as great as his business ability ... He ... deserved his legend more than most Americans. His peculiarities were marked and did not lessen as he grew older. A small, genial man, physically energetic, neither so distinguished-looking nor so finished as his friend, he was exactitude personified ...' He maintained a rigid

[1] Anna Robeson Burr, *The Portrait of a Banker: James Stillman, 1850–1918*, New York 1927, pp. 51, 94, 183, 188–94.

daily routine between office, club and his own and James Stillman's residences, seldom leaving New York except for his annual fishing trip to Canada. Even the solemn Stillman teased him about his eccentricities. Latterly he used to sleep at night locked behind a steel grating; on one occasion at Metis a 'poor demented fellow' stole the butler's coat which had the key in the pocket.[1] Burr mentions Sterling's reluctance to accept a fee from Stillman who was also his client; Farrer on 19 August 1892 appealed to Sterling to charge commission on Lefevres' business; it was small and not worth bothering about but they appreciated Sterling's help and would prefer it to be on a more business-like footing: '... we cannot even growl at you! ...'

A constant factor in Sterling's make-up was his thalassophobia. Although coming from a seafaring Connecticut family he would not even cross a ferry, much less take a sea voyage. In his letter of August 1890 Gaspard feared there was little chance of Stephen bringing him over with him to England the following month. In his later years Sterling was completely cut off from personal contact with Stephen and for long periods from Stillman; even the latter could not persuade him to visit him in his Paris house. Gaspard, however, would see him in New York and at Metis, and would also visit James J. Hill in St. Paul or in Quebec province when he too had a fishing lodge there on the St. John River. Thus, and by voluminous correspondence, was liaison maintained and the disadvantages of vast distance to some extent overcome.

JAMES J. HILL: JOHN S. KENNEDY

Some nine years younger than Stephen, Hill had at one time apparently had ideas of retiring from the 'Manitoba' presidency at fifty. John S. Kennedy had written to him in 1887: '... I know your views about yourself, that you are determined not to continue in your present position after you have attained your fiftieth year, and I think you are right ...'[2] Five years earlier Stephen, before his own most strenuous days on the C.P.R., had registered 'an affectionate protest' at Hill's hours of overtime on the St. Paul, Minneapolis and Manitoba: '... Though you are yourself only a little softer than steel, you, too, will break down ...'[3] evoking the appreciative but irrefutable rejoinder:

---

[1] Mr. Eric Reford to the author, 12 May 1971.
[2] Pyle, op. cit. vol. I, p. 433.   [3] Ibid. p. 340.

... I cannot close without thanking you for the kind personal interest you express. Our work is increasing with the ratio of the development of the railway, and it seems necessary for us to be always on the alert to any movement that will fortify our position or increase our revenue, and the familiarity with the situation which is necessary cannot be gotten except by personal acquaintance. We were very opportune in getting possession of the Red River Valley before other lines got a foothold. It is from there and Manitoba we draw our earnings. I would certainly rejoice if I could have more time to rest and be with our children, who are getting to an age when I might be of use to them, but our property is nearly all new, and unlike old roads, whose staff has been doing the same things at the same places for years. A failure to take in the whole situation owing to lack of knowledge or judgment, and under plea of temporary convenience or some other cause—matters are given a wrong direction and in the hurry of increasing business a precedent is established which is hard to change, or it is entirely overlooked and a permanent injury is the result. Every day's observation convinces me that in a new country a railroad is successful in the proportion its affairs are vigilantly looked after. There is no substitute for hard work, and the value of a railway is its capacity to earn money ...[1]

In 1888, when he would have been fifty, far from thinking of withdrawal, Hill was seeking fresh fields to conquer, and his old friends of the 'Manitoba' enterprise were ready to follow where he led. It was indeed to be a case of standing by him through thick and thin. Kennedy had told him in 1886: 'My confidence in your judgment and integrity is such that I am ready to the extent of my ability to go into anything which you ask me to, in which you are yourself interested, and of which you have the controlling direction' ...[2] just as Stephen, in the discussion already quoted (p. 23 above) on the Pacific extension, wrote: ' ... I have so much confidence in the soundness of your judgment in such matters that my inclination is always to accept your views, largely because they are your views'.

Among the reasons that made Stephen and his close friends stand by Hill through prolonged periods of uncertainty, personal regard and faith in his managerial flair stood high. There was also their own heavy financial involvement to consider; to show the slightest lack of confidence might well have brought down the whole pack of cards. There were to be moments of sheer exasperation when, in the intervals between the long explanatory letters from Hill, they were not kept informed; when appeals for money

[1] Ibid. pp. 340–1.   [2] Ibid. p. 408.

came at short notice and without prior consultation, or when action was taken with more regard to railroad politics than to sound finance as viewed from the City of London. Although Hill and Stephen met at intervals, or Farrer acted as go-between, the very distance at which Hill operated, with management of the expanding railroad network as his first and daily concern, made for occasional misunderstandings. Farrer in particular could react—perhaps over-react—with pungent comment.

Gaspard Farrer early developed the defensive attitude towards Stephen which no doubt partly accounted for his posture of caution *vis-à-vis* Hill. That he had shared some of the agonies of Canadian Pacific crises is indicated in a letter of 25 September 1885, written to an uncle who evidently contemplated investing in this new project:

... One word with regard to Mr. Stephen; he has been much abused but I know that he has made large personal sacrifices for the general good of shareholders and would have been a richer man today had he never had anything to do with the Canadian Pacific; in my short city experience I have never come across anyone so scrupulously upright (it seems to me almost wronging him to write thus) or one on whose judgment I would sooner rely, and if this is correct, his opinion is worth that of all the bankers of London, New York and Amsterdam—for he knows the facts the best. He is now on his way over and if there are any points on which you would like information I know he will be delighted to give it, it is his great wish to have as much light thrown on the affairs of the Company as possible. Please forgive this long epistle—I have watched the road from its birth and can't help thinking everyone must be as interested in the success of the Canadian North West as your affectionate nephew ...

Of Hill, on the other hand, Gaspard would write, as he did to John S. Kennedy on 3 September 1887 regarding a scheme for terminal facilities: '... Mr. Hill seems so impressed with the humanitarian desire to give every American, British, Dutch and German investor the inestimable advantage of lending their savings to the "finest road in the finest country in creation" that he appears to be in danger of inverting the pyramid ...' He was glad to think that Kennedy was still on the 'Manitoba' Board: 'I don't suppose any Western man yet born does the worse for being backed by a little Scotch prudence ...' Born at Blantyre, Lanarkshire, John Stewart Kennedy had emigrated to America in 1850, the same year in which Stephen came to Canada, finally settling in New York in 1856 and pursuing a successful banking career. By the time that Hill and his friends were taking up the railroad that became the 'Manitoba' Kennedy had amassed a fortune of half a million dollars; participation in the 'Manitoba' enterprise—Stephen allotted to him the fifth share which he had at his disposal for the purpose of raising the necessary capital—earned for him the nickname of 'the Scotch millionaire'.[1]

JACOB SCHIFF

In his letter of 13 March 1888 to Oliver Northcote (quoted above p. 18) Gaspard Farrer mentioned a syndicate which had been formed to dispose of a quantity of 'Manitoba' $4\frac{1}{2}$ per cent bonds, going on to say: 'I should think Hill must be working infinite damage to the credit of his property by his methods of finance . . .' After his visit that year to St. Paul and to Stephen at Metis he wrote to Hill that if the 'Manitoba' wished to dispose of a million dollars' worth of $4\frac{1}{2}$s 'unsold under Kuhn Loeb's option' his firm—Lefevres —would make a bid. There was a limited market in London for the road's securities which were quoted on the Stock Exchange, but nothing was being done to popularise them; this, he felt, could be done. Barings were the people to handle them in London, although he assumed the sum was too small for them. There is implicit here some resentment that Hill should be dealing with Kuhn Loeb, who were the following year to handle also extension bonds of the Eastern Railroad of Minnesota, the 'Manitoba's' link with Duluth.

The New York banking house of Kuhn, Loeb and Company meant at this time Jacob H. Schiff, son-in-law of Solomon Loeb, one of the two German-born founders. Schiff had joined the firm in 1875 and by 1886 was on intimate terms with James J. Hill; in that year he handled the previous 'Manitoba' loan issue. Schiff wrote to Kennedy that this had been a great success in New York and demand in Europe far exceeded allocations there.[2] Schiff's biographer, Cyrus Adler, publishing in 1929—nine years after

[1] RA GV C273/74, Lord Mount Stephen to Sir Arthur Bigge, 16 October 1908. See Heather Gilbert, *The Unaccountable Fifth*, in *Minnesota History*, Spring 1971; Dolores Greenberg, *A Study of Capital Alliances* : *The St. Paul and Pacific*, in *Canadian Historical Review*, March 1976; also index references to Kennedy in Gilbert, vol. 1. He was to hand over his New York firm to his nephew J. Kennedy Tod.
[2] Pyle, op. cit. vol. 1, p. 410.

JOHN W. STERLING
(from *The National Cyclopaedia of American Biography*,
by permission of James T. White & Co.)

Schiff's death at 73—quotes the unanimous verdict of three men on their late associate, that his financial achievements rested upon both his unusual grasp of problems and his unusual courage; that while essentially conservative, he often went in where others feared to tread; and that nevertheless he had rarely made a mistake in business judgment.[1] One of the three quoted—the others were Edouard Noetzlin and Max Warburg—was Robert Fleming, Aberdeen born London financier, regarded by George Stephen as one of the greatest authorities in the City of London on transatlantic investments.[2] Adler goes on to say of Schiff:

He would come to believe in a man, and doing so would accept that man's judgment even in matters of very large import. His complete confidence in [Sir Ernest] Cassel, the empire-building vision of James J. Hill, [Edward H.] Harriman's dynamic personality, the reserve and caution of Stillman, the close ties of family and affection with the house of Warburg in Hamburg all went along to influence what were in the aggregate vast business transactions.

Stephen was later to link Cassel's name with that of Fleming as being particularly knowledgeable about American securities; Gaspard Farrer took Cassel less seriously. Harriman—ultimately the giant of the Union Pacific Railroad—was perhaps the most controversial character of his period in American railway history; his prolonged battle with Hill over spheres of influence in the west will be dealt with presently. It would be too much to say that this situation preconditioned Farrer to find Harriman a congenial acquaintance; at the time it came as a surprise to him.

Although Schiff became a director of the Great Northern in 1893, he did not do any considerable financing for it, if only because Hill's Great Northern policy, as Adler points out, and as Farrer often complained, was to secure capital, whenever possible, from the limited circle of stockholders, rather than from the general public. The railroad was managed from St. Paul although the company had a fiscal office in New York. On one point Farrer and Schiff were in complete agreement: that Hill played his cards at times too close to his chest. Schiff wrote to Hill on 28 June 1893 that the New

[1] Cyrus Adler, *Jacob H. Schiff, His Life and Letters*, London, 1929, 2 vols., vol. I, pp. 24–25. See also Kuhn, Loeb and Company, *A Century of Investment Banking*, New York, 1967.
[2] See references in W. Turrentine Jackson, *The Enterprising Scot* : Investors in the American West after 1873, Edinburgh 1968.

York office appeared to be kept in the dark, whereas it should know months ahead with what it had to deal. On a later occasion Schiff declared that if a proper system could be not inaugurated to keep the New York office informed, it would be useless to have New York directors or a New York office.[1] Many years later, after Hill's death, Farrer had occasion to congratulate Edward T. Nichols, who had been in charge of the Great Northern's New York office, on his election as a director of the Chase Bank:

... In your Railroad capacity you have always been so considerate to us here that there would be no justification for my giving you the sly digs which I enjoyed passing on to our late lamented friend. You may remember his general antipathy to bankers, who by his talk one would think he believed to have but one 'raison d'être', viz: to get their hands into his Railroad till and sweep it clean. I often used to tell him, and you will soon find, that a Banker's calling is nothing but a profession of altruism, always doing business today for nothing in the hopes that the account may be valuable tomorrow; but tomorrow never comes. If you Railroad men come into banking in the end, it is only after the heyday of life has been spent in railroading, at a time when you have made your piles and are thinking only of how you may best distribute them for the good of humanity ... (8 February 1917)

Judging by the verdict on Schiff quoted above, he might have been Stephen's ideal banker. 'A successful banker needs two things,' Stephen once told Macdonald, 'caution and courage'.[2] He was thinking of his friend Sir John Rose, a professional banker, who had just died, and who 'had the former in a high degree but was totally wanting in the latter'. In this connection it is interesting to read the assessment of James Stillman by Anna Robeson Burr; Stillman always spoke of himself as a 'merchant banker': he was, says Burr, the 'banker-merchant' type *par excellence*, but in an age when these were 'grave gentlemen with side whiskers and string ties', Stillman had certain added qualities, certain audacities and breadths of view, which later on were to make them gasp. This 'quick, quiet, accurate youth' had early shown the chief characteristics of the banker; he was 'cool and wise and loyal, above all loyal' with the loyalty which instinctively put bank or business first.[3]

[1] Adler, op. cit. vol. I, p. 84.
[2] Macdonald Papers 271, 7 October 1888.
[3] Burr, op cit. pp. 47, 50–51.

Jacob Schiff's main concern had been the financing of American railroads, in the sense which included Canada and Mexico. In 1882–3 his company, Kuhn, Loeb, was involved in the Canadian Pacific's Stock Syndicate with its linked Contracting Company. A further quotation from Sir John Rose's letter to Sir John A. Macdonald of 1 February 1883 (see vol. I, pp. 113–16) gives a more precise idea of this participation:

Leading Houses in New York, here [London], Paris and Amsterdam have taken firm $10,000,000 of the ordinary stock, and at a price which will give the Company over £1,000,000 sterling. They have the option to purchase $20,000,000 more at enhanced rates making in all $30,000,000. If the public will subscribe for the first $10,000,000 now offered, which there is a probability of their doing, the new Syndicate will take the remainder in two calls of $10,000,000 each. This would give the Company between 3 and £4,000,000 in cash, and that sum with the balance of the subsidy and a part of the Lands including those sold to the Canada North West Land Company should be sufficient to complete the Road. An affiliated organization in the shape of a construction company propose undertaking the entire remainder of the work for these figures and the balance of the stock:—less $10,000,000 reserved to meet future outlay for Rolling Stock, Improvements &c.

At the time success seemed assured. Schiff wrote to Ernest Cassel on 19 June 1883: 'The American public is buying Canadian Pacific stock very eagerly. Since we took the management [of the sales] into our hands on behalf of the committee, six weeks ago, we have sold almost the whole second option of 100,000 shares, and the last option will probably be called within a few days'.[1] He was particularly attracted by the C.P.R.'s financial policy of raising money through issues of stock rather than increasing its bonded debt and thereby its fixed charges. As regards the 'construction stock' in which he and Cassel each had an interest, Schiff wrote to the latter in July 1883 that these shares would probably fluctuate widely during the next few months, since there was a large speculative supply, but he felt, nevertheless, that the road, with its three thousand miles of line and eighteen million acres of good land, was not unduly capitalized.[2] After the financial crisis of 1884 which dashed all Stephen's hopes, Schiff's interest in the Canadian Pacific became merely academic.

[1] Adler, op. cit. vol. I, p. 198.   [2] Ibid.

GREAT NORTHERN COMPLETED: WALL STREET CRISIS

On the eve of the great American panic of 1893 the Great Northern, its Pacific extension nearly completed, seemed to be going from strength to strength, although the Canadian Pacific's agent in Amsterdam saw it in a less favourable light. Gaspard Farrer wrote to Stephen on 1 June 1892 of Boissevain's enthusiasm over the C.P.R. and its President Van Horne:

... even that astute gentleman would be staggered at the virtues which our Dutch friend has been attributing to him. He sings a different tune over G.N. and made me shiver all down the backbone by the shakings of his head and accounts of Jim Hill's doings. I suppose the fact is that he and Hill have fallen out.

Despite his occasional carping at Hill, Farrer on 22 and 24 August 1892 was writing to a merchant of St. James's recommending both 'Manitoba's' and Great Northern as an investment: (Even the large holders did not transfer all their investment from the old road to the new.)

... Mr. Hill expects to have his trains running to the coast by 1 January 1893. The money for completion is provided and the cost has been within estimates. Mr. Hill writes that when finished and in operation earnings of the past year will be not only maintained but increased; and we have always found his statements more than realized by results.

I am often asked why the road should be better than many of its neighbours; in my opinion because the directors are the chief owners of its stock and because it has been the policy of the Company from its inception that no one should make a dollar out of it except as owner of its securities: hence there are no inside shows, no equipment companies, terminal companies, Express companies etc. etc. owned by Directors and leased at extravagant rentals sucking out the life blood of the property, —but every cent the Company can earn belongs to and reaches its proprietors,—that coupled with able management in operation and finance has been the secret of its success ...

Mount Stephen was at this time in Scotland for the grouse-shooting season. Using the nickname by which his intimate circle referred to him, Farrer told Sterling on 19 August:

... Lady Boss writes me that the Boss is in fine form and though he will not shoot himself walks all day on the hills with the shooters and comes home as fresh as the youngest. We are expecting Mr. Van Horne in about a week. Both he and the Boss more enterprizing than ever. We rejoice for their sake that matters are so prosperous . . .

Farrer believed quite sincerely, if not unquestioningly, in the future of the Great Northern, his faith resting on the value of the property as he knew it at first hand. He wrote to Hill on 7 January 1893 hoping they might see him in London 'now that you have got your line through to the Coast. How relieved you must feel to have finished that heavy work'.

Acknowledging on 18 March 1893 an offer of 'Manitoba' 4½s from New York, Farrer wrote to J. Kennedy Tod that his firm would have accepted, being confident of placing them in London, but supposed that Tod's 'Jew colleague on the [Great Northern] Board'—i.e. Jacob Schiff—would have reacted unfavourably had he not 'shared in the plunder'. The 4½s were already being offered in London 'and will doubtless all find their way over as have the Willmar and Sioux Falls Bonds. But why' he wanted to know 'is *Hill* in such a hurry for his money, to want it before the Bonds are ready? Would you let me have a line on this point and whether he has formed any plans for the future? A friend recently back from the States gives a poor account of his, Hill's health, excitability and trouble with his arm, but I hope these are passing evils . . .'

He wrote himself to Hill on 24 March, regretting that the latter had been prevented by pressure of business from carrying out his intention to pay them a visit that winter, and reporting 'surprising progress' in the Great Northern's credit as evidenced by some brisk buying. All the Willmar and Sioux Falls Bonds had been re-sold by Kuhn, Loeb and Company to Hill's friends in London at from about par to 103½ and now stood at 109–10. The 4½s also were doing well and might also soon all be in London. The guaranteed stock was unobtainable; but—postulated Farrer—'your objection to having the stock here can't apply to the *bonds* . . .' Hill might bear his London friends in mind; they would prefer to buy direct from the Company rather than pay Schiff and friends 2 or 3 per cent: 'we know, because we and friends were the buyers from Kuhn, Loeb'.

The line from Willmar, due west of Minneapolis, south-westerly to Sioux Falls, Sioux City and ultimately to Yankton on the Nebraska border, had been recently gathered into the Hill system, giving, as Hill wrote to Donald A. Smith in 1893, the shortest and practically the only direct line from the large pine forests of Minnesota—the largest left standing east of the Rocky Mountains—

to a connection with all the east and west lines crossing southern Minnesota and Northern Iowa, as well as direct connection with the Nebraska, Kansas and South Western lines at Sioux City.[1] This protective shield on the Great Northern's eastern flank was eventually to pave the way for the Burlington purchase.

Why was Hill in such a hurry for his money in March 1893? By the close of the previous year, in the midst of a confused political situation in the United States, the far-sighted had already detected the approach of a crisis in national finance. But for the record harvest of 1891, coinciding with a European grain famine, it would have come earlier in the wake of the crisis of liquidity which had overcome Barings in London in November 1890. But bountiful harvests brought their own financial problems in the form of provision for transport and storage, and of the circulation of money from the city banks to the farming areas at the appropriate time, even if this would gradually percolate back from the country banks as the crops were marketed. In previous seasons Hill had advanced to the farmers who used his road considerable sums on the security of the crops; this had of course paid dividends discernible in traffic returns. The increased exports of grain had however been accompanied by record imports into the United States from Europe at a time when, if the post-1890 withdrawal of European capital had eased off, there was still some reluctance in London to invest in transatlantic enterprises. In April 1893 rumours of a currency crisis began to circulate in America, the basic question being the ability of the U.S. Treasury to redeem its own notes in gold. Assurances first by the Secretary of the Treasury and then by the President himself served only to feed suspicion and on Wall Street the mounting reaction of panic set in. Pyle quotes an undated letter written about this time from Hill to Mount Stephen:

Under ordinary conditions it would be safe to depend upon sales of treasury securities, and surplus earnings; but uncertainty of the Government's silver policy disturbs all finance and might in emergency compel us to sell securities so much below value as to affect the general standing of securities previously sold, reacting on the Company's credit, or forgo doing what might be greatly to the Company's advantage. The sole object of the present issue is to furnish the Company with five millions of cash working capital, avoiding any sudden necessity for using its credit, leaving it very strong under all conditions that may arise.[2]

[1] Pyle, op. cit. vol. 1, p. 466.   [2] Ibid. p. 491.

The first week of May saw the collapse of the whole stock market, and a general run on cash from the banks. In this situation of general liquidation Hill cabled on 5 May to Mount Stephen a summary of the Great Northern's position:

Through line completed and paid for; Company owns Coast line 183 miles with large terminals at all important points costing $5.3 million upon which no mortgage or bonds; also an interest of $1 million in the line to Portland, owned jointly with Union Pacific; $600,000 in coal and other properties on the coast; about $2.3 million in bonds, and $2 million in bills receivable, $1.5 million of which will come into the treasury as bonds on connecting and proprietary lines. Our Company has no floating debt.[1]

This brief for the purpose of encouraging the friends who were Mount Stephen's usual sources of capital for the various enterprises in which he interested them may have done something to comfort those who were already in Great Northern: only the stoutest hearts would be ready to venture into further investment, for the tide of inevitable repercussion was already beginning to beat upon the further shore. Writing to his father on 23 May 1893 when the tempest had subsided a little, Gaspard Farrer quoted Francis Le Marchant, his partner in Lefevres, younger brother of the senior partner Sir Henry Le Marchant:

... Francis tells me the panic here last week was worse than anything we had at the time of the Baring crisis, that is to say, people were more frightened. The recovery for the moment has been remarkable, so sharp that we anticipate some reaction ...

On 23 June 1893 Jacob Schiff wrote to James J. Hill:

The demand for money to move the crops must necessarily greatly add to the tension already existing, and it behooves everybody to be most careful in getting his house in order before the autumn demand be upon us ... I have never experienced a similar state of affairs since I have been in business and I only hope the worst may be over, though I am not at all confident.[2]

Schiff's biographer observes that in reporting to correspondents on the financial situation, Schiff tended for the most part to see crop conditions as the determining factor; next came political conditions; the fluctuations of the stock market were the least significant.[3]

---

[1] Ibid. p. 477.   [2] Adler, op. cit. vol. I, p. 32.   [3] Ibid. p. 29.

Although movements in the mercurial environment of Wall Street or the City of London might well of themselves generate the most devastating financial cyclones from time to time, necessitating the keeping of a weather-eye open, the state of the crops in the American and Canadian farmlands was a recurring theme in railroading circles, being reported on at intervals throughout the growing season. Early estimates might by the end of harvest be completely falsified; abundant crops might of themselves cause the price of grain to sag, with unexpected repercussions in the business world. As to political considerations, the policies of a political party or the whims of an incoming President might have results as crippling as an international war—as evidenced in the American anti-trust legislation and the manner in which it was interpreted at different times.

The reaction in the London market anticipated by Farrer came and was repeated throughout the summer of 1893. He wrote to J. Kennedy Tod on 19 July acknowledging the latter's report on the situation in New York, which was not encouraging, and amplifying the cable he had sent regarding the position on his side. The first American railway collapse of this period—that of the Philadelphia and Reading—had made the London stock markets uncomfortable: there was no demand for investment securities nor did the American speculative list arouse any enthusiasm; distrust was growing all the time, developing the previous day into uncontrolled panic. Things looked better today but might still be a long way off permanent recovery. '. . . the general public will not buy freely till your currency question is settled and then only if your markets are continuously good . . .' There was a general impression in London that some great calamity was impending in the American market— he hoped Tod would give them due warning—but Farrer himself thought that the situation could be explained by stringent money and the weak position of some other railroads. Seven days later came Black Wednesday on Wall Street; the wholesale importation of foreign gold; the equally violent recovery affecting prices both of securities and of commercial products.

HILL APPEALS TO MOUNT STEPHEN FOR FINANCIAL AID

Mount Stephen had had a sudden appeal from Hill, and the Canadian Pacific too was in need of help. At Lefevres, Gaspard as usual was impatient of Hill's peremptoriness, writing to Mount Stephen on 22 August 1893:

What rubbish about 'short sales'. Hill has obviously borrowed the money already and is being pressed to repay. However we will lend a hand if we can. Enclosed is a copy of the telegram sent you this afternoon so that you could, if you wished, get posted forthwith as to (1) the financial position of Hill's road (2) the possibilities of Van Horne's requirements. You will recollect that the balance of your N[ational] P[rovincial Bank] loan (£48,000) becomes due 31 August. It would be advisable to repay this in any case; and we will see to this providing for whatever stock is not taken by the market. My cousin [Le Marchant] thinks that there would be no difficulty then in *your* getting £50,000 or perhaps £100,000 from the Bank for say six months fixed. It would be very desirable that the collateral should be mixed and quoted in London—not all guaranteed shares—if Robinson [of National Provincial] were to ask Scrimgeour [broker] what market there was for them the answer would not be reassuring. Robinson would look to us for information in a general way as to St. Paul, Minneapolis and Manitoba's position so we should wish to be satisfied on this point . . .

Farrer expected no difficulty as to collateral if the loan were to be for £50,000 only; if for £100,000, and the American market position did not improve, it would then possibly prejudice any later attempt by Van Horne to raise a large sum on the same sort of security. He went on:

If you were to lend Hill the money ought you not to have his gold note with a twelve months option on say G.N. shares at a low price. I hear 6% interest 5% commission and options at low prices on the collaterals are the terms which many rich people are offering to pay—the Union Pacific whose advertisement in this week's Chronicle is paying 8 p.c. interest and 5% commission and the security is excellent. But I suppose you would hardly wish to Jew Hill, but I hope you will leave plenty of room for yourself and us in case we do anything to help Hill. My cousin says Robinson may ask our endorsement so that he may have some one at hand whom he can worry if need be, and I think I could persuade my cousin to assent.

Please understand that we have not said a word to Robinson yet and my cousin may be quite mistaken in thinking we can do anything at all for you or Hill (except taking care of the Debenture Stock on which you may count). The amount unsold is £130,000 in addition to which we are carrying for the dealers £40,000. I had already arranged with Bishopsgate Street [i.e. Baring Brothers] that next time the dealers send in to bid it would be wise to offer them £100,000 as "all" and we and the Barings would take the £30,000 between us . . .

Farrer then referred back to a proposal, made to Hill a year earlier, either by Mount Stephen and himself or by the firm of Lefevres, that guaranteed shares of the 'Manitoba' should be deposited at the National Provincial Bank in London. He had written to Sterling on 19 August 1892 that J. Kennedy Tod wanted to activate the London market for 'Manitoba' shares but that Hill preferred the stock to remain in America. Farrer's firm were accustomed to acquire their shares through Sterling from New York, where these were not always readily available. Now Farrer could not refrain from adding:

Is it not vexing to think that if Hill has assented to our plan proposed a year ago domiciling guaranteed shares at the N.P. he might now have applied there and got his money comfortably as a *customer*. I cannot help chuckling to think of how he has now come grovelling after the way he has behaved . . .

The following day he wrote again to Mount Stephen acknowledging two letters and enclosing a copy of a telegram sent that afternoon asking for Mount Stephen's final decision about collateral for the loan being applied for that week by Le Marchant from the National Provincial Bank:

. . . It will be best to offer ample margin say 50% at least. As to terms he will suggest 1 p.c. above Bank rate and a minimum of 6 for six months fixed. It would not be wise to ask for a longer time . . .

Le Marchant—a director of the National Provincial—had reminded Gaspard that there was nothing in the transaction for Lefevres; he could not put forward the application for the bank's favourable consideration and at the same time benefit by it:

My cousin has given me a warm half hour over Hill's shortcomings. I wish that gentleman had been present. Does not all his action the past few years show that there should be some one on the Board in New York in English interests: Mr. Sterling for instance if he would accept. With a property of that magnitude "one man finance" and "one man management" is never advisable—and Tod and Schiff are only there to rob . . .

He assured Mount Stephen that he would do his best to get the money there or elsewhere—unfortunately Robinson himself was away otherwise he should have felt more confident—'but in these times you must not rely on my hopes or expectations . . .'

Le Marchant's application to the National Provincial was apparently unsuccessful. The next expedient being considered appeared to be the purchase outright by his London friends either of a quantity of 'Manitoba' guaranteed shares or of other securities held by Hill and deemed inadequate when offered as collateral for a loan. Farrer wrote to Mount Stephen on 28 August 1893:

No doubt there is a turn in guaranteed shares whether at 85 or 90: but perhaps the most unsatisfactory finale will be if Hill is relieved of a block of shares which I imagine neither you, [Donald A.] Smith and certainly we do not want and at a price which Hill does not like.

When Tod cabled he offered on Hill's account $250,000 Neba Consols 6s at 110 flat New York and $250,000 Montana 6s at 103—If Hill still has and cares to sell the Consols at 103 London we would probably take them ourselves, or the most of them, and should be willing to wait better times to sell them. I wired this afternoon to ask you this.

The tone here distinctly better, but no business. I send copy of this to Aberdeen in case you have left Ellis before the post arrives.

Gaspard's handwriting was not of the clearest, but in view of later events it is reasonable to guess that at this critical juncture, before leaving for an autumn holiday in Scotland, Mount Stephen should pay a flying visit to his friend Charles Ellis.

CHARLES ELLIS

It is not clear how Mount Stephen came to know Charles Ellis so well; after the latter's death in 1906 Gaspard Farrer was to tell John Sterling: 'I am afraid the Boss will feel his loss badly. I think Charlie Ellis really liked him better than anyone else, and though they did not see a great deal of each other owing to one living at Haslemere and the other at Brocket, they wrote constantly, and I have no doubt that Charlie Ellis thought more of Lord Mount Stephen than of anyone else . . .' Four years earlier Farrer had written to Sterling of Ellis: 'There is nothing he would not have been able to accomplish if he had been compelled to work'. Of apparently considerable independent means, and well-connected, (he was the third son of the sixth Lord Howard de Walden) Ellis was a bachelor 'not on very good terms with his relations'; an expert and indefatigable naturalist, who established a remarkable botanical garden at Frensham Hall in Surrey of which Gaspard wrote: 'There is no place like it in England; only ninety acres in all and every inch of it planted with some tree or shrub gathered from all over the world'. More of a scientist than merely an eccentric, Ellis was to become at the very end a virtual recluse, but one gets the impression that all along he had preferred nature in the raw to the human species. 'He was certainly the most individualistic character whom I have ever met', Gaspard told Sterling in 1906, 'and in spite of his strong prejudices and dislikes attracted by the force of his character the affection of a large number of friends'. Sterling had never met Ellis, but knew him well by repute; to Hill he was known personally. He was one of those friends of Mount Stephen who could generally be relied on to make large investments in time of need, and to hold on to them.

From a diary which Ellis kept on a youthful trip to Canada and the United States in 1860 one learns a good deal about him: he was travelling with the eighteen-year-old Prince of Wales on a State visit, but not being officially a member of the suite had time for his own pursuits and roamed more widely over American rivers and railroads. He was probably present at the levee which George Stephen attended in Montreal (vol. 1, p. 8) but one cannot be sure: a typical diary entry after a one-and-a-half hour visit to Cape Breton Island was: 'H.R.H. was received by the volunteers. I went into the woods and caught some Fritillaries . . .' He was not over-impressed by the Falls at Niagara but ' . . . I caught a garter snake crawling across the road at about 10 p.m., the first that I had ever seen at night'. The diary reveals his wide technical knowledge —botanical, zoological, mechanical, nautical—and his open-minded grasp of the transatlantic idiom; his sensitivity to sight, sound and taste: he delighted equally in a procession of salmon-fishing canoes on the Saguenay or in a prettily-decorated ballroom; 'the sound of the axes in the still summer evening' or 'my first mint julep . . . a tremendous composition'. He was delighted rather than deterred when he 'Got some hawk moth caterpillars on a tomato'. He was careful about money: he bought a mackintosh ($9) and some Indian canoe sketches ($6); changed a £10 note ($48.20c.—9 per cent premium). Though there were lots of furs and curiosities to be sold, they were dearer than in England 'so I was not tempted'. He noted that 'They made us pay two shillings at a turnpike' and that 'Peaches are 18 cents the bushel in Illinois and Michigan'. He was ready for adventure: 'We expected to meet Comanche Indians and so were obliged to keep away from the

Chapparals, where they might be lurking but none appeared much to my sorrow'. He was however absentminded; he was apt to leave behind in hotel rooms anything from his portmanteau to his pet snake or his 'two remaining bats from the Kentucky cave'. During a stormy voyage home 'My eyeless fish from Kentucky and my white crawfish got smashed up, also all my ferns . . . Horned toad died yesterday . . .' There is a whimsical entry regarding the last lap of the journey, on the train from Plymouth to Oxford: 'one of my dear little alligators departed this life after surviving the dangers and hardships of an Atlantic voyage—it expired ingloriously in my carpet bag, about Didcot'. Happily, however, 'my other pets, viz one alligator, two horned toads, a small snapping turtle, two snakes from Niagara and Montreal, one snake from Halifax, a black rat from the *Ariadne* and two beavers have all arrived safe at their destination'.[1] Ellis was then twenty years old. He was probably a visitor in the 1880s to Stephen's Quebec fishing lodge; in the latter's Will, one of the items specially mentioned was 'The picture in black and white of Causapscal given to me by the Honourable Charles Ellis'.

GREAT NORTHERN WEATHERS THE STORM

By the beginning of September 1893 the seasonal drain of currency to the grain-growing areas had ended and was in reverse. The stock market cycle which owed its motivation to human opportunism rather than to nature in the raw moved inexorably round through the stages of liquidation, low-price buying, profit-taking, stagnation, and finally recovery. But the Great Northern's two competitors in the West, the Union Pacific and the Northern Pacific, along with several other American railroads and numerous commercial enterprises, were bankrupt. To Sterling in New York Gaspard wrote on 17 November 1893 in more cheerful vein about Mount Stephen, back from Scotland and 'bursting with energy. I think there is likely to be a good demand for the Canadian Pacific Preference Stock and quite expect to see it selling at 94–5 before another six months are over'. But he finished: 'We are dreadfully disgusted at getting no news from Hill'.

This omission was shortly repaired, and on 25 November he was

[1] *Diary of Charles A. Ellis 1860*, unpublished, in the possession of the late Lt. Col. the Hon. A. C. Campbell.

acknowledging a 'full and satisfactory message' from Hill regarding the Great Northern's financial position, sent by cable in answer to an enquiry by Lefevres. This had put the firm in a position to speak confidently on the Company's prospects—not possible hitherto for lack of information. The Great Northern's strong cash position would, he hoped, enable Hill to 'work comfortably through what must be a trying year looking to present dulness in trade and such ugly competition as Union and Northern Pacific Roads must be when in the hands of Receivers'. The G.N.'s annual report had not yet however been vouchsafed, and Gaspard went on to prod Hill gently:

An ill-conditioned devil named Wilson, city editor of the "Standard", has been damning the road in maps in a Review of his called "Directors' Review" and his article in these times of want of confidence has attracted some attention: but this will soon pass away when we have your report. We are earnestly hoping you will come over in January. Your presence here would help the credit of your road immensely—there are so many points which can be talked over which cannot be discussed by letter. We think your 4% Bonds ought to sell at par and want to see them there . . .

He added a characteristic message to Mrs. Hill, for whom he had a quite unreserved admiration, and 'I hope to be out in the Spring with Lord Mount Stephen and intend then to exact from your little girl her promise of violin playing'.[1]

The annual report was already on the way and on 1 December 1893 Farrer was sending a copy to a firm of stockbrokers in the City with an enthusiastic commentary, highlighting the favourable points as he wished the compilers of the balance sheets would do: 'Whatever Wilson may write there is no road in the United States so lightly capitalized considering the property involved'. The following day he was reporting to Sterling: '. . . Stock Exchange is booming, such as we have not seen it since '89. Canadian Pacific Preference Stock $91\frac{1}{2}$ and I hope will be 95 before another three months'.

FARRER 'LOOKS AT STATISTICS'

It has been mentioned that Gaspard Farrer had a passion for statistics: that might be amplified to 'the concise presentation of

---

[1] That the violin-playing daughter was Charlotte, who later married George T. Slade, was confirmed to the author by Charlotte's daughter, Mrs. Georgiana Slade Reny.

statistics giving the maximum amount of useful information within the smallest possible compass'. He waged a life-long campaign in this cause—largely ineffectually, as on 23 September 1932 he was still pleading with Robert Winsor, Jr., a son of a long-standing business acquaintance in the Boston firm of Kidder, Peabody:

Do not trouble to send me masses of statistics, just half a sheet of notepaper to say what the present position is and what the prospects seem to be.

It sometimes seems to me that your financial community have gone statistic-mad—judging from the masses which some of my American friends are kind enough to send me; statistics got together at great labour and expense, and which, to me at least, are perfectly useless, and I should think to my banking friends who compile them. Statistics are essential for the Management, to know where and how earnings are coming in and, still more important, where money is leaking out in operation, but after all they are ancient history. What you and I want to know is what is going to happen tomorrow, and the really most important issue for us is the character of management, its efficiency and honesty . . .

Farrer was much impressed by the railroad operating sheet evolved by James J. Hill to be presented monthly (there was also an annual version) enabling the G.N. President to 'drop on to an offending spender instantaneously . . . Once familiar with the principles it does not take ten to twenty minutes a month to grasp the contents'. He explained these principles in a letter of 30 November 1897 to J. Douglas Fletcher:

Taking the average cost per ton mile, the unit of Railroad business, you will see the relative cost on the different divisions, cost in the corresponding period last year, and the comparison of each division to the whole; if anything unusual strikes you, carry your eye up to the train mile cost and you will see at once where the saving or additional expense occurred i.e. in station service or train service etc. etc; and that discovered you can spot the details of expense or saving higher up the sheet. If the explanation of variations in ton mile cost do not lie there, it will be found in the average number of tons moved per train—i.e. average train load, the line in the sheet following average cost per ton mile. Take for instance Eastern [Railway of] Minnesota: the ton mile cost was .28 or slightly over 1/8th of 1 penny per ton mile, yet the train mile cost is high owing to station service 47.28 as against average of 12.9 on G.N. all divisions, the fact being that this bit of road forms the neck of the bottle through which traffic on the whole system filters to and from the Great Lakes; hence average train load of 551 tons, against 304 for the whole system, but the cost includes terminals on the lakes where the expense of handling in transhipment is incurred.

The cost on different divisions varies of course according to the nature of country and traffic, but sight of the sheet stimulates a healthy rivalry among the various divisional superintendents, and enables one to tell exactly what the cost really is. The sheet is in fact an instantaneous photograph taken monthly of the work of every man who is spending money, of every cent he spends, and where and how he spends it . . .

Gaspard admitted 'I once showed the sheet to my cousin Tom who rather jeered; but it is the device slowly evolved during the past eleven years of a man who is acknowledged today as the first railroad operator in the United States, and who has been signally successful under conditions where all others have failed . . .'

The letter shows the very real appreciation Farrer had of Hill's task. When he wrote thirty-five years later to Edward Tuck, an American financier long settled in Paris, where he performed for the Great Northern very much the same service as did Mount Stephen in England, that Hill was never safe off the beaten track of the railroad proper, he was not in this particular instance thinking of Hill's excursions into finance, but of ventures such as the boats on the Great Lakes, and the later steamships on the Pacific, which he described as 'disastrous' and especially of the Iron Ore holdings at Mesabi, Lake Superior, of which Farrer wrote sadly (and it was his last word on the subject) 'In the case of Ore he deceived me badly, and I like to think he deceived himself as much . . .' With this letter of 6 October 1932 Farrer, in retrospective mood, was sending to Tuck some early communications from Hill on the subject 'which, together with our experience of the man for many years, seems some justification for my, alas mistaken, optimism about the investment . . .' This ingrained faith in Hill, inculcated no doubt in early days by Mount Stephen, struggled throughout their association with the sporadic doubts which from time to time assailed Farrer's mind. These were sometimes proved to have been mistaken, and they were never allowed to mar their relationship; having let off steam in a letter to Mount Stephen, Sterling or Tuck, Gaspard would indite an epistle to Hill in the most diplomatic terms, with no more, on occasion, than a mild protest that the railwayman was doing himself less than justice.

This situation cropped up repeatedly in respect of the 'Manitoba's' or Great Northern's reports. As early as 23 November 1888

GASPARD FARRER
(by permission of the Provost and Fellows of Eton)

Farrer had begun to react to the 'Manitoba's' annual report by sending Hill his own memorandum of the main points of interest to investors, who would look at it from their own angle which was not necessarily that of the railroad operator. This had little or no effect, for on 2 July 1895 Gaspard was still writing as follows to Hill's son-in-law, Sam Hill, enclosing Wilson's latest article on the Great Northern in the 'Investors' Review':

> That the revenue accounts and balance sheets in the annual reports are unintelligible to the ordinary reader is certain, as I have frequently told your father-in-law, and more attention is paid to this point here in England than appears to be the case with you; in fact a Mr. Pothonier on whose recommendation 1500 guaranteed shares have recently been sold told me only this afternoon that this was the reason that had determined him to get his clients out as soon as he could do so profitably.

Evidence that the Great Northern was in fact in good shape is provided in the last sentence of Gaspard's letter to Sam Hill: 'The traffics are most encouraging'. Had Pothonier been merely a hostile journalist little weight would have been attached to his reaction: Farrer told Sam Hill that Wilson's power had 'largely vanished from his excessive pessimism'. But Pothonier was a colleague of Robert Fleming, whose opinion Mount Stephen valued so highly; moreover they were both associated with one Trotter of James Capel and Company, who handled G.N. shares in London, in the London and Scottish American Investment Trust.

The arrival of the 1894–95 Great Northern annual report later that year threw Gaspard into a state of despair. He was fully aware that the obfuscation was partly intentional, with one eye on the politicians and on the Interstate Commerce Commission, which since an Act of 1887 had sought to curb the railroads' freedom of action, particularly over the fixing of rates. He wrote to Mount Stephen on 26 November 1895:

> Mr. Hill's report has just arrived, based on the same lines as hitherto only more so; as a conundrum to puzzle a Railroad Commissioner or populist politician it beats all previous performance; but as a record of the year's operations and position of the Company per June 30 it is impossible to regard it seriously; instead of distributing it broadcast to our friends my instinct is to bury it—bury it deeply; surely it does Mr. Hill's work and the property a maximum of injustice—after fifteen years' familiarity with the figures I can only pray that no one will ask me

to explain how they are reached; the ordinary investor must be hope-
lessly befogged . . .

To begin with, the gross and net earnings revealed in the report
were considerably higher than those cabled ten days previously
from New York and reproduced in the London papers. Farrer then
launched into an exasperated comparison of individual figures
with those on the previous year's report, pointing out several
inconsistencies. He cited an omission of particular interest to London
investors:

Take again the Minneapolis Western, a point likely to attract notice
here; the Bonds have been issued to the public by public prospectus; not
a word of the sale or application of proceeds; even the existence of the
bantling ignored.

Surely what we all want is a simple record of the machine as a *whole*;
its liabilities to the public as a whole; with continuity in the exhibition
of figures so that any one can follow the changes from year to year.

Such a record I will endeavour to compile during the next few weeks
and will send you. Meantime do not think that the above is some pious
opinion of my own. It is merely a reflection of the feeling of investors
here who have not the advantage of knowing Mr. Hill or the property,
who have no feeling for or against the Company, but who require justification before embarking on their own and friends' money; and so far as
I can judge the like feeling prevails in New York. We fortunately know
Mr. Hill and know the property and have faith in both; but I confess my
own is in spite of the reports.

Several times lately I have heard Manitoba and Denver 4's classed
together; the latter a second class bond on a second class property with
a minimum of earnings behind and the meanest of dividend records; ask
the reason—"Well, the public like Denvers, you see they are easily
followed" and so they are so far as figures permit; enclosed is the report,
just compare it with that of the G.N., and there are many other U.S.
RR reports as clear.

You will remember too that except monthly gross earnings the report
is the only official information issued; there are no monthly statistics
as with the Vanderbilt Roads. The public will never give their confidence
unless Mr. Hill will take them into his—and the G.N. wants all the
confidence it can get; it is a heavy debtor—heavy in proportion to
earnings; this year more than 80% of income is required for fixed charges;
last year all was so absorbed; and dividends were charged against profit
of former years. I should have said so in the report, in words as well as in
figures; the investor is a patient beast and will stand anything so long as
he can understand . . .

By the following year Farrer was able to write to Hill on 26 September 1896 (the diplomacy is fairly apparent although the 1895–96 annual reports appeared to have the additional merit of coming out earlier):

I like them much better in their present form than any previously issued: what you say under your own signature is always interesting and particularly so this year: probably the point that people here will mainly latch on to is that the regular interest and dividends have been paid out, material improvements and additions to the properties effected and this without any change in the capital account. Pages 14 and 15 are excellent— I will write you in a few days some points that occur to me for your future consideration . . .

The promised further comment was written on 6 October 1896, after consultation with Mount Stephen, and ran to several pages including a section on suggested layout of the salient items:

Lord Mount Stephen asks why not commence the report for the year with operations of the year—i.e. with earnings and their disposition. Will you then consider starting off with the total . . . [as on Hill's page 14] . . . and some such table as follows . . .

Then came a proposed layout, which after the total results of the year detailed the receipts and expenditure:

This shows at a glance the relation of net income to Bond Interest and to guaranteed and other dividends; each class of security holder sees at once what margin of income there is behind his own investment.
 Then proceed as you commence with a paragraph re changes on capital account and expenditure on capital account followed by a table of receipts and expenditures drawn to balance as overleaf . . .
 Then follow with paragraphs such as you have on pages 5, 6, 7, 8: it is well worth going into these details with the fullness in this report as they give a reality to the figures; then your general remarks as on page 9 and 10—by the way the first para p. 10 is a puzzle: it sounds well but I can't get any forrarder with it.
 Then omit page 12 and 13 but give greater prominence to p. 14 i.e. larger print adding a column alongside the "Total" columns giving the "totals" of the preceding year . . . p. 15 is excellent and I do not see how it could be improved.
 Then as to Balance Sheet will you consider the enclosed? I have been unable to fill in all the figures as I cannot make it balance with the material before me, but it will serve to show the principle in my mind; . . .

These are the few points that occur to me as tending to greater lucidity and enabling one to work easier from one report to another. We all feel that the better people understand your work and position the better they will like it.

At the same time, writing to Tuck regarding some other matters on 14 October 1896, Farrer mentioned that he had been at Hill about the annual report and asked Tuck to 'plug away at him in the direction of persuading him to give the security holders his full confidence'.

Hill responded on 16 October with what was obviously a spirited defence, stressing the problems of the man on the spot and evoking from Gaspard a conciliatory reply on 10 November:

... It is true; I wrote with an eye to security holders and them only: you have to take the wider view and remember State Legislatures as well, of whose ways I am entirely ignorant, and I have no doubt whatever that maintenance of rates is more important to the property than any other consideration.

You will however recollect that my suggestions on Income Account merely entailed a rearrangement of your own published figures, and whatever be the shortcomings of the local politician one can hardly suppose him incapable of simple addition sums.

Possible for the politician, possible for the shareholder. Yes, that also is true; but to sell goods we must display them temptingly in the window within easy reach of every passer's eye, while the politician bent on mischief will ferret out the fat things for attack conceal them as we will behind the blinds.

But I write in ignorance of so many facts patent to you that if your judgment does not fall in with mine there is an end of the matter, indeed your big shareholders, or such as I who know you well, care little enough what the report contains or omits; we should sleep as well if no report existed so long as you are at the helm; but I am always thinking of the day when you determine to follow Lord Mount Stephen's example and take life easier; much as I dread the time from a selfish view it is folly to expect you will continue indefinitely to bear such a burden of work as you have of late; and equally useless to think that those who take it up— your sons I hope—will at once obtain the confidence which all repose in you.

Any change that will at some future day make the work easier for your sons is in the right direction, and changes can be best made now with your judgment to guide and control.

That is what was and is in my mind.

INTERPRETING HILL

Although it is fairly clear that John W. Sterling never actually joined the Great Northern Board as representing English interests he did from time to time have an opportunity of interpreting Hill's plans to Mount Stephen, or conveying the latter's suggestions to Hill, Sterling being one of the few people to whom Hill felt he could speak openly. Early in 1890 one of these interviews took place, apparently on the subject of making Great Northern securities more readily available in London. Farrer writing to Sterling on 15 February mentions a cable he has sent briefing him for this meeting, pointing out the success achieved in London with Canadian Pacifics at this time. There was no reason, he wrote, 'why G.N. credit shouldn't stand as high here after a bit if our friend makes up his mind to carry out his understanding and so continue his association with Sir George [Stephen]'. There is no further enlightenment as to this obviously delicate negotiation; certainly the association continued. About this time the future of the Soo Line (the Minneapolis, St. Paul and Sault Ste. Marie) was under consideration, his London friends hoping that it would fall to Hill who had made an offer for it.[1] Van Horne, however, opted to retain it for the Canadian Pacific. This incursion of a Canadian-owned railroad into American territory was to lead to difficulties over rates, an issue of popular politics which the United States Government wished to keep firmly under its own control.

The transatlantic correspondence between Mount Stephen, Hill, Farrer, Sterling, Tuck and others over the years revealed most of the important developments in which they were involved, one source filling the gaps left by the other, sometimes by direct quotation from a letter just received from the next party. Personal meetings at crucial points might replace the act of putting pen to paper, but the need, or at least the desire, to keep each other informed, sooner or later caused this replacing switch to be put in operation that all might go forward in line. Certainly the cross-fire of comment serves to illumine these relationships-at-a-distance.

OUTLOOK UNCERTAIN

As the next new year got under way after the alarms of 1893 Farrer replied on 27 January 1894 to a communication from

[1] Gaspard Farrer Letter Books, Farrer to Stephen, 3 May 1890. See also Gilbert, vol. I, pp. 250–1.

Sterling on the subject of the Twin City Stockyards Company—one of the less fortunate enterprises in which Mount Stephen and Sir Donald Smith as well as Farrer's own firm were investors—'The Boss is continually recurring to the comfort your care has been to him' adding in a postscript:

> I too think we are "bumping along on the bottom" and are likely to see better times: and I am glad you write so to the Boss as he needs cheering: he has been very low and refuses to see light ahead. I may be too much influenced by stock markets which here seem ripe for improvement, but I think he is unduly depressed about the future price of wheat which can hardly remain at present [low] level even though as seems likely the U.S. ceases to be a factor in European supplies. That ruffian J. J. Hill is behaving as badly as usual . . .—The Boss still expects him over—I shall believe in his coming when he is here.[1]

Lady Mount Stephen had written on 4 January to young George Cantlie, who was working in the C.P.R.'s Montreal office: '. . . Times are very bad here as well as in Canada and the US. No one knows what will happen next, & all of us who have our incomes depending on "investments" are badly shorn of our incomes, but better times will come, & we must wait for them'. She added a kindly word of encouragement:

> Don't mind if promotion is slow in the CPR, be sure it will come, and you will I know be ready for it when it does come. I do not know if your Uncle has ever told you of the time when he arrived in London at the age of 18, without a single friend, and only a very few shillings in his pocket, going from house to house to seek employment, and oh the rebuffs and refusals he met with!! When I say from house to house I mean the drapers' shops. He often shows me the houses from which he was sent away "We don't want any new shopman". At last by dint of perseverance he got into a shop, where the dining place was so dirty he could not stand it & left tho' he hardly knew where to go to, & after he got into a place in St. Paul's Churchyard, & once there, he worked so hard that his health gave way, but he had no home to go to, & remained there till he went to Canada. I tell you all this, that you may see what *perseverance* can do. "Once put your hand to the plough don't look back . . ."[2]

---

[1] Omission after 'usual' believed to be: 'i.e. re Van H.' Over the next few months there are indications that Hill was complaining of the C.P.R. President, probably over the question of rate-cutting on the Soo Line.
[2] Letter in the possession of the Hampson family.

Farrer was writing to R.R. Grindley of the British Bank of North America on 13 January 1894: 'I fear there is a hard time before Canada with these miserable prices for farming products'. As to the price of wheat, the Canadian Prime Minister, Mr. Mackenzie Bowell, in the course of a correspondence with Lord Mount Stephen on the subject of ocean freights—he was again trying to achieve for Canada a new fast line on the Atlantic—wrote on 17 January:

... The competition in wheat from India, Egypt and other eastern parts points to the necessity of more mixed farming in Canada. Our producers must adjust their methods to these changing conditions of trade.[1]

Whereas towards the end of 1893 Farrer had been writing cheerfully to Sterling of the booming sales in London of Canadian Pacific Preference Stock, by June 1894, when Mount Stephen was once more in Montreal, he was reporting a complete stalemate in that security. Taking counsel with John Baring and Francis Le Marchant and with Thomas Skinner, he concluded that rather than drop the price, which might frighten holders and still fail to bring in fresh buyers, C.P.R. ought to cut the dividend from 5 to 3 per cent. He thought that in view of exceptional loss of late by floods in British Columbia, this might not be badly received. Mount Stephen's response was to propose 2½. With the aid of these London friends an issue of Debenture Stock was placed with brokers that month, and by 21 June Mount Stephen was cabling better prospects from Montreal. Replying that day Gaspard wrote:

I gather Hill sees some light ahead; and that you see no reason why future C.P. earnings should bring about a fall in the Preference Stock. Markets here are more cheerful today ...

By 28 June Farrer was reporting to Mount Stephen that things on the London market looked more promising: dealers were more interested in the C.P. Preference than for some time although a good deal of caution was still evident with regard to Overseas investments. He forecast:

A month's decent traffic would set everything right. After the many collapses we have had of late and with Denver and Norfolks [Denver and Rio Grande and Norfolk and Western Railroads]—both mostly held here—known to be hanging on by the eyelids it is not surprising that

[1] Mackenzie Bowell Letter Book 119. (PAC).

people are ready to be frightened. The Montana Central Bonds are quoted today 101–3. Marked later on at about 100 on the market and the balance placed . . .

Mount Stephen at Metis was having little time for the salmon. On 30 June Gaspard acknowledged a cable message and replied:

I hate to think of your fishing holiday being broken up and ten days of hot travelling substituted, but I am not surprised that you have decided to go and looking to the momentous questions looming up for both properties, especially Canadian Pacific, I am greatly relieved that you are to post yourself on the situation first hand.

Gaspard himself had been across the Atlantic that spring; it seems certain that during Mount Stephen's journey to the Pacific and back, doubtless with a stop at St. Paul, discussions took place on a venture that had been mooted over a year before, and had indeed been in Hill's mind for much longer. Although he had decided, on balance, to build his own road to the Pacific, he had never quite given up the idea that a closer connection with that other American transcontinental, the Northern Pacific, would be beneficial to both systems if only from the point of view of eliminating unnecessary competition. Hill had already been approached to come to the rescue of the Union Pacific but had declined; now the Great Northern was faced with the opportunity of taking part in the reorganization of its more immediate rival, the bankrupt Northern Pacific.

III

Northern Pacific

HILL CONSULTS MOUNT STEPHEN

In May 1893 Hill had written to Mount Stephen:

I cabled you a few words about the Northern Pacific. That Company has run its length and will have to be entirely reorganized, wiping out all present and preferred shares. There are two very strong parties, including the very strongest financial concerns here, who will take up the reorganization provided we will name half the new board and find men to manage the property . . . We will not invest money in it, but our position in traffic matters is so well recognized that the parties feel safer with our coöperation than in any other position.[1]

This was written before there was any mention of bankruptcy. In August 1893 the Northern Pacific's creditors applied for the appointment of receivers, alleging that the company was insolvent, and receivers were duly appointed. It was clear, however, that radical reorganization was required, and the Northern Pacific people turned to John Pierpont Morgan, who had already successfully carried out other such rescue operations. Morgan and Hill had been acquainted for some time although without any business connection. Once approached by Morgan, it was Hill's instinct to turn to Mount Stephen, and he wrote to him in October 1894:

If the Northern Pacific could be handled as we handle our property and all the wild and uncalled-for rate cutting stopped, it could be made a great property. Its capacity to earn money is good, and with all unnecessary expenses, commissions and train service abolished, it would, I think, astonish even its friends. You will recall how often it has been said that when the Northern Pacific, Union Pacific, and other competitors failed, or went into the hands of receivers, our company would not be able to stand; and that they, having nothing but expenses to pay, would destroy our business. Now we have had them all in bankruptcy and in the hands of receivers for more than a year; and while the Northern

[1] Pyle, vol. 2, pp. 4–5.

Pacific has been forced to issue $5,000,000 receivers' debentures, we have gone along and met not only their competition but that of the 'Soo' line and the Canadian Pacific Railroad on coast traffic, which is really more destructive than Northern Pacific if we followed it down, and in addition we have had the worst conditions of business and other matters affecting our company, and still we hold our own. I hope you will not consider this as self praise, for it is not so intended. The quality is in the property, and careful management and constant effort will bring it out . . .

He went on to say that on 1 November the Great Northern's treasury would show a credit balance of nearly half a million dollars over and above the amount necessary to pay all the coupons due on the first of January next. Even this was too small a margin for such a large company 'but in view of what we have come through in the way of panics, strikes, floods, storm, and fire, I think it shows the real strength of the company more than anything else could'.[1]

Five days later Hill wrote again to Mount Stephen analysing in detail the property and liabilities of the Northern Pacific and outlining more fully the task that would face them were they to commit themselves:

To handle the property in the courts and hasten a reorganization would require actual control and a strong party. The amount of work to be done would be very great, and the men who could be of use are very few. The advantages to our company would mainly come from the freedom from competition and needless friction and expense in operation, all of which I think would be worth to us about $600,000 or possibly $750,000. When they went into the hands of receivers a year ago, timid people said, 'Now the Great Northern meets its Waterloo, with its competitors in the hands of receivers and released from fixed charges &c'; but you will bear in mind our difficulties . . . during the past year, and still we are prosperous and in good financial condition while they are asking the court to pay their shortages. I speak of this to show that we can get along without them and against their operating at an enormous loss. At the same time the control of an empire such as lies between Lake Superior and the Pacific Ocean, which is served by the lines of both companies, would render the future reasonably secure for both properties, and its value should not be overlooked . . . There are many other matters of detail of which I could write, but unless there is a probability of our doing something it is hardly worth while taking your time. However, I am reasonably satisfied that if the Berlin people or any other holders of Northern Pacific securities do not realize how much more we can do with the property than any other

[1] Ibid. pp. 7–8.

organization without exception, they will surely realize this before they are done.[1]

The large European investment in the Northern Pacific ensured that a good deal of interest was taken in its circumstances across the Atlantic. It had seemed—like the Great Northern—such a magnificent property. On 23 September 1889 Jacob Schiff had written to Ernest Cassel that, granted proper management, there was no doubt that the Northern Pacific was the most promising enterprise on the American continent. Schiff had no very great opinion of Villard as a business man, but in the years 1889–90 he made substantial investments in his railroad.[2] By 1893 Villard was virtually out of the picture. Mount Stephen, back in England, had enlisted the help of Gaspard Farrer in determining the current position of the Northern Pacific. As usual, Farrer had found the published statistics somewhat obscure, but on 25 October 1894 he sent Mount Stephen a rough account of the property and its indebtedness, complete accuracy being impossible. He succeeded in tabulating the main items: lines owned—4,600 miles, including leased branches and terminals; total bonded debt—$171,056,500; total annual charge—$9,790,270; land grant earned and unsold— 38,500,000 acres; sum due for land sold—$5,000,000. He enclosed a map showing the relative positions of the Northern Pacific and Great Northern lines, and a separate sheet giving details of bond liabilities.

On 26 October Jacob Schiff wrote to Ernest Cassel about the difficulties of railroads in general and those of the Northern Pacific in particular:

The N.P. reorganization appears to be the most difficult task of all, and it will no doubt take several years before a sound reconstruction of that company's finances can be accomplished. E. D. Adams, who is at the head of the N.P. reorganization committee, is very able as you know, but he has a herculean task before him. In my opinion, your friends of the Deutsche Bank could do nothing better than to induce Mr. James J. Hill to interest himself in the affairs of the Northern Pacific Company. No one else so thoroughly understands everything concerning the traffic of the territory through which the N.P. runs, and he has proven in the management of the affairs of the Great Northern what can be done by thorough attention and management on strict business principles, even in the face of the most adverse circumstances . . .

[1] Ibid. pp. 8–10.   [2] Adler, op. cit. vol. I, p. 84.

It would certainly be of immense advantage both to the N.P. and to the G.N. if the two systems should come into close relationship, and it would increase the net earnings of both companies, but especially of the N.P., many hundred thousands of dollars if—instead of the competitive trains now being run and the many expensive duplicate agencies now existing—under harmonious relations, trains were arranged under a mutual understanding and joint agencies were established . . .

He cited the benefits that had accrued from a similar arrangement between the Chicago and North Western and the Chicago, Milwaukee and St. Paul following the election by the stockholders of a number of men in common to both boards, and continued:

Our own relations with the Northern Pacific reorganization committee are of the friendliest character; in fact, we have been, and are, accumulating considerable amounts of the higher grades of Northern Pacific securities, and I believe if you could see your way to make the above suggestion to the Deutsche Bank we could find many ways to interest ourselves jointly with you in the reorganization, to mutual advantage, but please do not understand that I would desire you to broach the subject to Doctor Siemens unless this be perfectly agreeable to you.[1]

Cassel, a naturalized German, had come in contact with Schiff while on business in America on behalf of his firm, Bischoffsheim and Goldschmidt, of London, England. The two corresponded constantly for forty years from 1880, and Cassel became involved personally in a number of ventures in which Schiff had an interest.

On 28 December 1894 Schiff was urging Hill—the latter not unwilling but still hesitant—to bring about a virtual consolidation between the two properties, and on 31 December wrote to him with what Schiff's biographer terms 'a detailed financial plan of such magnitude as to put it at that time among the very first of great railroad transactions. He proposed in effect an issue of $150 million bonds, which he thought would take care of all the Mortgage Bonds outstanding, as well as of the Trust Notes and Receivers' Certificates, and leave a reserve of $25 million to $30 million for necessary improvements and additions. His idea of the relationship of the two companies was that the Northern Pacific, as reorganized, should be leased to the Great Northern Company, with a division of the joint earnings; upon the new basis, the Northern Pacific should be able to take care of $6 million of fixed charges'.[2] Hill replied on 4 January 1895:

[1] Ibid. p. 85.   [2] Ibid. pp. 86–87.

I think I fully appreciate the situation as it affects both companies. A very large saving could be made in Northern Pacific operating expenses and waste of revenue, and further by reducing all unnecessary train mileage. The net result would be so great as to astonish you. The work of looking after this could not be done anywhere else than on the ground, and it would require an organization which could not be made in a day. I am sure you feel in our own case that we are doing our work with fair economy, and that we are improving from month to month; still no one knows better than I do how far we are from doing as well as could be done. A difference of ten cents in the average cost of moving one ton of freight one hundred miles on any line will make a difference in our net revenue of $1,000,000; and I think the difference in our average cost per ton per mile and that of the Northern Pacific last year would have given them over $3,000,000 more net revenue than they earned.

I have gone over their mortgages carefully and spent what time I could spare evenings on their reports, but I am not clear as to many of their worthless branches.

It is beyond doubt a very desirable thing to do, and at the same time one that calls for the greatest caution and wise forethought in making a plan of campaign, and after the work of reorganization was carried out, the real hard drudgery would begin in order to secure an organization that would get the results which should be had to justify the work.[1]

It was obvious that the financiers were more ready to go ahead than was the practical railwayman, on whom the success of the enterprise, in the last instance, so much depended. Later that month Hill was in New York, and in February saw Cassel in London. Gaspard Farrer reported to Sterling on 2 February that they did not seem to 'get much forrarder. I dread the G.N. taking on more responsibilities and would not give a twopenny damn for the $50 millions (Hill) dangles before us—in fact nothing but the necessity of preserving our own skin would make us move. Gwinner [of the Deutsche Bank] is to be here shortly—J. J. Hill can think of nothing but N:P though so far he does not seem to have formulated any plan. We have scarcely heard a word about his own road . . .' Meanwhile Gaspard was busy on a tabulation for Mount Stephen of Great Northern statistics, and was having the usual trouble. He sent the result on 7 February with the comment:

Overleaf are Hill's figures as I understand them—considering the times even if reality is blacker than I paint we should not be surprised: but one

---

[1] Pyle, op. cit. vol. 2, pp. 10–11.

can understand that others who have not the same opportunities of personal contact thinking the business a bit "dark". Obviously judicious bookkeeping has been necessary to produce the result he reaches in 'Income a/c' report . . .

In other words, the figures proved nothing, but the road was in shape to undertake anything that Hill felt was possible.

Back in the United States Hill reported to Mount Stephen on 19 March 1895 the results so far of conferences with E. D. Adams, the American representative of the Deutsche Bank and chairman of the N. P. reorganization committee:

Since our arrival in New York, which will be two weeks tomorrow evening, I have spent most of my time on Northern Pacific matters and have had several interviews with Mr. Adams, during which I have gone over the entire situation with him as it was discussed in London and also covering about all the ground relating to the property, its value as a railway, present and prospective. I also made up a comparative statement from the Railroad Commissioners' Reports, showing the results on the basis of operating cost of the Milwaukee and St. Paul, the Chicago and North Western and the Great Northern. Applied to the business of the Northern Pacific, the result shows that it would be necessary to get better results than either of these in order to place the Northern Pacific where it could pay the obligations necessary to an acceptable reorganization and at the same time leave the new company on a basis of net earnings which would enable it to pay its interest charges beyond question, even if a failure of crops or other temporary cause reduced its income.

I have urged on Mr. Adams, and I am sure that he agrees with me, that the market price of the bonds of the reorganized company will be the measure of the company's credit, and the importance of having the bonds so good that the holders will not be at all anxious to sell them. There would be much difficulty in building up the credit of the new company in the face of so many bondholders watching the market with a view to selling on every little rise.

This last consideration was an important one not only in this instance but throughout Hill's association with Mount Stephen, and may have had a good deal of influence with Hill in his desire to limit the market circulation in London of his own securities. With these in the hands of his friends—Mount Stephen, Ellis, Lefevres, Tuck, Donald Smith and a few others—Hill could make his calculations with fewer imponderables. He went on:

Mr. Adams has evidently worked very hard since he went into the committee, and I find he has acquired a great deal of information which is more or less valuable and which must really have taken a great deal of time and labour to work out. At the same time the whole question comes down to, first, a determination of what the company can be made to earn *net*; and, then, the best and most practicable distribution of these earnings to the new bonds and stocks by an equitable merging of the several classes into the new company's securities. I think I have shown Mr. Adams to his satisfaction that the Northern Pacific can be made to do better work than it has ever done in the past . . . (*sic*) and a reorganization made on these lines will be creditable to the makers and profitable to all who receive the securities.

I may be mistaken, but I think I could see in Mr. Adams's mind a somewhat remote desire towards a *unification* of the two corporations. However, with the past experience of the Northern Pacific in operation of its lines, and the small proportion of net to gross earnings, it was not easy to devise any plan of reorganization that would meet the expectations of the bondholders and at the same time be on a really safe basis looking to the future credit of the company.

The Adams committee seem to have made a really good plan for that company, if they can get some *good men* to handle the property on a basis of good economy. It makes little difference what else is done if a property is not handled with close regard to expenses and income.[1]

At this point Hill had not actually seen Edward Adams' plan, which was evidently being submitted first to the Deutsche Bank in Berlin. On 10 April 1895 Gaspard Farrer wrote to Hill:

Mr. Adams' plan has this week reached Lord Mount Stephen from Berlin: a work of art: but why is the title omitted? "A scheme to scale and reorganize Great Northern in the interest of Northern Pacific". We have read it; & reread it: before dinner as well as after: yet such is the case. Plainly he or we need educating.

As we understood the pivot on which all your talk in London centred was *reconstruction of N.P. on the base of Great Northern credit*.—Yet Mr. Adams for the sake of symmetry to his paper structure sweeps away in an hour the work which for seventeen years you and your friends have been toiling to build up fabric and foundations.—Surely he has forgotten that he is the suppliant, not you.

And the scheme is as unpracticable as unreasonable, as no one can know better than a man of Mr. A's ability: one that might have emanated from a running broker of Wall Street penetrated with the idea that Great Northern is collapsing, and its owners, tottering under the burden of

[1] Ibid. pp. 11–13.

undigested securities, seeking means to unload on international markets. We are quite unable to fathom his motives, anyway we gather from your cables that you regard it as we do—so further criticism is needless, but Lord Mount Stephen wished me to write and say how it strikes us in principle . . .

Farrer concluded his letter, after reporting well of 'Manitobas' on the London market, 'Your traffics are most encouraging'. A week later he was writing to Mount Stephen about Hill's Minnesota Western bonds which he and John Baring were anxious to launch in London; both were confident of making a success of an issue. This was proceeded with in due course and Farrer was able to tell Hill on 1 May (Hill was then in England again) that Minnesota Western bonds had been well subscribed for; he hoped that, after changing hands since their first issue at 2–3 premium, they would in the course of a few weeks all have 'found their final resting place and be no more heard of till 1911'. As if to underline his support of the Great Northern's position, Farrer had tabulated for Mount Stephen, and sent to him on 23 April, a comparison of Hill's earnings and expenses over 1893–4 with those of the Canadian Pacific, also doing well in the markets of both London and Berlin, after a recent setback. He found that 'Roughly Hill's gross earnings *per train mile* last year were 37c. greater than Van Horne's, net earnings 21c. greater, the difference practically consisting of the 15c. per train mile spent by Hill in maintenance in excess of Van Horne'. Moreover, these calculations were favourable to the latter in that they were based on a year's C.P.R. figures, but only on the last six months of Great Northern.

DISCUSSIONS IN ENGLAND

In his letter to Hill of 1 May, Gaspard said that he had arranged for Hill to accompany him that weekend to Brocket Hall, the country home in Hertfordshire which Mount Stephen had two years earlier leased from Earl Cowper, son of Lady Palmerston. It had been the home of Lord Melbourne, Queen Victoria's Prime Minister, passing to Lady Palmerston when Melbourne died in 1848. Mount Stephen thus became a near neighbour of the third Marquess of Salisbury at Hatfield House. Since 1892 the Conservatives had been in Opposition; first Mr. Gladstone and then Lord Rosebery had been leaders of the Liberal Administration.

Lord Salisbury was to regain the Premiership on 25 June 1895 after an episode in which Mount Stephen was, if not directly involved, at least on the sidelines; this will be the topic of a later section of this chapter. Meanwhile, the comings and goings of that spring across the Atlantic of those trying to resolve the future of the Northern Pacific were gradually centring on London. Hill and Farrer were to stay at Brocket from Sunday to Monday, and on that day, 6 May 1895, Hill and Mount Stephen were to meet E. D. Adams and Dr. Siemens of the Deutsche Bank. Retailing this news to John Sterling on 4 May, Farrer described the spread of speculation, originating in Kaffirs, on the London market: '. . . in short, optimism is the fashion . . . a grand moment for a slump if any ill news cropped up as it is the city rather than the public who hold the baby at the moment'. On the same day he wrote to Harry Stikeman, of the British Bank of North America in Montreal, that Morgans in London had recently sold a large amount of American securities, indicating a revival of interest in United States securities generally.

As a brief for these preliminary meetings Farrer had drawn up a memorandum, presumably for the benefit of Mount Stephen, suggesting 'a scheme fair to both parties, and with special regard to the influence which Mr. Adams' impressions of the Great Northern position would entail on him'. First he listed the inherent advantages: the common advantage of the two systems working in harmony instead of in competition; the advantages possessed by the Northern Pacific in its denser traffic and consequently larger gross earnings, and in its larger land grant; then those offered by Hill: the credit of association with the Great Northern and the financial help thus made available, and Hill's 'effective management which will in part, may in whole pass away with his retirement'. He continued:

Balancing these one against the other, and assuming Mr. Hill's method adopted of eliminating for the present unprofitable leased lines and dealing with owned lines only—about 3,500 miles—it seems reasonable to apply future net earnings *first* to direct Northern Pacific Bonds and such new capital as is required to place the property on a sound physical and financial footing *in amount per mile equivalent to G.N. present requirements for interest per mile* a proposition thought to be indubitably safe being applied as a fixed charge, *second* in equal division between N.P. and G.N.

6

From this he concluded that on the basis of the Great Northern's fixed interest per mile, some $5,150,000 could be achieved for the Northern Pacific to pay charges on, say, $120 millions of Bonds 4s and dividends on $7,200,000 of 5 per cent Preference Stock, in fact, assuming a limit of safety this could be done with a total of $4,500,000. He noted that Mr. Hill had arrived at much the same conclusion, although by a different process apparently, and imagined that Mr. Adams would consider this a minimum. He reworked the sum on the slightly different basis of G.N. interest plus dividend per mile, achieving a distributable total a million dollars higher; Mr. Hill, he thought, might consider this a minimum. He added:

Any such principle as the above would facilitate eventual consolidation if hereafter thought desirable, and would leave Mr. Adams a free hand now in apportioning the new securities among the Bondholders whom he represents—

thus going some way to meet Mr. Adams' suspected leanings. He feared that in any practicable scheme the Northern Pacific's capitalization per mile—a weak point—must still largely exceed that of the Great Northern, but on the other hand this would in time be set off by the former's larger land grant assets.

FIRST LONDON AGREEMENT: OPPOSITION

On 14 May 1895 Farrer reported to John Sterling in New York what must have been the background to a cable message announcing that on 10 May agreement had been reached in London:

... You never saw two more excited men than Lord M.S. and Hill last week. I did not attend their interviews with Siemens and Adams but was with them at all other times obtaining thereby a liberal education—it struck me that Adams was away too smart for Hill in negotiation and no terms would have been reached but for the Doctor's and Lord Mount Stephen's intervention ...

What was afterwards known as the first London agreement was drawn up at Mount Stephen's London house. The text, addressed to Edward D. Adams, Chairman of the Reorganization Committee, Northern Pacific Railroad Company, was undersigned by James J. Hill, Lord Mount Stephen and Edward Tuck, and countersigned by the Deutsche Bank. It was accepted subject to formal ratification by his committee by Adams and proposed, on behalf of a majority of the capital stock of the Great Northern, that the latter company should guarantee payment of principal and interest of new Gold Bonds, secured by mortgage lien on the Land Grant and Railway of the Northern Pacific of such amount as would be required in reorganization, up to $175 million, with a maximum annual interest of $6,200,000. The N.P. bondholders were to obtain a decree of foreclosure and have the property bid in by a committee of their own. The current outstanding stock was over $80 million, and in addition to its floating debt it had had $121 million of bonds outstanding on which no interest had been paid for two years. Now a new company was to come into being with new bonds to a total of $100 million or over and the same amount of capital stock. The Great Northern, in return for guaranteeing principal and interest, was to have half the capital stock. The agreement—which at this stage was still only tentative—provided for joint use of certain tracks and terminal facilities, and for the amicable and equitable interchange of traffic.[1]

Opposition, both public and private, was expected. For some time the American public had been suspicious of anything that smelt of monopoly in railroad operation. This had become, as has been mentioned, an issue in popular politics. The Sherman Antitrust Law of 1890 forbade combinations in restraint of trade, although this had not yet in practice been applied to railroads unless these were obviously 'parallel or competing'. In Hill's view, a combination such as was proposed—and this was using the term in a somewhat loose sense—could not but benefit all concerned, including the public; the only alternative was the natural law of the survival of the fittest, with its implication that the weakest would go to the wall. It was, however, a private protest that set the law in motion. A stockholder of the Great Northern, Thomas W. Pearsall, claimed that the arrangement would depreciate the value of his holding by making the Great Northern the guarantor of a financially unstable system; he accordingly brought suit in the Federal Court to restrain those responsible from carrying out the agreement.[2] The matter was first referred to the circuit court of Minnesota, whose legislature had in 1881 passed an Act, amending in more forceful terms an earlier measure of 1874, providing that

[1] Ibid. pp. 14–17. The seven clauses of the agreement are here given in full.
[2] According to Albro Martin's biography of James J. Hill, it was Hill himself who got Pearsall to bring suit.

"no railroad corporation shall consolidate with, lease or purchase, or in any way become owner of or control, any other railroad corporation, or any stock, franchises, rights, or property thereof, which owns or controls a parallel or competing line". The question was, did the Great Northern's original charter, ante-dating the Act, exempt it, and even if it did not, were the two railroads in fact parallel or competing in the sense of the Act? The circuit court decided in the Great Northern's favour, whereupon an appeal was lodged with the Supreme Court of the United States. Meanwhile the Attorney General of Minnesota brought a similar suit which resulted in an unfavourable decision in the Federal Courts.[1]

MAINTAINING GN CREDIT PENDING NP LITIGATION

In England, Mount Stephen and Gaspard Farrer set about the task of maintaining the credit of the Great Northern while the Northern Pacific matter hung fire. Farrer was only too anxious to have an opportunity to handle more of Hill's securities, and wrote to Hill on 11 June 1895:

... In our judgment the Sterling 4s and the Consols [Consolidated Mortgage] the former especially, will be the measure of the Company's credit here: and we believe the best assistance we can render you, both in your own affairs and the N.P. business, lies in keeping these two issues up at a good level and with a good market. Thanks for the offer of help which you cabled Lord Mount Stephen. We shall accumulate some stock in advancing the price but we will take care of this ourselves without bothering you.

Under the circumstances we do not wish Montana Extension Bonds introduced and quoted here in competition especially as asking for a quotation for an issue of $7,800,000 merely to sell a few hundred thousand would seem a mistake in policy from the Company's point of view, and might lead to misunderstandings here.

We think however we could place the [Montana] Bonds abroad, and possibly among one or two insurance companies here without causing comment in the London market, unless you preferred to sell them in New York . . .

All the $400,000 Consols, he said, had been sold, mostly in London, a few in Paris, and they had managed to advance the price; this he had been arranging with Nichols of the New York office of G.N.

---

[1] Adler, op. cit. vol. I, p. 87.

to save Hill trouble. Gaspard's eye was as ever on the statistics and he ended his letter: 'Your May traffic very satisfactory—best ever for May'. On 13 June, apparently acknowledging a cable from Hill, Farrer wrote that he was 'pleased you're satisfied, but please remember the tide has been with us; good earnings on your side and increasing confidence among buyers here; it might lead to disappointment if you expected too much from our individual efforts, but something we can do to help and will ...' He was rather afraid that Mount Stephen, in his recent cable to Hill, had got carried away over the possibility of getting Sterling 4s to par and repaying collateral. '... Assuredly it would have been flattened out had I been present when he sent it, to accord closer with the dry facts of the situation of the moment; still I look forward to the future and am hoping for a $20 million year for 95–6, my wonder being whether you have rolling stock to handle such a traffic'.

Although Farrer might be restrained in his letters to Hill, and might seek to restrain Mount Stephen, his own enthusiasm overflowed in a letter to Oliver Northcote, late of J. Kennedy Tod of New York, now living in Bedfordshire, to whom he wrote on 14 June 1895:

... As to Hill's property in general you will recollect that the bad times struck it just as the extension to the Coast was in progress and when, consequently, it was financially in its weakest position, yet, notwithstanding, it is one of the few roads in the United States that has maintained its dividends. Since July last, though times have been bad enough, traffics have shown continuous increases, the total for eleven months being $1.7 million increase, that for May being the largest May take in the Company's history; now business is fairly on the mend all along the line; Hill cables this morning—"Crop outlook largest and best condition ever seen, without mishap should reach 60 million bushels, increase first week June $80,000"—so we may fairly expect good traffics for the next six months.

Looking at the matter from another point of view I have always considered one of the weakest points in Hill's position was the limited number of his clients. Now this Northern Pacific matter is going to be the biggest advertisement St. P.M. & M. securities have ever had; already we find inquiries from quarters where none have ever yet been held; all points to the probabilities of holders of the Bonds being largely increased in number. If anything comes of the deal and its results are successful, it means so much more profit for Great Northern and therefore so much more behind St. Paul, Minneapolis and Manitoba. If practical (difficulties) arise St. P.M. & M. is still untouched, the Guarantee falling exclusively on Great Northern.

That all this will be as apparent to the public as to us who follow things closely cannot be expected yet something will permeate. Barring accidents I cannot see what is to prevent St. P.M. & M. Sterling 4s going to par, and 4-½% Consols to 110%.

On 26 June Farrer reported to E. T. Nichols in New York that the Stock Exchange had granted a quotation for an additional $400,000 worth of Consols, but suggested putting a time limit on the exchange option at present open to holders of '7s'—was there any reason, he asked, for granting them indefinite put and call on the Company? Farrer was confident the Bonds could be raised to 110, but did not care to do this if it would benefit the '7s' only, 'especially as we should be tempting them to sell out on our backs'. In a postscript—Gaspard was much given to postscripts—he added that he had discussed the matter with Lord Mount Stephen: 'We both think it most desirable in the interest of the Northern Pacific deal to keep Manitoba credit at the highest level possible and that this exchanging option should be terminated without delay to enable us to raise the price of the Consol. Bond. Please consult the President'. Further letters and cables on this subject followed, Hill being unwilling to terminate his offer so soon; he then suggested waiting until after current redemptions. On 5 July Hill cabled that the Montana 4s would be sold in New York, and not offered in London. On the 8th came a cable from Nichols agreeing to terminate the exchange privilege on the 25th. Two days later Farrer was asking Nichols to send him regular traffic statistics. (It was at this time that he was corresponding with Sam Hill about the unintelligibility of the Great Northern reports.) Meanwhile Mount Stephen and Farrer were still in touch with Arthur Gwinner of the Deutsche Bank in Berlin, working out technicalities, keeping Hill in the picture. Farrer wrote, for example, to Gwinner on 17 July: '... Lord Mount Stephen was unwilling to enter into the question of the disposition of land proceeds, considering that a matter for your goodself to settle with Mr. Hill, but it has occurred to me that no provisions should be inserted in the Mortgage diminishing the land's effectiveness as a lever for converting prior liens'. This letter mentioned a 'departure from the London agreement'.

At the middle of August 1895 it seemed that the crop movement was slow to accelerate, while on the London stock market there was a state of unprecedented stagnation in American securities. Writing of these matters to E. T. Nichols on 20 August, Farrer commented that mining speculation had for the moment killed all other business. Although the grain traffic might hardly have begun, 'the rise in copper ought to set things humming on your Montana lines'. For some years Cassel and through him Schiff had been investing in the Anaconda copper company of Montana, and soon Hill, through Schiff, was to follow suit.[1] Mount Stephen's involvement came later.

Before the Circuit Court's decision on the Northern Pacific plan, alternative courses of action were being discussed. On 21 August, acknowledging in Mount Stephen's absence in Scotland a message from Sterling, Farrer suggests that the latest idea was the device of a proprietary company, the difficulty here being to frame terms on which Great Northern shareholders were likely to consent to this without depriving such a company of the necessary measure of control. Hill had become suspicious of the Deutsche Bank's desire to alter the original terms of the London agreement, and this, Farrer thought, tended to colour his statements on the legal situation. 'We here entirely acquit our German friends of the deep designs which Hill imputes . . .' he told Sterling. G.N. counsel was now on his way over to England so that there was some hope of early clarification. On 27 August Gaspard assured Hill, in answer to his of the 12th, that neither Mount Stephen nor he ever contemplated relinquishing G.N. stock except to the control of and for the benefit of a proprietary company of which G.N. shareholders were owners, but they entirely agreed with Hill that a direct guarantee of the *railway* company was better in every way, both for Northern Pacific and Great Northern. He continued:

Your letter to Lord Mount Stephen about your own finances was interesting and I am delighted with your idea of repaying Collateral Trust Bonds by the issue of Stock retaining Sterling 4s in the Treasury for future emergencies. I hope you will also consider getting rid of the Preferential rights on existing Stock: 6% on a Preference is out of date in these days and a Preference Stock comes dangerously near a fixed charge so far as the credit of a company is concerned; besides no more money is required to pay 5% on $50 millions ordinary than would be necessary for a 4% on 25 millions ordinary if the Preference is retained: in addition you obtain the advantages of simplicity and wider markets: if you thought some

---

[1] Ibid. pp. 155–6. In 1892 the Anaconda Company of Butte, Montana, built its own smelter; previously the Butte copper ores had had to be sent overseas.

compensation necessary, perhaps you might be able to give 120 ordinary for 100 Preference. Today you are paying $1,550,000 per annum on G.N. proper securities Bonds and Stocks; 4% dividend on $55 million ordinary would increase this payment by $350,000 per annum and 5% by $950,000 per annum.

Once your finances are fixed on some broad basis I would like to see every dollar earned over 5% put back in the road till wooden trestles were unknown, terminals in every centre increased beyond all seemingly reasonable requirements and in short the position of the company generally physically and financially impregnable; it is folly to suppose the road can a second time have the benefit of the knowledge and life's devotion which you have given it.

But perhaps all this is premature in view of the modifications which Northern Pacific matters may entail—anyway you must excuse my making the suggestion but you have instilled into me some of your own keenness for the old property.

This bold attempt at explicit advice signalled a much closer interest in the road on Farrer's part now that he was more heavily involved financially through his Lefevre firm and in advising others. Writing again to Hill on 31 August he hoped that Mount Stephen, returning shortly from Scotland, would have further news from Hill about Northern Pacific affairs.

Keeping a keen watch on the Great Northern's monthly figures, he wrote sadly to Charles Ellis on 18 September that Hill's gross receipts for July and August were disappointing. Bad news was not withheld from Ellis, although on the same day he penned a more optimistic assessment to a London broker. Almost immediately a cable brought better traffic news, and Farrer added a note to his letter of 19 September to Mount Stephen: 'Hill's second week September $136,000 increase'. The following day he wrote to Hill himself of his delight at the September earnings—'real bumpers!—I am determined to have Sterling 4s at par before the year is out but must avoid all signs of manipulation . . .' He suggested to Hill on 2 October that when the annual report was issued, an extract should be sent to the Press for publication merely stating, without comment, the gross and net earnings, net income, fixed charges and dividends paid. The next day he wrote again at length, acknowledging on his own and Mount Stephen's behalf Hill's long letter and memorandum of 12 September which had helped to clear their understanding of the situation. The favourable decision of the Circuit Court had just been received: now they awaited the

Supreme Court's verdict on the appeal. He told Hill: 'All you write goes to show how essential to proper management is a knowledge not only of local circumstances but of local sentiment also ...' Sterling 4s stood at 96–98, the Bonds at a record 97, 4½s at 108–110, and Lefevres were ready to bid for more. By 26 October Farrer was reporting to Hill that the London market had again been overcome by a wave of mining speculation, but the Great Northern securities were keeping up well and the limited demand was still better than in the days when G.N. was hardly known in England. He was inclined to be scathing about Anacondas, which had just missed the boom. In a second letter of the same date Farrer asked Hill what his capital requirements were likely to be 'that we may be prepared to help you. You may be sure you will not frighten us . . .' The Hill girls and some friends were in England and he added: 'Your daughters . . . even dare to ridicule my interest in your sacred operating sheet!'

He was impatiently awaiting the annual report for the year ending June 1895. Hill cabled at the end of October that it would be out the next week, but Gaspard on the 30th was trying to impress on Sam Hill that it should be published more speedily:

... it is a small matter, and our impatience seemingly pedantic, but I remember your father-in-law once telling me that it was attention to *small* matters that made the difference of success or failure in Railway management.

I am sure that greater attention to small matters affecting the credit of the Company might raise that credit to an appreciably higher level; and one of these details is prompt publication of the report.

It shows that the accounting department is efficient and in full control (and I have always understood that there is no better Railroad accounting in the U.S. than yours) and creates the impression that the management is anxious to take into confidence at the earliest moment all its clients, Bond as well as Stock holders. I have sometimes thought that in the labour involved in turning out the real meaty article you have forgotten to dish it up with the sauce that tickles the appetite of the fanciful investor. In this country, Railway dividends are declared, subject to audit, about a fortnight after the close of each half-year and the audited accounts published about a month later, so you must make allowances for English impatience.

When Farrer wrote to Mount Stephen on 26 November 1895 the letter quoted on page 65, the Great Northern annual report had

just arrived. He was still working on his own promised compilation
in mid-December, getting additional information from Nichols in
New York. Both he and Mount Stephen had been taking a rather
more than academic interest in a recent *cause célèbre*, the Minnesota
Wheat case, the salient point at issue being the 'reasonable' profit a
carrier could expect to claim. This was obviously in Gaspard's
mind when on 17 December he finally sent to Mount Stephen a
complicated tabulation comparing the operations of the Great
Northern with those of the Chicago, Milwaukee and St. Paul and
with the Buenos Ayres Great Southern, the most important road
in Argentina, managed from England. His main conclusion lay in
the disparity of rates between the G.N. and the Southern: the latter
carried six times more passengers per mile operated than the G.N.
but for half the haul, and for a lesser rate, the average receipt per
passenger being but a third of that of the G.N. On the other hand,
G.N. freight tonnage was more than double that of the Southern
and the haul longer, but the rate was less than a third, the average
receipt per ton carried being but half the average on the Southern.
Had the rates obtained on the Southern prevailed on the Great
Northern, the latter's net passenger earnings would have been less
by $841,000, but net freight earnings more by $29,641,000—that is,
the G.N. could have earned $28.8 millions more net money.
Regarding Judge Kerr's decision in the Wheat Case—based on the
effect on the carrier tried by the test of what is reasonable profit on
a reasonable capital—Gaspard had written to Hill on 8 November
1895:

I cannot say that Judge Kerr's decision has cleared my mind as to the
real principles on which "reasonableness" of rates should be determined;
the problem seems insoluble; but as the lines on which cases have been
decided here differ somewhat from your own wheat case I think you may
like to hear what our decisions have been ...

Lord Mount Stephen thinks the concluding paragraphs of your
judgment are a sop to the popular feeling. I hope so. If the principles
apply to bumper harvests, the converse with poor crops should also
apply; yet everyone knows it would be practically impossible to raise
rates in and because of lean years.

Meanwhile Jacob Schiff was trying to persuade Hill that the
Great Northern's plan for the Northern Pacific should be abandoned
without waiting for the Supreme Court decision. Writing to Hill on
18 November he admitted that some of his associates were of the

opinion that nothing should be done until the verdict of the Supreme Court were known, but he himself had come to favour an independent reorganization of the Northern Pacific—that is, by individuals instead of by the railway company as such.[1] Hill did not agree. Pyle quotes a letter written at the end of 1895 to Mount Stephen in which Hill stressed the strong position of his own railroad at that time, compared with other Pacific lines and particularly with the Northern Pacific:

... Our company is the only Pacific line paying a dividend on its shares, while three out of five lines other than our own are in process of reorganization, which must wipe out many millions of the capital invested in those enterprises. Every other Pacific line except our own received enormous sums of money or lands or both as subsidies, while our line, or rather our company, has gone on steadily paying dividends to its shareholders for fifteen years, and all this time the dividend has been earned during the year in which it was paid except in 1889 and 1894, the deficiency for these two years being made up from former surpluses, without materially reducing such surplus ...

The Northern Pacific has had large earnings during the fall months. Their car equipment, while not such large cars as our own, is greater in number and they have rushed everything to market, while we have encouraged holding in country elevators and have advanced money to help carry the wheat so held, to ensure a steady winter traffic. I think we will have on the line and in farmers' hands to come forward on January 1st fully 25,000,000 bushels, while the Northern Pacific will not have over 5,000,000 bushels. I think, therefore, that our earnings will hold up longer, while those of the Northern Pacific relatively will fall off after the holidays, and next year the parties who are now shouting huzzas for independent reorganization will have another song to sing. At any rate, there will be a more solemn note in their music long before they reach a reorganization on any basis ...

Quoting the latest Northern Pacific figures, Hill concluded: 'From the above I estimate that with such changes as we could make in from twelve to eighteen months on the Northern Pacific, we could rely with reasonable safety on earning a good dividend on the preferred shares at the end of the first year'.[2]

On 30 November 1895 Farrer had been assuring Nichols in New York that business in London was resuming its normal course 'and barring fresh political disturbances, we hope soon to be able to report

[1] Adler, op. cit. vol. 1, p. 87. [2] Pyle, op. cit. vol. 2, p. 19.

further sales . . .' On 14 December this trend still continued; Farrer told Nichols that demand for all high class bonds had improved; Manitoba Sterling 4s, that favourite yardstick, were firm at 95½–96. Four days later the name 'Venezuela' hit the headlines. The controversy between Great Britain and Venezuela over the boundary between the latter and British Guiana was of long standing but had gained in urgency by the discovery of gold in the disputed area some ten years earlier. The United States had been prepared to respond to Venezuela's appeal to act as arbiter, but Britain had consistently declined to accept this intervention. On 18 December Britain learned that President Cleveland had laid before Congress the diplomatic correspondence, and had recommended the setting up of an independent commission whose findings the United States would consider to be binding upon Britain. In the end arbitration was agreed to and the final verdict went in Britain's favour; meantime the air of Wall Street was 'blue with curses'[1] while the London investment community was 'stirred . . . to its depths, and threw on the American market a load of liquidating foreign sales'.[2] President Cleveland's public espousal of the Venezuelan cause aroused 'indignant astonishment' in England,[3] and war between the United States and Great Britain seemed hardly beyond the realms of possibility.

On 21 December 1895 Farrer wrote to E. T. Nichols elaborating on a cable already sent as a consequence of the uneasiness in London over the financial situation, particularly the position of gold, in New York. He feared that there was little prospect of selling the railway bonds in London in the immediate future and this fear was evidently shared by Barings, with whom Lefevres had been selling the bonds on joint account. But on 24 December Farrer made a point of writing to one of the brokers whom he was accustomed to keep posted as to Great Northern developments, reporting that Mr. Hill had just cabled that the past half-year's earnings had been little short of $7 million of which $6 million had been remitted to New York from the West since 1 July, sufficient to pay the interest on the entire bonded debt, direct and guaranteed, for a twelve-month and still leave a million dollars towards dividends on the

---

[1] An American correspondent quoted in Arthur D. Elliot, *The Life of George Joachim Goschen, First Viscount Goschen 1831–1907*, London, 1911, 2 vols., vol. 2, p. 203.
[2] Alexander Dana Noyes, *Forty Years of American Finance*, New York, 1909, p. 249.
[3] Lady Victoria Hicks-Beach, *The Life of Sir Michael Hicks-Beach*, London, 1932, 2 vols., vol. 2, p. 22.

'Manitoba' and Great Northern share capitals. Feeling, perhaps, that this painted too rosy a picture, Farrer added a postscript: 'It is of course the good half of the year'.

Writing to Hill on 24 January 1896, still on the question of the last annual report about which Hill and Mount Stephen had been corresponding direct, Farrer sought to be placatory:

... Anyway I fancy you and we here are not far apart on this matter, and that ten minutes talk would prove it; discussions by letter are rarely satisfactory even between Ministers of State apparently—How ridiculous all this squabbling is! Six weeks since not one in ten thousand people here knew where Venezuela was and to this day not one in fifty thousand cares a twopenny damn where the boundary is fixed so long as the question can be settled with honour—I suppose the same could be said of your people. It is very disappointing that year after year panics and dislocation of business should recur chiefly owing to the action or inaction of politicians, when apparently international tariff and currency difficulties might all have been satisfactorily settled by a little common sense and unselfishness ...

He acknowledged Hill's New Year gift of 'beautiful apples which I and sundry small nephews and nieces have highly appreciated' and made a lighthearted reference to the return home from Europe of Hill's daughters. He was equally appreciative of Hill's sending the Great Northern operating sheets for 1894–5 and early 1895–6: 'they are full of interest and when we next meet I am hoping to get a quiet half hour with you that I may thoroughly grasp the physical conditions which affect the composition of the figures in each division'. He assured Hill that, as to the annual report, 'I agree your work needs no justification and am sorry you should think me disgruntled: had I three years ago been able to forsee the conditions under which you would have to do that work I should have said the results you *have* obtained would have been impossible for anyone else but yourself—they are just great—and it was not the work but the representation of it to which I took exception. I wrote Ld. M.S. that that did you *in*justice; I thought and think that the report might be made simply clearer: the ordinary investor is excusably ignorant, often stupid, always lazy: he does not want masses of detail but a simple result as a whole: the closer figures can be reduced to an object lesson the better he is pleased—I know well the farce of attaching too much importance to form, that it is not the figures but what is behind them that is material: but form and figures do have a bearing on credit; that is the side I see daily: the only side on which I am able to form an opinion or would venture to make you a suggestion ...'

By 1 February 1896 Farrer had to report to Nichols that Manitoba Sterling 4s were down to 92; there was however some demand for 4½s and he made a tentative bid for these. The public, he said, were taking very little interest in the American market; only bonds of undoubted standing were being bought for investment, although among the professionals there was a certain amount of speculation.

NEW PLAN FOR NP: SECOND LONDON AGREEMENT

By early 1896, still awaiting the Supreme Court judgment, Hill had a fail-safe plan for the Northern Pacific worked out. On 15 February he sent it to Mount Stephen, and its provisions were largely the basis of what was to be the second London agreement. Hill wrote:

Bearing in mind the opposition to the consolidation of the interests of the two companies which has grown out of the public discussion, lawsuits &c, during the past summer, I think it would be well to avoid for the present any discussion of the proposed unification of interests. My plan would be for a party of the friends and large shareholders of the Great Northern to buy all the consolidated bonds of the Northern Pacific to be had in the market. We should secure one-half the issue if possible ... I think I could make up a party to take the whole transaction in America, but as it would be very profitable I would prefer to distribute it among some of our good friends abroad.[1]

Thus the plan aimed to substitute stockholding by individuals in their private capacity for that by a corporation, thereby satisfying the law. There followed conferences in New York and in London, involving the same parties as had been in the original scheme. Jacob Schiff wrote to Robert Fleming on 10 March; 'The Northern Pacific plan is about ready to be issued through Morgan. The G.N. is not in it'.[2] On 16 March 1896 the plan was made public: it provided for the sale of the property at foreclosure, and the organization of a new company with $80 million common and $75 million preferred stock, and the issue of a maximum of $130 million prior lien 4 per cent bonds and a maximum of $60 million 3 per cent,

[1] Pyle, op. cit. vol. 2, pp. 23–24.
[2] Adler, op. cit. vol. 1, p. 88.

these bonds to be issued by degrees, as required. A syndicate comprising J. P. Morgan and representatives and friends of the Deutsche Bank subscribed $45 million to underwrite the scheme, plus $5 million to make immediate improvements in the property.[1] On 30 March the Supreme Court did in fact reverse the decision of the Circuit Court, finding the original scheme unlawful.

Hill was not a member of the syndicate but by agreement with Morgan he and his friends had the right to take such portions of stock as were not subscribed for by the old Northern Pacific stockholders. This turned out to be initially about $16 million; they could from time to time acquire more, and did so to the tune of $10 million, making a total of $26 million, representing a large but not actually controlling interest.[2] On 30 April Gaspard Farrer wrote to Charles Ellis telling him that an interest of $100,000 had been reserved for him, saying 'I beg you will keep this matter to yourself. The guarantee is a business risk with possible, and I hope assured, profits attaching, the participation obtained for you by Mr. Hill being offered you as an old supporter of his property but not as a "right" to you in your capacity of a Great Northern shareholder in which all other shareholders would expect to join'.

The plan provided that for the first five years both classes of stock would be vested in a voting trust of five, headed by J. P. Morgan, the voting power of the trust expiring on 1 November 1901. Another provision—the right to retire the preferred stock at par on any 1 January during the next twenty years—was to have unforeseen repercussions in the saga of the 'Northern Pacific corner' five years later.

Unfortunately for the record, the full tale of Hill's visit to London was contained in a letter from Mount Stephen to John Sterling; writing to the latter on 4 April, Farrer did not repeat it. Writing to one of the brokers on 20 April, Farrer referred to Hill's 'flying visit' and to the 'week's incessant talk'. Drawing the broker's attention to the Great Northern's half-yearly statement to 31 December 1895 just published in *The Times*, Farrer admitted that this was the 'fat half' of the year but believed that the condition of the property and its capacity for cheap operation were as satisfactory as its earnings. Even if a repetition of the 'phenomenal crop' of 1895 could hardly be expected, he thought that owing

[1] Pyle, op. cit. vol. 2, p. 24.
[2] Ibid. pp. 24–25, also p. 103; J. J. Hill to the St. Paul *Globe*, 22 December 1901.

to the increase in general business, earnings were likely to be maintained. Reporting on 4 June to E. T. Nichols that he had had a chance to sell the rest of his last batch of G.N. '4½'s and so had let them go before the annual balance, Farrer assessed the general prospect referring to the current bimetallism controversy:

Business in American shares has long ceased to exist here and of late there has been a feeling about that looked like developing into a debacle in Bonds: as may easily occur yet if your politicians declare for silver: many issues can be had today under their present quoted prices if only buyers could be found: however there is a brighter side too and if the country was unmistakably to declare for gold we should probably have a decided boom in U.S. things. Morgan who has just sailed has been vehement in protesting that none but a gold man is possible for President: but he has too many bonds to sell to carry conviction, and a few houses such as Samuel Montagu, Stores, Seligman, all prophesy silver as more or less of a certainty. I still have faith in the good sense of American people, if not in its Senators, but I confess to being weary of object lessons.

GARNET WOLSELEY: THE C.-IN-C. APPOINTMENT

On 14 May 1895, four days after the signing of the first London agreement concerning the Northern Pacific reorganization, Field Marshal Viscount Wolseley—he had been awarded his Field Marshal's baton late in 1894—wrote from London to his wife who, with their daughter Frances, was sojourning at Homburg:

... Met Mount Stephen and walked about with him for some time and then home with him to see my Lady. She has not been well but is now all right again. He is very anxious you and Frances should propose yourselves to pay him a visit whenever it may suit you to go to Brockett [*sic*] Hall ...[1]

It was only the following day that it occurred to him to write to Frances: '... I forgot to tell your mother that Mount Stephen said it was generally accepted that this was the Duke of Cambridge's last year of office ...'[2] In 1895 Wolseley's term as Commander-in-Chief, Ireland, was drawing to a close just as it was being rumoured that H.R.H. the Duke of Cambridge, after some forty years in the post, was at last retiring as Commander-in-Chief of the British Army. Mount Stephen was not alone in taking it for granted that

[1] W/P24.   [2] Ibid.

Wolseley would automatically succeed him, although Garnet himself was by no means certain of it, and with reason. One of his obvious rivals was Lord Roberts, completing an extended term as Commander-in-Chief, India, and newly a Field Marshal. The others were the royal Duke of Connaught, third son of Queen Victoria, who had made the Army his career, and General Sir Redvers Buller, then Adjutant General at the War Office, an old 'Wolseley Ring' member. Buller had, in fact, been all but appointed before the change of Government that year. The Queen wished the Duke to have the appointment, and had set her heart on Wolseley going to the Embassy at Berlin.

Already Wolseley had been discussing his chances with his old friend Sir Henry Bulwer (nephew of Lord Dalling, former Ambassador at Constantinople, he had succeeded Garnet as Governor of Natal in 1875) who wrote to him on 18 May 1895 that it was clear to him from what Wolseley had told him that the outgoing Secretary of State at the War Office, Campbell-Bannerman, had every intention of disregarding Wolseley's claims, probably as part of an understanding with the Duke of Cambridge when the latter's unwilling consent to go had been obtained.[1] The Duke and Wolseley had never exactly seen eye-to-eye over the question of modernizing the Army; in his letters to his wife Garnet generally referred to the Duke as 'old Bumble Bee'. So far as the general public was concerned, the choice would have lain between Wolseley and Roberts; when Lieut. General Sir John McNeill wrote to Lady Wolseley that Buller ought to have the post if only because the country was so divided between Wolseley and Roberts, he was not alone in voicing this solution.[2] For long Wolseley had been to England 'our only General', but since Kandahar 'our other General' had been catching up fast. Roberts, however, had virtually disqualified himself two years earlier by angling for the appointment of Commandant at Aldershot; Campbell-Bannerman had then put him down as an 'arrant jobber and intriguer' . . . a good soldier and capable administrator but 'altogether wrong in his political notions, both British and Indian'.[3] There were, indeed, a great many considerations involved in the business of appointing a successor to the Duke, both political and military, not least the probability that future reorganization at the War Office would sooner or later result

[1] Ibid. [2] LW/P 21.
[3] John Wilson, *C.B. A Life of Sir Henry Campbell-Bannerman*, London, 1973, p. 180.

in the abolition of the post of Commander-in-Chief. As it was, a limited term of five years was now proposed. The fullest account so far published is contained in John Wilson's biography of Campbell-Bannerman; it is proposed here to concentrate on a rather different angle, as seen from the Wolseleys' point of view and in correspondence with Lord Mount Stephen. It might however be said at this stage that Campbell-Bannerman, both during his first spell at the War Office when Wolseley was Adjutant General, and in his second and longer term when Wolseley was in Ireland, had proved himself on the whole sympathetic to the latter's opinions, while at the same time developing a liking for Buller which Wilson concludes was perhaps too uncritical. Lady Wolseley, too, had got on admirably with the Campbell-Bannermans of whom she had over the years seen a good deal at their favourite continental spa of Marienbad, although her temporary defection to Homburg might have incurred the cynical censure of C.B. who noted at one time the fashionable trend in that direction of his fellow-countrymen.[1] At all events, he had given her to understand, in the course of a correspondence in 1893, that he had Wolseley in mind as the next Commander-in-Chief.[2]

Wolseley himself was out of the country when on 21 June 1895 the Rosebery Government fell, hours after the announcement of the Duke of Cambridge's resignation; he had joined Sir John Pender's yacht *Mirror* for a cruise which included the opening by the Kaiser of the Kiel Canal. In his letter to Louisa of 23 June he noted the Duke's resignation but had nothing to say of the Government's defeat or its possible repercussions.[3] It would indeed have been uncharacteristic of the curiously frivolous correspondence which over the years passed between the two to have skimmed more than the froth off the day's news. Apart from the question of his appointment, and the related one of their consequent place of residence, the problem generally uppermost in their minds at this period was that of their daughter's future. Frances was proving increasingly difficult, not only to marry, but even to live with: this is a topic which will be dealt with presently in the context of her relations with her godfather, Lord Mount Stephen. On 28 June Garnet wrote to his wife to ask 'if I am made C-in-C what would you say to my having [Cecil Fielden] as an A.D.C.? Now talk this

[1] Ibid. p. 142.   [2] Ibid. pp. 184–5 and 209.
[3] W/P 24.

over, please, with Frances and let me know your views . . .'[1] He seemed more concerned about forwarding his daughter's latest possibility than with his own ambitions. His doubts are reflected in his letter to Louisa of 6 July, but again he relates the possible 'blow'—if he is not appointed—to his daughter's future. London was obviously nearer the centre of the marriage market than Berlin or Calcutta, the Indian Viceroyalty being the third contingency.[2] Louisa repeatedly adjured him to think only of his own career; she was by this time distinctly out of sympathy with her daughter.

What had in fact happened on 21 June 1895 in the House of Commons was known afterwards as the cordite debate: the War Office spokesman on the Opposition front bench, St. John Brodrick, speaking to the Army Estimates, had challenged the War Minister, Campbell-Bannerman, over an apparent shortage of ammunition and of the explosive cordite. Caught off guard—as indeed were the Government Whips when it came to a vote—C.B. fumbled the issue, and almost before it was realized what was happening, the Rosebery administration was defeated. Over the next few days, alongside Lord Salisbury's main preoccupations of forming a minority government which he could keep in power until an election should be held, and of ensuring the continued survival of the Army without its frustrated vote, there was performed an elaborate ballet aimed at preventing Buller, the Rosebery nominee, from being, by a last stroke of Campbell-Bannerman's pen, appointed Commander-in-Chief. It was known subsequently as the affair of the seals. The War Minister's seals of office were a necessary appendage to an instrument of appointment. On 25 June the new Prime Minister sent his private secretary to wait upon the retiring Secretary of State for War and suggest that he hand over his seals, only to achieve the reply that 'the Sovereign might demand the surrender of Seals which She had granted, but that no demise of the Crown had yet been announced'.[3] The Commission appointing Buller had in fact been made out, with the reluctant approval of the Queen and the even more hesitant acquiescence of Buller. The latter had pressed Wolseley's prior claim and his own inadequacy as a 'first man' (as opposed to a 'second man')—a perceptive self-assessment.[4] He had

[1] W/P 24. [2] Ibid.

[3] This version from the Earl of Midleton (formerly St. John Brodrick), *Records and Reactions, 1856–1939*, London, 1939, pp. 83–93.

[4] C. H. Melville, *Life of General Sir Redvers Buller*, London, 1923, 2 vols., vol I, p. 274.

had the added embarrassment of discussing the matter with his old
chief, forced by conflicting loyalties to assume complete ignorance of
official intentions.

Wilson writes that C.B. was the last man to wish to 'jump' an
appointment. He agrees, however, that his subject had an acute
sense of humour. A rather similar manifestation had earlier
been displayed by Lord Salisbury when the question of a
successor to the Duke of Cambridge had been discussed before
the change of Government. On learning of the proposal to appoint
Buller, St. John Brodrick had tackled Campbell-Bannerman,
asking 'Are you going to pass over both the Field-Marshals?'
'Why not? Won't your party support it?' Brodrick had
advised the War Minister to ask Lord Salisbury, doubting if
'both of our greatest commanders being in the early sixties, he
would have military or civil support for such a slight'. Next day
Lord Rosebery put the question to the Leader of the Opposition:
'All he got was the cryptic reply: "I gather the appointment is not
to be vacated till November 1st" (we were then in June), "and it
will rest with the Government then in power" '. On being pressed
further, Salisbury would only repeat 'Surely the Government then
in power must decide'.[1]

Both Lord and Lady Wolseley, still in suspense as June gave way
to July, were writing around to friends in the hope of gleaning
some information, and Garnet passed his replies to Louisa. Sir
Henry Bulwer's brother, Sir Edward, wrote to Garnet on 13 July:

I was very sorry to hear from Lady Wolseley's letter to my brother that
your chances of succeeding H.R.H. were not good. I confess that I had
been a little alarmed at the well known favour felt by Lansdowne and
Brodrick for Roberts—at the same time there was a general impression
that it would hardly be profitable to pass you over for him. It would be
in the interest of the public service such a monstrous proceeding and
so detrimental that it was felt it could hardly be done. At Devonshire
House the other night I had a long talk with Derby and though he was
very cautious not to commit himself, I felt from his manner that there
was some hesitation about your chances. Griffiths also told me that
Grove was rather desponding and now I gather from Lady W.'s letter
that it is Buller. Well I called on Buller the other evening (only Monday
last) and we got talking. At that time I don't think he knew anything
about it. He told me he had been kept on as Adjutant General for two

[1] Midleton, op. cit. p. 88.

years longer. He was strongly in favour of a Commander-in-Chief [the recent Hartington Commission had proposed abolishing the post] and I don't think ever thought that he should succeed to that—moreover at . . . our dinner Campbell-Bannerman spoke to me quietly some time and among other things I gathered from him that he himself had hovered between you and Buller but that Buller had urged your claims very strongly. Owing to the Government collapse however the whole matter dropped . . .

. . . You have been so mixed up with the present organization of the Army from the very beginning that any impartial person would say that you ought to be the first Commander-in-Chief in the new conditions . . .[1]

As to 'the well known favour felt by Lansdowne and Brodrick for Roberts': Lord Lansdowne in 1888 had exchanged the Governor-Generalship of Canada for the Viceroyalty of India, where Roberts was Commander-in-Chief. He was, in the words of David James, biographer of Roberts: 'to become one of Roberts' closest personal and public friends. Small, precise and reserved, a man who could unburden himself to very few, Lord Lansdowne was the beau ideal of the patrician pro-consul. He and Roberts took to each other at once and their correspondence, which started the day the former landed in Bombay, was to continue for a quarter of a century until death'.[2] Lansdowne was later to write: 'I loved [Roberts] as I have loved few people in this world. Of all the men I have ever met he seemed to me the most absolutely genuine and sincere . . .'[3] Lansdowne was now Secretary of State for War in Lord Salisbury's new administration; Brodrick was Under-Secretary of State in charge of War Office business in the House of Commons. While Financial Secretary at the War Office from 1886–92 Brodrick had witnessed the resistance of the Duke of Cambridge (whose many virtues he nevertheless acknowledged) to the 'Wolseley school of modern thought', and wrote: 'From 1886 onward, the skirmishes between the Duke and Wolseley, if the issue had not been so serious, somewhat made up to me, during five years, for rarely having the time to attend ordinary places of amusement'.[4] In his memoirs, he shows himself entirely sympathetic towards Wolseley; this would probably have surprised the latter.

From Sir John Pender, the cable and telegraph magnate, Wolseley heard on 14 July:

[1] W/P 24.
[2] David James, *Lord Roberts*, London, 1954, p. 221.
[3] Ibid. p. 490.   [4] Midleton, op. cit. p. 81.

I saw Brodrick but he knew nothing, but I learned from him that he had arranged with Lord Lansdowne to go to Homburg with Lady Hilda until parliament opened so you may see him there. What I learn confirms what you tell me but I cannot conceive any such injustice being done. I was told that this was arranged by C.B. with R.B. before Resignation was talked about. I believe Devonshire is the man who will decide the question. I believe him to be a straight man . . .[1]

Following his letter to Lady Wolseley already quoted, Sir John McNeill wrote to Wolseley from St. James's Palace on 16 July:

From all I can gather I think you had better lie low for the present. Of course this will be a Cabinet question, if 2 or 3 names are submitted I think your chance is very good. If one name only is submitted I feel sure Her Majesty will confirm the decision of ministers, in any case she will initiate nothing.[2]

Garnet added a note to this letter for Louisa: 'This all means that the Queen will not raise her finger to help me. Burn this as Her name is mentioned in it'. He added a covering letter on 17 July, from Dublin: 'I don't gather much comfort from J. McN.'s letter, but my note to him has not done me any harm . . .' He was finding his work in Ireland tedious, whether the office work which had kept him busy until 1 a.m. that morning and had begun again at 6 a.m., or the official visits such as that to the Hibernian Military School for which he was just about to start. Lord Roberts, due to succeed him there, was coming on 1 August to look over horses &c which he might wish to take over.

On 19 July Garnet wrote to Louisa from the Curragh Camp, County Kildare, having been to 'some silly Garrison races'. McNeill, whom Garnet frequently criticized, had committed the indiscretion of telling Buller that Wolseley doubted his loyalty; Louisa shared his disapproval and her husband commented: 'had he thought for a moment, he must have realized that what he said was calculated to create an ill feeling between Buller and me'. Even the poet Alfred Austin—not yet the Laureate, but already the self-appointed chronicler in verse of Wolseley family events—contributed his theories on the issue. Referring to him as 'little Austin'—a favourite term of contempt—Garnet nevertheless seized upon one of the poet's ideas, telling Louisa:

[1] W/P 24.   [2] Ibid.

... he is right, I think, in believing that Buller was preferred to me because he has as Adjt. Genl. always made things pleasant for them: he has never urged great reforms upon either the Duke or the War Minister that would displease the former or curtail an increase to the latter's Budget. The fact is, that for the five years he has been A.G. the Army has only gone forward in the grooves I got it into but he has made no progress for it or given it any new ideas or new system... In dull times when no war is in the air, this is what commends itself to any administration Tory or Radical... An Army must go forward, it cannot stand still or mark time as ours has been for the last five years without danger and without falling behind others...[1]

In this letter of 19 July he made an oblique reference to the cordite debate when he accused Buller of being prepared, for the sake of pleasing his political masters, to say that there was enough small arms ammunition, 'when it is well known we have not and could not obtain it if we suddenly wanted it'. He adverted again to this topic in his letter to Louisa of 21 July, saying: '... I could not do those sort of things in my old age even to obtain employment... leaving the nation like Sampson [*sic*] when his hair was cut off...' He still professed to be more concerned for his wife's and daughter's interests than for his own, although he could not help adding that in his vanity he thought that it would be better for the army to have him for five years rather than Buller.[2]

More cheering news came from Colonel Spencer Childers who wrote to Wolseley on 19 July: 'I am sure that Cecil [Colonel Edward Herbert Cecil, son of Lord Salisbury] has shown my letter to his father, who has told him to say only enough to let me see between the lines that there is not any likelihood of the Campbell-Bannerman project being adopted...'[3] But more than anything Garnet appreciated 'a nice letter from Mount Stephen' written from Brocket on 19 July and sent on to Louisa on the 21st with the suggestion: 'If you can spare the time write Ly. M. a few lines to say how much you appreciate the kindness of feeling which characterises every line of her husband's letter. There is no *arière* [*sic*] *pensée* in his friendship. It is genuine...'[4] Mount Stephen wrote:

... I have been, in a quiet way, trying to find out exactly how matters stood. It seems clear that the late Government had actually offered the post to Buller and if they had remained in power he undoubtedly would have got the appointment... Lansdowne is a great admirer of Roberts

[1] Ibid.   [2] Ibid.   [3] Ibid.   [4] Ibid.

but would hesitate, I think, to make him Chief. I *suspect* the old Duke has recommended Buller, not I suppose that he considers him the better man for the place—he cannot possibly pretend to believe that—but perhaps on the ground that Buller is quite competent to fill it and his appointment would avoid offending the pro-Roberts party in the Army. I also suspect that the politicians might have a hankering preference for a man of less influence and less overshadowing personality so that the Secretary of State would become completely "Boss". But be that as it may, I'm afraid the politicians interact as they always do, and decide the matters in the way most agreeable to themselves and without much consideration for anything else. If Buller is not appointed, you are, I think, sure to be offered it. Lansdowne is a very straightforward cons- cientious fellow and not in the least likely to be swayed by St John Brodrick. He will probably be more influenced by the Duke of Devon- shire and Chamberlain than anyone else. I saw McNeill in London yesterday and he told me that Lansdowne had sent for you but that you did not draw much encouragement from anything he said to you which does not surprise me and shows that the question is still in abeyance, and that there is still a chance for you.

I would gladly have gone to Lansdowne on getting your letter but I know him too well to believe that my doing so would have done anything but harm. Further I should be very chary about doing anything that could possibly be considered unbefitting, as a friend of yours.

I think you acted wisely in not staying in London and so giving occasion for gossip and ill-natured remarks. In short, you have done all that you could properly do—you could not as you say go on your knees to Lord Lansdowne and beg him to give you the appointment. If Fate has decreed that you are not to get the appointment we shall indeed be very grieved. But you must not consider that your life and work are ended by any means. Time will show, as it always does, that our bitterest disappointments carry many compensating advantages and you may be quite sure, your case will be no exception . . .

P.S. If you can think of anything that I can do in this matter do not fail to let me know.

Louisa replied to Garnet on 23 July: '. . . I thought Lord Mount Stephen's grasp of the whole matter most surprising for a civilian in fact far clearer than that of the soldiers who have written to you, but then this has become a politicians' question and no doubt little Harry [Northcote] has coached him up . . .'[1] Lady Wolseley was feeling the strain of this prolonged suspense to such an obvious extent that even her unsympathetic daughter was moved to confide

[1] LW/P 17.

to her mother's maid that she was sorry her mother had this anxiety just now, 'which I thought wonderful', wrote Louisa to Garnet, 'but she never offers me any sympathy . . .'[1]

Writing from the Carlton Club on 20 July, Alfred Austin reported that he had it from a very high authority that it was doubtful that C.B. had appointed Buller. This was sent by Garnet to Louisa with an undated and disgusted comment: 'Is not the enclosed note like A.A.? There is not a grain of information in it, and yet his Delphi-like pronunciations are meant to sound oracularly as if emanating from the source of all knowledge . . .'[2] Then came two letters, written on 26 July by a soldier, Major-General L. V. Swaine. The first, after listing the military considerations: that the Army was divided between Wolseley and Roberts, and that therefore it was better to appoint neither, and that since it seemed that the intention was to have not a Commander-in-Chief but a Chief of Staff with clipped wings—in which case a Field Marshal was not called for— veered to the political, voicing the feeling that both Field Marshals were too outspoken, and that the Cabinet would prefer a plodder to a genius. He had heard a rumour that Wolseley was not on particularly good terms with Lord Salisbury: he didn't know—the idea was new to him, but for his part he couldn't conceive of Lord Salisbury's bringing personal feelings into the question, even if this were true. The letter from Childers quoted above disposes of this consideration. Swaine himself was a Conservative, a member of the Carlton Club, and he now put forward the bold suggestion that the time had come for Wolseley to unfurl his political colours . . . 'play a trump card'. Remarking that on the one occasion when Wolseley had sat in the House of Lords he had occupied the cross-benches, Swaine pursued: 'You must consider your age, that in October you will be unemployed, that there are no special berths for a Field-Marshal, and that the Conservatives have a long spell of Government before them . . .' This he had been assured of by an influential Conservative. If Wolseley were to write at once to the Secretary of the Carlton Club desiring him to put him up for membership, he would be elected—as a member of the House of Peers—without a ballot on Tuesday week. On hearing that Wolseley had done this, Swaine would do the rest. Garnet's open condemnation of the Home Rule policy of the late Ministry would be sufficient recom- mendation. Swaine's second letter contained the rumour that

Lord Elgin, Viceroy of India, was thinking of resigning (this Garnet already knew of: in fact the rumour proved untrue) and the news that the British Ambassador to Berlin *had* resigned. This was expected, and Swaine asked 'Why not go in for the Berlin Embassy? ... It would be a great compliment to the Emperor, and although it might not be fully to your liking, it will be a post brim full of interest and hard work ...'[1]

Another letter written to Wolseley on 26 July was from his colleague Sir Evelyn Wood, a peripheral 'Ring' member lately Commandant at Aldershot, whom Wolseley was accustomed to criticize bitterly on occasion. Wood reported that Lord Salisbury was said to be in a great dilemma; he was being much pressed to appoint the Duke of Connaught, but being told on the other hand that to do so would create a very bad effect in the country.[2] Wolseley was getting desperate and was ready to accept any suggestion. He wrote to the Carlton Club, although he attached little importance to it; he told Louisa on 28 July that he had been writing around regarding other possible employment. He was feeling disgusted with the Army and was keenly resentful of the reports that the late Government had meant deliberately to discard him.[3] His wife, equally on tenterhooks, and irritated in addition by Frances, ranged in her letters of 28 and 31 July over the possibilities of their future ... India ... Germany ... or they might 'subside into Ebury Street with a parlourmaid'.[4] But on 29 July there had been another ray of hope: Lady Mount Stephen had written to say that Lord Lansdowne had called at their town house, 25 St. James's Place, but unfortunately the Mount Stephens had been away at Brocket. She had no doubt that the visit was connected with the appointment of Commander-in-Chief, 'our affection for Lord Wolseley' being well known to Lord Lansdowne. She supposed the latter would now write and make an appointment to see her husband. This he did, but meanwhile, on 31 July, Lord Mount Stephen wrote to Lord Lansdowne. Unfortunately this letter is not among the Lansdowne papers at Bowood but is merely noted in a letter book as dealing with Canadian

---

[1] Ibid.
[2] Ibid. A Great War anecdote is told of Sir Evelyn Wood in Charles Carrington, *Soldier from the Wars Returning*, London, 1965, p. 78. After Loos, recruits were anxious to get to France: 'One of my friends overcalled his hand by appealing to a great-uncle whom he had never met, a very elderly field-marshal, and received this reply or words to this effect: "Field Marshal Sir Evelyn Wood acknowledges receipt of a letter from 2nd. Lieutenant So-and-So, and begs to inform him that he (the FM) spent many years at the War Office combating the baleful effects of private influence".'
[3] W/P 24.   [4] LW/P 17.

affairs.[1] It is, on the whole, unlikely that the letter had anything to do with Wolseley, but that it dealt with an entirely different, and Canadian, subject in which Mount Stephen was then interested, namely that of getting a British Government subsidy for an Atlantic freight line. That same day the Canadian Prime Minister, Sir Charles Tupper, was writing to the Colonial Secretary, Joseph Chamberlain, recapitulating a discussion of the previous day on the whole question of Canadian freight services.[2] Donald A. Smith's letter to Tupper of 18 December 1895 shows that Mount Stephen was involved in these negotiations,[3] which culminated in the promise of a subsidy and the calling for tenders for the new Atlantic steamship line. The Allan Line tender was accepted, but before the contract was signed the Conservative Government fell in July 1896, the Liberal Party under Sir Wilfrid Laurier was in power, and the Atlantic project was abandoned.

The 1895 episode of the appointment of the Commander-in-Chief showed Wolseley in both the worst and the best light. With hindsight, the protracted correspondence and Garnet's reactions to it, and the whole intricate process of testing the water and reporting throw out many clues for the interpretation of later events. All these must one day be dealt with by the definitive biographer of Wolseley. To Mount Stephen, years afterwards, fell the task of—if not picking up the pieces of the once-glamorous general, whose active service stopped too soon and whose wars were always too little—at least consoling the declining years of his friend. In 1895 Wolseley's future was still full of promise, his public reputation high. His judgment could still be acute, but there was something in him that was failing. This does not appear to have been remarked by anyone at this time, not even by those who did not support his candidature.

On 31 July 1895 Garnet wrote to Louisa enclosing two further letters: the first from Frederick Maurice, a younger military devotee of whom Garnet was very fond and who was to be his first biographer: 'So like himself', Wolseley commented 'full of honest enthusiasm and of courage that equals the enthusiasm: not always discreet nor always wise in public matters. Above all meanness and yet very suspicious of others and inclined to attribute men's actions to unworthy motives and to see conspiracy in their conduct'.[4] This

---

[1] I am indebted for this information to Mr. J. R. Hickish, F. L. A. S., Agent at Bowood, 20 December 1969.
[2] Tupper Papers 648 (PAC). See also Mackenzie Bowell Letter Books 119–21.
[3] Tupper Papers 666.   [4] W/P 24.

may have been a perceptive assessment of Maurice: it was a fairly accurate reflection of Garnet. The other letter, from Swaine who was glad to know that what he had heard rumoured of Wolseley's relations with Lord Salisbury was not true, reported that both John Morley and Lord Wantage said it would be impossible to pass Wolseley over: an ungracious act after all his services. Lord Roberts, he said, was now quite out of the field, so that Buller remained his only rival, 'and as both you and Lady Wolseley are liked by the Queen—how they got to know this I can't say—your chances seem to be looking up . . .' If not, Swaine was hopeful of the Berlin alternative. He concluded: 'I am glad that Lord Lansdowne will have your letter on Wednesday for I expect everything will now be rapidly settled in order that Lord Salisbury, who is sure to see the Emperor at Cowes, can give him a direct answer if His Majesty enquires of him who is to succeed Malet . . .'[1] Wolseley had not in fact written to Lord Lansdowne; the reference is to a letter he had written to another military colleague, Major-General Sir John Ardagh, a personal friend of Lansdowne, but in the hope that Ardagh would show it to Lansdowne.

'It is the suspense of all these possibilities that is so trying' wrote Garnet to Louisa on 1 August,—mentioning the Ardagh letter '—Poor Damocles'.[2] He enclosed Evelyn Wood's letter of 31 July: Wolseley's chances, Wood thought, had materially improved in the last few days, although he did not think Lansdowne had yet made up his own mind: 'I fancy he realizes clearly now, perhaps more clearly than he did, how unwise it would be to put in any one who knows little or nothing of the English Army'.[3] Lord Roberts was of course an Indian Army man: a race apart, in the eyes of those who had not served in the sub-continent. Henry Bulwer also wrote on 31 July, recalling the affair of the seals. He had heard from General Clive that it was said Lord Salisbury's aim was to prevent C.B. appointing Buller. Bulwer concluded : 'Lady D. N. whom I saw last week told me that as far as she could make out from the S.s. nothing had yet been decided or would at present be decided. But I daresay she has written to you herself'.[4] This was presumably Lady Dorothy Nevill, daughter of the third Earl of Orford, whose memoirs record a good deal of social and political history as witnessed over her long life.[5]

---

[1] Ibid.   [2] Ibid.   [3] Ibid.   [4] Ibid.
[5] *The Reminiscences of Lady Dorothy Nevill*, ed. Ralph Nevill, London, 1906.

The poet Alfred Austin, also writing on 31 July, had decided that India was the best alternative: 'I have more than once said that I should like to see you Viceroy and what you say only strengthens that view. I shall accordingly seize any occasion that may arise to urge it on those circles where the decision rests . . .'[1] Garnet forbore to comment, but did not take this too seriously for he wrote to Louisa on 3 August: 'I am still in correspondence with lawyers about our house in Pont Street. Would you be content to live in it if we were made Bumble Bee's successor? It would be scarcely big enough I am afraid. Let me know what you think'.[2] Coleridge Grove, Wolseley's military secretary, reported on 2 August that the Duke of Connaught was definitely out of the running: the Government had made up its mind not to have him. He added: 'The general public is only just beginning to wake up about the matter and that only gradually and partially. But as it does, so does the movement in your favour gain strength . . .' The trouble was, he said, that so many gave the matter no attention at all.[3]

Mount Stephen, writing from Brocket on 2 August, was cautiously optimistic; Garnet sent the letter on to Louisa on the 4th, but the enclosure from Lansdowne which it mentions is not now with it. Mount Stephen wrote:

I *doubt* if the Duke of Connaught will be offered the vacant place. He may get it 5 years hence! I think *your* chances are better than when I last wrote, but one never can be certain of anything in dealing with politicians until it is actually done.

The enclosed from Lansdowne came this morning. It gives me an opportunity of seeing him at his own request. I shall go up on Tuesday (Monday is Bank Holiday) and will find out all I can. I wish I knew the Duke of Devonshire as well as I do Lansdowne. Lord Salisbury I feel pretty certain would favour your appointment.

But if fate has decreed otherwise the Governor General [*sic*] of India would be a fitting end up to your active career . . .

Mount Stephen's impartial friendship with both British and Indian Army people would not have admitted to any difficulties on this score. He went on:

Your views as to the supreme importance of economy are in full accord with what Donald Stewart has been telling me for years. Fighting Russia and keeping up little wars with the Tribes on the frontier are foolish if not wicked devices to secure honours and decorations &c. &c. He says he has

---

[1] W/P 24. [2] Ibid. [3] Ibid.

never been able to find out how it came to pass that we had any one at Chitral to be relieved at an expense to India of over £2,000,000.[1]

This was followed on 5 August by a letter from Brocket: 'Just a line to say that I have reason to believe you will be the new Commander-in-Chief. Rowdy Lane was here today: he, at all events, thinks so'. Major-General Sir Ronald Bertram Lane was then Extra Equerry to the Duke of Connaught. Garnet sent this on to his wife, having scribbled on the back: '. . . I have only this moment received this from Mount S. It is so encouraging that at the risk of misleading you I am now telegraphing to you the word "Good" which I hope you will remember means "things look well" . . .' and on the front: 'Keep this secret, but merely say when asked that of course you naturally assume I am to be Old Bumble Bee's successor'.[2]

On Tuesday 6 August 1895 Mount Stephen saw Lord Lansdowne. The following day Garnet wrote to Louisa from County Kilkenny:

. . . Just as I was starting off this morning for my day's manoeuvring I received a note from Mount Stephen written after his interview with Lansdowne. It was so cheering and hopeful that I sent it to you by post this morning and telegraphed to you "*good*" which by our "code" stands for "things look well". I hope that word may not have misled you to imagine the matter is settled in my favour. When you receive Mount S.'s letter you will have in your possession all that I based my telegram on. I think it means that Kerry [their code-name for Lansdowne] told him it was at least tolerably certain. I begin to think it is so, or I would not have sent you my telegram of today.

He added that he had just received a loyal letter from General Sir William Butler, one of the 'Ring', author of *The Great Lone Land*.[3] Louisa's reply on 7 August to the telegram (it is not clear whether one or two had been sent) showed that she had indeed remembered the code:

Your "good" telegram has just arrived . . . We understand it to mean that you have heard something encouraging but not *decisive* and we think that Lord Mt. S. must have sent you a satisfactory account of his interview with Lord L. yesterday. If so Lord Mt. S. must, I think, have telegraphed it to you, as I don't think there was time for his letter to reach Kilkenny . . .[4]

[1] W/P 24. This 'minor siege' resulted in one KCSI, one VC, three DSO's and one CB.
[2] W/P 24.   [3] Ibid.   [4] LW/P 17.

Lord Lansdowne himself had already made up his mind to recommend Wolseley. Lord Salisbury had written to him on 5 August relaying the Queen's views: first, that Roberts was absolutely impossible. '. . . I told her . . . that you proposed to recommend Lord Wolseley . . . She recognised Lord Wolseley's claims but demurred strongly to his great imprudence and his fondness for a clique. She then talked of the Army's preference for the Duke of Connaught . . .'[1] In 1890, when presumably there seemed little hope of dislodging the Duke of Cambridge except by the most devious means, 'the Queen had enthusiastically endorsed a suggestion by Wolseley that the Duke of Connaught should be appointed as Commander-in-Chief, but had been told by her Conservative Ministers that he must fill other commands first, and not as Ponsonby put it, jump "into power by what may almost be termed violent means"'.[2] Her Majesty still suspected 'that the Government think (most foolishly) Arthur would be as retrograde and old-fashioned as the dear Duke of Cambridge, whereas he is the very reverse, and it is too shameful keeping him out of all important places on account of his birth'.[3] The latter quotation, in a letter to Sir Henry Ponsonby in 1893, related to the question of the Aldershot command, which the Queen then hoped would lead to her son's appointment to the Army's highest office.

That Wolseley judged it politic to revive this suggestion in the letter he wrote to Ardagh for Lord Lansdowne's eye is revealed in the letter that the Secretary of State for War wrote to him on 7 August:

Ardagh mentioned to me your readiness to stand on one side in the event of its being desired to make the Duke of Connaught Commander-in-Chief and your idea that in this event employment might be provided for you in India or at Berlin. I have no reason for supposing that there will be an early vacancy in India but I at once made Lord Salisbury aware of your readiness, in the event supposed, to go to Berlin . . .

Lansdowne had now heard that the post at Berlin was open to Wolseley, but continued: 'In making this intimation to you I feel bound to add—and the Prime Minister approves of my doing so— that you would in my opinion be the proper person to succeed

---

[1] Lord Newton, *Lord Lansdowne, A Biography*, London, 1929, p. 131.
[2] Wilson, *C.B.* p. 182. Sir Henry Ponsonby was Queen Victoria's Private Secretary.
[3] Wilson, p. 182.

H.R.H. the Duke of Cambridge as Commander-in-Chief, and that
if you are *en disponibilité* I should ask you to accept the appointment.
It would not be fair to you that the offer of Berlin should be made to
you while you were in ignorance of alternative possibilities . . .' He
added that it would give him very great pleasure to have Wolseley
as his principal military adviser.[1]

Garnet copied this secret letter in pencil for Louisa, signing it
'Kerry' and added that he had just sent her a telegram: "Hurrah,
strictly secret". The relief was almost overpowering; 'Thank God
for this new mercy to me', he wrote '—I think you had better come
to London at once and look out for a house with stabling in which
we could live comfortably as we did when in Hill Street . . .' He
was writing to accept the appointment of Commander-in-Chief in
preference to Berlin. '. . . Do please both you and Frances thank
God for this new blessing which I know comes from Him. It is
raining in torrents. Goodbye. I will write more fully by next post'.
The next day he wrote postponing his election to the Carlton
Club.

Wolseley gave but one lingering look in the direction of Berlin,
when he received a message from the Queen that the German
Emperor was very anxious that he should go there; he could stay
there until he was seventy, 'removed from all the toil and worry of
that War Office. But to give up my profession even for £7,000 a
year was serious and I kept thinking of Frances and her future and
how much better placed we would be in the matrimonial market in
London'. He ended this letter of 9 August to Louisa 'always assuming there will be no material alteration in the position of C-in-C'.[2]
But he was forced to agree when Lord Lansdowne wrote, acknowledging his acceptance: 'You must clearly understand that changes
in the position of Commander-in-Chief are inevitable'.

Louisa's spirits were quite restored by the ending of the suspense
and the prospect of house-hunting in London—a favourite pastime.
Both she and Frances were at Brocket in September:

. . . Charming party, very good house, unpretentious outside and full
of comfort inside, and even of architectural features. The M.S. were as
nice as nice could be. Sir D. Stewart and Earls Waldegrave and Selborne
were there—no women . . .[3]

---

[1] W/P 24.   [2] Ibid.   [3] LW/P 17.

ADVICE TO A NEPHEW

On 28 February 1896 both Lord and Lady Mount Stephen were
writing to their nephew George Cantlie, now the CPR's Stationery
Agent at Montreal, on receiving news of his engagement to Beatrice
Campbell: letters full of affection and good advice. Lady Mount
Stephen was 'sure she is all you say and you must think so all your
life', (as indeed he did) 'be "steadfast and true" and God will be
with you both. I am so glad your dear Mother is pleased . . .' There
followed an encouraging homily on the economics of housekeeping,
then: 'We were astonished at what you have been able to save the
CPR in stationery! It is marvellous!! I should hope and think that
Sir Wm. Van Horne would at all events give you an increase of
1,000 $ a year at once . . .' Mount Stephen also, after wishing them
every happiness, said he was 'much gratified to hear that you have
given satisfaction to your chiefs in your present position'. There
were echoes of his own mother as he continued:

The only sure way to obtain advancement & promotion to higher
places is by doing thoroughly well the work you have on hand whatever
it may be and waiting patiently for your chance, which is sure to come in
the end. Sir Donald Stewart after 18 years in the Indian Army was still
a Captain. The waiting happened, he got his chance and is now a Field
Marshal. There is a Spanish proverb to the effect that "the stone fit for
the building does not lie long in the road".

If you are to achieve a success as a railway man (& remember the
highest positions are open to ability & character) you will find it necessary
to concentrate your whole mind on your work to the exclusion of everything else. You will have no distractions of any kind & you will always
be most particular to do everything requisite to inspire the confidence
of everybody above & below you with whom you come in contact.
Your engagement may be a great help to you in all these matters . . .'

On 22 April he was able to write and congratulate George on his
promotion to Superintendent of Car Service. He enclosed a letter
for Beatrice: ' . . . Had my dear wife been spared she would have
written to you herself and told you how pleased we had been by
the numberless letters we had received from friends in Canada all
speaking of you in unrestricted terms of praise . . .'[1]

[1] Letters in the possession of the Hampson family.

IV

The shape of things to come

'WE have been quite anxious again about her Ladyship', wrote Gaspard Farrer to John Sterling on 4 April 1896, just after the conclusion of the second London agreement on the Ncrthern Pacific and the departure of James J. Hill, '—the old trouble—she is really better today but a recurrence of the evil is only too probable unless a rigid course of diet and Carlsbad is adopted'. The Mount Stephens were at their town house in St. James's Place, and there seemed, in fact, no prospect of moving Lady Mount Stephen even to a continental spa.

As Lady Mount Stephen's illness progressed, Garnet Wolseley, now at his post at the War Office which was then in Pall Mall, took to calling on his friend on his way to or from work. Louisa, having set up her menage at 4 Grosvenor Gardens, had joined her daughter at Lowestoft where Frances was recuperating after an illness vaguely attributed to the drains at the Royal Hospital, Dublin. Garnet wrote on 9 April:

I sat with Mount Stephen yesterday afternoon from five to six and tried to cheer him up. But I am sure he has given up all hope. Three doctors were there with her and she had had a bad night. Sir Donald Stewart and Lord Waldegrave were with him also, and strange to say at times the conversation became actually amusing and he laughed as if she was only dressing to go out and that he was waiting for her. I called there this morning in fear and trembling lest I should hear she had died. The butler said she was worse, although she had taken nourishment.

Of course at any moment this obstruction might come away and she might recover, but poor dear good woman, I think myself there is absolutely no hope.

I shall go there again this evening.[1]

Next morning when he wrote from the War Office it was to say:

[1] W/P 25.

Poor Lady M. died this morning about 8 a.m. One of our oldest and best friends gone. I called there, as I have done every day since I knew of her illness, on my way here. I am going back at 5 p.m. to see him and try to cheer him up. It will be a great break-up there and although I cannot quite make up my mind whether her loss will or will not be a serious matter to him, still it means a new life, a new departure to a man of 64 or 65 years of age. [in fact 66] He cannot begin anew and it will take him some time to carve out new grooves for his daily occupations. I fancy he will go as he intended to fish in Canada with John McNeill.

He told me yesterday that Alice was so highstrung in nerves that she would not even take enough rest. In fact he seemed to think that her overwrought excitement prevented her from being as useful as she might otherwise be. I can quite understand this with her, especially as she knew that when the poor Lady was quite well, the best and most cordial relations did not exist between them. He said that Lady M. had the evening before begged Alice to lie down and had turned to him as if in chaff and said 'You don't keep her in order or she would obey you better . . .'[1]

But Louisa had already had a telegram from Beverley MacInnes, Mount Stephen's secretary, and was writing to Garnet that day, 10 April: ' . . . I feel very sincerely grieved. She was *always* a kind friend, *always* the same . . .'[2] A few hours later she wrote again: 'Before getting your "gram" this evening I *had* written to Lord M.S. I wonder if he is very heart-broken? . . . It is nearly 29 years when she was so kind to me when you & I arrived in Canada, a bride and bridegroom . . .'[3] Many years later Frances added a note to this letter of her mother's: '[Lord Mount Stephen] was truly very heartbroken over the death of his first wife. She was one of the kindest of women'.[4] Always quick to criticize her mother, Frances resented the implication that her godfather, obviously not given to public demonstrations of affection, might be inadequate in this respect. Garnet had set Louisa's mind at rest on this point, for she wrote to him on 12 April: ' . . . Poor Lord M.S. I feel *glad* though that he regrets the dear kind Lady. Poor Alice, I have written to her today . . . I am glad you lunched with the lively Miss Agnes . . .'[5] Garnet had written on the 12th, saying that the funeral was next day:

---

[1] Ibid.   [2] LW/P 22.   [3] Ibid.
[4] Frances was permitted by the literary executor to see her mother's letters and annotated some, not always accurately. That her father's letters were not similarly annotated suggests that they were withheld from her; they contain many criticisms of her, as did her mother's, but Frances' attitude to her father was entirely sympathetic.
[5] LW/P 22. 'Miss Agnes' was Sister Agnes Keyser.

I told him yesterday that I thought he had better go away for some time, and said why not go out with McNeill as you had intended to fish in Canada. He replied, I couldn't. I was never on that river without her, and I should be reminded of her every moment. However I feel it would be much the best thing he could do, for I think he is a man who would require some engrossing pastime such as good salmon fishing, to make any place away from his ordinary surroundings bearable for more than a day. I don't know that he would find enjoyment as you or I should in the meanest little foreign town that possessed the "aroma" of antiquity about it . . .[1]

On the 14th they both wrote to each other, Louisa hoping that her husband was 'not cold and wet at the funeral' and Garnet saying '. . . I reserve an account of the funeral yesterday for when we meet. Poor dear Stephen, he looked ten years older . . .'

When Gaspard Farrer told Sir Donald Smith on 8 April 1896 that he was writing in place of Mount Stephen, owing to Lady Mount Stephen's illness, on a matter which concerned both the Great Northern and the Canadian Pacific, he must have reflected, as he conveyed his message, on the relief which 'Lady Boss' had felt when her husband finally broke his official connection with the latter enterprise: '. . . Lord Mount Stephen explained that he was no longer in the position to say what the views of the C.P.R. Board might be, or offer any advice, but would write to you personally stating in general terms Mr. Hill's wish and his own hope for some arrangement which may be mutually satisfactory . . .' Farrer had doubtless seen a good deal, during the anxious days of Canadian Pacific construction, of the work and worry suffered in the Stephen household. He tended to take up a specially protective attitude towards 'Lady Boss'; on 9 September 1891, for example, when Mount Stephen was doing a particularly exhaustive tour of both his rail systems, Gaspard wrote to him: '. . . Give my love to dear Lady Boss—I hope she will not overtire herself travelling. I am longing to have you both back again . . .' or on 9 June 1894, when the Mount Stephens had evidently had a difficult voyage across the Atlantic, and Mount Stephen was planning an American trip: '. . . I do hope that "Lady Boss" stays in Canada and that the return voyage will be less of a terror to her and anxiety to you . . .' Now all his concern was for Mount Stephen, and indeed all the latter's immediate circle were rallying round with proposals for his distrac-

[1] W/P 25.

tion. On 23 May Farrer wrote to John Sterling: '... He has just returned from a two days visit to Mr. Ellis which he has much enjoyed: he sees Morgan this evening and then returns to Brocket. Alice and Harry hope to get him on some of the House of Lords Committees after Whitsuntide. They have let their house in Seymour Place and are to live in future at 25. He is very well'. This all-too-precipitate move to share his town house in St. James's Place with the Northcotes was accompanied by the establishment of Alice as hostess at Brocket Hall. For the moment Mount Stephen submitted.

Writing to Hill on 4 July Farrer thought it possible that Mount Stephen would go out to Metis in the Spring, in which case he would accompany him and would hope to take a trip on the Great Northern: '... The Boss is wonderfully well and cheerful and is spending the middle of the week in town and Sundays at Brocket. He will probably go to Sir John McNeill at Colonsay for ten days in August and afterwards to Aix with Lady Northcote ...' On 13 August he confirmed to Hill that Mount Stephen was with McNeill on Colonsay, 'an island off the West coast of Scotland with no telegraph and steamers but twice a week—he will be glad to get back ...' To Sir Donald Stewart, the 'old Warrior', he wrote on 18 August: 'the Boss seems in good form but rather low at the thought of Aix. I shall be rather surprised if he does not dislike it quite so much in reality as he does in anticipation'. He told John Turnbull, Mount Stephen's man of business in Montreal, that the latter had quite enjoyed his 'Scotch trip' (18 August 1896) and on the 26th reported to Sterling that 'The Boss writes cheerfully from Aix and so far seems to like the place. He is undergoing a course though no one knows quite what there ...' Some success seemed to have been derived, as on 21 September Farrer told Charles Ellis: '... The Boss is back, particularly vigorous, says his rheumatism is gone and proved it by walking me down to the City this morning about five miles an hour'.

Mount Stephen's words to George Cantlie on 30 September 1896, three weeks before his nephew's wedding: '... I now write to wish you and her a long and happy life, each being everything to the other until the end ...' had a melancholy ring. A portrait of his first wife remained on the table in his study for the rest of his life, being then bequeathed to Alice. His advice as to work was as vigorous as ever: 'I recently read a criticism on a newly published life of Millet the famous French Painter from which I cut the enclosed quotation from Millet's own words, long before he became famous. They so exactly express my own views of life that I send them to you & beg you will not forget them'. The sanctifier of French peasant life (whose *Angelus* and *Gleaners* in reproduction used to point the moral in at least one old-type country school in the north-east of Scotland) had said:

My program is work. That is the natural condition of humanity. "In the sweat of thy brow thou shalt eat bread" was written centuries ago. The destiny of man is immutable, and can never change. What each one of us has to do is to seek progress in his profession, to try and improve daily in his trade, whatever that may be, and in this way to surpass his neighbour, both in the superiority of his talent and in the conscientiousness of his work. That is the only path for me. All else is a dream or a lottery.

Mount Stephen's advice as to personal financial management was: '. . . your wife will be a wiser counsellor in all such matters than anyone else . . .'[1]

FARRER AND GN FINANCE: DULUTH AND WINNIPEG

Throughout the summer of 1896, apart from reporting to his friends on Mount Stephen's health and spirits, Farrer's main preoccupation was with the election campaign in the United States and its effects on the stock market and on the future of the American enterprises in which they were all interested. The Republican candidate, William McKinley, stood for gold; the Democratic William Jennings Bryan led the free silver movement. In his letter to Hill of 13 August, Farrer remarked that Mount Stephen 'like you is confident that the silver craze will die and McKinley be elected. I hope you are right'. He was busy dealing with the aftermath of the Northern Pacific agreement, and wrote to John Sterling on 12 August acknowledging a cable about scrip calls:

. . . probably the Boss has told you that he has kept none for himself but has distributed a fair amount among his own friends for whom he is buying the later call or rather at the moment has left us to pay, he being away in Scotland. I was therefore anxious to know on our own account as well as on his what further payments were possible or likely . . .

[1] This letter is in the possession of the Hampson family.

The Boss is expected back at the end of the week. Our market here is very nervous about U.S. securities and the repeated assurances of New York bankers that McKinley will get in and all be well would have more effect if unaccompanied by determined efforts to sell. The last few days there have been loans negotiated by people and on security that reminds one of August–September 1893. This severe slump and panic has certainly taken firms here by surprise, firms even such as Rothschilds, Morgans, Speyers etc. and from what indications we have I gather the same is true on your side. Hill for instance would hardly have been talking about his scheme had such a collapse been in his mind.

I am afraid you will think I am rather a sorehead—and so I am. We had learnt to expect *one* American panic per annum but this six months business is trying till one gets accustomed to it.

'Even millionaires are running round hat in hand', wrote Farrer to Hill on 13 August, while assuring him 'Your Sterling 4s have stood up as well as any bond in the list' . . . As to Hill's 'scheme' which concerned the Great Northern's securities: Farrer had written to him on 23 July on the subject, Mount Stephen having shown him a letter of Hill's dated 3 July, and asked him to write briefly 'the points that occur to us on what appears an excellent scheme'. First, as to maintaining the stock a preference stock:

We assume you have good reasons for this and there is much to be said for disturbing holders as little as possible; at the same time there is a certain awkwardness in having a Preference stock that is preferred to nothing, and a 6% Preference on which but 5% dividends are paid; moreover the rights under the scheme offer some inducement to present holders to relinquish their nominal preferences for an ordinary share, and it is easier to get $25 million of shares to consent to a change than it will be to get the consent of twice that amount of shares at some future date as your letter seems to contemplate.

Secondly, as to a proposed special dividend of 10 per cent:

Is this necessary? it would certainly seem a pity to pay it if involving a sale of Treasury Bonds.—Judging by investors here 5% per annum is sufficient; the regularity of dividend to which holders have become accustomed being a more important factor than the rate of return. Personally I am always dead against parting with more good cash than is necessary.

The third and last point concerned providing part of the money for repaying collaterals from the company's cash reserves:

This is a matter which you alone can decide when the time comes according to the needs of the Company which you can then foresee; the only points before us here are as to outgoings the requirements in connection with the possible purchase of the Duluth and Winnipeg Railroad, as to incomings the inadvisability of viewing the Sterling or other Treasury Bonds as necessarily liquid assetts immediately available if the present financial and political conditions in the United States continue or become less favourable. . .

The possible purchase of the Duluth and Winnipeg had been the subject of Farrer's letter of 8 April 1896 to Sir Donald Smith (quoted on page 116); both Great Northern and Canadian Pacific were interested in this bankrupt line, which was eventually incorporated by the Great Northern with its Eastern Railroad of Minnesota in its Northern Section. Its importance lay in its access to the developing Mesabi iron range on Lake Superior. The Duluth and Winnipeg affair provided one of those occasions on which Mount Stephen obviously preferred to stand on the sidelines, hoping somewhat naively for a harmonious solution. Van Horne, as President of Canadian Pacific, exhibited a much more restrained persona than he had done as general manager in charge of construction; this did not prevent him, however, from perceiving that Hill was at times behaving with a deviousness that Mount Stephen was slower to acknowledge. But sometimes the humour of the situation was to Van Horne almost worth the exasperation he experienced. In the case of the Duluth and Winnipeg Mount Stephen had at an early stage suggested Sir Donald Smith as mediator.[1] Farrer hoped that Hill would be able to proceed with his scheme that Fall, in a more assured business climate, enabling his shareholders to 'welcome the scheme as the bonus that in fact it is.' 'What delusions there are on this gold and silver question!' he wrote in conclusion. 'The issue appears to me the simple one of paying or failing to pay debts, and the adoption of silver would merely add to the difficulties (pace friend Tuck) which the general fall in prices has brought about . . .' Edward Tuck had a theory that the United States had a vast reserve of gold: Gaspard was curious to know where it was, what the amount, and how Tuck arrived at it.[2]

[1] See Van Horne—Stephen Letter Book 1894–8 (PAC).
[2] Gaspard Farrer Letter Books, Farrer to Edward Tuck, 14 October 1896, referring to a letter from Tuck to Mount Stephen.

EASTERN OF MINNESOTA: LOUIS W. HILL

Farrer's letter to Hill of 23 October 1896 shows that the new scheme for Great Northern securities was then still hanging fire. He acknowledged Hill's 'interesting letter of 1st.' on the political situation:

indeed your opinion on this matter is the only one in America that I would value; we have had plenty as you may imagine "of the soothing sirop kind" but orders to sell have accompanied even the profoundest convictions.

Lord Mount Stephen has shown me your letter to him: no doubt we shall hear from you again as to what you have decided as to the details of your financial plan—it would be a great convenience to share and bondholders here if they could make whatever changes become necessary through Barings instead of individually having to send their securities to America—perhaps you will bear this in mind when the time comes . . .

A few firms have been buying back shares these last weeks but no evidence yet that the British investing public are in the market . . .

He remarked on the rare circumstance that a rise in the price of wheat had actually taken place while the crop was still in the hands of farmers, who would thus reap the full benefit, and thanked Hill for his latest operating sheets which he was looking forward to dissecting. On a cursory glance what struck him most was that on the Eastern Minnesota Division the average cost per ton mile was down to the average for the whole road, and the train load considerably above the average.

Writing to E. T. Nichols of the Great Northern's New York office on 6 February 1897, Farrer said he had heard that Hill might be coming to England in March, and very much hoped he would: 'The rest during the voyage does him good and we are anxious to hear about his new deal, as to which we are very much in the dark at present'. Again political developments were bedevilling progress on the stock market: this time the aftermath of the Venezuelan affair. Just as a 'nice business' was commencing in Sterling 4s and other good American securities, 'the news of the Senate's action on the arbitration treaty reached us. It is very unfortunate, and would seem as if your political parties were bent on destroying confidence in your Government'. The previous day he had written to Charles R. Hosmer, who did the Commercial Cable Company's business in Montreal, 'Certainly the American people have been putting their

English friends' faith in them to a severe test these past few years'. (Farrer's Lefevre firm had handled the first English business of the Commercial Cable Company in which at this time Mount Stephen had an active interest. The majority interest was held by John W. Mackay of New York, a C.P.R. director. The Company, then going from strength to strength, owned three Atlantic cables as well as land lines.)

Hill did make the trip, Farrer writing on 23 April to Oliver Northcote at Luton: 'Hill seemed to us in very good spirits about his own affairs; but as to general business in the United States there seems to be little enough confidence in America itself and none here. Personally I feel hopeful, but nobody encourages me . . .' When in London Hill had obviously discussed with Mount Stephen and Farrer the prospect of making an issue of Eastern Minnesota Debenture Stock. Farrer was more than once called upon to interpret British stock market terms to his American friends—such as 'put' and 'call' or 'contango'—and soon after Hill's departure he was writing him an essay on 'Debenture Stock'. The Great Northern's counsel, Grover, was clearly puzzled by some document that had emanated from the London discussions. Farrer explained to Hill on 11 June 1897:

The U.K. public like the term 'Debenture Stock'. It is like the Queen's stamp on the sovereign, which does not add an iota of intrinsic value to the gold, but at once enables it to pass current among everybody as a £ Sterling; and no other name but Debenture Stock would do as well . . .

He enclosed a memorandum fully explaining the usage and its history, and then discussed its particular application to the proposed Eastern Minnesota issue. He went on:

As you are aware Lord Mount Stephen considers that securities in this market had better be wholly confined to this market; and this is the course we should ourselves prefer; but if you desire New York to participate and wanted say $5 million a simultaneous issue might be made by your friends in New York of say $2.5 million in Dollar Bonds suited for that market and £500,000 Sterling Debenture Stock by Barings here . . .

I am very keen that the Debenture Stock scheme should be worked out; with Eastern Minnesota it is on a small scale, but it would be a good test of what might be done hereafter for the Company's credit on a wider basis for which I have plans floating in my mind. I believe you have no idea what could be done for your credit in this way . . .

The issue would be guaranteed by the Great Northern and St. Paul, Minneapolis and Manitoba Railroad Companies. Farrer wrote a second letter to Hill on that day suggesting that Nichols should 'quietly not to raise rumours' take steps to get a quotation in London for Great Northern shares, and in answer to Hill's letter of 2 July wrote on the 17th regarding this that it was not a case of dealing in shares in the present state of the market, only to *get* an official quotation to keep existing holders 'quiet and happy'. If later U.S. railroad earnings generally improved and the American political situation was more satisfactory 'a wider distribution might be possible and we should be in a position to take advantage of the possibilities'. His judgment was that the application should be made before the contemplated big distribution by the Great Northern on the grounds that it would evoke less criticism than if it came after, when 'people would be sure to think the orange had been sucked dry and as J. S. K[ennedy] would express it we were "letting the Street have them"'. English people so far were buying very selectively from only the oldest-established American railroad securities; the one new company to make a successful issue that year had been Commercial Cable for whom Barings had acted. He congratulated Hill on his latest net earnings, particularly gratifying as gross takings had not yet increased: 'prospects do seem very bright, indeed if this rise in wheat holds and present harvest prospects are realized I doubt if even your politicians can upset the apple cart'. Farrer did not see his way at that time to accept Hill's invitation to make a trip out, but promised to cable if he could come later. Writing again on 21 July about the Debenture Stock he hoped that Hill would manage to get down to Metis for a rest. Farrer in fact went out to Metis that summer, but without Mount Stephen who never went there again, and saw something of Hill.

October and November 1897 saw urgent messages flashing back and forth across the Atlantic in connection with the Eastern Minnesota issue and with the Great Northern's quotation on the London Stock Exchange. On 11 October Farrer cabled to Hill that the sooner the new issue was out the better; he had been putting out feelers among a few friends on the basis of the terms discussed and expected to see 'Estevan' (Mount Stephen) the following day. On 13 October he cabled again: 'Good progress here. When will you be ready? Should like issue this month ...' He wanted to know—and he repeated this in a letter of the same date to John Sterling in New York—whether Hill could include the new equipment which he contemplated purchasing under the Mortgage, as owing to the amount per mile being high it was desirable to assure the English public that the entire proceeds of the loan would be devoted to the specific property in question and all that property subject to the lien. Barings wanted to have one of the well-known New York Trust Companies as Trustee.

Farrer then wrote on 14 October to Louis W. Hill, the twenty-five-year-old son of J. J. Hill, who was slowly—much too slowly, Gaspard thought—being allowed to work his way up on the railroad. Louis had been present at discussions in St. Paul on Gaspard's recent visit, and was now asked to tell his father that the application for a London quotation for Great Northern had gone forward; this was for future use—at present the price was too high for the English public. Farrer wrote again to Louis on 16 October, copying the letter to Sterling, regarding the Eastern Minnesota Debenture Stock Mortgage, and more urgently on the 27th; he was anxious to have the necessary documents to make the issue; had he had them on his return from the United States he could have gone to the public at once and probably had the money by now. He continued:

At the moment all markets are unhinged by the change in the value of money; owing to German demand for gold and the low rate of U.S. exchange the Bank of England has been gathering in supplies and altogether through sales and borrowings has taken about £4 million off the market; this action has tightened up rates for the time, but it is artificial, and as soon as gold export demand is less acute the above money will probably be released and conditions again become normal.

Following the bland statement that 'Lord Mount Stephen is a good deal engaged with his own affairs just now'—this will be enlarged upon presently—Farrer reported that he had had some talk with him about 'the future capital changes which your father has in mind and the principles of which Lord Mount Stephen entirely approves'. This referred to the proposal, carried out the following year, to increase the Great Northern share capital from $25 million to $50 million. Hill had sent him cables regarding an offer of the Deutsche Bank to act for them:

we presume your father means to limit their services to German markets though his cable said "London"; a London registry would be of no use;

the public here are accustomed to certificates on the New York register and will not use others; the London register of the Canadian Pacific has been an entire failure and the number of shares forced on to it in the first instance have since tended constantly to diminish; moreover excellent ally as the Bank would be in Germany it has no influence or following in this country; and lastly if any work here has to be done for the Company its old London friends in Bishopsgate Street would be very much upset and disgruntled if the business were taken out of their hands without cause.

The application for the quotation of G.N. Shares is now before the Committee; some objection has been raised owing to the scarcity of dealings, but we have no doubt these difficulties will be overcome and a quotation granted in a few days . . .

Farrer was keeping an anxious eye on the American political scene: Tuesday 2 November was the presidential election day, and on the 4th he expressed his fears as to the result to Louis Hill. Had he been superstitious he might have regarded as a good omen the granting on the 2nd of a London quotation for Great Northern shares. He reported an enquiry for the shares on the 4th; as it was desirable that stock should be forthcoming to meet any such demand, Barings and Lefevres had agreed to furnish a few shares from their own holdings. The Deutsche Bank had written to Lord Mount Stephen, but, Gaspard repeated, they did not understand the habits of investors in England. He had cabled to Louis that day asking if any spare shares were available, in case of enquiry.

On 4 November Gaspard also wrote to Sterling, telling him that Hill had cabled that his Eastern Minnesota arrangements were all ready, but awaited the collection of the last lots of Duluth and Winnipeg Bonds. This railroad had just been acquired by the Eastern of Minnesota, and the inherent complications, legal and otherwise, were holding up the Eastern issue. Writing to J. J. Hill on other matters on 26 November he referred to recent Press comment on the Great Northern's annual report, adding 'Lord Mount Stephen is delighted with the idea of your squatting on $2,500,000 U.S. Government and £500,000 Consols, and says "Tell Mr. Hill it is none too much; none too much for a big concern like his".' He ended the letter with a plea for Louis:

I have been writing several times to Louis and intend keeping this practice up if he at all responds. I am anxious that he should be interested and follow all G.N. matters on this side and the more he grasps the finance questions the better pleased we shall be: and now that I have mentioned him with you let me say that which I have sat down to write to you half a dozen times and as often got up with nothing done feeling that you would only call me a d—d meddling fool for my pains,—but I am really concerned as to Louis' position and work in the office, or rather the want of them, because I know how utterly weary and demoralized I should myself become under similar circumstances: I mean going down daily to the office without definite task and purpose. You will remember what a high opinion Lord Mount Stephen formed of Louis, of his thoughtfulness and sobriety, of his judgment, and Lord Mount Stephen does not often make a mistake in these matters. I cannot but think that it would be a great help to Louis if he had some definite work and responsibility and I am sure he would do it well: but he is such a modest good fellow that he will never push himself forward and will need all the push and encouragement which you can give him to bring out his merits. And now will you forgive me for meddling in a matter that is no concern of mine— You have been so very kind to me that I have ventured to tell you a point that struck me as an outsider and which I do not feel sure that you realized in the same way . . .

Farrer's letter to Hill of 1 December indicated that they were still awaiting the last of the Duluth and Winnipeg Bonds. On 4 December he recapitulated to John Sterling the latest developments:

On 27th J. J. Hill cabled "Sterling advises today better progress in outstanding Bonds", and again 1st "Am advised can sell New York Eastern 4s Bond at 93½ net to Company; at even price assured prefer Debenture plan; cable me your views and wishes", to which we replied "We have been ready waiting two months past, do we understand that you are now prepared to offer us the business on terms my letter to you September 25 but so as to net Company 93½ and that you are in position to authorize issue here immediately?"

The same day, Gaspard recalled, he had cabled Sterling enquiring as to the likelihood of Hill's advice as quoted above and asking about the position regarding Duluth and Winnipeg Bonds; Sterling had replied:

"Hardly likely. Three large holdings Duluth and Winnipeg Bonds outstanding" for which we thank you. We still await reply from J. J. Hill.
As you know, I have always feared that at the time Mr. Schiff advanced the money for the Duluth and Winnipeg purchase some understanding was made as offering Messrs. Kuhn, Loeb and Company the first chance to buy the subsequent issue of Eastern Minnesota 4s; it would have been a natural stipulation on Mr. Schiff's part and one that I should have

made in his position, still it is hardly conceivable considering the way Mr. Hill has been negotiating with me.

Please excuse this long story; I thought you might be able and willing to help me, and it was therefore better to put you in possession of all the facts so far as we know them.

The return of William McKinley as President of the United States with a comfortable majority disposed of one of Farrer's worries; the problem of the Eastern Minnesota 4s dragged on. On 4 December 1897 he wrote to Louis Hill:

Referring you to copies of cables which have passed between your father and ourselves I am sure you will understand our reluctance, in the mere hope of capturing business, to give your father a light hearted assurance which future circumstances now unforeseen might prevent our fulfilling, and so disappoint and perhaps inconvenience the Company. You will remember that during my stay in St. Paul your father authorized me to arrange with Messrs. Baring for the issue subject to the conditions which I then wrote and which he approved. Since my return we have been awaiting the completion of the work on your side necessary prior to such issue, and have been refusing other business offers to keep ourselves free for Great Northern. But we are still without the Mortgage Deed and other promised documents essential before we can give an opinion. As soon as we receive them and your father tells us he is in a position to deal we will promptly let him know whether we can do the business for him or not . . .

Two days later he cabled Hill himself: 'Have seen Barings re Easterns. Subject to approval Mortgage satisfied could do as well for you here were we in a position to issue now—Lefevre'. It should be noted that 'Lefevre' was Farrer's telegraphic code name; his firm of Lefevres does not up to this time appear to have been involved in this particular issue although they were holders of Great Northern. Repeating this cable to Sterling on 11 December, Farrer was able to add Hill's answer: 'Sterling making every effort possible. Expect hear matter closed every day. Will advise you at once'. Gaspard added: 'This seems to show that my suspicions were unfounded. I hope they are'. On the same day he acknowledged Hill's cable, saying: '. . . Your Sterling Bonds are quite firm now round 96, and if we can conclude the Eastern of Minnesota business with you shall put the Sterling 4s to par, which I think we could do with very little buying, probably £50–£100,000.' Hill had also sent the September operating figures for Great Northern: 'most satisfactory'. Farrer wanted to know to what extent, if any, improvements on the Eastern of Minnesota and Montana Central which he had seen in progress during his recent trip were included in the ton-mile costs.

At last, on 17 December 1897 Farrer was able to write to Nichols acknowledging a copy of the Eastern Minnesota Mortgage, which their lawyers were now examining. On the 22nd he sent some lengthy comments to M. D. Grover, the G. N. Counsel at St. Paul, as well as sending a copy to Shearman and Sterling in New York, and to Hill. To the last he wrote: 'We think an issue should be made here the second or third week in January'. He had already cabled him for a prospectus letter. Then came one of those jolts—not unexpected, for Gaspard had already had his suspicions but had dismissed them, but nevertheless requiring all his diplomacy to counter—which caused Hill's London friends to have their reservations on occasion about his methods. On 16 February 1898 Farrer wrote to Sterling, enclosing for his private perusal the recent cables that had passed between himself and Hill; he did this in recognition of Sterling's help in connection with the Eastern Minnesota business. They were as follows:

Received from Hill 27 January: 'Sterling wires hopes close finally Tuesday. Leaving for St. Paul tonight'.
Sent to Hill 1 February: 'If currency 30 years assured think premium unnecessary: suggest altering Deed giving Company option redeem at par plus interest after 30 years'.
Received from Hill 4 February: 'Am offered 95 plus interest new Eastern Bonds. What do you think Debenture Stock would realise net London? I feel bound to you for what you have done this and other matters. If thought best sell Bonds here will secure for you half participation less commission. Give me your views fully'.
Sent to Hill 4 February: 'Thanks for friendly message. John Baring away till tonight: will reply fully tomorrow. Do you wish Eastern issue precede or follow Great Northern Stock Operation and are you in position to enable Eastern issue to be made at once'.
Received from Hill 5 February: 'Think Eastern can be made at once; action cannot be taken in Great Northern before March 1st culminating June, July. Prefer Debenture plan but cannot consistently overlook firm offer made here. Bonds would be placed with big Companies closing transaction quickly, you having half participation. Just received other offer for whole of any issue Eastern may have: will keep matter waiting your reply'.

Self . Gian : Alge

PRINCESS MAY OF TECK, MISS GIAN TUFNELL,
PRINCE ALEXANDER GEORGE OF TECK, CANNES 1892
(*from a photograph in Queen Mary's album, by gracious permission
of Her Majesty Queen Elizabeth II*)

Sent to Hill 5 February: 'Private: Barings and selves bid you subject our approval Mortgage 95 per cent par value plus interest with division profits after 2½ net to us for £1,030,000 Sterling Debenture Stock, to be domiciled with Barings. If you accept mail us prospectus letter, certified copy Eastern Board minutes authorising Mortgage and issue Debenture Stock, and certified copy Great Northern and Manitoba minutes authorising guarantees. Will materially help if interest dates made March and September 1. Reply'.

Received from Hill 6 February: 'Have offered nothing here. Kennedy Senior offers 98 and interest net; may do better. Whatever is done you will be compensated'.

Sent to Hill 7 February: 'If you consider New York bid for issue in New York best for Company's interests we will not pursue matter further'.

Received from Hill 8 February: 'Will do nothing until reach New York Wednesday. Will cable you then'.

Farrer told Sterling that the message of 8 February was the last, although he had heard since from Hill from St. Paul. He does not say what he had heard, presumably because Sterling would already know, or because Hill was cabling on an entirely different matter. He had in fact before 15 February received a cable from Hill for transmission to H. W. Forster, M.P. of London E.C. with whom they had been negotiating in connection with the transfer of Forster's Kaslo and Slocan Railway Company securities to the Kootenay Railway and Navigation Company. This minor rail system, in a mining area of the Selkirk Range in British Columbia just north of the American border, promised to provide Hill with a connection in the north west area of Washington Territory. This was not something in which Mount Stephen was directly involved.[1]

On 23 February 1898 Farrer told Sterling that Hill had cabled Mount Stephen that he had sold his Eastern Minnesota Bonds in New York at par plus interest: 'presumably this means the Net price the Company has received. I shall be very much interested and obliged if you can confirm. The price is a good one, certainly higher than we could have afforded to pay here, and I would venture to think that the purchaser has since wished that he had never been born ...' He still did not know for certain who had bought the issue, and on 2 March wrote to ask Oliver Northcote whether he had heard any details of the sale: 'I rather gathered that your

---

[1] Farrer to H. W. Forster, M. P., 15 February 1898.

former firm [J. Kennedy Tod] and Mr. Kennedy had bought them . . .'

At least Gaspard had the satisfaction of writing on 23 April to Louis Hill:

A line to tell you how pleased Lord Mount Stephen and myself are to learn from your father of your appointment of assistant to the President: we do not understand what your special duties will be but we are both entirely confident that whatever they are they will be in safe hands.

My own belief is that there is nothing in which you can so much assist your father as in harmonizing relations of G.N. and N.P.: their real interests, viewed from the broadest point, are identical, and it is only personal elements that now create friction. I remember Lord Mount Stephen once having to gain confidence under difficult circumstances; he never missed a day without finding some excuse for dropping round for a friendly chat and frank communication: and he very quickly succeeded: and I am sure you would equally soon succeed in gaining the confidence of Mellen and Northern Pacific officials, and most of these troubles which are now worrying your father would disappear.

However you will be the best judge of what is wise and practicable: but one thing is certain that it is possible for you to do much informally which from your father's position is difficult or impossible for him.

Will you please remember me to your mother and tell her we will do our best to take care of Mr. Hill while he is here.

'If I could do L.W. over, I wouldn't change a thing', James J. Hill was to say of Louis many years later. His feelings for his other son, James Norman Hill, whom Gaspard Farrer similarly tried to instruct in the art of personal relations, were rather different.

SOIL FOR DISCONTENT

Charles F. Mellen was President of the reorganized Northern Pacific, Edward D. Adams Chairman. When Farrer wrote, on 16 August 1897, to H. R. Cooke, a broker of Manchester, that one of the reasons for the high credit in New York of Great Northern shares (then standing at 130, and Manitobas at 120) was its harmonious relations with the Northern Pacific, he was slightly stretching a point, describing the potential rather than the actual. He told Cooke:

. . . It is hard to exaggerate the importance of this: Mr. Hill . . . has always told me that with co-operative management he could save $3 million in working expenses between the two roads. We have known Mr.

Hill for twenty years and he does not enthuse; indeed he has always done better than his promise. The saving to the N.P. will be greater than to the G.N. N.P. fixed charges are now down to $6.2 million; [previously quoted as $9,790,270—i.e. when no dividend was paid] 4% on the Preferred Stock would require a further $2.8 million, or say $9 million in all. Net earnings (N.P.) have reached (in booming times) to over $13 million, and this in days of fierce competition with the G.N.—so you see there is considerable possibility for the future for the N.P., and a dividend on their Preferred not so far off as recent earnings might lead a casual observer to think. We regard N.P. Prior Lien 4s as good beyond question, and the 3% General Lien as a fair speculative Bond for those who want 5% interest . . .

A few days earlier he had been recommending Northern Pacific 4 per cent Prior Lien Gold Dollar Mortgage Bonds to his brother Frank as 'a good investment now, and if J. J. Hill's life holds for a few years, likely, along with all the Company's securities, to go much higher'. On 25 August he wrote in the same terms to another broker: 'prior lien 4s safe under any circumstances but N.P. 3s, though a fair risk at 5 per cent, not a bond you should lock up for your old ladies and forget'. It gradually became more evident, however, that Hill did not have as much influence in the councils of the Northern Pacific as he had expected, and that the latter became increasingly suspicious of the Great Northern. Meanwhile in 1897 the other great victim of the years of depression, the Union Pacific, after an abortive attempt at reorganization in 1895–6, was in process of being incorporated as a new company. In November it was bought at foreclosure by a syndicate brought together by Jacob Schiff of Kuhn, Loeb and Company, and a new giant appeared on the western railroad scene: Edward H. Harriman.

THE GN'S LONDON IMAGE: NEW ISSUE

It may well have been these events that prompted Gaspard Farrer, on 24 November 1897, to forward the Great Northern's annual report to the Editor of *The Economist* 'in case you care to take notice of it in your paper. Its issues, and more especially those of its leased line, the St. Paul, Minneapolis and Manitoba Railroad, are held to a considerable extent in this country, but being purely investment securities they do not attract the notice given to the speculative rubbish'. He drew the Editor's attention particularly to the continuity of dividends, the St. P. M. & M. having paid 6 per cent without a break since 1882, and the G.N., starting at its organization in 1890 with 4 per cent, having subsequently increased this to 5 per cent and lately to 6 per cent. He went on: 'I believe I am right in saying that the Great Northern, Lake Shore and Michigan Southern, Boston and Albany, Delaware Lackawanna and Western are the only United States Railways of importance that have been strong enough to maintain their dividends without diminution during the past six years of depression; the Great Northern is certainly the only one West of Chicago'. Picking out a second point to emphasize he concluded:

> You will notice that the secret of the Railway's success is its heavy train load, and I enclose you some comparative figures of the Northern Pacific, its neighbour and rival, to show what an important effect in Net Earnings close operation in this matter makes. It costs no more to haul loaded than empty cars, and no more to haul long trains than short ones. There is no commoner waste in the operation of Railways than the running of needless train mileage.

He offered to supply more information if required, and added a postscript: 'I may say I have known Mr. Hill for twenty years and have paid constant visits to the property during this time'. For the analysis of N.P. figures he had been indebted to a kindred spirit at the St. Paul headquarters, R. I. Farrington; this had been sent on by Hill. Just over four years later, writing to congratulate Farrington on becoming Second Vice-President of the Great Northern, Farrer declared: '. . . the knowledge that the Company's finances have the advantage of supervision by your cold grey eye is a matter of comfort to me'.

On 27 November 1897 copies of the article which duly appeared in that week's *Economist* were sent both to Farrington and to Hill. To the latter Gaspard said: 'I did not write it, or should have put some of the points a little differently . . .' On 1 December Farrer told Hill that Mount Stephen thought the article ought to be circulated to British shareholders in Great Northern and the 'Manitoba'. Hill had in mind a rights issue for the following spring, offering the existing stockholders $25 million in new shares, share for share at 60, repaying with the proceeds their $15 million worth of Collateral Trust 4s; later he hoped to replace the 'Manitoba' securities with Great Northern. Once again politics intervened. For some time Americans had been giving more than moral support to Cuba in its efforts to achieve independence from Spain. The final spark to the powder-keg came on 15 February 1898 with the sinking of the American battleship *Maine* in Havana harbour. America wanted war with Spain and President McKinley, against his will, went along with the tide. It was a short war, lasting from April until August, with victorious America acquiring the Philippines in the course of it, but repercussions on the stock market were inevitable and were duly chronicled by Gaspard Farrer.

He had written to Oliver Northcote on 2 March 1898: '. . . I do not share your views about Spain and think war is the last thing that she wishes for; indeed with 100,000 to 200,000 men locked up in Cuba, she is in a very weak position' . . . Northcote had no doubt been thinking of the United States Army, some 30,000 strong; in the event most of the fighting took place between two inadequate navies. Farrer went on to say that Hill had cabled him some weeks since that he hoped to announce his plan for the calling in of Collateral 4s on March 1st, culminating in July; he had now heard from other sources that this had been postponed to September. He thought that under any circumstances 'we may count on the melon being cut during the present year. If he is wise he will postpone the offer of converting Manitoba shares into Great Northern for another year. With the addition of 25,000,000 G. N. Stock through the melon operation, there will be quite enough of that security to digest for the present'. Writing to C. R. Hosmer of the Commercial Cable Company on 12 March (he was feeling somewhat disgruntled because someone unknown had just sold half a million dollars' worth of the Company's bonds in London, taking advantage of his own careful publicity for these) Farrer reminded him that in the event of war people would be sure to fear the cutting of cables, regardless of the fact that even if cut, a temporary interruption of business would be the limit of the Company's loss—not the destruction of property. Four days later he wrote to John W. Mackay in New York: '. . . War scares and dearer money have brought about a fall in the price in most of our high class investment securities and have checked the buying of Commercial Cable Debenture Stock: but this is temporary . . .' By 5 May he was able to assure H. R. Cooke of Manchester that although the Cable Company prices had fallen a little in common with other securities, the war had brought the largest business the Company had ever had, on both landlines and cables. He had already told Cooke on 19 March that Great Northern was doing better than ever, 'indeed is piling in money'; now he could report on Hill's promised visit. During the ten days Hill had been in London they had been able to go 'through and through all G.N. matters' and his forecast to Cooke of August 1897 had been fully justified. The railroad's business was increasing apace, with net earnings mounting up even faster, in proportion, than gross; improvements planned for 1898–9 would be met out of revenue (not, as in England, charged to capital account) and in a year's time it was hoped that G.N. operating costs would be lower than on any other road either in the U.S. or in the world. As soon as the war was over they would proceed with the new issue; probably that was all that could be attempted that year but when a favourable opportunity arose it was hoped to replace the Company's obligations in the way of 'Manitoba' shares and bonds with Great Northern shares. If Cooke had followed G.N. affairs of recent years he would know that the net earnings were 'real available sums and not book entries . . .'

On the same day Farrer repeated all this to his father, with more emphasis on the 'Manitoba' securities of which Sir William Farrer was a holder, adding:

A study of the origin of these earnings shows that the country tributary to the new lines in the extreme west is coming rapidly to the front as a tonnage producer; in fact the western divisions have already passed, in relative proportion of earning capacity, some of the older divisions along the Red River Valley, and give promise of becoming the most profitable of all; this is satisfactory as justifying the heavy capital expenditure of 1891–4, and is of real importance as diversifying the sources from which income is derived, and making the Road less and less dependent on a single harvest and the price of wheat . . .

He went on to say that the Great Northern was yearly rising in the estimation of both the financial and the railroad world:

For instance during my stay in St. Paul last autumn I found Pennsylvania Railroad officials examining into Great Northern books and operating methods and I have since heard from them that they were much pleased with what they learnt. Now Mr. Hill tells me that Hughitt of the North Western has asked permission to make a similar study; these are small matters perhaps but all tend to show recognition and appreciation where formerly incredulity or denial existed . . .

It is doubtful whether Sir William would have appreciated the mention, at the time, of Marvin Hughitt of the Chicago and North Western—a railway with a strategic position in the west—who was associated with Jacob Schiff in the reorganization of the Union Pacific.[1] Gaspard wrote again to his father on 10 May, explaining that the earlier letter had been written with a view to his 'Manitoba' holdings, that is to the G.N.'s obligatory charges (as the G.N. guaranteed the 'Manitoba's') but supplemented it now with a sketch showing the effect of these capital changes on his interest in G.N. shares:

The issue of new shares at 60 will raise the amount outstanding to $50 million and the conversion of St. P. M. & M. shares a further $25 million or to $75 million in all; obligatory charges will thereby be reduced to $4.5 million per annum while 6% dividends will require a further similar sum.

Mr. Hill contemplates then increasing his dividend to 7%, the maximum which he considers the States legislatures will permit . . .

This Gaspard thought should be quite possible. As to a reasonable value for the shares,

Mount Stephen with his usual buoyancy thinks 150–160, knowing that all large holders such as Hill, himself, Donald Smith, Kennedy, [D. Willis] James, Tuck, [Charles J.] Paine &c. will subscribe for and hold their new shares. I am not so sanguine; when wheat falls as it will, and Klondyke booms are over, people will not feel so good as they do today; but there is no doubt the power of the U.S. to absorb its own investments is far greater than people here imagine, and America is becoming yearly less and less dependent on European support. I think we may feel very well content if the $75 million with 7% dividends attains to a 5% basis, say 140; and this does not seem to me impossible under conditions of moderate prosperity and when once the shares have reached a final resting place.

Hill's visit to London in April 1898 was apparently quite unmarred by any hard feelings about the Eastern Minnesota issue; after all, he had made the best bargain and they were his shareholders. Gaspard had written to him on 25 March 'I am glad you are coming', and had sent him some 'light literature for your perusal aboardship'—to wit, a comparison of Great Northern and Canadian Pacific operating figures: 'perhaps you will tell me when

[1] Adler on *Schiff*, vol. 1, p. 50.

you arrive how far the conclusions are accurate and complete. Unfortunately I have no material either from G.N. or C.P.R. for a comparison of the items of cost'. On Hill's departure Gaspard wrote to Louis on 30 April: '. . . It is blowing a gale from the South West this morning.—I'm afraid your father will have a rough start. We have enjoyed having him here'.

By 26 May 1898 Farrer was complaining to Louis Hill that the New York cables to the London papers were making daily, and usually inaccurate, mention of the Great Northern's financial plans. He hoped that the scheme might be brought out and settled up 'as soon as possible before your State Legislatures or legal officers have time to ask for injunctions or create difficulties of any kind'. On 21 June he told Louis that they had received circulars regarding the new stock; so far he had heard of no rights offering in the London market. The same day he spelt it all out for his father: he might disregard the circular so far as it referred to Seattle and Montana shares : Papa would remember that some weeks ago a circular was issued informing them that Seattle and Montana shares had been handed over to Trustees for the benefit of Great Northern share-holders . . . [part of the proceeds of the new issue was devoted to the Seattle and Montana purchase][1] 'you will now be asked to resign your rights under this Trust such resignation to be taken as consideration for 40% of the amount you would have had to sub-scribe for the new G.N. shares at par. All this is a mere dodge to get round the law which forbids G.N. shares being issued for less than their par value . . .' Acknowledging James J. Hill's letter of 21 June Farrer wrote on 6 July: '. . . In these days when everything is booming in the North West and Cuban victories are begetting enthusiasm I am comforted to think that you are sitting at the tiller and on the till . . .' He wrote to Louis that day also, again acknowledging a letter of the 21 June, with enclosed statistics. The increase in wheat acreage, he said, was very remarkable, and would 'give you a pretty lively work next October and will make your brother [James N.] and his officials on the Eastern [Minnesota] sit up. What a clearance the high prices have made of stocks on hand . . . it is wonderful under the circumstances that your traffics are keeping up as well as they do . . .'

Farrer then pressed Louis for information on other recent developments: how was the Fosston line progressing (a branch from

[1] Pyle on *Hill*, vol. 1, p. 477.

the ore lands into Duluth) and when would it be open for business? The *Commercial Chronicle* had reported that the Spokane Falls and Northern Railway (in the north-east of Washington Territory, running north to the boundary in the Kootenay district) had been bought by the Northern Pacific; (Louis had cabled Lefevres on 17 June: 'Have purchased Spokane Falls Northern ...' in connection with the Kootenay deal); was this a joint purchase with the Great Northern? Farrer thought it could hardly have been bought by the N.P. on its own account, without G.N. consent and approval. Pursuing the latter topic on 14 July, Farrer was obviously determined to plunge Louis in at the deep end of railroad finance. The Spokane Falls and Northern had in fact been bought by the Great Northern; Mount Stephen had shown Farrer a letter of J. J. Hill's written from New York; Farrer asked Louis:

Have you decided how to finance permanently for this road? Your Sterling 4s are in some demand and the price at the moment 101 bid ex interest in a small way. Financing on Stock would be preferable but as a good quantity will have been put out this year, especially if the Manitoba exchange takes place, I wondered whether you would approve issuing a 4% plain Bond at or about par to Great Northern shareholders repayable say in ten years but convertible at holders option after three years (i.e. subsequent to the next Presidential election) into Great Northern Stock. This would make the charge for finance light until the new Road has been put into standard physical condition and would give your shareholders a nice option without committing them at the moment to a further addition to their holdings in a *Share* security, moreover if they chose to sell as the price would be materially below the present quotation for G.N. shares it might induce a fresh set of buyers to come in and so eventually broaden your lists of shareholders.

In the same letter he had posed the question: 'How do you propose to get your present Stock made into Ordinary? We suppose the conversion must be optional and that when you raise the dividend to 7 it will be only so raised to holders who relinquish the Preference ...'

The rights issue was a great success, Hill's London friends not only taking up their own allocations but acquiring such other blocks as they could through John Sterling in New York. For example the Royal Victoria Hospital in Montreal, founded and endowed by Sir George Stephen and Sir Donald Smith in 1887, took advantage of the opportunity to sell their rights for $504,000.[1] These were probably all purchased by Lefevres and Barings on joint account and distributed in London. Farrer's letters to James J. Hill of 20 and 29 July 1898 record negotiations with Sterling—a Trustee of the Hospital—for the purchase of one block of 4,000; Lefevres and Barings kept a few for themselves, some went to 'old friends of the Great Northern, such as the Admiral'—Admiral of the Fleet the Earl of Clanwilliam: one of the Mount Stephen circle generally thus referred to, in the same way as Field Marshal Sir Donald Stewart was 'the old warrior' and Farrer's brother-in-law, Commander Eddie Hunter-Blair, was 'the Captain'—and the balance among investors believed to be permanent holders. Farrer had written to Stewart on 19 July saying that Lord Mount Stephen had asked Lefevres to reserve for him 'any amount' and told Hill that he was cabling Sterling that they could probably use more at the same price, 60 New York; they had disposed of the 4,000 at a minimum profit, and therefore considerably below market quotations. Writing to Oliver Northcote, who had evidently expressed some surprise at the success of the Great Northern's latest operation, he said on 5 August: '. . . You must not forget that Hill is now regarded as the first Railroad man in America, and that the moral effect of all his old supporters taking up and holding their new allotment of stock is irresistible . . .' He added that all indications were that that season's crop was the biggest the G.N. had ever had to handle. He had commented to Sterling on 29 July that rights sales in New York had been excellent; he emphasized this point to Harvey Cooke of Manchester on 4 August: '. . . Demand comes almost entirely from America where confidence in the property and its management has been steadily growing'. He told Cooke that notice had been given for the redemption of the 4 per cent Collateral Trust Bonds on 1 September.

On 6 August 1898 Farrer wrote to Hill regretfully declining an invitation for a trip on the railroad: 'You know how keen I am about everything connected with the old machine . . .' but there was too much unfinished business in London, 'including Kootenay'. There was some possibility that they might meet in New York in the autumn. This apparently faded, as Farrer, writing on Kootenay business on 28 December, asked 'Are you likely to come over next

[1] W. Sclater Lewis, *Royal Victoria Hospital 1887–1947*, Montreal, 1969, p. 122. See also Part I, The Founding of the Hospital.

spring? I want to have a gossip with you about all Great Northern matters and shall run out as soon as the snow is gone unless there is a chance of seeing you here'. By 15 February 1899 he was writing gloomily to Hill of the state of the London Stock Market where he was gradually disposing of the Kootenay Debenture Stock; it was disgusting, he said, the way in which English people were selling their American investments, good and bad indiscriminately: 'The Boss and I will soon be the only holders here of G.N. left. He is in great form and looking forward to your visit'. He himself was to come out in March or April. On 27 April Farrer wrote to Charles Ellis that Hill was at Brown's Hotel, Dover Street—a London haunt beloved of transatlantic visitors—for a few days only, and on 29 April to John Sterling that Hill was to return 'on Wednesday in company with Mr. Schiff'. One of Hill's sons accompanied him on this occasion, as Farrer told Sterling on 3 May: 'Hill left this a.m. in good spirits—also Schiff. Nothing could have been pleasanter than my relations with both father and son ...' The subject of their conversations on this visit will be treated in the next chapter; it is proposed now to catch up on a little social history.

A NEW CHAPTER OPENS

When Gaspard Farrer wrote to Louis Hill on 27 October 1897 that Lord Mount Stephen was 'a good deal engaged with his own affairs just now' he was playing upon words in a manner that Louis may, or may not, have appreciated. But for a last-minute postponement the 27th would have been the wedding-day.

On 21 April 1897 Lady Wolseley, who was at Brighton, wrote to her husband in London that she had been to lunch with Miss Ellen Willmott at Warley Place in Sussex. Described by Miss Gertrude Jekyll as 'the greatest of living women gardeners' Miss Willmott was to achieve lasting fame with her book *The Genus Rosa*, published in instalments between 1910 and 1914. Besides her large garden in Sussex she had another in the Rhone Valley; Miss Jekyll's biographer classified her as 'beautiful, erratic, an artist, member of the Bach choir'.[1] Wrote Lady Wolseley of her visit to Warley: '... Ld. Mount Stephen was lunching there. Can he be thinking of Miss Willmott? He was in high spirits. She seemed distraite. She told me Lady Somers, *aged 67 or more*, is making desperate efforts to

[1] Both quotations from Betty Massingham, *Miss Jekyll*, London, 1966, p. 81.

marry him!'[1] By 4 December 1897 Garnet, writing from a Brighton hotel to Louisa at Grosvenor Gardens, was able to make a comparison between some friends he was seeing there: '... Mrs. H.— a good companion for H.'s old age ...' and 'Our friend George Stephen' who 'did better, but then he was rich and a noble Ld. ...'[2]

In the second week of October Mount Stephen became engaged, not to Miss Willmott, but to Miss Gian Tufnell, daughter of Captain Robert George Tufnell, R.N., a Lady-in-Waiting to Princess Mary Adelaide, Duchess of Teck. It was on account of the last illness and death of the latter that the wedding was postponed for a month. The Princess, mother of the future Queen Mary, had been in indifferent health for some time,—she had undergone a serious operation in the spring—but, according to her biographer, 'After paying a short visit to Lord Mount Stephen at Brockett Hall, in Hertfordshire, the Princess returned to White Lodge very much better in health ...'[3] It was during this visit, in mid-October 1897, that the host became engaged to the Lady-in-Waiting. On 13 October the Duchess of Teck's daughter, Princess May, then Duchess of York, wrote to Gian from York Cottage, Sandringham:

Dearest Gian,

Your letter was indeed a surprise to us all! I do not know why dear Mama thought I should scold you, on the contrary if it is for your happiness I think you are quite right and I send you my very warmest congratulations in which the Duke joins. How curious that you should have become engaged to Lord Mount Stephen just when my Parents were at Brockett—I hope to see you at White Lodge on the 23rd. when I will offer you my good wishes in person.

I remain
dear Gian

Your very affect*ate*
May

[4]

As the Duchess of Teck had only ended her previous visit, to Appleby Castle, on 9 October, Princess May had some reason for being both surprised and curious. The present writer has no information as to

---

[1] LW/P 23.
[2] W/P 26.
[3] C. Kinloch Cooke, *A Memoir of HRH Princess Mary Adelaide Duchess of Teck*, London, 1900, 2 vols., vol. 2, p. 310.   [4] RA GV CC44/193.

Mount Stephen's previous acquaintance with Gian Tufnell, although there was every opportunity for them to have met in English society, and the Duchess of Teck's visit to Brocket in 1897 was presumably not her first. Gian became her second Lady-in-Waiting in 1895, but had been a member of her suite for longer than that. For some years Gian's aunt, Lady Wolverton, whose house at Coombe Wood, Kingston-on-Thames, was near White Lodge, had been among those who regularly and happily came to the financial rescue of the Duchess of Teck, a delightful personality who habitually lived beyond her resources. They were also engaged together in a number of charitable endeavours.[1]

The link with the Princess May, four years younger than Gian who was born in 1863, was more personal and stronger. In his life of Queen Mary, James Pope-Hennessy follows the course of Princess May's engagement, first to the Duke of Clarence, 'Prince Eddy', eldest son of the Prince of Wales (later King Edward VII), who died shortly afterwards in January 1892, and then to his brother George in 1893. Through all the significant stages Lady Wolverton and her niece were on the sidelines. In September and October of 1891 the Teck family were staying with Lady Wolverton and Gian at the Foley Arms Hotel at Malvern spa in Worcestershire. Pope-Hennessy notes the melancholy fact that in the course of sightseeing in this pleasant neighbourhood the Princess May visited Worcester Cathedral and was shown the tomb of Arthur, Prince of Wales, son of Henry VII, who died during his father's lifetime and whose young widow then married his brother Henry VIII. It was when staying afterwards at Coombe Wood that the Princess May received the not unexpected summons to Balmoral, the prelude to her engagement to Prince Eddy.[2] After the latter's death it was Lady Wolverton, co-operating in some royal engineering, who from March until May 1892 entertained the Tecks at a villa at Cannes, where they were visited by the Prince of Wales and Prince George.[3] The bereaved Princess gradually revived in health and spirits and was to continue her contacts with Gian in happier circumstances. Recording Gian's marriage, Pope-Hennessy writes: 'She was one of Princess May's few really intimate friends, for they were bound to one another by the strongest of all ties in friendship —a common memory of much past happiness amongst those now

[1] James Pope-Hennessy, *Queen Mary*, London, 1959, pp. 176–7.
[2] Ibid. pp. 202–3.   [3] Ibid. pp. 232–3.

dead. With Lady Mount Stephen, Princess May could recall the
life at White Lodge, with all its ups and downs; the wit, vitality
and benevolence of the Duchess of Teck; the gay sojourns and the
laughter at St. Moritz; the whole fabric, in fact, of her own lost
youth . . .'[1] Princess Mary Adelaide's Journal, for example,
records some of these carefree days at St. Moritz in August 1894,
following the birth on 23 June of Princess May's first son: '. . . In
the morning May went out and I, with Gian, called on
Madame de Planta at her delightful *châlet* . . . with Gian and Sidney,
gathered flowers. To my delight, we found some of the sweet
wild pinks! . . .'[2] In August–September 1895 there was a social
sojourn in Scotland, where the Duchess of Teck took the waters
at Strathpeffer, in Ross-shire, attended by Gian, and visited
neighbouring houses where friends were assembled for the grouse-
shooting season. They went on to stay at Hopetoun House, Dalmeny,
going into Edinburgh on 28 September to witness the Duke of
Cambridge's last review of troops as Commander-in-Chief in the
Queen's Park near Holyrood Palace. The Earl of Hopetoun had
just returned home after six years as Governor of Victoria, and the
Duchess, evidently recalling earlier happy visits, seemed overjoyed
to be back at Hopetoun: '. . . We have our dear old rooms . . .' It
was very much a family affair; on 19 September 'joined boys and
Miss Roche and Gian at football . . .'[3] The vision of the ample
Duchess thus disporting herself is indeed delightful.

After the October 1897 visit to Brocket the Duchess had returned
to White Lodge, as quoted earlier, very much better in health.
Princess May, just back from a visit to Ireland, had hoped to see
Gian there on the 23rd. On that day, however, the Duchess began
to feel unwell and died on the 27th. Afterwards a letter was found
in her blotting book, written from White Lodge on 25 October to
her Comptroller, the Hon. Arthur Walsh:

Dear Mr. Walsh,—I think I asked you to come on Wednesday next in
the morning and stay to luncheon, but if equally convenient to you I
would like to propose to you to dine and sleep here on Wednesday
instead, arriving about tea-time. We have asked some of our neighbours
to meet May at dinner that evening, and the *fiancé* Lord Mountstephen
is coming to dine and sleep, so you will have to help us entertain our
guests. With love to Clementine, whom I would have invited, had I a

[1] Ibid. p. 410.   [2] Cooke op. cit. vol. 2, p. 281.   [3] Ibid. pp. 288–94.

spare corner in which to stow her away, I am ever, dear Mr. Walsh, your sincere friend,

> Mary Adelaide.

P.S. Please telegraph reply.[1]

The Mount Stephen wedding took place quietly on 27 November 1897 at St. Margaret's, Westminster. It was described to Queen Victoria by the Hon. Harriet Phipps, Woman of the Bedchamber, in a letter dated 29 November from Kensington Palace:

Madam,

I have just had the honour to receive your Majesty's telegram and at once write to say that the wedding took place rather quietly on Saturday at 2 o'clock at St. Margaret's Westminster. The Church was decorated with white flowers and Palms and instead of, as is usually now the custom, the bridegroom awaiting the bride just below the Chancel for the first part of the Ceremony, Lord Mount Stephen and his best man, Sir John McNeill, stood close to the Altar much concealed by the Palms—and someone near the Church door told me after that the bride gave rather an agonised look for a moment not seeing he was there!! Miss Tufnell looked very nice in a plainly made white satin dress with a Brussels lace veil. She had no long bridal train, perhaps out of consideration for her four tiny little Bridesmaids—the foremost of whom was little more than a baby of apparently about 3 years old, too young to pay any attention to the Bride, so that Sir John had to do bridesmaid as well as best man and hold the Bride's gloves! The Service was partly choral. The Bishop of Peterborough and the clergyman of the Church near Brocket officiated. I sat in a Pew just behind Sir Stafford and Lady Northcote, with Sir Donald and Lady Stewart, Lord and Lady and Miss Wolseley, Princess Victor Hohenlohe and Countess Valda Gleichen. Lady Somers, General Higginson, Mr. Yorke, Mr. and Lady Margaret Douglas and a few others were present.

I thought Lord Mount Stephen looked shy, (as indeed he told me he should be) but I thought quite nice and not too old, and when they came down the Church from the Vestry and the Bride's veil was up so that I was able to see her I thought she looked radiantly happy and smiling. They were to cross yesterday for Paris where they spend a week's honeymoon and then return to Brocket till January when they go to the Riviera for 2 or 3 months as she likes warmth. Sir Stafford and Lady Northcote were to start this morning for Rome for a couple of months but I do not know whether the gale has not delayed all these arrangements.

[1] Ibid. p. 314.

Lady Northcote, who as well as Lord Mount Stephen I saw last week, told me she likes the new Lady Mount Stephen really very much and thinks she is suited to Lord Mount Stephen and will make him happy but the engagement came upon her quite as a surprise. The difference in age is so great it seems to me rather a venture, but I sincerely hope it will turn out well . . .[1]

There is some reason to believe that the apparent precipitancy of Mount Stephen's second marriage was not unconnected with the somewhat 'managing' disposition of his adopted daughter Alice Northcote, who had assumed the position of mistress of his establishments. It is said, for example, that she resented the acceptance of Gaspard Farrer as virtually a son of the house, with a room always reserved for him. At all events, Frances Wolseley records that her godfather took this opportunity to make financial provision for both Alice and herself. The town house in St. James's Place was given over to the Northcotes while Mount Stephen acquired 17 Carlton House Terrace, one of the original Nash terrace houses built on the site of Carlton House on the Mall, after its demolition in 1829. Shortly afterwards Harry Northcote was appointed Governor of Bombay, being elevated to the Peerage in 1901 as the first Lord Northcote, and was subsequently Governor-General of Australia.

Frances Wolseley appears to have been jealous of Gian, but perhaps more in retrospect than in actuality at the time of the marriage. In her rather repetitive memoirs she refers twice to the occasion when in her girlhood (she was nine years younger) she met Gian while the latter was staying with the Sidney Glyns at Farnham in Surrey. Gian was Sidney Glyn's niece. Frances writes of being 'thunderstruck' years after to find Gian married to her godfather; as she was present at the wedding, this tends to invite reservations about her account of the early meeting:

It was during our tenancy of the Firs, Farnham, that I first knew Gian Tufnell, who was many years later to become the second Lady Mount Stephen. Her Uncle and Aunt, Mr. and Mrs. Sydney Glyn were spending some weeks at Farnham and she and a Parisian girl named Evelyn French, the niece of Mrs. Glyn, were both staying with them. The contrast of these two young women was very great, for Gian was plain, somewhat awkward mannered, clad too, always in tailor-made English coats and skirts. Her boots were the thickest of the thick. The French

---

[1] RA Z199/167. Sir Stafford and Lady Northcote were Harry and Alice; Henry Stafford Northcote had been knighted in 1887, the year of his father's death; he was the second son.

girl on the contrary was fair and graceful, "put on her clothes well" as my mother expressed it, followed the latest style of hairdressing, the "dernier cri" of town costume and moreover, she was an elocutionist of the highest merit . . .

But even Frances Wolseley possessed a latent sense of fun and inborn honesty; she relates how the Glyn boys teased their French cousin, pretending that her most ordinary remarks were rehearsed. At breakfast, the cue as to what she would have to eat produced the desired stock response: 'Du Lar-r-rd, mon onquelle . . .' Evelyn would capture Garnet Wolseley, a not unwilling victim, to listen to a French military recitation entitled 'La Trompête'.[1] Writing to his wife on 16 September 1893, while on a cruise calling at Breton ports, Garnet reported meeting Mrs. Glyn and her son George 'bound for Dinard to stay with her sister Mrs. French. So I shall see Mademoiselle "du lard mon *oncle*" . . .' Perhaps unconsciously Frances reflected her parents' views. Although Garnet was to appreciate Gian's hospitality in later, more difficult days, neither he nor Louisa held her in such high regard as they had the first Lady Mount Stephen. For one thing, Garnet could never enjoy Brocket when he had to share it with Royalty: he wrote to Frances in 1898 when setting out thither when the Duchess of York was to be a guest: '. . . A little Royalty goes a long way with me and I had that little yesterday . . .' But according to Frances: 'weekend parties at lovely Brocket received fresh impetus from the added zest of Lady Mount Stephen's personal friends who joined the usual habitués . . .' Gian never appeared to intrude upon her husband's relations with his god-daughter; in fact it was after his second marriage that these relations became closer. This, again, must be relegated to a later chapter.

[1] PVW 118/188.

V

Moving towards a climax

BALTIMORE AND OHIO

... From Cincinnati in a comfortable sleeping car to Bellaire where we began the famous Baltimore railroad said to be the finest scenery of any railway in the world. It is 376 miles long, the whole way through rocky glens and valleys sometimes 300 ft. above the river—passing by the Potomac, Monongahela, Youghiageny and Cheat rivers of which the last is the finest scenery with the exception of the junction of the Potomac and Shenandreith at Haysas Ferry—Killed some fan tailed grouse and squirrels ...

So wrote the young Charles Ellis in his diary in October 1860. When Gaspard Farrer told him on 9 May 1899 that he would reserve 2000 Baltimore and Ohio Railroad shares for him this signalled Ellis's participation in James J. Hill's latest venture: the readjustment of the finances and operation of this oldest and once strongest of American trunk lines. Founded in 1827 and gradually extended until in the 1870s it reached New York, the Baltimore and Ohio had since the late 1880s been periodically in trouble. J. P. Morgan had carried out an apparently successful rehabilitation for its owners in 1887 and at the instigation of Hill, whose London friends bought a considerable quantity of the stock, became involved in the rescue operation of the late 1890s. Jacob Schiff had also been interested in the road from time to time, and became a director in April 1899. After five years of control by a voting trust of five men the rehabilitated property came under the control of the Pennsylvania Railroad.[1] Hill's part was largely advisory; he and Morgan had picked the trustees and his friends could be relied on to hold their stock, which in London was handled by Speyers.

On 9 September 1898 Farrer had referred, in a letter to Louis Hill, to the interest aroused in London by the sale of B. and O.

---

[1] Frederick Lewis Allen: *The Great Pierpont Morgan*, London, 1949, pp. 88–9; Adler on *Schiff*, Vol. 1 pp. 143–8; these versions do not exactly tally.

Preference shares; writing again on 5 November he mentioned Louis' father's offer of B. and O. participation. He wrote to John Sterling on 25 November 1898 thanking him for an offer of B. and O. 4s which they were glad to accept; he had not written sooner as Lord Mount Stephen had the matter in hand and Gaspard 'feared creating confusion'. He added: 'I am off this p.m. to Brocket for a shoot. Lord Mount Stephen is looking extraordinarily well and young and in excellent form'. He wrote to Sterling on 10 December:

Following Lord Mount Stephen's instructions we cabled the British Bank [of North America] on the 8th inst. to pay you $90,000 against delivery of 1500 B. and O. Preference Shares. If you will kindly let us know the interest due to Lord Mount Stephen, we will send you a cheque for the amount.

Lord Mount Stephen tells me that you have written that the stock is to be tied up till 31st December 1899; we understood that sales were prohibited for one year from date of purchase i.e. until *September* 99 and in fact we have seen a letter from Messrs. Speyers of this city to that effect. The difference is not very material and I should not like either my name or Speyers to be quoted in the matter, but we should be interested to learn, if you can ascertain which date is in fact correct.

Farrer's letter of 6 January 1899 to Sterling, presumably on behalf of his Lefevre firm, reflected the popularity of the Baltimore and Ohio securities: '. . . The liquidation of the B. & O. 4% syndicate results in a very satisfactory business for us thanks to you; I hear the new Securities are likely to be delivered about the end of March'.

As soon as the snow was gone Gaspard had indeed crossed the Atlantic; this visit had looked like being conditional upon Hill's inability to do likewise. In the event they returned together in April, much of their time on board ship being devoted to discussing the recent Baltimore and Ohio developments. Gaspard promised Sterling on 29 April to furnish him 'an epitome of many conversations I have had on the matter with Mr. Hill'. He reported that they had had a pleasant trip and that Hill was the better of the rest. There was much more talk during Hill's time in London, Farrer telling Sterling on 3 May that Hill had left him to place jointly with Barings among their friends 20 to 25 thousand Preference shares at 73—but only among those who would hold them for a couple of years, the time Hill had estimated it would take for the

B. and O. to find its feet again. Farrer got the impression that Hill was satisfied his friends could come to no harm and that they had every chance of making big money. Hill himself was prepared to forego his own chances of profit so long as he retained practical control of the voting power without having to put up fresh money. Farrer in fact told E. T. Nichols on 11 October 1899 that Hill was placing his B. and O. shares at their disposal.

By 21 August Farrer had been able to assure a stockbroker friend that B. and O. 3½ per cent Prior Lien Gold Dollar Bonds, along with St. Paul, Minneapolis and Manitoba Pacific Extension First Mortgage Bonds, came into the category of 'old ladies investments which may safely be locked away and on which you need never expend another thought'. If a 'more sporting venture' was desired, B. and O. 4 per cent Preference shares could be recommended alongside Great Northern, although 'You must understand that neither of these two last stocks are selections for the nimble ninepence and both would fall away in price with a general reaction in the American market; but both are the shares of sound properties and we believe there is big money in them for the permanent holder. All four are quoted on the London Exchange . . .' He explained that the B. and O. was an old and fine property with an established traffic but which under inefficient and dishonest management had become bankrupt and disorganized. It had been recently placed on a sound footing financially and the technical operation turned over to good men and under close supervision. For the past two years it had been in receivers' hands, net earnings being just sufficient to pay the dividend on the Preference shares in full; none had however been paid nor was it certain that one would be paid during the current fiscal year ending June 1900; earnings were now expected to increase and 'unless we are much astray there will be within the next two years a large divisible surplus for Ordinary as well as Preference shareholders . . .' He wrote to Hill on 29 August of his gratification that B. and O. earnings were mounting up; Speyers were rightly doing their best to discourage speculation in the Ordinary shares . . . 'I don't forget that you put the time as two years off for their new policy to work out . . .' By 3 January 1900 Farrer was advising Lord Clanwilliam, 'the Admiral', that B. and O. Preference had advanced too far to make them worth purchasing; on 19 February he told him that the company had just declared a dividend of $2 on its Preference stock, indicating that it was doing well. He felt obliged to write to Charles Ellis on 12 January 1901 that 'our St. Paul friend' had sold the whole or the greater part of his B. and O. Preference shares; this did not alter Farrer's view—or indeed, he believed, Hill's—about the company's soundness 'as a speculative investment' but as Ellis had bought on the knowledge of Hill's association, he was letting him know in confidence. He further informed Ellis on 25 March 1901 that he believed the Pennsylvania Railroad was adding substantially to its B. and O. holding, but proved that his own confidence was as firm as ever by accepting on 11 February, on behalf of Lefevres, Edgar Speyer's offer of a further $100,000 worth of B. and O. securities.

GREAT NORTHERN PROSPEROUS

Before leaving for America in 1899, Farrer had been telling Hill (as quoted in the previous chapter) that English investors were selling their American investments, both good and bad. Three days later, on 18 February, he reported to Hill that selling of Great Northern in London seemed to have stopped for the moment. On his return from his latest trip over the road he wrote to Ellis on 27 April full of enthusiasm:

... In operation, which has always been Hill's strong point, I am satisfied the G.N. can furnish cheaper transportation than any of its competitors while for the first time in my experience the business in sight seems to me to have—temporarily—got a bit ahead of the road's capacity to handle it to the best advantage ... Immigration along the line is very heavy—and the Hill sons seem likely to be able to carry on the management when the old man tires ...

Writing to a stockbroker on 14 October 1898 he had quoted the results of a comparison with the dividend capacity of other lines. Having listed the Great Northern's statistics for fixed charges, dividend requirements and other expenses, and net earnings for the past financial year: '... you will notice that G.N. fixed charges are comfortably low, and that net earnings per mile that would pay 5% on G.N. shares [in fact 7% was paid on the $75 million capital] would pay but 3.4% on the ordinary shares of the Chicago, Milwaukee and St. Paul, but 1% on those of the Chicago and North Western, and would not quite suffice to pay the Northern Pacific Preference dividend in full'. He was writing with this information in anticipation of the position after the 1898 proposed conversion of 'Manitoba' shares into Great Northern. In this connection he wrote to Hill on 6 January 1899: '... We are delighted at the way in which stock has come in and I hope it has not involved too burdensome an accumulation of stock in your hands'. Commenting that the latest G.N. earnings were excellent, he added: 'you certainly are a most satisfactory custodian of other people's money ...'

He wrote to Hill in more jocular vein on 16 August 1899, having just received a message ending 'outlook very promising': 'I can only account for this unwonted lapse into enthusiasm by the early prospect of seeing your daughters again ...' Mrs. Sam Hill, who had been in poor health after, or perhaps before, a rather damp visit to Scotland, had just left for home 'in buoyant spirits such as I have not seen with her before and I sincerely hope this may mean that her trip here has done her permanent good. We all at home liked her much: the gentle dignity of her ways constantly put me in mind of her mother'. Hill had followed up his enthusiastic cable with a letter of 18 August, acknowledged on the 29th with one of Gaspard's statistical calculations enclosed. Hill's operating sheet 'fully accounts for and justifies your recent "lapse". By Jove it is a magnificent record of operation: more than you ever promised or I thought possible ...' Some of Gaspard's own enthusiasm spilled over next day into a letter to Charles Ellis; perhaps because of his awareness that the road would soon have to spend more in order to increase its capacity, Farrer was thoroughly in favour of Hill's underestimating net earnings, for public consumption, but Hill's own figures had been sent to Ellis: '... the *real* net income being $14,500,000. I am urging him to smuggle some of this out of sight, so if he approves the suggestion, the report for the public may, and I hope will, show a considerably reduced amount ... Hill himself is in extraordinary spirits about his outlook for general business: meanwhile he is continually getting down his cost of operation, lately to a point which neither he nor anyone thought possible so few years ago'. He spelt this out to Hill on 30 September: '... As to the future: it is evident that additions and improvements in sight and inevitable will fully absorb all net earnings in excess of interest and dividend requirements for several years to come ...' To one of his stockbroker friends he had written on 21 August 1899: '... The Company pays 7% dividends but earnings are much in excess of distributions and though dividends cannot well be increased some means will probably be found to give holders from time to time additional indirect benefits . . .'

Mount Stephen, meanwhile, had taken Gian to Homburg for a month. Gaspard told Hill on 16 August: ' . . . The Boss writes in great form from Homburg and tells me that on his return he will race me any distance and back . . .' On 2 September he reported further: '. . . The Boss is back at Brocket very fit and in great spirits over your earnings . . .' As regards the possibility of increasing returns to the shareholders, this had a political aspect which is hinted at in Farrer's letter to Hill of 7 October, which enclosed another statistical exercise of a hypothetical nature; he had submitted this first to Mount Stephen, who described the figures as 'very comforting, so perhaps they will amuse you: of course we both realize that the policy they indicate is impracticable both on account of the local Legislatures as well as because it would raise shareholders' expectations unduly'. The memorandum showed the possible result of an annual 5 per cent stock bonus in addition to 7 per cent cash dividend as at present paid, together with the effect on capital account of replacing bonds maturing during the next twelve years with stock. There is a hint at this time that Hill was already looking to the more distant future of the enterprise which he had so successfully built up, but it is too early still to anticipate the steps which he was shortly to take in an attempt to safeguard this. At this juncture Gaspard was delighted to hear that Hill's sons, Louis and Jim, had again achieved a measure of promotion. On 9 October he wrote to Hill again on getting further good news from Mount Stephen:

The Boss has told me of your 16 millions of net earnings: it is a magnificent showing: no one appreciates the dollar side of the business more than myself: but please remember that I appreciate the other side also, as I realize to the full that this success is the result not only of ability but of a lifetime of self sacrifice and unceasing toil and devotion to the property. I wish I could think I could ever be of service to you or yours—if ever I can be sure to apply to a drone of a shareholder but Sincerely yours, Gaspard Farrer.

In a postscript to a letter to Hill of 8 November 1899 Farrer reported: 'We know of about 2000 G.N. shares recently bought in New York on London account: quite an unusual amount'.

On 5 May 1899 Garnet Wolseley had written to his wife: '...
Yesterday I had a note from Mount Stephen saying he wanted to
see me about your Northern Railway shares. They are he says now
worth £20,000 and we can now have 102 more shares at par. The
£600 at Cox's [Bank] will buy 30 more shares, of the remaining 72
we will sell one half to pay for the other half and the result will be
an addition of £3,000 to the above £20,000 ... and your yearly
income from it will be about £810 (pounds) ...'[1] The Wolseleys
were among the many friends whom Mount Stephen advised about
their investments; their expenditure was less well regulated,
although at this stage the business of trying to marry their daughter
was thought to justify an apparently extravagant way of life. The
Great Northern shares had previously stood in Garnet's name, but
he was gradually handing all these matters over to Louisa; his
deterioration in health since 1897 will be dealt with presently.
Meanwhile, his letter to Louisa of 24 June 1899 provides further
evidence that Mount Stephen's stay at Homburg that August was
to prove beneficial: '... met Mount Stephen and we had a long
walk together. But his pace is about a mile an hour which does
not suit me, so I was glad to end my walk by myself ...'[2]

MOUNT STEPHEN BABY

Very different was the tone of the letter Garnet wrote to his wife
on 25 September 1899:

I give as many guesses as old de Sevigny gave her daughter in that
memorable letter of hers & you would never guess my news. Lady — is
going to have a baby!!! Who is it? Our Lady of Brocket! Do please write
a line to M.S. to congratulate. Since the days of Sarah there has never
been anything more wonderful. A withered up old maid married to a
man of 70! I heard it a few minutes ago from Mrs. Glyn ...[3]

The following day he wrote again: '... Alice Northcote has asked
me to stay from this Saturday to Monday with her at Hardwick
House, Pangbourne ... She makes no allusion to the *baby of
Brocket* ...'[4] Louisa replied to the first: '... Fancy the Stephen
baby. What a wonder—I will write & congratulate certainly. One
must not write as if it were a surprise though ...'[5] Garnet pursued
his train of thought on 28 September: '... I shall be curious to see

[1] W/P 28.   [2] Ibid.   [3] Ibid.
[4] Ibid.   [5] LW/P 25.

how Alice N. takes the approaching baby in the Brocket family. From what Mrs. Sidney Glyn said last night when I dined with her, Lady *M.S.* was a little nervous at first about telling her ...'[1] Alice appears to have been lent Hardwick House by Charles Rose, son of Sir John; the party included 'Col. Lugard of the Niger and of West African fame'. Lady Wolseley duly wrote her congratulations, and sent the letters which both Mount Stephens wrote in reply, with her own comment, to her husband on 29 September: 'These are nice letters which you will like to read. I am very glad they are happy & hope they may have twins every year!' Mount Stephen had written:

Thanks so much for your more than kind note. Yes it is quite true that we are expecting the arrival of a new claimant for board & lodging about Feby. next who will you may be sure be warmly welcomed.

It was sweet of you to write such a charming letter every word of which I know came from the heart. You and yours are now among the oldest of my friends & your friendship I value as a precious treasure. Again thanking you for all your kind wishes. My love to my Goddaughter ...

He added a postscript: 'I fancy you *see* but little of the Commander-in-Chief in these days. I am still hoping for peace. The war, if it comes, will very soon be a most unpopular one though old Kruger is a most tiresome old man'. His wife's letter, signed 'Giana Mount Stephen' ran as follows:

I cannot resist writing too—for your kindest of letters has given us both much pleasure. I do think George is indeed blessed with the best of friends and so am I for I maintain that what is his is also mine.

I think & hope the coming person—of whichever sex—will be a great happiness to George. I know it will be to me—for the very idea of it fills me with delight & Feby. seems a long way off for that is the earliest I can look forward to. Again thanking you for all you say to George—he was *so* delighted with your letter.[2]

[1] W/P 28.
[2] LW/P 25. War in South Africa came on 11 October, following President Kruger's ultimatum. Goldwin Smith was to write to Mount Stephen on 31 March 1900: '... What you say about Kruger is perfectly true. He managed his case ill ...' and on 15 January 1903: '... You sum up the case when you say that you always thought Milner the author of the war. Race feeling would have subsided, and all would have gone well in time had not an insolent and conceited bureaucrat, a stranger to the country, gone in with his Jingo policy to stir up strife and bring on all these disasters. It is a warning to us to get rid, if we can, of British Governors ...' (first quotation from *Correspondence of Goldwin Smith*, ed. Arnold Haultain, p. 354; second from Cornell MS.)

Disappointment, unfortunately, was to follow. On 16 March 1900 Gaspard Farrer wrote to James J. Hill: '. . . We are grieving today over Lady Mount Stephen's misfortune: the child arrived this morning a still-born daughter. It is hard luck for them and such as he does not deserve'.

GARNET WOLSELEY: DECLINE AND RETIREMENT

No one to date has written the definitive biography of Field Marshal Viscount Wolseley; the daunting mass of his daughter's papers demands the attention of a psychologist–historian, and the sociological aspect of the Wolseley story has yet to be satisfactorily examined. The present writer, being neither psychologist, sociologist nor military historian, proposes merely with a minimum of digression to deal with the Wolseley family's relations with the Mount Stephens.[1] Lord Lansdowne's biographer, Lord Newton, records that when Wolseley became Commander-in-Chief 'he set upon his task full of initiative and enthusiasm, until unfortunately a serious illness early in 1897 left him with a loss of memory and an impaired capacity for work . . .'[2] Frances Wolseley's memoirs state that the operation after which Garnet repaired for convalescence to Brighton in February 1897 was 'a serious one for tuberculosis of the glands', and refer to 'a large swelling in his neck'. She writes of the sojourns that followed in a succession of Sussex houses:

There was a terrible restlessness about my poor parents, neither of them were well and because their great ambition, that of marrying me well, had not been accomplished, they seemed to have come to the end of their resources. He too had suffered from his illness to such a degree that his memory was much impaired and yet he felt active and able bodied enough to continue his work and did manage to accomplish it throughout the S. African war.[3] A bitter and crushing blow came tho' when he realised that his supreme command of the Army in England wld. be an obstacle to his being given any active service work and too that

---

[1] In a foreword to her manuscript memoirs, dated June 1924, Frances Wolseley wrote: 'I am very desirous that most of what I have here recorded should be published some day'. Marjory Pegram's *The Wolseley Heritage*, London, 1939, sub-titled The Story of Frances Viscountess Wolseley and her Parents, was written at her instance during her lifetime and published after her death. Wolseley's biographers do not deal with this topic.
[2] Newton on *Lansdowne*, p. 137.
[3] This is inaccurate; Wolseley retired at the end of 1900.

his old rival Lord Roberts was likely to win higher recognition than himself. All this added a sorrow, a despair to those last years of official life which should have been such a golden ending to a selfmade career.[1]

That Frances was aware of the other frustrations of these years, resulting from the diminished status since 1895 of the Commander-in-Chief *vis-à-vis* the Secretary of State for War (then Lord Lansdowne) is indicated in an earlier note in her memoirs, but neither she nor her mother really appeared to take an intelligent, as opposed to an occasionally emotional interest in Garnet's work, nor are Frances' recollections always reliable. It is not proposed to comment further on the organizational changes in the War Office, nor to go into the question of preparedness for war, particularly the South African War beginning on 11 October 1899. Lansdowne's biographer writes: '. . . when the crisis . . . came in 1898, Lord Lansdowne did not hesitate to jeopardize his political future by threatening to resign unless the very moderate demands made by himself and by Lord Wolseley were acceded to . . .'[2] From the Wolseley papers it appears that relations between Lansdowne and Wolseley became more and more difficult as political and military considerations clashed.

Writing from Brighton on 7 February 1897 to Louisa who was still in London, Garnet complained: 'I cannot understand why it is that I remain so weak for although I am nearly 64 I ought to be able to walk my ten miles with ease . . .'[3] and to Frances two days later: '. . . at moments I am as weak as a baby and as devoid of all backbone as a jellyfish. Then I perk up and feel young and lusty as the eagle of the Bible . . .'[4] On 15 March he was back at the War Office, commuting from Brighton, although he soon found this too tiring and a base was again found in London for weekdays, Louisa remaining in Sussex. Garnet wrote to her on 16 March that he was to lunch next day with Mount Stephen, adding that at the War Office 'the plot thickens around me'.[5] He wrote more fully on 18 March:

. . . I am much amused at finding everywhere a certain amount of surprise at my return to work at all. It was currently reported in the clubs that I

---

[1] PVW 119.
[2] Newton, op. cit. p. 191 and Midleton *Memoirs* p. 93: 'the combination of Wolseley and Lansdowne enabled more to be accomplished for the Army in the three years which intervened before the Boer War than in any previous period of our history'.
[3] W/P 26.   [4] Ibid.
[5] Ibid.

had gone off my head, some said had only lost my memory, others that I was dying of diabetes . . . In fact, speculations as to my successor were rife . . . I lunched with Mount Stephen and Alice yesterday . . . He is looking so well and so young for his age . . . He wants me to go down to him in the country which I may do by and bye if I find (myself) worn out in town . . .[1]

Quite apart from his work, Wolseley's social engagements at this time hardly indicated either mental or physical decline. On 22 March he was dining at Grillion's—a club 'founded for the purpose of preventing the political differences between the leading men of the two parties resulting in permanent social estrangement'—and on the 25th he was guest of the evening at the Omar Khayyam Club. Two days later—a Saturday—he was with the Breakfast Club before going down to Brighton, and met with them again on 10 April. The next time he attended, on 1 May, he regaled them with observations on Gibraltar, where he had just been on an official visit. For these diary notes (and for the quotation on Grillion's) we are indebted to the man who acted as polycladous Boswell to Wolseley as to countless others, that superclubman of the Victorian era, Sir Mountstuart Grant Duff, one time Governor of Madras and Under Secretary of State for the Colonies. In his *Notes from a Diary*, published at intervals over nearly half a century, are enshrined probably most of the dining-out anecdotes of the day; a veritable Ruth in the harvest-fields of the club tables, he seized upon the bon-mots dropped in his direction by carefully-elected Boazes and garnered them for posterity. These club meetings were not the place for friendship as such but for brilliance of conversation. On 2 November 1896 Grant Duff noted after dinner with the Literary Society: '. . . as I had Wolseley on one side and Fletcher Moulton on the other, I had no reason to complain'. (John Fletcher Moulton, later Lord Moulton, brilliant mathematician, Judge, Member of Parliament, Fellow of the Royal Society.) Meeting Lord Mount Stephen—then Sir George Stephen—at the Cosmopolitan Club on 20 February 1889 he had asked him if it was he who gave the name of Banff to the 'watering-place surrounded by magnificent mountains' which a friend had recently described to him. (His own estate of Eden was on the borders of Banffshire and Aberdeenshire.) 'He said "Yes. Ever so many stations on the Canadian Pacific have

---

[1] Ibid.

got Banffshire names. We have a Balvenie, Kininvie, and others, the pronunciation of some of which puzzles the people in these regions not a little"'.[1] Perhaps the last recorded entry on Wolseley —at the Breakfast Club on 11 July 1900, less than five months before Garnet's retirement and the year before Grant Duff's death—is the most delightful. They were discussing 'the current craze for attributing the works of Shakespeare to Francis Bacon . . . Wolseley said that he had once remarked to the Queen that some people now doubted whether Shakespeare had written his own plays. "Oh! don't talk to me about that", she replied, "that was Lord Palmerston's nonsense"'. Interred within the picturesque ruins of Elgin Cathedral, Grant Duff's flat tombstone is inscribed, not as has been reported 'Mountstuart requiescat' but even more appropriately, 'Mountstuart in pace'.

August 1897 found Wolseley on leave, cruising in the Hebrides on Sir Donald Currie's yacht, attended by a doctor and 'dear Maurice—who wants sea air badly' (Sir Frederick Maurice). From Islay he wrote to Louisa: '. . . My neck all but healed. How nice it will be to give up these bandages'.[2] On 21 September, moored in the Clyde and apparently making public appearances, he told Louisa of the difficulty he was finding in making speeches: '. . . what I fail in is memory . . .' he misses points he meant to make, invents, and is lost. His neck is still not healed.[3] Louisa was again preoccupied with efforts to marry her daughter. She wrote to Garnet on 26 August: '. . . I am quite ready to spend the winter in a Scotch shooting lodge, but what about Frances. We must marry her first! Oh! when will that be! . . .'[4]

Living alone in London during the week, except when he was away on manoeuvres or on tour, Wolseley saw a good deal of Mount Stephen during his last years at the War Office. From Brocket he wrote to his wife on 3 and 4 July 1898 complaining of the dullness of the house party: '. . . the whole society strikes me as being unnatural, out of tune, unreal and consequently oppressive . . .' The only gleam of amusement to be captured was in contemplation of the new butler 'very like John Morley!'[5] On 22 October 1899, eleven days after the declaration of war, he and Frances were to travel down to Brocket together. Owing to dense fog Frances was late for the train at King's Cross, and when Garnet arrived at Hatfield

---

[1] No doubt Stephen was thinking of the place Canadians call *Craigellat'chie*.
[2] W/P 26.   [3] Ibid.   [4] LW/P 23.   [5] W/P 27.

station he found a War Office messenger with 'disquieting news from South Africa' which demanded a decision. This was the day after the Boer victory at Elandslaagte. But apart from a complaint to his wife that Gian provided no railway time table in his room and 'How I hate this ribbed paper to write on—I shall divorce you if you ever introduce it into your house', his letter of 22 October contains mainly the usual waspish comments on the house party: John McNeill 'irrepressible'; Lady Rosslyn 'hideous'; the American Ambassador 'clever, but *very* vulgar and ignorant of the world's ways'; 'My Lady here looking drawn somewhat above and inflated a little below. The Boss grows younger looking . . .'[1]

On New Year's Day 1900 Wolseley was looking forward to retiring in October. On 7 February he wrote to Louisa from his rooms in London:

I came home here from the War Office tired and weary and fell asleep for an hour in a chair. Then went to dine with the Mount Stephens. *He and she and I*, quite pleasant. She improves much on acquaintance and although there is nothing much in her—I mean in her head, for her waist makes you realise she has much in her body—she is bright and pleasant and very amiable and genial. In fact I not only had a pleasant and good dinner but I enjoyed myself and for the time forgot little Lansdowne and the War Office and all the worries and troubles of my life . . .[2]

Five days later he was writing of an interview with Lansdowne when he had offered his resignation (which was not accepted) since the Cabinet would not agree to his demands for South Africa. Roberts had by then gone out there as Commander-in-Chief and was at odds with Buller whom he was superseding. '. . . But I have had a snooze before dinner and a pleasant evening with good cheer at the Mount Stephens . . .'[3] The one bright spot at this time was the sudden if evanescent show of affection and concern by his daughter. In the earlier letter above he had written of her: 'She is coming to write very much as you do, with a great sense of humour and real wit'. In the note of 12 February, when even the American Ambassador was in favour, having 'kept us all alive with his amusing ways and stories', he concluded: 'Fondest love to Frances who grows nicer every day because she is more affectionate'. Although Frances omitted from her writings any evidence of criticism of herself by her father, and never wrote critically, if sometimes

[1] W/P 28.   [2] W/P 29.   [3] Ibid.

sadly, of him, Garnet had been quicker than Louisa to spot that deficiency in her nature which made her unsatisfactory as a daughter and (except once) unsought as a wife. Her growing indulgence in close female friendships, persisting long after the age at which such might have been considered normal, may in some measure be traced to the inhibitions of a Victorian child who found it difficult to be at ease with her seldom-seen and mutually devoted parents. She was no rebel against society's pattern; she liked living in style and would have liked to be mistress of her own establishment, with appropriately ample means. She appeared to have cherished life-long mild regret about the Irish landowner whom she refused to marry early on, after thorough appraisal, on account of a certain gaucherie in society and the inadequacy of his rent-roll. Later she was to refer to her mother's 'vulture-like' personality, and was to ferret out the conflicting evidence which pointed to Louisa's having been born illegitimately either to a married woman whose mind became deranged on finding herself pregnant, or in mysterious circumstances within the Erskine family. Her accepted father's name (they were mutually devoted) was Alexander Erskine Holmes, but Louisa was four years old when he married and always used the name of Erskine. Mount Stephen's attitude to the gradual estrangement of Frances and her parents will be dealt with presently.

In April 1900 Garnet had the sadness of attending 'poor Donald Stewart's funeral'.[1] For Mount Stephen there was some consolation in the knowledge that he had been a faithful steward of his old friend's worldly possessions. He wrote to Garnet on 19 April: '. . . The dear old Warrior's estate comes out better than I expected —over £100,000 in clean liquid securities. This, I am told, is three times the amount he brought out of India. I am very glad . . .'[2] In 1880, when Stewart got the command at Kabul, Wolseley had thought Roberts, albeit junior, the better man professionally. In later years, while his dislike of Roberts increased, he came to share to the full Mount Stephen's affection for Stewart; they had got their Field Marshal's batons together in 1894.

Increasingly now Garnet leant upon the two sources of comfort in a crumbling world, his wife and Mount Stephen. Even the latter could not dispel Wolseley's positive distrust of Lord Lansdowne. Garnet wrote to his wife an 13 July 1900: '. . . I lunched yesterday with the Mount Stephens and met little Lansdowne there . . .'[3] In

[1] Ibid. [2] PVW 119/538. [3] W/P 29.

September Garnet was at Brocket again:

... Where I sleep is on the ground floor, my window looks out upon a garden full of flowers and yew hedges—It is the room in which Lord Melbourne died. In the bathroom through which you enter it, is a bookcase filled with delightful old works & nice old bindings & book plates of the Lamb & Lewis families that would delight Frances. They tempt one to steal ...

He had been for a drive with the Mount Stephens in the direction of Hatfield House:

This country round here as you know was a great forest and is still much wooded. Being very undulating in feature it is a lovely bit of *green* landscape to drive through, the cottages and farmhouses—many being as old as Hatfield House—are all of that deep and dark brick that tones so well with the brilliant foliage that bounds the view in every direction.

Lady M. looks very very thin & pale & drawn—can it be the beginning of another baby? I hope so, for our old friend's sake ...[1]

That he felt soothed and welcome is clear from the letter he wrote next day, 22 September: '... Lady Mt. S. was very nice and I think liked having me there. I should say, she would find it dull at Brocket without company ...'[2]

With his unwilling agreement, Wolseley's retirement was postponed until 30 November 1900. But he wrote on 7 November to Louisa, whom he was about to join in Sussex, of his 'blank, blank future ... If I had kept my money and not poured it on Fred believing his stories of future fortune, I should meet you on that road singing and dancing, but instead of joy being in my heart I hate even talking over my private affairs ... What an end to all my ambition—I staked and lost ...'[3] Garnet had always been generously devoted to his own family, to his sister Caroline, a chronic invalid, and to 'poor Fred', the brother who was always about to make his fortune in Australia with the Wolseley sheep-shearing machine, but died after a lingering illness having absorbed, instead, a good part of Garnet's. Even Mount Stephen gave the latter little encouragement to talk about his debts; instead, he added, over the years, to his gifts to Frances. On 17 January 1901 he wrote to her that he was proposing to give her £5,000 6 per cent Bonds of the Pillsbury Washburn Flour Mills of Minneapolis: 'They are a perfectly safe investment and will yield £300 a year. The dividends

---

[1] Ibid.   [2] Ibid.   [3] Ibid.

LORD STRATHCONA
(from *Record of the Celebration of the Quatercentenary of the University of Aberdeen*)

are payable half-yearly, and will I hope make you feel comfortable. I have not mentioned the matter to anyone, and think it will be better to keep it to our four selves. People are always so ready to "chatter" about such things, that it is nearly always better to keep them to oneself. Let me know who your banker is, and I will give instructions for the Bonds to be delivered to them for safe-keeping, on your account. It is a great pleasure to me to be able to do this for you and render this little service. Your affectionate Godfather, Mount Stephen'.[1] The previous year he had invested for her the £1,000 which had been his christening present, plus interest of nearly £600, in the Amalgamated Copper Company, saying at the time: 'I hope this will turn out to be a profitable and safe investment for you. I wish you had ten times the number of shares ...'[2] Later he had to extricate her from this, and 'Pills' turned out to be for a time something of a disappointment. Railway securities were to become her main source of income.

Wolseley's retirement was only the beginning of his battle to justify his record at the War Office. Even before the setting up of the Royal Commission on the South African War under Lord Elgin, to which Wolseley gave evidence and which eventually, in 1903, published an ambivalent report, there came in 1901 'Army Night' in the House of Lords and the public confrontation with his late Secretary of State, Lord Lansdowne.[3] On 25 January of that year Wolseley, his mind divided between his professional reputation and his financial position (he considered his pension inadequate) lunched with the Mount Stephens in London. He wrote to Louisa:

... After luncheon he and I had a talk and I thanked him for his kindness to Frances, but he said it was always what he had intended doing. He made no allusion to anything else. I said I was anxious to get some Directorships. He said don't be in a hurry & be very careful. I said that I would do nothing without asking his advice. I said I hated being idle: he answered, that feeling would soon wear off. He never asked in even the most indirect fashion about what we owed or gave me any opening for dwelling upon the matter. He may have been shy—I know I was. He talked a great deal, & very sensibly about my speech & said he hoped I would get someone to begin the "ball" by bringing the matter before the House, so that it should not begin with me. That I could not be too

[1] PVW 119/565.
[2] PVW 119/540, Mount Stephen to Frances Wolseley 18 May 1900, and 119/538 Mount Stephen to Garnet Wolseley, 19 April 1900.
[3] Hansard (Lords) 4 and 5 March 1901, also 15 March.

complimentary to my successor &c &c—et voila tout—It was then time for me to go to the House of Lords & we went together in a hansom for which I paid. He wanted to pay, but I had my shilling ready first. I told him I had seen in the Press how liberal he had lately been to an Institution in Aberdeen. He said he thought it was so much better to give away money in your lifetime than to leave it for Charity in your Will!! . . .[1]

On 4 March 1901 the Duke of Bedford set the ball rolling with a Question on the duties of Commander-in-Chief. Wolseley's speech to the House of Lords lasted for one and a half hours and occupied eighteen columns in *Hansard*. It does not read as the work of a man in his dotage, nor of a man launching a vendetta. He said at the beginning '. . . My arguments are not directed against individuals, but against a military system which I have honestly tried for five years and found wanting . . .' In replying, Lord Lansdowne, then Foreign Secretary, chose to make a personal attack, alleging that Wolseley had not given the system a fair trial, that he had not used to the full the powers he had, had initiated proposals or called for papers '. . . fitfully, and only when the spirit moved him . . .' He referred to a paper in which Wolseley had enumerated his duties with notable omissions. On Garnet's moving for papers to be laid before the House the debate was presently adjourned to 15 March. He was not without his supporters on both days—these included Lord Rosebery—but his motion was defeated 62–38.

LORD STRATHCONA

A member of the Elgin Commission was Lord Strathcona. Raised to the peerage in 1897, Sir Donald Smith had since 1896 been Canada's High Commissioner in London. The Canadian Government, in face of some initial opposition, had by December 1899 sent one contingent to join the British forces in South Africa and promised another. Strathcona then made his magnificent gesture of contributing at his own expense the force of four hundred recruits from Manitoba and points westward that became known as Strathcona's Horse.[2] Strathcona was a master of the magnificent gesture, some of his exploits being regarded with affectionate amusement by his cousin Mount Stephen. He was already aged 75 when he became High Commissioner and in spite of attempts at

---

[1] W/P 30.
[2] Beckles Willson, *Life of Lord Strathcona*, Toronto, 1915, p. 517 ff.

resignation from 1911 onwards still held the office when he died in 1914 at the age of 93. He was unremitting in effort rather than indefatigable; indeed, Gaspard Farrer's reports to friends over the years give the impression of a man almost wantonly dissipating his last physical resources. On 20 July 1888 Farrer told James J. Hill that Sir Donald was 'far from well' but would not rest. He was then Member of Parliament for Montreal West; in 1886, after five years away from Ottawa, he had been approached by the city of Winnipeg to be their candidate, but before he had returned a definite reply was persuaded instead by James Alexander Cantlie, the husband of Mount Stephen's sister Eleonora, to stand for Montreal West, but as an Independent.[1] He wrote to Sir John A. Macdonald on 11 June 1890:

... What little I know of local politics does not inspire me with much hope in the future of those who are residents in this part of the Dominion and I am greatly inclined to follow the example of Stephen who has almost entirely withdrawn his interests to the other side of the Atlantic and I hope to effect this ere long ...[2]

On the contrary he was destined to become even more embroiled, if not in Quebec provincial politics at least in those of Manitoba (the vexed question of the Manitoba Schools Act) and on a national level. He was mooted for Prime Minister to succeed Sir Mackenzie Bowell, but here he did draw the line; Sir Charles Tupper came back from London to fill the post and Smith opted for the High Commissionership.[3] He was then both President of the Bank of Montreal and Governor of the Hudson's Bay Company.

On 8 February 1893 Farrer wrote to the man he referred to as 'Uncle Donald': '... I do hope you are better and taking better care of yourself—you really looked tired out when you left London ...' (Beckles Willson quotes King Edward VII's remark at a garden party: "Here comes Uncle Donald, but where is 'Our Lady of the Snows?' "[4]). He told Hill on 4 July 1896: 'Sir Donald is in great form over social functions: shook hands with over 500 people at an afternoon reception at the Imperial Institute on Dominion Day and subsequently dined 150 at the Westminster Palace Hotel making speeches till midnight ...' On 4 August 1899 there was a similar report to Hill: 'Lord Strathcona presides most afternoons

[1] Ibid. pp. 420–1. [2] Macdonald Papers 265.
[3] Peter B. Waite, *Canada 1874–1896 : Arduous Destiny*, Toronto, 1971, pp. 265 and 271. [4] Willson, op. cit. p. 564.

and every evening at some meeting or another, and speechifies with great aplomb on art, music, medicine, science, university extension, French Employment, and every other interest that is glad to enlist the dear old gentleman's presence—and purse'. On 23 March 1901 Farrer told John Sterling: 'Lady S. has been very ill, is still in bed but is recovering. Ld. S. has also been ill and has at the moment pleurisy in both lungs but is nevertheless attending deputations to his majesty and other functions, going out in the bitter east winds though the doctors have forbidden him to leave the house and have warned him that he does so at the peril of his life'. To Louis Hill he wrote on 17 July 1902: '. . . We have had rather a disturbed summer here owing to the King's illness [King Edward VII's coronation had to be postponed from 26 June to 9 August] and though many have now left Town, London is still swarming with Premiers and Princes—giving our excellent friend Lord Strathcona a grand opportunity for banquets without end, and speeches to correspond . . .' On 20 August 1902 he told Sterling: '. . . Lord Strathcona is by way of being in Scotland, which means that he occasionally runs up there for anything from 12 to 24 hours. He has been tremendously busy entertaining Colonial Premiers and Bigwigs of all kinds—altogether in his best element and I think looking remarkably well. Lady Strathcona is going off to Carlsbad . . .' Beckles Willson relates that Sir Thomas Shaughnessy, then President of Canadian Pacific, once told an Anglo-Canadian gathering in London: 'You will be gratified to learn that, yielding to the earnest entreaties of Sir Thomas Barlow, Lord Strathcona has decided to relax his energies. He has succumbed to the united pressure of his medical man, his family, and his friends, and has been induced to promise to leave his office at 7.30 each evening instead of 7.45'.[1]

Strathcona's connections with Scotland were well nourished during these years. He built himself a substantial eyrie in Glencoe, the 'glen of weeping' from which he took his title in its Gaelic form. In 1899 he became Lord Rector of the University of Aberdeen, elected by and representing the interests of the student body in that capacity until 1902. Succeeded then by Sir Frederick Treves the King's surgeon, he became Chancellor of the University for life. It happened that in 1906 the University of Aberdeen was celebrating its quatercentenary; although the papal bull sanctioning the

---

[1] Ibid. p. 575.

erection of the institution was issued in 1494, the founder, Bishop
Elphinstone's own charter detailing and setting his seal to the
actual plans was signed 17 September 1505, reckoned after the
introduction of the Gregorian calendar as 1506. This was a happy
coincidence, for although the University had laid more than
adequate plans for a fitting celebration, during which the King was
to open new buildings at Marischal College, it provided the occasion
for one of Lord Strathcona's most inspired gestures. He told the
Principal, the Very Reverend John Marshall Lang, that he 'wished
his contribution to the celebrations to take the form of a dinner or
banquet, at which he desired that not only all the Delegates and
invited Guests but all Graduates and other members of the University taking part in the Celebrations should be invited to be present.
(He) ... further indicated his desire that no apparent difficulties,
financial or otherwise, should be allowed to stand in the way of the
carrying out of his plan in the best possible manner'.[1] The committee in charge of the event were delighted: quite apart from
anything else they had faced the difficulty that there was no hall in
the city capable of holding the number of people expected to attend
the larger gatherings. Adjacent to Marischal College was a 2¾ acre
site recently subjected to slum-clearance by the Town Council;
hereon was erected a temporary building that would accommodate
2,500 at table and 4,740 in rows. It cost, in all, £3,400.

The Strathcona Banquet, which took place on the evening of
27 September 1906, remained a lifelong memory of sheer delight to
the students and recent graduates who were present. The more
important guests might well have witnessed many such, and perhaps
some of the older graduates (these dated from 1835; a graduate of
1831 was at the last moment unable to attend) but for many it was
something they would never see again. The novelist Neil Munro,
an invited guest, wrote an evocative essay on it beginning:

Ghosts of old graduates, long dead, that have known Barmecide banquets,
studying on a regimen of oats in poor attics by the frugal light of candles,
may well have haunted the Strathcona Hall that night, and, if ghosts have
any appetite, or can feel regrets for old unable years, they must have looked
wistfully upon this gigantic feast where all the culinary resources of the
South had been requisitioned to give the North one evening with Lucullus.
Among them (it is easy to fancy) must have been Dalgetty, who, it may

[1] *Record of the Celebration of the Quatercentenary of the University of Aberdeen,
25–28 September 1906*, ed. P. J. Anderson, Aberdeen, 1907.

be remembered, accounted for the unseemly haste of his eating at the Castle of Darnlinvarich by telling how he had learned to hurry at the bursary table of Marischal College, "when, if you did not move your jaws like a pair of castanets, you were very unlikely to get anything to put into them". And yet, however it may have been with the poor ghosts, those who really dined with the Lord Chancellor that night will doubtless remember the nature of their viands less than the circumstances attending their disposal, for public banquets are not so much an indulgence of the corporal appetites as the occasions for that human rapport which is ever more effluent after food and wine, otherwise a banquet were a barbaric and shameful rite . . .

The King was not present, but a special invitation had been given to His Serene Highness the Prince of Monaco, equally on account of his reputation as oceanographer and naturalist as because he chanced at the time to be passing down the east coast of Scotland in his yacht, on his way from an Arctic expedition. The Principal, replying to the toast of The University, like Neil Munro conjured up the vision of one of Sir Walter Scott's favourite characters: '. . . When I contemplate this vast concourse, and when I think of all that this hall given by our noble Chancellor—(cheers)—represents, then I cannot but feel that through this hall tonight there stalks the figure of old Dominie Sampson raising his hands and saying "Prodigious!" . . .'

Begun in state, wrote Neil Munro, the occasion 'ended somewhat drolly—which, after all, is the sign of success in all festivity, for ere its close half the company found themselves too far off and too much wrapped in the cloud of smoked tobacco to hear or see with certainty who spoke from the platform . . .' Andrew Carnegie, honorary Doctor of Laws,[1] proposing the toast of the City of Aberdeen, announced: '. . . I have given the eloquent speech which I had prepared, and from which I hoped to elicit your cheers, to the myriad-mouthed Press, and you will read it there in full tomorrow morning . . .' In the printed speech he referred not to a Scott character, but even more appropriately to a local Aberdonian worthy: '. . . You had in olden time a famous "Davie do a'thing",

---

[1] Ibid. pp. 137–8 (describing how at the graduation ceremony Andrew Carnegie was never actually 'capped'): 'Mr Carnegie, answering to his name, rose promptly and mounted the platform. But the emotion of the moment was for once his master. He looked up at the face of old Strathcona; their eyes met, and we knew that, for the instant, the whole world was lost to them. Mr. Carnegie instantly held out his hand and the Chancellor took it; but in doing so, he laid down the Mystic Cap and thus it happened that Mr. Carnegie was never created a Doctor! . . .'

but had your task of this week devolved upon him it is to be feared Davie would have found one thing beyond his powers. And what would Davie have thought had he been called upon to erect this hall in a few days, and what of the man capable of conceiving the idea of having such a structure which would have cracked his lamp had even Aladdin attempted it? The Chancellor wished to dine a few friends; and numerous as is this company, reaching almost the three thousand, they are only a few of the mighty host of Strathcona friends whom to know is to love . . . Is it not positively amazing what the Scot can grow to imagine, undertake, and accomplish if caught young enough and transplanted to the stimulating climate and conditions of Canada, the home of many of our English-speaking race? The North American continent appears the most fruitful developing ground in the world for the human plant provided it is started right—that means among the heather. Whether it be a railroad across the continent to the Pacific, or a monster hall in Aberdeen, it's all the same to the transplanted Lord Chancellor, who inherits the virtues of both lands and the foibles of neither . . .'

NORTHERN PACIFIC—GREAT NORTHERN—UNION PACIFIC

It has been mentioned above (p. 131) that following the 1897 reorganization of the Northern Pacific, Hill was disappointed with the measure of control accorded to him by virtue of his own and his friends' participation. Although the position of the road itself immediately improved, Hill was not satisfied that the results hoped for were being achieved under the chairmanship of Edward D. Adams, advised by the Morgan firm's Charles H. Coster. The latter, described as "a white-faced, nervous figure, hurrying from directors' meeting to directors' meeting; at evening carrying home his portfolio of corporation problems for the night"[1] suffered a breakdown in mid-1898 and died in March 1900. Hill wrote to J. P. Morgan in the Fall of 1898:

The sole object of myself and friends in signing the London agreement with your house and the Deutsche Bank was to bring together as nearly as possible the general policy of the Northern Pacific and the Great Northern, so that both companies could be operated on such lines of general policy as would preserve their mutual independence and allow each one to discharge all its duties to itself and to the public in such a

---

[1] Allen, op. cit. p. 104, quoting John Moody.

manner as to avoid unnecessary expenditure of money either in building
new lines or in the operation of existing lines. We believed this could only
be done by the holding of a large and practically a controlling interest
in both companies by the same parties.[1]

Gaspard Farrer's letter to Arthur Gwinner of the Deutsche
Bank of 21 July 1897 indicates that Mount Stephen had continued
in correspondence with the latter, tying up loose ends. Many years
later, Farrer was to tell the Northern Pacific president: '. . .
(Mount Stephen) was a firm friend in past days to GN and NP as well, and
did as much as anyone to bring the management of the two
properties together after NP was reorganised in the nineties . . .'[2]
On 10 November 1897 Farrer had written to Louis Hill of a long
interview which Mount Stephen and he had had that morning
with Adams, just back from Berlin and 'in good spirits, possibly
the effect of the refresher which we understand Mr. Morgan
presented to him from the coffers of the Northern Pacific . . .'
They had discussed one of the bones of contention between the
Northern Pacific and the Great Northern, the Fosston branch
from the iron-ore producing area on Lake Superior into Duluth
(see above p. 136). Adams had 'expressed cordial concurrence' in
James J. Hill's view that the Fosston extension was no breach of
the London agreement, that it had from the first been assented to
by those representing N.P. interests. Farrer had got the impression
that the N.P. chairman's main concern at that time was the settlement in New York city, as a representative of the road, of Colonel
Daniel S. Lamont, lately President Cleveland's Secretary for War.
'. . . I had heard before leaving America that he had arranged to
take up his residence there, and I confess I was then, and still am,
unable to see of what use he could be to the Company, except in
St. Paul and on the line of road. We presume, however, that the
step was taken with your father's approval and that he has good
reasons for it; perhaps when you write you would let us know what
it all means'. Farrer pursued these, among other topics in a letter
to J. J. Hill of 26 November 1897, acknowledging Hill's analysis
of the Northern Pacific's annual report. He ruefully commented
'. . . the Company's statement and implications show that the old
leaven is still there, and the sale of fresh securities still regarded as

[1] Pyle on *Hill*, vol. 2, p. 28.
[2] Gaspard Farrer Letter Books, Farrer to Howard Elliott, 6 February 1922. (Elliott
had returned to the presidency of the Northern Pacific.)

the legitimate method of raising funds instead of looking to the road's earnings'. Referring to the 'refresher' which had raised the spirits of Adams he continued: 'J. P. Morgan has recently sold here $1 million Prior Lien 4s . . .'—supposedly on behalf of his own firm—'and I hope is the result of converting General Mortgage 6s, and does not imply fresh borrowing . . .' On 1 December 1897 Farrer expressed satisfaction with Hill's letter of 22 November regarding Great Northern and Northern Pacific developments and proposed to send it on to Mount Stephen, then honeymooning in Paris: 'He will be specially interested to hear what you say as to your relations with J. P. Morgan & Co. and as to the position of Mr. Lamont'. Morgan had just sailed that afternoon but was expected back at the end of the month.

From time to time during 1898 Farrer kept his correspondents *au fait* with market trends in Northern Pacific: to Harvey Cooke of Manchester he wrote on 3 January that as to the dividend on the Preferred shares they were likely to do as well as, or better than his firm had forecast in October; they would themselves sooner hold N.P. than Canadian Pacific Preferred at equal prices, yet C.P. was selling at par and N.P. at 60. 'I do not in any way wish to detract from C.P. Preference Stock, but I am convinced that N.P. Preferred and Common are both selling below their values'. He told Oliver Northcote on 2 March: '. . . I am quite keen on Northern Pacific Preferred Shares and General Mortgage Bonds at the existing prices of 65 and 63 London respectively . . .' In February these had risen higher but by 19 March he was telling Cooke that there had since been a relapse; it seemed unlikely there would be any dividend on the Ordinary shares, though some prospect of this in the autumn depending on harvest results and other factors, including political; 'but as we adopted what is for us an unusual practice of recommending a share as a speculative venture I am anxious to put you in possession of the figures as regards the property, so far as they are known or we can estimate them'. On 5 May he assured him that they would pay the full 4 per cent dividend on the Preferred but that on the Ordinary was still uncertain. He wrote to Louis Hill on 18 May that Gwinner forecast a net surplus for the year of $3 million, after paying the Preferred dividend, but favoured putting this into a guarantee fund for future Preferred dividends 'and leaving the Common shareholders to subsist on hope'. On 4 June he told Louis that Morgans had that week sold the last of the 40,000 N.P. Preferred stock, and on 21 June commended Louis' 'conservative views' on the N.P. dividend distribution; it would be time enough to consider a dividend on the Common stock when a bumper crop was assured. He reported to Cooke on 4 August 1898 that N.P. continued to do well; those who had bought the securities since the reorganization had no cause for complaint and it was possible these might become worth a good deal more than at present. This cautious forecast—at a time when the early success of the reorganized Union Pacific was one indication that prospects for railroads in general were favourable—stemmed from a recognition that although the Northern Pacific property had great potential, Farrer was conscious of undercurrents of dissatisfaction and of the mounting frustrations weighing upon J. J. Hill.

On 25 November 1898 Farrer wrote more frankly to W. Stewart Tod of the New York firm of J. Kennedy Tod. He felt that the N.P. Common stock was then marked as high as it merited. There might, on the other hand, be a 4 or 5 per cent dividend any day if only the N.P.'s differences with the Great Northern—at the moment over the Oregon Railway and Navigation Company—were settled. He added that this particular case might readily be settled if Hill were agreeable. It was, however, being rumoured that Hill and his friends had decided to liquidate their N.P. holdings; if this were true the effect on the price might last for a considerable time. It was 'a monstrous pity' that Hill had failed to inspire J. P. Morgan and the Deutsche Bank people with sufficient confidence in his fairness to the N.P. property to persuade them to hand it over to his care, but it was now evident that they would never willingly run the risk. Regarding one of the other points at issue—that of the Lewiston extension (to connect the south-eastern extremity of Washington Territory with the main line)—Farrer believed that Charles F. Mellen, President of the Northern Pacific, was in the right. He wrote further to Tod on 30 November that neither Mount Stephen nor he had heard lately from Hill as to what he was doing with his N.P. stock. In reply to a query from Tod, Farrer said he was satisfied that whatever Hill might have done with his own holding, he had certainly advised some of his American friends to lighten theirs. 'This I would not care to cable but write it now for your own information only. This news was a surprise to us as we had hitherto thought his talk against Northern Pacific merely the consequence of irritation at being baulked of obtaining control. However we concluded that we had better act cautiously and as our prices opened a dollar above parity, we had no doubt in determining to leave the business alone for the present: though I still think the time will come to buy as an obstinate devil like J. P. M. is not likely to be treated to a game of this kind and he has a long enough purse to back his obstinacy. Today there has been heavy selling here on the rumour that J. J. Hill had severed his connection and sold his holdings. If true it is a pity that he has allowed his temper to get away with him . . .' It was not true.

As regards the Oregon Railway and Navigation Company, since it was last mentioned (pp. 19–22) the position had again changed. The Union Pacific, in receivership, had lost control and while the latter was in process of reorganization the Northern Pacific, jointly with Kuhn, Loeb and Company, had acquired 38,000 shares of O.R. & N. Preferred stock and meant to buy more in order to hold a clear majority.[1] Having discussed these plans with E. D. Adams and C. H. Coster, Jacob Schiff wrote on 9 February 1897 to J. J. Hill asking for his approval by wire:

Mr. Coster thought it would be best that the Northern Pacific, the Great Northern, the Union Pacific and the Oregon Short Line should each own and hold one fourth of the stock acquired and to be acquired. In view, however, of the efforts which it is reported have recently been made in Boston to pool the holdings of the Oregon Short Line stock in the interest of the Chicago, Burlington and Quincy (without much avail), I suggested it might be dangerous to admit the Oregon Short Line, for the present at least, into ownership of the Oregon Railroad and Navigation Company. This view was, upon discussion, adopted by both of the other gentlemen, and we thereupon concluded that all interests would be best served if the Northern Pacific retained one quarter of the purchase already made and received a like proportion in further acquisitions of stock; that Kuhn, Loeb and Company cede to the Great Northern Company a like one-fourth in present holdings and future purchases, and that the other one half remain for the present as an undivided interest, in the ownership of J. P. Morgan and Company and Kuhn, Loeb and Company, to be sold at their own discretion later to the Union Pacific and the Oregon Short Line (either or both) provided the purpose of the purchase can thereby be accomplished—viz, (1) the securing of the permanent independence of the Oregon Railroad and Navigation Company; (2) the election of a

[1] Adler on *Schiff*, vol. 1, p. 88.

management which shall be pledged to the maintenance of rates, traffic at all times to be directed by shortest routes.[1]

These aims, however, were not to be attainable, partly because the Northern Pacific management seemed determined to pursue an independent course in the western states, building rather than coming to terms over existing lines. E. H. Harriman, meanwhile, was becoming a dominant figure in the Union Pacific, demonstrating his faith in the enterprise by largely adding to his own financial stake in it. Among his colleagues on the Board was James Stillman. Events were gradually building up to the situation where the personal relations between Harriman and Hill were to be a vital factor, a factor which caused a good deal of uneasiness in Hill's London friends, remote from the scene of action. Early in 1898 the Union Pacific proceeded to reacquire some of the subsidiary lines which it had lost, and hoped eventually to regain control of the Oregon Short Line and Oregon Railroad and Navigation Company.[2] In May 1898 Harriman was elected chairman and chief executive officer of the Union Pacific; his relations with Jacob Schiff were to become closer, because of Kuhn, Loeb and Company's involvement with the Union Pacific, as Hill's became more tenuous. Farrer's letters of November 1898, quoted above, were therefore written at a time of some uncertainty.

On 3 May 1899 Hill and Schiff sailed for America together after the successful Baltimore and Ohio operation. How one wishes one could have overheard the shipboard conversations of this period! About this time the Northern Pacific and the Oregon Railroad and Navigation Company were at odds in the Riparia–Lewiston district, between the Columbia River and the south-east border of Washington with Idaho. Schiff wrote on 19 July 1899 to Harriman explaining what had been done during his absence in England to keep the Northern Pacific people from stealing a march, adding: 'At the coming election of the Navigation company, the Union Pacific will get into undisputed control, so that you personally can thereafter act as chairman of the executive committees of the three companies covering the line from Omaha to Portland' (the important Pacific connection).[3] There was further correspondence between

---

[1] Ibid. pp. 88–89.
[2] George Kennan, *E. H. Harriman: A Biography*, Boston, 1922, 2 vols., vol. 1, pp. 130–7.
[3] Adler, op. cit. vol. 1, p. 96.

the two and on 9 August Schiff told Harriman: 'Since writing you on Monday we have completed negotiations for the purchase of about 23,000 shares of Oregon Navigation Preferred Stock held by the Northern Pacific ... I became convinced that there was no use in fooling any longer about this matter, and that it was unsafe to permit this stock to remain in the hands of the Northern Pacific, having learned that some people were making the endeavour to purchase the Navigation Preferred Stock not only from the Northern Pacific but also from Mr. Hill ... Considering it most important that this large block of stock should not remain or go into hands where hereafter an attempt might be made to interfere with future plans for a unification of the Union Pacific properties, I thought it best to acquire it while we had an opportunity to do so, and I think, aside from every other consideration, that, based on the Stock's intrinsic value, we have made a very good purchase. As we shall now meet very soon personally again, of which I am most glad, there is no need that I go into further detail about this matter today, but I hope and believe you will be pleased with my action'.

Farrer's letter to Hill of 13 September 1899, on Northern Pacific matters, shows no awareness of these developments, but neither does he comment adversely at any later date. He reported the recent visit to London of Arthur Gwinner 'very bullish on Northern Pacific'; land sales had been unprecedented and within three months the last of the old 6 per cent General Mortgage Bonds would have disappeared; the next balance sheet would show $2,400,000 paid out of earnings for special improvements, though they hoped to reduce this sum to $1 million yearly in the future. Gwinner considered a 4 per cent dividend on the Common stock assured for next year and Charles F. Mellen, the President, had even hinted that more might be forthcoming for both Common and Preferred. Farrer commented: 'All this I hope is true as it will mean prosperity for Great Northern also. Not a word about possible reduction of rates and the effect on future net earnings; perhaps however this will not come while business continues on the boom; but the more I think over the matter the clearer I see that it is senseless to draw a hard and fast North and South line at Chicago and expect rates West to continue permanently twice as high as those East'. He wrote to Gwinner on 30 October 1899 acknowledging the Northern Pacific's 'splendid report'.

HILL-HARRIMAN RELATIONS

On 12 September 1899, meanwhile, Hill had written to Harriman, first sending the letter to Schiff for his information, suggesting a detailed plan for harmony of interests:

The change in plan of operation made necessary by the sale of the Northern Pacific's holdings of Navigation Company preferred shares, and that Company's withdrawal from the agreement, leaves the situation as regards the relations of the Great Northern and the Navigation Company in a position of too great uncertainty to be allowed to continue for any length of time beyond what is necessary to re-arrange a basis for jointly operating the Navigation Company's lines. As you are well aware, I have always considered it to be for the best interests of all concerned that the Union Pacific, Northern Pacific, and Great Northern should be placed as regards the Navigation Company where the interests of the first-named would be best served by a plan providing practically for the joint ownership of the Navigation Company in such a manner as to secure to it the support and benefit of all the traffic of the other three companies. During my recent conversation with you on the subject, you spoke of the desirability of the Union Pacific having its own line to Portland and the Pacific Coast. The same is true of the Great Northern, and to a less extent of the Northern Pacific. I think it goes without argument that each should and will have access to Portland and the Pacific Coast. I can speak with certainty for the Great Northern in that regard. An arrangement for all three companies to use the Navigation Company's lines would necessitate conditions of a permanent character, giving to each company as nearly as may be practicable under all the circumstances the same rights and benefits as would accrue under separate lines owned by each. This would include equal conditions applying to business east or west through the Huntington and Spokane gateways, and an equal division of the business which could properly be divided between the three companies. Local business of each of the three companies to and from the lines of the Navigation Company would readily take care of itself, as also the local business of the Navigation Company.

I think, with such an arrangement as I have outlined, the Northern Pacific would be willing to arrange for the business of the Union Pacific to go over its lines between Portland and Puget Sound. Possibly the better arrangement would be to include the Portland and Puget Sound business in the general arrangement.

In looking over this plan, it may appear to you that the Great Northern is assuming a great deal when it has not a mile of railroad at this time in the territory occupied by the Navigation Company, and the Union

Pacific has a large majority through the Short Line, of the shares of the Navigation Company, but I may urge on the other hand that the Great Northern would bring to the Navigation Company the valuable traffic of about 5,500 miles of railway in a new country which is very rapidly growing, and most of which the Navigation Company could not secure in any other way. This also applies to most of the Northern Pacific's 5,000 miles. The Great Northern and the Northern Pacific would also become in a measure guarantors of the bonds and stocks of the Navigation Company to the extent of whatever sum was agreed upon as the value of the Navigation Company, and this sum would be in any event not far from twice as much as it would cost to duplicate the property today. In other words, the owners of the Navigation Company would be protected in the occupation of the country, substantially without competition or diversion of the business, which one or more lines would greatly reduce and ultimately in my opinion force a reduction of the capital represented in the Navigation Company's property. I know that country fairly well, and I think that with 5 million dollars I could build a much better line from our road into Portland; and with, say, 2 million more, reach the most productive sections of the Navigation Company. This would call for an annual charge of, say, $300,000, which I feel very sure is much less than we would pay the Navigation Company for doing our business under such a plan as I have outlined.

I sincerely trust that you will take what I have said herein as a plain statement of the case as I look at it, and I also ask that you will endeavour to have the matter brought to an early conclusion, to the end that we may all shape our affairs to work to a common end and bring about such an arrangement as will be of permanent good to all concerned. If it is the wish of yourself and friends to hold the Navigation Company for your own use, and not to make it available for the Northern Pacific and ourselves, you are certainly in a position to do with it as you may deem best, or otherwise, and I only ask that we be informed at as early a date as is convenient whether we shall look forward to some such arrangement as I have outlined, or whether we shall take the matter up outside of the Navigation Company. I have included the Northern Pacific, for the reason that I would be unwilling to assume the burden of the Navigation Company jointly with the Union Pacific and leave the Northern Pacific free to divide the traffic as it would be able to do with an investment so much less than the Navigation Company's that the latter would be unable to meet it. I hope you will consider this fully and entirely on a business basis with a view to enabling us to arrive at something practical when I am again in New York, which I hope will be about the middle of October.

Pyle adds that Hill had still to convince the Northern Pacific management, '. . . big men . . . not . . . steeped in practical experience as he was . . .' Hill wrote to one of them (presumably Morgan's) in October spelling out his basic plan: '. . . I am pushing the question of a joint control of Oregon Railway and Navigation by the NP, UP and GN, to the end that we may all have the use of the Navigation Company's lines on fair and equal terms in perpetuity. This would undoubtedly be better than to build independent lines to Portland, if it can be done on a proper basis; otherwise it would be better to build'.[1]

Schiff, according to his biographer, did not believe that the differences between the two men were irreconcilable, and wrote to Hill on 25 September:

I duly received your letter with enclosure for Mr. Harriman, which I have delivered. Mr. Harriman has been much impressed by your suggestion, though, frank as I am always with you, I should add that I think he felt somewhat irritated by the mandatory tone in which your letter to him was written. I explained to him that you wrote in the midst of your preparations for your departure on your annual inspection tour, and that no doubt all you intended to do was to impress him with the earnestness you felt about the subject matter of your letter. I think Mr. Harriman understands this now, and I believe I am justified in saying that, aside from his thorough desire to work in harmony with you and have your friendship, able as he is himself, he has always recognized your great ability and the value of your experience and advice.

I have not the least doubt that there will be no difficulty whatsoever in making a satisfactory arrangement between the Oregon Navigation and Great Northern Companies. It is manifestly to the interest of the Navigation Company to have so valuable a connection as the Great Northern, while to the latter the connection with the Oregon Navigation Company for Portland and other points will be far superior to any lines it could construct and terminals it would have to acquire. The difficult element, as we all know, will be the Northern Pacific, with its aggressive and often intolerant attitude, but I believe and hope that with the influence you can yourself bring to bear, . . . [sic] and with the reasonable expectations of Mr. Harriman and the executive committee of the Union Pacific, it should not be so very difficult to bring the Northern Pacific management to a sense of the responsibility they should have, to prevent them from building needless duplicate lines, and to enter into such

[1] Pyle, op. cit. pp. 42–7. Hill's letter is quoted in full in view of the subsequent involvement of Mount Stephen and Farrer in the relations between Hill and Harriman. Pyle calls it 'an honest, businesslike presentation of the facts, not without occasional acidity and disclosure of possibilities of trouble if anybody wanted to make trouble. It undoubtedly affected profoundly the views of Mr. Harriman' (p. 46).

arrangements as should be equally satisfactory to them and the Oregon Navigation company.[1]

In 1899 Harriman had also become a director of the Baltimore and Ohio, and Schiff added: 'To guide the policies to be adopted in Baltimore and Ohio, you and Mr Harriman should likewise join hands, and, if you do so, with the experience you both have, I feel entirely confident as to the future of the property'.[2] Less than three weeks later, on 12 October 1899, Schiff wrote to Robert Fleming in London: '... The Union Pacific is doing splendidly, but as to that, all railroads are making fine showings ... The Union Pacific has now again gotten firm hold of the Oregon Short Line and the Oregon Railroad and Navigation Company, has (gathered) into its treasury practically all of the Common and Preferred Shares of the Oregon Navigation and all of the Stock of the Short Line, and also the latter company's A and B Income Bonds. The net earnings of the three companies for the past fiscal year have been almost $16 million, the fixed charges something like $6·7 million, showing something like $9 million surplus for the Preferred and Common Stocks of the Union Pacific. That is not a bad showing for a road which was sold under foreclosure less than two years ago'.[3]

Harriman's biographer Kennan describes how in 1899 the Union Pacific reacquired the Oregon Short Line and at the same time secured control of the Oregon Railroad and Navigation Company, thus increasing its mileage from 2848 to 5391 and recovering its lost outlet on the Pacific coast at Portland.[4] The control of the O. R. & N. was effected by issuing $27,460,000 of new U.P. Common stock and exchanging it for O.S.L. stock on the basis of share for share. As the Short Line owned a majority of the stock of the R. & N. Company, the U.P. thus obtained control of both roads. Later in 1899 the U.P. increased its own Preferred stock from $75 million to $100 million and its Common from $88,460,100 to $96,178,700 for the purpose of securing complete ownership of the two Oregon lines. The new shares of Preferred were used in retiring the Oregon companies' bonds, and the new Common shares were exchanged for all the stock of the R. & N. Company that the Short Line did not already possess. By virtue of these operations the U.P.

[1] Adler, op. cit. vol. 1, p. 89.
[2] Ibid. p. 144.
[3] Ibid. p. 98.
[4] Kennan, op. cit. vol. 1, p. 164 and F/N1, quoting *Commercial and Financial Chronicle*, 22 July, 2 September and 13 October 1899.

12

became owner of 98 per cent of the Oregon Short Line and 91 per cent of the Oregon Railroad and Navigation Company. Kennan adds that the Union Pacific spent large sums on the Oregon Short Line and R. & N. Company, bringing the lines up to the new U.P. standard.[1]

On 6 November 1899 Schiff wrote to C. H. Coster, J. P. Morgan's Northern Pacific representative: 'I can assure you, there is every desire on the part of Mr. Harriman, ourselves and the executive committee of the Union Pacific, to arrive at a permanent understanding with Northern Pacific and Great Northern interests, and I cannot see that there should be any difficulty in finding a basis just and reasonable to all interests concerned'.[2] Schiff continued, writes Adler, to 'act as a buffer between the two contenders', Harriman and Hill.[3] He told Hill on 29 January 1900:

As to your very ingenious Oregon Railway and Navigation proposition, I am going over it with Mr. Harriman and am trying to impress him with your ideas. This must and can be settled between you and Mr. Harriman, and I know there will be no difficulty about reaching something like your idea, provided you can get the Northern Pacific people to come into line. Mr. Harriman thinks, and in this I believe he is right, that it would be more desirable that the ownership of the stock should be divided up between the Union Pacific, the Great Northern and the Northern Pacific, in proportion to the sums they are to guarantee, and that the leases and guarantees should be made after division of such ownership, which would make the entire arrangement ironclad for all time. My own opinion is that the Northern Pacific should put its lines from Seattle to Portland into the arrangement, so that no necessity should be created hereafter for the Great Northern and Union Pacific, either or both, to build a competing line between Portland and Seattle.[4]

Hill was again planning to visit London and then Paris that year. Gaspard Farrer wrote to him on 16 March, acknowledging a 'many paged letter' in his own hand of 5 February, and saying: 'I do hope if you are ever good enough to write again you will remember to use your typewriter and save yourself'. The Great Northern showing was excellent: 'The only cloud on the sky that I can see at present is the low price of wheat and the high price of all commodities that a farmer needs'. He went on: 'I shall come out some time this year—if Parisian tourists have not already filled available

[1] Kennan, op. cit. vol 1, p. 166.   [2] Adler, op. cit. vol. 1, p. 98.
[3] Ibid. p. 90.   [4] Ibid. p. 91.

berths—and nothing would please me better than to accompany you on your return if my work here enables me to leave at that time. We here are all looking forward to your visit . . .' Finance business in the City was 'absolutely dead outside the War Loan. It looks as if we were in for a period of dearish money, accumulating evidence that the banking world has expanded its loans as far as it prudently can with the present state of gold . . .'

NORTHERN PACIFIC: TOWARDS FIRMER CONTROL

Hill sailed for England on 25 April and spent at least two days in London in the first week of May before going on to Paris. Gaspard expected to accompany him back to America later in the month. This was no doubt another period of endless talk and planning of which little or nothing was committed to paper, for much was to happen before these friends met again. The Northern Pacific must have loomed large in their conversations. Just before Hill landed in England Gaspard sent a long letter to Mount Stephen on 1 May 1900 commenting on, and returning, correspondence that had passed between Hill and the late C. H. Coster on the points then at issue between the Northern Pacific and the Great Northern— mainly alleged invasions of territory. Gaspard admitted that his comments must be read with reservations as they lacked the understanding that could be reached in personal interviews. He enclosed the latest maps of the two railroad systems—these are now at the end of the letterbook —'to show clearly the effect of each party's aggression on the other property I have marked in blue pencil on the Northern Pacific map the alleged Great Northern's aggressions of which Mr. Coster complains, and on the Great Northern map the alleged Northern Pacific's aggressions of which Mr. Hill complains'. One of the matters that demanded clarification concerned the acquisition of the St. Paul and Duluth Railroad: this came under Coster's complaints against the Great Northern, whereas Gaspard noted that the previous day's cables from New York had announced that control had been bought by the N.P. He proceeded to go through the lists in detail, conceding here and there that one of the respective complainants had a point, or that, on the other hand, the complaint was not justified: for example, that the plans for the Great Northern's Fosston branch antedated the London agreement and were acquiesced in by the Northern Pacific representatives.

Gaspard then continued:

The above deals with the several offences of either party which are still in dispute. There remains the Spokane Falls and Northern purchase and transfer to the G.N. which Mr. Coster puts forward as an act of virtue on the part of the N.P. and as evidence of its desire to live up to the London agreement even to its own detriment. I am unable to understand Mr. Coster's claim to the territory which this road serves as being as much N.P.'s as G.N. ... perhaps the best proof that the claim is not seriously made is the fact of Messrs. Morgan's action in transferring the control to the G.N., any other course must have led to open rupture between N.P. and G.N.

It will be seen from the above that the only two important extensions or acquisitions are:—

1. the G.N.'s Fosston line about which Mr. Coster was under misapprehension and

2. the Spokane Falls and Northern now happily disposed of. All others are comparatively small affairs about which a settlement should be easily reached if each party approaches the differences with good temper and a determination to settle . . .

Leaving details aside there is the larger question of the actual control of the N.P.; and on this subject it is unfortunate that the understanding which the Deutsche Bank and presumably Messrs. Morgan entertain is not that which Mr. Hill and you believed to have been reached. If Mr. Gwinner refers to the London agreement as the interpretation and limitation of that understanding, I would ask him if he thinks it reasonable to suppose that Mr. Hill, Lord Strathcona and yourself would at a critical financial time have subscribed large cash funds and otherwise assisted passively and actively to prevent dismemberment of the Northern Pacific system and to rehabilitate its finances for the sake of that degree of control which the Great Northern today possesses.

On 12 May 1900 Farrer wrote to John Sterling (Hill was then in Paris) acknowledging a letter of 27 April inviting him to stay with him in New York. Farrer's plans were still unsettled: he had meant to return with Hill 'but if the Boer resistance collapses as looks more probable the last few days we might have a burst of active business here which I could not well afford to miss . . .' He wrote again on 19 May that he hoped to sail on 25 August or 1 September:

News of Mafeking relief (from Pretoria only so far) reached London last night at 9.30 and at 4 a.m. this morning the crowds were still cheering in the streets. They have begun again now 11.a.m. and all main thoroughfares are surging with singing shouting flagwaving masses. I have never seen anything like it. The war has been hateful to us from the outset but the pluck and example of that little garrison is legitimate grounds for pride and enthusiasm.

Hill in Paris was pursuing business more than pleasure: in response to a telegram on the subject of Northern Pacific Bonds Gaspard replied on 15 May: 'You have never mentioned the amount of Bonds which you had yourself or were willing to spare, and there is nothing in your letter (to which you refer me in your telegram) that gives me any indication. If you will wire me in the morning the amount you can spare *for the Boss and my firm to divide between us* I will cable the payment to Nichols . . .' The side-heading *N.P. Bonds* was provided by Gaspard. Under the heading *G.N.* he wrote: 'The Boss has been down here this morning and has shown me your letter with the 9 months' figures.—You should not worry about the fall in the price of the shares—I don't believe it will frighten holders here: we have not had ourselves to sell or heard of a single share being sold in London; and we have had quite a number of little buying orders (executed in New York): not amounting to much in total but good buyers who are likely to hold. I find that eliminating holders of 5,000 shares and upwards the average of the balance is 280 shares—I would like to see it under 100 and it will get there before long . . .' The following day he acknowledged another message from Paris with the offer of Hill's interest: 'the Boss and my firm are very glad to take $125,000 each and we have today cabled to make the payments to Nichols . . .'

On 19 May 1900 Farrer wrote again to Hill in Paris: Hill had apparently been in consultation with Arthur Gwinner of the Deutsche Bank over the new scheme that was in his mind regarding control of the Northern Pacific and Farrer was glad to hear that Gwinner was favourable. He agreed there would be no difficulties about getting a party together to buy a block of shares: 'But is this necessary or advisable? If J. P. M. were willing that you should join the Board now with power to nominate a majority within the next year there is something to be said for leaving the voting trust to expire in the ordinary course. The purchase of a big block of shares and concurrent dissolution of the Trust and election of yourself is sure to create the maximum of flurry both in Wall Street and among local legislators'. Writing to a correspondent in Birmingham on 1 June he compared Northern Pacific favourably with Canadian Pacific as an investment: 'N.P. Preference shares are now selling at about 76½ New York'.

Gaspard made his projected visit to America in the autumn, seeing Hill there and returning to England accompanied by young Jim (James Norman Hill). He wrote to Hill on 13 October 1900: '... We had a first-rate trip over and I believe are the only two cheerful persons in the City today; it is difficult to account entirely for the fit of the blues that prevails but I think so far as American affairs are concerned if McKinley is elected we shall quickly see a revival of business. There is no bull account open here'. On 3 November Farrer wrote to James Norman Hill that he had concluded that the recent buying of Northern Pacific Common stock by J. P. Morgan *must* be on his father's account: 'I hope it is'. Jacob Schiff had on 25 October written to Crawford Livingston of St. Paul: 'As to Northern Pacific matters, I know little except that Mr. Hill, in a mysterious manner, hinted that it would not be long before he would control it'. In further letters to Livingston he indicated that he was no longer in Hill's confidence in the matter of Northern Pacific, and told him that it was evident that the Morgan firm was buying a great deal of the Common stock.[1] On 13 November Mount Stephen had received a somewhat cryptic cable from Hill, whereupon Farrer wrote to the latter that he had concluded that this meant that a few weeks or months more would see Hill in virtual control of the N.P.: 'My first thought was for you and one of pleasure that you should obtain your desire—my second for Mrs. Hill and for her feeling at fresh burdens of work undertaken—but I sincerely hope if work will be more worry will be less and that that will bring consolation to her, and compensation to you. It is splendid news for the Great Northern...' The N.P. voting trust had been dissolved.

Farrer wrote to John Sterling on 8 December regarding the Northern Pacific transaction: '... Your letters and messages to Lord Mount Stephen have been of great assistance to my firm and it would give my partners and myself sincere satisfaction if you care to take a participation of 500 shares in the amount allotted us by Mr. Hill and on his terms ... [i.e. at lower than market level] retaining 500 shares from our allotment when Mr. Hill makes delivery to you ...' Gaspard hoped to sail for America that day week ... the N.P./G.N. development had such great possibilities

[1] Ibid. p. 91.

for the future that he was anxious to get the matter straight; he would go first to St. Paul, then return to New York. On 11 December he acknowledged Sterling's cable: 'Bought through Drexel Morgan & Co. on confidential advice Bacon [Robert Bacon was Coster's successor at Morgan's] 4000 Common Stock about 16 5/8 2,600 2nd. Preference about 28¼ two thirds divisible between you and Estevan' [Mount Stephen] and replied that morning: 'Bank have instructions pay you $52,000'. The same day he confirmed that he was sailing for New York on 15 December. Gaspard spent Christmas with the Hill family—a memory he afterwards treasured; what he discussed with Hill is not revealed.

On 26 December 1900 Jacob Schiff wrote from New York to Crawford Livingston: '... Mr. Hill was here from Friday to Sunday and he came to my house just before leaving. I could not exactly make out whether he came here on Erie matters (he went home over the Erie Road), or in connection with other problems in which Morgans and he are interested'. Schiff's biographer comments: 'The former allies had reached the parting of the ways'.[1] Hill had just joined the Board of the Erie Railroad; in response to a query from Sterling Farrer had replied on 8 December that he did not propose to enquire of Hill about this development: Hill might think he wanted a participation on the same favourable terms as with the Northern Pacific. Lord Mount Stephen had agreed with this, adding 'that he attached no importance to Hill's joining the Board (except of course from a market point of view) and would sooner be guided by your judgment in buying Erie securities than by Hill's ...'

Farrer wrote on 12 January 1901 to a friend whom Mount Stephen was accustomed to advise on his investments: 'Lord Mount Stephen's predictions about Northern Pacific Common are quite likely to be realized but I am sure he did not intend to convey that a 6% dividend or any excess of the present rate of 4% was in immediate sight—next year or the year after if all goes well—but another such crop as was experienced last season might postpone an increase even longer ...' He recommended selling and pocketing the profit.

As regards the Northern Pacific, Hill was not yet 'home and dry'. Farrer wrote to him on 23 January 1901 that since his return from America he had been wondering how best to help him on this

[1] Ibid. pp. 91–92.

score: 'Lord Mount Stephen, we and our immediate friends own today some 30 to 40 thousand shares and as in the ordinary course of our business we lend money on the Exchange we propose to make a point of taking in N.P. Shares as collateral and of putting them into our name. I have spoken to John [Baring] who will follow our example and I expect in this way to get voting control of a fair line of the floating stock in this market in addition to our permanent holdings. The floating stock will of course be gradually transferred from our names as investors absorb or the stock gets to your side, but meantime it ought to have temporarily some 50 to 100 thousand shares in name friendly to G.N. which I hope may have the effect of strengthening your position with J. P. M.'

CHECK!

Besides his preoccupation with Northern Pacific Gaspard was beginning to be worried about a forthcoming (1901) Great Northern issue; only gradually did it become apparent that Hill had something else on his mind. On 19 February 1900 Gaspard had reported to 'the Admiral', Lord Clanwilliam, 'the best half-year in the Great Northern's history'. He quoted a recent letter from Hill regarding prospects: making all due allowance for imponderables such as the coming Presidential election, or a turndown in trade, Hill still found 'the underlying elements of our increased traffic practically unaffected, and it seems to me that we must have a continuance of growth'. Three days later Farrer wrote to the Editor of *The Economist*, evidently judging that the half-year's results could be utilized to give a booster to the previous (1899) issue. He reminded him of the last *Economist* article 'which caused wide satisfaction here and in the States' and hoped that 'in the interest of sound finance' the memorandum which he enclosed might be considered of sufficient importance to be used in some form: 'Financing on Share capital has been the exception instead of the rule and any effort in this direction appears to me worthy of encouragement which a notice in your paper would give'. His memorandum read as follows:

The bearing of the train load in Railroad economy is now the subject of comment in almost every American railroad report. Some years ago we drew attention in our columns to the fact that Mr. J. J. Hill President of the Great Northern USA had recognised its importance and commenced the physical reconstruction of his Road which he foresaw was necessary if prosperity was to be maintained under the present day level of transportation rates.

The issue of Great Northern Shares now being offered to existing shareholders at par remind us that the reconstruction of the Company's finances is not less remarkable. During the past few years over $35 million of securities bearing fixed interest have been replaced, and over 700 miles of Road have been constructed or purchased, by the issue of Share Capital. This is the line on which the Company's future financial policy will be shaped; it is in accordance with the best traditions of sound finance and has already reduced the Company's annual fixed charges to a third of the Net earning capacity of the property.

Whether viewed from a physical or financial point of view there is today no Road West of Chicago better fitted to produce cheap transportation or better able to withstand times of *commercial* depression than the Great Northern.

Gaspard invariably tempered his advice to investing friends with a concern for their individual needs, whether for regular income or long term capital appreciation. He told Mount Stephen's secretary, Beverley MacInnes, on 1 June 1900: '... I should consider G.N. Stock an excellent investment at present prices and should not hesitate to buy it either for myself or my friends but it is a *share* which many people do not like and is liable to considerable fluctuations in price according to the speculative feeling in the New York market ...' On 13 October 1900, after his return from America where he had discussed the subject with Hill, he sent the latter a copy of an 'inspired' article in *The Statist* which George Paish, the paper's American railroad leader-writer, had apparently been commissioned to write, after briefing by Farrer. He had asked Paish to call and had given him 'an afternoon of instruction directing his attention more especially to the change in the Capital position of the Company and to the percentage of "fixed charge" and "fixed charge dividends" to net increase now and in 1897' ... (These, he explained to Hill on 13 October, were more easily understood by bankers and brokers than "ton mile" and "train load" statistics.) 'The article so far as marked in blue pencil contains the pith of our talk (bar the care taken of the loading of the *passenger* trains over which I can picture Jim's grim smile) the balance being the writer's own lucubrations'. Paish had altered the figures slightly but it remained accurate enough. 'I hope you will be satisfied and that the horrid expense will be justified. So far as the report is concerned I took that published in the *Chronicle* as the text and cut out what seemed to me of lesser consequence so as to save expense'.

Still ruminating over the statistics of both Great Northern and Northern Pacific, Farrer wrote to James Norman Hill on 25 October 1900 enclosing some figures and wondering 'why the N.P., with some 1,750,000 more helping mileage than the G.N. conducts transportation per train mile all for two cents less'. Without the N.P.'s excess engine mileage the figure would be as low as 57 compared with the G.N.'s 64. He recalled that formerly the G.N. charged a fancy price for carrying coal, recouping itself with dividends from the coal company: was this still the case? He added: 'Lord Mount Stephen has cabled your father fully as to finance and as the two are in accord as to policy we have not troubled to communicate re Sterling Bonds and the market for them here'. Much of Farrer's correspondence with J. N. Hill at this time concerned the Alberta Railway—the old 'Galt road' from Lethbridge to Great Falls—which the G.N. was considering taking over but finally decided against. But on 3 November he returned to the subject of G.N. finance and the forthcoming issue: Mount Stephen and he seemed afraid that this would not be large enough: '. . . You will need it all and it would be a mistake in our judgment to get 10 now and like Oliver Twist be "asking for more" in another twelve months . . .' A week later he was harping on the old string of wider distribution for G.N. securities: the loyalty of old friends, sensitive to the company's needs, would be misplaced if it prevented it from getting enough money. The stock should be allowed to find its own level, the future being sufficiently secure, continued concentration now that amounts were large was a growing weakness: '. . . get strength in distribution . . . Please do not think I refer to Lord Mount Stephen—he is one of the few—the very few—who has the courage to speak out to your father and as regards stock issues thinks the more the merrier—but I know he agrees . . . about distribution'.

Writing to Sterling on other matters on 13 February 1901, Gaspard concluded: 'I believe with Stillman that the whole *share* market is too high and beyond the G.N. and N.P. Shares which we mean to keep I have not a Share of any kind and intend to stand clear . . . We can't imagine why Hill puts off his own issue; the writing on the wall seems writ large to our eyes'. He still did not appear to realize what was occupying Hill although there is a clue implicit in his letter to J. N. Hill of the same date. After reporting a piece of hearsay about the Northern Pacific: 'The Deutsche Bank recently issued a circular offering to exchange N.P. Voting Trust certificates for depositors' certificates and in one case . . . returned depositor certificates in the name of its own nominee instead of that of the owner'—he wrote: 'I shall shed no tears if the Milwaukee deal falls through . . .' For some years Hill had been concerned to find a rail connection that would take the Great Northern into Chicago: a possibility now offering was the Chicago, Milwaukee and St. Paul, but Farrer (as in the case of Hill's desire for control of the N.P.) instinctively shrank from further empire-building with all its attendant anxieties. He told J. N. Hill: 'We are quite anxious for April the date which your father tells us he proposes to make his own issue; it seems to me as if speculation in New York had passed all reasonable bounds and I shall sleep easier when the G.N. has obtained its money and got out of debt, though if half the stories current here are true $25 million at 65 will not get or at least keep it out of debt for long. I am now staggered at my own moderation in suggesting $60 million as the amount of fresh capital money you would require over the next five years! . . .' On 19 March he was able to tell the Admiral that the Great Northern was to issue a circular in New York that morning 'offering shareholders the right to subscribe at par less 20 (say 80) one new share for every four old shares'.

Farrer had observed to Sterling on 13 March 1901: 'I see Hill is in New York'. On the 23rd he wrote to him: '. . . It will be interesting to see what truth there is in Hill's Burlington story; it is pretty plain that any lease made at this late period of the day will be no gift to the lessors, and I expect that you will agree with me in thinking that the assumption of the liability it would involve (liability for supervision and management as much as pecuniary) is hardly a bull point for either N.P. or G.N. . . .' The same day he acknowledged Sterling's cable of the 20th: 'Can learn nothing definite except that Hill tells me confidentially that it is probable that the Burlington and Quincy will be leased by N.P. and G.N. Railways'. Acknowledging Sterling's letter of the 2nd, Farrer wrote on 12 April: 'You are right that the Q. purchase is considered a bull point in the present temper of the market and on paper rightly so, but past experience has shown that in rocky times the success or failure of the big railway properties has depended on management and supervision, and I confess to being neither big enough nor bold enough for these gigantic combinations, and am sufficiently parochial to be content with the modest profits from the 12,000 odd miles of G.N. and N.P. . . .'

Farrer's letter to Hill of 20 April 1901 was the diplomatic Gaspard at his best, exasperation kept well in hand: 'Lord Mount Stephen writes me that he has received a cable from you announcing that the Chicago, Burlington and Quincy has passed under the joint control of the Great Northern and Northern Pacific . . .' While protesting that no amount of profit for Hill's shareholders was worth the cost of a night's rest or day's extra work for him '— we all owe too much already to your unceasing care and devotion; —' he continued 'however the decision is yours and is made and I can but hope that it will involve less sacrifice for you than would at this distance appear . . .' His next thought was for Mrs. Hill, and there was a kind message about Gertrude, one of their daughters, and another observation on the family circle. There follows the cryptic remark: '. . . if ever again you talk to me about Jonahs I shall confront you with a Theban Mount Stephen'. He went on: 'The Admiral writes me from Cannes about the new shares: so far as I can make out he is ready and anxious to sell his last shirt sooner than miss any of his allotment. The Boss has offered me Metis for the summer . . . I hope I may see you . . .'

VI

Northern Securities: hostage to fortune

ON 23 March 1901 Gaspard Farrer had written to John Sterling:
'. . . The Boss writes me piteous letters from Cannes; he hated
going there, and is obviously bored to extinction by the life; but
Lady Gian was really looking seedy and needed a change and I
hope it will have done her good . . .' and on 12 April: '. . . The
Boss is back and is looking well and he tells me Lady Gian (is)
much better and with appetite returned. Unfortunately it is certain
that he will not go out himself: but he has again offered me Metis
and I am greatly tempted to go. Would there be any chance of
your coming up there with me? It would be delightful if you
would'.

The plans for Metis went ahead: Mount Stephen's former
butler, Cole, was to sail on 6 June for Montreal on the *Parisian* to
arrange for provisions and to prepare and run the establishment.
Farrer was to follow in the *Lucania* to New York on 15 June,
accompanied by his brother-in-law, Commander Edward Hunter-
Blair, R.N. (Retd.)—known thereafter to the Metis circle as 'the
Captain'—'an excellent fellow and good company'; Farrer told
Sterling on 1 May 'you will like him'. He had asked Cecil Baring,
then based in New York, but the latter was to be in England at the
time. Mount Stephen thought there was 'plenty of fishing for three
and possibly four and has ordered three canoes . . .' John Turnbull,
Mount Stephen's man of business in Montreal, was to help with
arrangements, including delivery of a small sailing yacht, to be
hired or purchased for Farrer in Montreal. Sterling would join
them on the journey from New York to Montreal, arriving at Metis
on Monday 28 June.

Gaspard had dined on 30 April with Lord Revelstoke (John
Baring), just back from America, to hear the latest news. Baring
had met both Sterling and his great friend there, and Gaspard told

Sterling: 'his personal feeling towards Stillman is of the pleasantest and he has returned convinced that Stillman is the strongest man he has met in New York . . .' 'Visitors', wrote Stillman's biographer Burr, '. . . left his office with a great sense of confidence. Always at the back of his mind there was the wish to stand well in the eyes of men whom he respected, there was the hope, the idea of power . . . he always admired the English bankers and their sturdy sense of caste; . . .'[1] Stillman did not admire Andrew Carnegie, whose steel interests had just passed with others to J. P. Morgan's giant new U.S. Steel Corporation, giving rise to a wave of speculation on both sides of the Atlantic which Gaspard Farrer deplored. The latter concluded his letter of 1 May to Sterling: 'Am glad you have got a good allotment in the Burlington syndicate. It ought to prove good business'.

Farrer was to write only once more, on 24 May, to Sterling before sailing, and between these two May letters much had happened. He explained that 'Northern Pacific and such like matters' had been occupying his attention to the exclusion of all other correspondence. '. . . I shall have much to tell you when we meet but shall leave it till we meet—apart from the serious business aspects it has served as an interesting study in human nature— not always edifying though sometimes ludicrous . . . I am afraid the after effects of this miserable business will be serious here . . .'

The Northern Pacific 'corner' of May 1901 was closely linked to the Burlington purchase because control of the N.P. meant half-control of the C.B. & Q.[2] As has been mentioned (chapter 1, p. 18), James J. Hill had early realized the importance of access to railheads at the heart of the system if a transcontinental traffic was to be successful. The Chicago, Burlington and Northern had since 1890 been under the control of the Chicago, Burlington and Quincy; in 1899 the latter bought it outright and at the same time purchased all the lines east of the Mississippi hitherto leased by their company. In 1897, after the Northern Pacific reorganization, Hill had discussed with his London friends the possibility of getting control of the Burlington but was dissuaded. The first tentative overture to Charles Elliott Perkins, President of the Burlington, was in fact

[1] Burr on *Stillman*, pp. 94 and 185.
[2] For the detailed history of the Burlington, see Richard C. Overton, *Burlington Route: A History of the Burlington Lines*, New York, 1965.

made by E. H. Harriman on behalf of the reorganized Union Pacific; Perkins was not responsive. Following the death in August 1900 of C. P. Huntington, who had merged the Central Pacific with the Southern Pacific and developed the latter, the Union Pacific had purchased Huntington's interest in the Southern Pacific, becoming a formidable competitor for the Great Northern. The Burlington, however, remained discouraging to the advances of Harriman, who was backed by a syndicate comprising also Jacob Schiff, James Stillman and George J. Gould of the Missouri Pacific. During 1900 this syndicate had bought on the market a certain amount of Burlington stock, but being unable to get enough, this they later sold. J. P. Morgan, meanwhile, had tried to persuade Hill that the road to go for was the Chicago, Milwaukee and St. Paul; only when it proved impossible to make a deal with the latter did Morgan agree to Hill's trying, on behalf of both Great Northern and Northern Pacific, to come to an arrangement with the Burlington. Early in 1901 Burlington shares began noticeably to change hands: the numerous small holders who had frustrated Harriman's attempts were at last selling. Preoccupied with the purchase of the Southern Pacific, Harriman failed to realize that Hill was seriously pursuing the Burlington. Perkins, faced with the certainty that he must give way, preferred to treat with Hill, but only at a price: $200 a share in joint N.P./G.N. 4 per cent Bonds, or $200 in cash. An abortive attempt by Harriman to achieve one-third participation was rejected by Hill as likely to defeat the whole object of his operation, and on 20 April 1901 a formal offer to purchase was submitted. This was on 29 April commended to the Burlington stockholders and duly accepted. The company was to maintain its separate identity. Perkins wrote to his wife on 20 May 1901: 'The C.B. & Q. deal is now practically settled . . . It is a great trade all around, and future generations will say so'.

Writing to Mount Stephen after the formal offer had been made in April Hill admitted that the price was high but this could not have been avoided; he himself was in no doubt about the value of the deal:

The best traffic of the Great Northern and Northern Pacific is the cotton and provisions west- and the lumber and timber east-bound. The San Francisco lines run through the cotton country from New Orleans through Texas and Arkansas. The great provision centres are Kansas City, St. Joseph, Omaha, Chicago, and St. Louis, none of which are reached directly by the Great Northern or Northern Pacific. Both companies have to divide the through rate with some other line to reach those important points ... The Burlington lets us into these districts and commercial centres, over better lines and with better terminals than any other road ... It is true we pay a great price for the property. This could not be avoided. Seventy-five million dollars or $80,000,000 of the Chicago, Burlington and Quincy is held by small holders, many of whom got it by inheritance. The average holding of the stock by the Company's books is 68 shares in the hands of nearly 15,000 stockholders ... Our plan is based on securing not less than two thirds of the 'Q' shares which enables us to form a new company which will lease the property to the present company, the rental being the interest on the bonds paid for the purchase; the stock of the new company to be divided between the Great Northern and the Northern Pacific equally, $50,000,000 to each. The new bonds to be payable at our option any time after five years.[1]

As might be expected, the Union Pacific people, particularly Harriman and Schiff, watched with alarm as Hill's negotiations for the Burlington proceeded. On 8 April 1901—while Hill's London friends were still largely in the dark—Schiff indited a characteristically florid protest to Hill:

Lest you might misunderstand my position and sentiments, it is proper that I should say to you, that wherever our business interests may place us, I feel it is too late in our lives to personally go apart. Friendships have little value, if they are only determined by personal interest and go to pieces upon the first clashing of interest; on my part, I can assure you, this will never be the case, as far as my esteem and attachment for you are concerned.

I have never had in anything so large an interest as in the Great Northern Co., to which I have held on until now, under every condition, these many years, because of my implicit faith in you. I have always spoken frankly to you, and I say now to you, that the manner in which this proposed acquisition of control of the Burlington has been proceeded with has not been in the best interests of the Great Northern shareholders. Since you have deemed it well that the Burlington be controlled partly by the Great Northern Co., your judgment, as to this, is to me final, but I am afraid you have permitted others to induce you, because of the personal advantage and profit they will get therefrom, to pay an exorbitant price, rather than to follow lines through which much might have been saved to the companies which acquire control.

As to the Union Pacific, it must take care of itself, as it will be able to

[1] Pyle on *Hill*, vol. 2, pp. 119 and 126; the name Chicago, Burlington and Quincy was usually abbreviated either to 'Burlington' or 'Q'.

do, but in any event, I want to feel that nothing has come between us, for I would truly be less happy if such could ever be the case, and I am

As ever, your friend, Jacob H. Schiff.[1]

By the beginning of May 1901 J. P. Morgan was in Italy, Hill had gone to the Pacific coast, Farrer in London was planning his fishing holiday. No one, in the market mood that had followed the launching of the U.S. Steel Corporation, appeared to be surprised when Northern Pacific Common stock advanced from 102 to 131 and Preferred from 101 to 109; in any case the Burlington purchase alone might have produced this result. Complacently both the N.P. Company itself and the firm of J. P. Morgan joined in the selling. Hill afterwards recalled that at an earlier Great Northern board meeting he had replied to a director who wanted an assurance that the N.P. would not pass into other hands, that he and his friends, together with J. P. Morgan, held some $35-40 millions of N.P. stock out of a total of $155 millions—a larger proportion than was customarily held by the controlling interest. He could not visualize anyone setting out to purchase in the market the quantity necessary to control $155 millions of stock.[2] This, however, since mid-April, was exactly what E. H. Harriman had been doing, most of the stock passing through the hands of Kuhn, Loeb and Company. Hill, in Seattle, was at last alerted and, travelling by special express, was in New York on Friday 3 May, going at once to Schiff's office. The latter told him that Kuhn, Loeb and Company were buying Northern Pacific on orders from the Union Pacific. Still unbelieving, Hill investigated further. On Saturday 4 May he got Robert Bacon to cable Morgan for authority to buy at least 150,000 N.P. shares, preferably of the Common stock.[3] (It will be recalled—page 95— that the second London agreement stipulated that the Preferred stock could be retired at par on any 1 January for the next 20 years.) By 3 May Kuhn, Loeb had told Harriman that they had bought for Union Pacific account about 370,000 shares of Common and 420,000 of Preferred—about $79 million worth, a majority of the total but not of the Common. To the last moment Harriman seemed unconvinced of the importance of having a majority of the Common, but on Saturday morning, 4 May—he was himself ill at home with what turned out to be appendicitis—he gave orders

[1] Adler on *Schiff*, vol. 1, p. 100.   [2] Pyle on *Hill*, vol 2, p. 141 ff.
[3] Kennan on *Harriman*, vol. 1, p. 300 ff.

to one of the Kuhn, Loeb partners to purchase a further 40,000 shares of Common at the then inflated price. He heard no more until Monday 6 May, and then what he heard came probably under Gaspard Farrer's heading of ludicrous. Before executing Harriman's order the partner had wished to consult Schiff; Schiff, an orthodox Jew, was at the synagogue and told the partner not to proceed; that he would be responsible. Schiff's decision was, says Kennan, based on the belief, supported by legal opinion, and believed to be shared by James Stillman, that as they already had a clear majority of all shares (6,000 more than half) there was no need to pay extravagantly for more.[1] Believing this to be true, Harriman gave no further order, and could afterwards claim that he had bought no shares that week. Meanwhile on Monday 6 May Morgans were scooping up N.P. Common at prices which were advancing to 130, continuing on Tuesday, when the Common reached $149\frac{3}{4}$: they were therefore branded as main contributors to the debacle. By Tuesday evening, 7 May, they had their 150,000 Common shares—30,000 more than required—and stopped buying although they still lacked a majority of Preferred and of the total. As both classes had equal voting rights, the U.P. interests would be entitled to name a majority of directors at the next N.P. election in October 1901, although they could not prevent the retirement of the Preferred the following January, which would leave them with only a minority of Common stock.

There followed the less edifying phase: dealers who had sold

[1] See Adler on *Schiff*, vol. 1, p. 106: Schiff to J. P. Morgan 16 May 1901: Schiff wrote that in the forenoon of Friday 3 May, 'the earliest opportunity', he informed Hill that the U.P. interests had got upwards of 40 per cent of the entire capital stock of the N.P., telling him that their only purpose was 'to bring about the harmony and community of interest which other means and appeals to him had failed to produce, and I asked him to give your partners these assurances, and appealed to him to do what was in his power to bring about this result'. That evening, he continued, Hill came to his house, remaining until after midnight 'and repeatedly assured me that there would be no difficulty in accomplishing what I had proposed. Evidently, however, Mr. Hill must have put no credence in the statement I had made to him of the ownership by U.P., for on the following Monday the frantic buying began . . .' Pyle (vol. 2, p. 147) mentions an offer to Hill at this stage of 'position and power' if he would accommodate U.P. interests. Albro Martin in his biography of James J. Hill states that according to Mrs. Hill's Diary, Hill left St. Paul, where he had been for a week, on Saturday 27 April, reaching his New York office, in the same building as Schiff's, on Monday 29th. There Schiff met him and made the offer (presumably the one referred to by Pyle) that Hill should head all their combined concerns if he would part company with Morgan.

Useful insights into the character of Jacob Schiff—particularly as regards his 'stifling orthodoxy'—are given in David Farrer, *The Warburgs*, London, 1975. For example, (p. 204) 'One Sabbath day (a grandson) picked a rose to present to his grandfather. Schiff responded: "You have killed something on the Sabbath." '

short—i.e. more than they held, expecting prices to fall—were faced on Wednesday with a rise of 50 points and even at that price a shortage of N.P. shares; they were therefore forced to sell other stocks cheap to raise money. By Thursday 9 May, N.P. Common was selling at up to $1,000 a share while other securities plummeted: U.S. Steel from 46 to 24. At this point the responsible leaders of the financial community weighed in with measures to halt the panic. The railroad giants prepared to settle for a compromise solution, which included U.P. representation on both N.P. and Burlington boards. J. P. Morgan was empowered to choose the new members of the N.P. board in advance of the annual election, and nominated Hill, Harriman—who also became a member of the executive committee—William Rockefeller (then a director of the Milwaukee, as well as being the financial genius of Standard Oil), Hamilton McK. Twombley (a director of the Chicago and North Western, he was also appointed to the Burlington directorate, along with Harriman, Schiff and Gould to represent Union Pacific interests) and Samuel Rea, Vice-President of the Pennsylvania Railroad.[1] This is not the place for further analysis of this power-struggle: Schiff, in another fulsome apologia of 16 May 1901 gave J. P. Morgan his viewpoint, in which it emerges that while Harriman seemed bent on actual control of the N.P. Schiff merely wished to influence N.P. and Burlington policy; this belongs to the Hill story. Hill later, giving testimony in a court of law, said that had the Union Pacific gained control of the Northern Pacific and with it half the Burlington, they would very soon have had control of the Great Northern also; 'it would have almost destroyed the value of the Great Northern property or its shares for its shareholders . . .'[2]

The Northern Pacific 'corner' demonstrated the advantages of having the bulk of the Great Northern's interest in the N.P. in a few hands. Hill's biographer Pyle provides a somewhat journalistic account of the crucial days: 'Exactly as the four associates made all their arrangements to buy the St. Paul and Pacific, and pledged their "fortunes and their sacred honour" without a word in writing, so Mr. Hill and Mr. Morgan agreed to stand by each other, let come what might . . . J. P. Morgan . . . asked Hill and his friends not to sell out . . .' to which Hill replied that 'myself and friends would stand without hitching. And they did'.[3] They did indeed.

---

[1] This was known as the Metropolitan agreement, the meetings having been held at the Metropolitan Club in New York.
[2] Pyle, op. cit. vol. 2, p. 145. [3] Ibid. pp. 148–50.

On 8 May Gaspard Farrer relayed to Charles Ellis a cable message received that morning from Hill that Union Pacific interests were attempting to gain control of the Northern Pacific and by so doing oust Great Northern interests: 'Mr Hill begs that we and other G.N. friends will hold N.P. shares regardless of price or that if any wish to sell they should give him the opportunity of buying first'.

HOLDING COMPANY: PRELIMINARIES

Once the immediate difficulties were surmounted, Hill bent his energies towards ensuring against any repetition of recent events. The Quebec fishing holiday—Hill was at his home on the St. John River and Farrer visited him there—was hardly a retreat from business. Before sailing for England again Farrer went over the Great Northern, returning by the Northern Pacific as far as Butte, Montana. He reported to Edward Tuck in Paris on 13 August 1901 that crops both east and west of the mountains were better than he had ever seen them in America: 'more like crops in this country'. On 10 August he dwelt at length to John Sterling on the pleasures of seafaring:

We were landed at Plymouth at 11 a.m. on Thursday after a perfect ocean trip. I wished continuously that you had been with me both for the sake of your company and as evidence to you of how well the Atlantic can behave—the sea like a mill pond from start to finish and after the first two days which were rather too hot a perfect temperature enabling one to loll about the decks from morning to midnight in thin flannel suit without overcoat or rug ... Plymouth is a lovely harbour and as we sailed in on a glorious morning we met hundreds of fishing smacks on their way out and mingling with these a number of H.M. Fleet returning after the Naval manoeuvres. It was as pretty a sight as man could wish to see ...

... I ran down to see the Boss yesterday p.m. and tried to give him a fair exposition of each party's contentions. He agrees with you ... their involvement is the best guarantee for their seeking a peaceful settlement on strictly business lines; my own feeling is that Morgan will be able to control Hill if Stillman Rockefeller & co. are willing and able to control Harriman. Many many thanks to you and Bloss for all your hospitality and kindness. I can't tell you how much I enjoyed having you at Metis.

But before planning for the future got much further there was the aftermath of May to be reaped: the disposal of the large block of

Common stock acquired by Morgan's on the 6th and 7th. On 12 August Farrer wrote to Lord Strathcona enclosing a cable from Hill. He was going to Brocket that afternoon to ask Lord Mount Stephen what he was prepared to take, and would then communicate with Strathcona: 'The million to which Mr. Hill refers is £1,000,000 sterling. He asked me whether I considered his London friends would take up to that amount, but at the time I left nothing definite was settled as to the terms of his scheme, and I need hardly tell you my reply was non-committal. However, he needs help now, and I personally shall do anything I can in my small way to assist him'. He added a postscript: 'The stock Mr. Hill is asking his London friends to take forms part—as I understand—of the $15,000,000 nominal bought last spring by Messrs. Morgan at Mr. Hill's instance and at a cost which Mr. Hill told me averaged 122. I presume the Great Northern Company will have to shoulder the difference between that price and 115, the scheme in my opinion is more advantageous for G.N. shareholders than for those of Northern Pacific'.

Hill's scheme, discussed with Farrer 'as we sat catching flies that afternoon on your verandah' (a phrase from a later letter to Hill) was to safeguard their investment by putting a majority of the stock —in Hill's words—'where it could not be raided again as it had been. We wanted to put it in a corporation that was not a railroad company—a company that would hold it as an investment, and the larger the company the more difficult it would be to secure a majority of it'.[1] In other words, he visualized a holding company, into which the stock of both Great Northern and Northern Pacific— or a majority of it—would be put. Writing to Lord Revelstoke also on 12 August, Farrer repeated what he had told Strathcona, adding: 'In effect we are being asked to become a relief committee to the Morgan pool and it will be obvious to you that the Holding Company's securities can be bought cheaper by the purchase of G.N. shares at today's market price than by taking over N.P. Com. at 115 and subsequently exchanging them. Nevertheless I shall do what I can to help and hope you will do the same. What will your firm take? I am communicating with Mount Stephen and Strathcona and Ellis. I don't know to whom else I can apply. As the Great Northern will eventually disappear from the list I think you might fairly stipulate that your subscription should be conditional on

[1] Ibid. p. 164.

your remaining bankers for the Holding Company in London as you now are for G.N.' In a postscript to Revelstoke he added that on Hill's asking him on what figures he could rely in London—Hill supposed at the most a million—Farrer had replied that it would depend on the terms, which had not been settled when he sailed for England.

The following day, 13 August 1901, Farrer wrote to Charles Ellis at his Piccadilly address that he would come to see him that afternoon on the chance of finding him. He wrote also to Edward Tuck, then at his Chateau de Vert Mont at Rueil in France: 'Lord Mount Stephen showed me a letter he had from you in which you write that you would be glad to hear details of Mr. Hill's scheme if I have anything to report'. He enclosed a copy of Hill's cable, saying: 'I imagine that the stock which he is now asking his London friends to take forms part of that bought last Spring by the American pool to secure a majority of the Common. His proposal is not really to buy N.P. shares at 115, at which price they are cheap, but to buy Holding Company's Shares at par,—a proposition which one can hardly lay before clients as a matter of business.—However I personally shall do all I can to help him . . .' On 14 August Farrer replied to Hill, care of E. T. Nichols at the Great Northern's New York Office, copying the letter to Mount Stephen:

Referring to your cable message received on the 12th, we like the principle of your scheme, though the terms as regards N.P. appear to us open to criticism.

As to your London friends co-operating to relieve the Morgan Pool by buying what amounts to a purchase of Holding Company's Shares at par: your proposition is not one of business, nor one which we could put before our friends as such. I have however communicated a copy of your message to Lord Mount Stephen, Lord Strathcona and Lord Revelstoke, and cabled you a reply on behalf of my own Firm.

If you succeed in getting in 42,000,000 of N.P. Stock on the basis of 115, you will have done well, and will then be in a better position for future negotiations with the Harriman Schiff party, but I shall be surprised if they ever consent to come in on the terms which you are now asking your own friends to join you in accepting.

Lord Revelstoke had written at once from Aix, where he was on holiday, and Farrer acknowledged his letter on 16 August: '. . . The capital of the Holding Company will be of an elastic nature, capable, if all Hill's schemes are carried out, of almost limitless expansion. For the moment, he does not propose to do more than offer to take in all Great Northern shares on the basis of 180, and the 42 million N.P. Ordinary on the basis of 115. I have seen your Francis [Baring] today and am now cabling to Hill the extent to which your Firm are willing to assist him'. The same day Farrer wrote to Ellis: 'I have this afternoon cabled some assistance to Hill, and have added in my message as follows:—"Except for this help you must arrange balance on your side. I will cable in case your other old friends who are well disposed can help you later, but in any case the amount will be small, and you had better not count on it at all".' Ellis had obviously not yet made up his mind. Farrer told Lord Revelstoke on 17 August: 'Hill does not specifically reply in regard to your Firm's offer, but says he has taken the whole 50,000 himself, trusting to us, yourselves, Estevan, and others to help him so far as we can. As I think you know, I cabled him early this week that we would take 5,000 shares, for which he seems grateful. I have since heard that Sterling also takes 5,000. Stephen seems wheeling into line, and I think will help at his own time and in his own way, and I have little doubt that Strathcona and Ellis will follow his lead ... The message concludes "have no idea of changing from Barings as London representative"'.

For Mount Stephen this was obviously one of the occasions when a lack of previous liaison produced a feeling of irritation with Hill. On 17 August Farrer brought Sterling up to date with developments:

... We have had a lively week passing cables between ourselves, Mount Stephen and Hill. Nobody here seemed anxious to take the initiative in relieving the Morgan Hill pool of the baby so on the principle of "bis dat qui cito dat" I cabled him on Tuesday that we would take 5,000. Since then I have persuaded Barings to offer Hill a twelve months advance of $500,000—and I think Estevan, Ellis and perhaps even Beaumont (the two latter following Estevan's lead) may help later.[1] Estevan has very naturally resented being called upon to stand and deliver at a moment's notice and without preparation, and messages that have passed have shown some feeling. This morning's cables however show that this is disappearing. Your own subscription is splendid and will do much towards relieving the tension.

Lord Strathcona arrives in town tomorrow and writes me that he will

[1] Note: Hill's biographer Martin has evidence that during the Barings crisis of 1890 (see Gilbert, vol. 1, p. 256) Hill offered help to the tune of £50,000 sterling. W. B. Beaumont was a friend of Mount Stephen and of Ellis.

assist. Your message to Estevan this morning giving us Bacon's assurance that the N.P. Common majority is certain is a great relief. It is the point on which I have always been uncomfortable and upon which even at this moment am not entirely satisfied. Hill cables me that he is starting for Maine to see Harriman. I hope he will have the good sense to meet him fairly. There will never be permanent peace unless Hill makes reasonable concessions in the Burlington–Union Pacific country, and if he does that I do not see why the Harriman Stock should not come into the Holding Company. I know you will agree that this is right and will do anything you can to assist if ever opportunity should occur.

The set against the big man [J. P. Morgan] here has been very decided, fostered it is said by the enemy, as a result his paper has practically disappeared, bills having matured and not being replaced. You will readily believe that his name is not the only one criticized and paper and commitments of all parties concerned in this miserable squabble is being closely scrutinized here.

On the same day, 17 August, Farrer wrote to Strathcona at 25 Grosvenor Square, repeating some of this information: that Lefevres were willing to take 5,000; that Barings had offered Hill a personal advance; that conferences between Mount Stephen and himself and 'sundry messages between Lord Mount Stephen and Mr. Hill' had caused him to cable as quoted in his letter to Ellis, that total help could not be guaranteed. He copied two cables received that day from Hill: the first, the sense of which he had communicated to Revelstoke: 'To secure shares and plan have taken whole 50,000 and trust yourself Barings Estevan and others will take 20 or 25 of it'; the second: 'Yours received. See previous message today. 5,000 shares you take will help. Deeply grateful for your good will. The Holding Stock will sell above par at once. Leaving for Maine tomorrow to meet Harriman'. Farrer continued:

Lord Mount Stephen has very naturally resented having the pistol held at his head, and being asked at a moment's notice and without preparation to enter into heavy commitments. I think however he would be inclined to assist with his influence and perhaps with fresh money as and when he can conveniently get it together, but on this point I shall know further by Monday . . .

Gaspard was leaving town that evening for Sunday, but could come and see Strathcona on Monday. In a postscript he added the news that Sterling had taken 5,000 N.P. shares.

Late on the Saturday night, 17 August, came a more cheerful

cable from Hill which Farrer paraphrased on the Monday for
Lord Revelstoke: '. . . Hill cables in good spirits,—already sees his
Holding Company's shares selling well above par. Something has
occurred to change his temper. He mentions: "matters already look
as if my burden will not be heavy" and again "leaving to meet
Harriman". Either of these sentences may be significant as you will
understand, and may account for his good spirits. He cabled late on
Saturday asking me to say—will not need "John's kind offer" of
which I have informed your people'. Mount Stephen was in
Aberdeen, where he was about to receive the Freedom of the City,
and Gaspard wrote to him at the Palace Hotel there on Monday 19
August relaying Hill's further news: "Buy any shares Common
you can up to 115 . . ." Hill wanted Lefevres to have their 5,000
"for the benefit you will derive". Acknowledging three letters from
Mount Stephen, one of 17 and two of 18 August, Gaspard replied
to some specific questions regarding Burlington securities and
obligations, the fourth answer being: 'In case of default of one or
other of the Guarantors, the other may take over the defaulter's
half-share in the Burlington property, becoming thereafter
responsible for the defaulter's liability'. Mount Stephen was
clearly going very minutely into the whole question. Farrer told
him that their friend Beaumont had agreed to help, but that he
had nothing further from Ellis: 'Lord Strathcona has just been in
and I think will follow your example, though he obviously is not
keen to add to his investments. I suggested leaving the matter
till he gets out to New York, and he will do that, or possibly cable
Sterling to take up to 5,000 . . . I will keep you posted in case of
further developments'. He was dining that night with Louis Hill
who was in London en route for Southampton.

MOUNT STEPHEN'S SCOTTISH BENEFACTIONS

Mount Stephen's hesitation was not entirely—if at all—due to
pique. Cash resources in the hands of men of such means were not
allowed to lie idle: they were invested to the best advantage, and to
switch investments required time and thought. Within the last two or
three years Mount Stephen, now over 70, had already been making a
number of financial dispositions in line with his belief that it was
better to give while still alive than to make posthumous bequests.
He had just received the Freedom of the City of Aberdeen on 27

August 1901 as a result of a gift to the Royal Infirmary there of
£25,000.[1] He had written to Lord Provost John Fleming in November 1900 saying that he wished to do something for the institution in which he had been a patient in 1846. The Infirmary was
just completing a scheme of improvements undertaken to mark
the Queen's Diamond Jubilee, but which had so exceeded the
estimated cost as to leave a debt of £24,665 on a total of £75,297.
A new building was therefore named the Mount Stephen Medical
Pavilion. In 1902 Mount Stephen transferred to the Infirmary
securities of the nominal value of $100,000 to yield an annual
income of £1,000. Later, in 1907, he was to give £10,000 to the
endowment fund and in 1908 £26,758 to be spent exclusively on
certain permanent improvements: three new operating theatres
and a casualty and outpatient block.[2]

Moreover, in July 1901 Mount Stephen had just set up the Trust
that bears his name for the benefit of certain ministers of the
Church of Scotland. To quote from the Deed of Trust:

I the Right Honourable George Lord Mount Stephen, a Baron of the
United Kingdom of Great Britain and Ireland, taking into consideration
the reduction that has taken place in the Stipends of the Parish Ministers
of the Church of Scotland during the last fifty or sixty years and being
desirous of restoring the Ministers of some of the Parishes in the vicinity
of the Parish of Mortlach my native Parish to a position of greater
independence and having transferred to the Scottish American Investment
Company Ltd. whose registered office is in Edinburgh to be held by it as
Trustee for the purposes aftermentioned seventeen hundred shares of
one hundred dollars each of the Preferred Stock of the Great Northern
Railway Company of Minnesota U.S.A. it is hereby declared that these
shares . . . are to be held in trust always . . .

The stipends of ministers of the Church of Scotland were at that
time partly regulated by 'Fiars prices'—the average prices of the
different kinds of grain of one year's crop, judicially determined
by the Fiars Court. For 50 or 60 years corn prices had been falling
to such an extent as materially to reduce clerical incomes. Mount
Stephen therefore proposed to establish a fund from which £100

---

[1] Minutes of Aberdeen Town Council, 7 January, 17 June and 27 August 1901.
Aberdeen Daily Free Press 8 January 1901. Lord Strathcona was made a freeman of
Aberdeen in October 1901.
[2] Short history of Aberdeen Royal Infirmary published at the opening in 1935 of the
new Royal Infirmary at Foresterhill. See also *Aberdeen Daily Free Press* 12 December
1900 and 27, 28 and 29 August 1901.

sterling should be paid annually to augment the stipend of the parishes designated.[1] In addition to earmarking $170,000 worth of Great Northern shares for this purpose, Mount Stephen also, on his visit to Dufftown in August 1901, announced a plan to provide 25 or 30 annuities of £16 (or more if the fund established permitted) for elderly residents in Mortlach and Glenrinnes. He himself nominated the first seven beneficiaries, leaving the further administration of the scheme to trustees.[2] He also endowed 100 beds at the Aberlour Orphanage to the tune of £35,000, representing an annual income of £1,000, and gave £5,000 to Dr. Gray's Hospital, Elgin. The Northern Pacific 'corner' had demonstrated anew how vulnerable the best of investments could be; to be lauded for his largesse only to find one day that the basis had crumbled was unthinkable. Yet this very cloud was to hover over him for a period of years in the not-so-distant future.

HOLDING COMPANY: SUPPORT IN ENGLAND

Meanwhile Farrer on 19 August was passing on the latest news to Charles Ellis. Of Hill he wrote: 'Obviously something has occurred to put him in good spirits. Possibly he finds friends there willing to lighten his load, and possibly his reference to Harriman may indicate a disposition on the part of the enemy to come to terms'. Ellis had informed him that Beaumont was prepared to help and Farrer had cabled Hill accordingly. Next day he was able to acknowledge Ellis's letter of 19 and telegram of 20 August: '. . . we have cabled Hill "Ellis will take any part 5000 N.P. Common Shares if required"'. If Hill accepted this offer, Farrer would see to the sale of any securities Ellis decided to realize. This produced from Hill the reply: 'Thank Ellis for good will. Think all will be taken here. Will write'. Farrer commented to Ellis on 21 August: 'I should not be surprised if after all he takes advantage of your offer, at least to some extent'.

Meanwhile Farrer was also keeping Tuck informed. He wrote on 20 August of his active cable correspondence with Hill: 'mainly

---

[1] Register of Deeds and Probate Writs, Books of Council and Session, Vol. 3136, Register House (Legal Section) Edinburgh. See also A. J. H. Gibson, *Stipend in the Church of Scotland*, Edinburgh, 1961. The Trust was to be administered in Edinburgh by Robert Fleming's Scottish American Investment Company. In 1902 and again in 1907 other parishes were added to the scheme.

[2] *Aberdeen Daily Free Press* 26 August 1901. *Dufftown News* 14 September and 12 October 1901.

in respect of the 50,000 N.P. shares which he was seeking to place here in London. Finally he took the entire amount himself trusting to us to relieve him of a part. This we have been able to do. His last messages are buoyant in tone. He reports "everything now closed" (which I take to mean that a majority of the G.N. and N.P. Common have assented to come into the Holding Company on the terms mentioned) and confidently anticipates that his Holding Company shares will sell well above par as soon as the scheme is made public. I agree with you that the merit of the Holding Company is its simplicity, and I hope that eventually the right to come into it will be offered not only to all G.N. shareholders but to all N.P. ordinary shareholders on the basis of 180 and 115 . . .' He wrote also to 'the Admiral', Lord Clanwilliam, on 21 August, not mentioning the Holding Company but merely telling of his recent trip over the Great Northern with Hill: both property and country were in better shape than ever: 'Bar accidents, we may look forward to the best year the Company has ever had'. He invited the Admiral to come and talk on the subject. In the same sense he wrote to one or two others, but was more forthcoming to Cecil Baring in New York (21 August):

Before this letter reaches New York you will probably have heard something of Mr. Hill's future plans. Should they work out as he expects they will involve an increase of the Share Capital of the New Company during the next five to ten years, rendering it desirable for him to seek fresh markets and a broader following.

I had some talk on the subject during my recent trip with him to the Coast and suggested his following up the line which the acquisition of the Q . and relations with Perkins and Hunnewell [Chairman of the old Burlington board] had opened up. There are no better holders than New England investors, and no Firm which commands their confidence as does that of your Boston friends. [Kidder, Peabody & Company] I had hoped to find Winsor still in London, but he had sailed before I reached home. Could you broach the subject to him? Any action on the part of K.P. will of course depend on their taking a like view of the properties and their future as we ourselves entertain; if they do not there is an end of the matter.

In my ignorance of whether the business would suit or in what way it could be made profitable to them my letter is purposely vague; I cannot do more than indicate the bent of Mr. Hill's mind as it was when I left America.

He added the inevitable postscript: 'You will recollect that it is well to keep a blind eye for some of our friend's peculiarities; his loyalty to the *property* we have never seen reason to question during the 21 years we have been connected with him and it'.

To Hill himself Gaspard wrote on 22 August:

I have sketched out to Lord Mount Stephen your ideas of the future of the Holding Company—with the share capital eventually absorbing all G.N. and N.P. shares, as well as the Bonds issued for the Burlington purchase. He is pleased with the simplicity and breadth of the scheme—but is impressed with the desirability of making an early effort to secure new markets, and so increase the number of the faithful. He concurs with you in thinking that out of this country there are no better holders than the New England investor—I am confident that in New England Kidder, Peabody and Co. can reach more of the class which you require than any other Firm, and John tells me that Winsor is the live man,—and a very live man too—in that concern . . .

He told Sterling on 28 August that they were now awaiting Hill's return from vacation; Nichols had cabled that nothing would be made public before then. He went on:

Mr. Hill declined Baring's offer of the twelve months' loan, and further replied in response to Ellis's offer to take 5,000 shares that he did not expect to need his assistance. Under the circumstances, we did not press Beaumont to follow Ellis's suit, though I think he would have taken 5,000 if we had made a point of it. I was particularly glad of your subscription of 5,000, as I am sure it influenced Lord Mount Stephen and Lord Strathcona and it will do a great deal towards strengthening your influence with Mr. Hill. He cabled me last week that he was leaving New York to meet Harriman—I shall be interested to hear the result of these two worthies' conferences . . .

Gradually over these months Farrer's letters revealed most of the background to the formation of the Northern Securities holding company. He wrote on 30 August 1901 to another friend in London clarifying some points: the price of 115 New York meant 118 or 119 here, and the condition of purchase at that price was that the holder should exchange each $100 share (for which he had paid $115 New York) for $115 worth of stock in the new company that was about to be formed for the purpose of holding the majority of Great Northern and Northern Pacific stocks. It was expected that the stock of the new company would commence with 4 per cent dividends, and quite possibly there might be no increase on this rate for some years. 'Under the circumstances, you will see that you are investing in a *share* paying but 4 per cent for the present but with a possibility of an increase in the future if all goes well'. If his friend still wanted it after absorbing this information, he would reserve stock for him: Gaspard's letter to him of 10 September showed that he did.

HILL–HARRIMAN AGREEMENT

That Farrer still had doubts about the wisdom of the Burlington purchase came out in his letter of 3 September 1901 to Charles Ellis:

... It is to be hoped that something more reasonable than "manifest destiny" guides Hill in undertaking liabilities such as he has done in the case of the Burlington Road. It is quite possible Tuck may be right in saying we should have been outgrown sooner or later by our ambitious neighbours, but supposing they had absorbed the Burlington at the high price paid instead of ourselves, it seems to me that would have driven the [Chicago and] North West and Milwaukee and St. Paul into our hands and on conditions where we should have fixed the price instead of the seller.—But these are big and difficult questions, and one would not like to put one's own judgment against that of Mr. Hill, whose knowledge of traffic conditions is better than anyone's.

The following day he acknowledged a cable from Sterling which he was to relay to Lord Mount Stephen. It would be interesting to hear, he wrote, 'what concessions Hill had to make to procure Harriman's acquiescence to the arrangements you shadow out'. On 7 September he copied for Ellis a cable just received from Hill: "Harriman has turned over their proxy to Morgan for October election. That shows justification"—'presumably', commented Farrer,'justifies Hill in thinking that Harriman is satisfied'. On the 9th he told Ellis: 'Hill cables this morning "Kindly show my letter to Estevan and Ellis. U.P. arrangement very satisfactory. Business outlook improving daily and will exceed any estimate we have made. N.P. shares taken by me largely over applied for"'. Farrer wrote to Hill on 11 September, thanking him for the various messages: 'You have done wonders: as we sat catching flies that afternoon on your verandah my wildest expectations never rose to the possibility of Morgan's obtaining his enemy's proxy. I am hoping that the next news will be that their 37 millions have come into the holding Company'. (See above p. 193: he referred to the

Northern Pacific shares purchased by U.P. interests before the 'corner'.) Writing further to Hill on 16 September on the subject of Harriman's proxy he said: 'It is a comfort to have it but with no opposition there seems no reason to use it and some for avoiding its use if delivered as from Union Pacific'. Turning to the future:

Your forecast of August 31 has excited my imagination and I am trying to reconcile the seeing of visions with the realities of cold cash. We have so often discussed the question of the Company's cash that you must be sick enough of it and I only recur to it now because I see clearly that if through misfortune Jim and Louis had to take up your work the state of the till would have a bearing on the ease with which the regime in St. Paul could be continued. Financial chances which you may take they must not dream of risking—I know you will agree with me. Assuredly Great Northern has no shareholder better pleased to pocket his jingling tingling golden minted quid than myself, but I do earnestly hope you will resist pressure to increase dividends till the new Compy. is past the transitory stage and established in public estimation and cash resources— independent of bankers and even of its own shareholders except when times are ripe and shareholders in the mood. The Boss is back from Scotland where he has been receiving freedoms and making speeches! Outside your own home you have no truer personal friend—on your side the water or on this—moreover to G.N. a splendid advertiser with a keen eye to the Company's interest . . .

That Gaspard Farrer, despite his doubts about the Burlington purchase and its concomitants, was anxious to further Hill's plans is evidenced by his letter of 11 October 1901 to Robert Bacon of J. P. Morgan's regarding the Bonds (Great Northern/Northern Pacific) which financed the transaction: 'Would it be of any advantage to you to have the C.B. & Q. Joint Bonds quoted in London? About $1 million have been placed here within the past few days to my knowledge, and there appears to be a small demand for a bond paying a clear 4 per cent'. He would arrange this if Bacon were to send the relevant papers. There was also the more personal diplomacy to be pursued. He wrote to J. N. Hill on 12 October that Jacob Schiff had been in London for ten days, having sailed for home on the 9th:

He talked freely to Lord Mount Stephen regarding Northern Pacific matters, the gist of which I think you may like to hear. He earnestly protested that he and his friends had no intention of interfering with your father in any way in the management of the Road, either as to its policy or operation, but were determined that they would never give up the power they had of being able to elect their own Board in case the Union Pacific was ever attacked through the Burlington. He did not regard the retirement of the Preferred Stock by the issue of Bond or Debenture as legally possible. I do not however myself see how he and his friends could resist the retirement of Preferred by an issue of Ordinary Stock to existing holders, and if your father's contemplated holding Company is carried through successfully and becomes established, I see no reason why he should not call upon his holding Company's stockholders to provide the funds necessary for taking up the proportion of N.P. Ordinary to which the holding Company would be entitled; but as you know, I myself would sooner remove the cause of the trouble than place the enemy in a minority by means which seem to be within our powers.

To Robert Bacon he had written on 11 October that Schiff had been talking freely: that he had no desire to disturb Mr. Hill in either operation or policy of the Northern Pacific but was determined not to relinquish the power he and his friends professed to hold of turning Mr. Hill out in case the U.P. was ever attacked through the C.B. & Q.: 'I am in hopes that means may be found of keeping the peace other than those of holding the rod over Mr. Hill, and I am glad to think the balance of power remains with your Firm to make a fair settlement to all properties—the only kind of settlement that can be lasting'. On 5 November he was thanking Bacon for his message about a N.P. settlement: 'it is the best of good news and let me assure you that your courtesy and thoughtfulness in advising me is appreciated to the full. In conjunction with other G.N. shareholders here, I believe that these troubles could not have been satisfactorily adjusted without the intervention of yourself and your Firm'.

NORTHERN SECURITIES COMPANY

On 12 November 1901 the Northern Securities Company was incorporated under the laws of the State of New Jersey with a capital of $400,000,000. Hill was voted President and of the fifteen directors six represented the Northern Pacific, four the Great Northern, three—including Harriman—the Union Pacific and two were independent. All holders of Great Northern and Northern Pacific were invited to exchange their shares in these for the stock of the new company on the basis of $180 for every $100 of G.N.

and $115 for every $100 of N.P.[1] Harriman exchanged all the
Northern Pacific securities he had acquired for about $82·5 million
worth of Northern Securities shares.

On 13 November Farrer wrote to Charles Ellis: 'Hill cables this
morning to thank you for your support and adds: "80,000 G.N.
shares deposited more than required. At present have application
for more holding Company's Stock than will be required to take up
N.P. Preferred"', and the following day copied to him Hill's cable
of that morning: "N.P. directors today unanimously voted retire
Preferred at par January 1st. giving holding Company all N.P.'s
Shares. People here are paying 200 for G.N. turning same into
holding Company. Situation very gratifying. I have no doubt
holding Company will repeat G.N. only in larger way". Again on
15 November he quoted Hill's cable of that morning: "N.P.
Common shareholders to have option of subscribing at par for
N.P. Convertible Debentures to the extent of 75/80ths of the
nominal value of their holdings".

To Sterling on 16 November Gaspard wrote acknowledging a
cable message

which coming from so sane and judgematical a Philosopher was a relief to
me though I am still puzzled to see where Hill and his friends propose to
find some $40 million of fresh *cash*. All this means further concentration
of shares in a few hands instead of distribution as I think would be wise.
I wish to goodness he had given Preferred as well as Common the right
to exchange on the basis of 115. The possible profit which you fore-
shadow for Common Stockholders under this present scheme appears to
be dearly earned if it leads to added concentration of holdings and
overloading of individuals. You will think me a d—d pessimist but 40
millions *is* a big sum for those less parochially minded than we Britishers
and to me is none the smaller from the loans that are now running here on
New York account and the constant applications which I fear of for more.
Am just off to Brocket for the Sunday with your message in my pocket.

But first he relayed to Ellis—without indicating the source
—Sterling's 'reassuring message' regarding the demand which 'our
correspondent believes awaits the new securities [Gaspard footnoted this "and rights"] to be issued under the scheme as soon as
the details are made public'. His correspondent, he assured Ellis,
was 'so sane, well posted yet outside banking business', yet did not

---

[1] Pyle, op. cit. vol. 2, pp. 167–8. Kennan on *Harriman*, vol. 1, pp. 329–30.

'condescend to explain where Mr. Hill and his friends expect to find that unconsidered trifle of $40,000,000 hard cash in case the public are less responsive than he anticipates'. On 19 November he advised Ellis to read the latest *Statist* ; Farrer knew the writer well and was confident that he had not the material on which his tables were based; he consequently believed this to have been supplied 'from headquarters'. He had reason to know that J. J. Hill had been in communication with the paper.

Although he had no hesitation in revealing some of his doubts to Ellis, it was to Sterling that Gaspard wrote most freely. Referring to Sterling's message of the 15th about Northern Pacific 'holding off the market', Farrer confessed on 23 November that it seemed to him that Hill & Co. would be fairly extended by January 1 in finding $40 million more or less to repay N.P. Preferred and that if Harriman & Co. took advantage of the situation to offer their or rather the Union Pacific's holdings in Northern Securities 'we might have very uncomfortable half hours as Hill would not be in any position to protect his market. I shall be delighted if Harriman & Co. stick permanently to their holdings believing that this will prove a restraint upon Hill and a protection to us'. Farrer thought that this would necessitate 'a more frank exhibition of accounts etc. etc. On many of our friend's methods you and I are already in accord and it seems to me impossible to have seen the (?) of his operations during the last year as we have, without having received a severe shock to one's confidence in his judgment . . .' The self-deprecatory outburst that followed could only refer to the circumstance that after years of close connection he was about to become Lord Revelstoke's partner in Baring Brothers, while remaining a partner in Lefevres: 'No, it's such d—d rot that my ears refuse to burn—if John does not know better he ought to—and soon will—the only ability I have ever shown in life was in early recognition that I had none & the squatting in consequence on the coat tails of Stephen, Sterling, Hill & Co. from which wild horses will not dislodge me . . .'

In this frame of mind he wrote on 5 December 1901 to one of his broker acquaintances on the subject of Great Northern and the holding company: 'During the twenty years we've been connected with the Company no-one has ever yet sold its securities but has had cause to repent it afterwards, and so it will be now'. He was not referring to what the price of the stock might be next week or next month, 'but to the intrinsic merits of the properties and their present and potential earning capacity, of which I have some special knowledge, and these are factors which in the long run must govern the price of the securities. It may take some little time for the public to get accustomed to the new securities, but I have little doubt but that after a while there will be a better market in 400 millions of stock round about par than there ever has been or can be in 125 millions selling at 180'. He added: 'It may interest you to know that Mr Hill's original plan for the exchange into the Northern Securities Company's Stock was to limit it to the majority of Great Northern Stock which he and half a dozen friends hold, and it was only on the earnest representations of myself and others that he consented to extend the option to every shareholder. It shows how difficult it is to please all parties'.

Farrer had great hopes that John Sterling might have opportunities of exercising a moderating influence upon Hill *vis-à-vis* Harriman, and apparently wanted him to become a director of the holding company, but Sterling was not keen. There is a trace of Schiff's attitude in his letter of 17 December 1901, acknowledging Sterling's of the 6th: 'You are the only person who can talk about your joining the Northern Board. My own feeling had been that there must have been some influence at work on Hill during the last year of which we had had no previous experience: and in this case one naturally looks to the Banking interest which did make or at least is reported to have made the big haul out of the Burlington deal: and it was in the hopes of counteracting influences of this kind that made me so cheerfully willing to sacrifice you—the instant my letter was posted it occurred to me how selfish it had been . . .' It was not to Sterling's taste to have to deal with such a situation: clearly he did not fancy the role of buffer between two such potentially explosive forces. Jacob Schiff had written to Ernest Cassel on 11 November 1901: 'Although the Union Pacific is in the minority in this holding company, it will nevertheless exercise a potent influence upon the management of the two Northern lines, on the strength of its rather large holdings. In addition, the Union Pacific has made a territorial agreement with the two companies which protects it against any invasion and gives it the extensive use of important lines on the northern Pacific Coast. I believe the whole arrangement is of the greatest importance and advantage to the U.P. and justifies in every way our attempt last Spring to preserve the Union Pacific from damage'.[1] These were presumably the concessions agreed by Hill at his meeting with Harriman in September.

OPPOSITION: LITIGATION BEGINS

The Northern Securities charter had been drafted with care: in what was becoming an age of amalgamations, despite the Sherman Anti-trust Act, it was the first example of railroads so arranging their affairs. It was not an amalgamation: terminology was all-important; but the case of Northern Securities was to make American legal history. A week after the granting of the charter Governor Van Sant of Minnesota called upon all the other governors of the States through which the Northern systems ran to unite in opposing the holding company by all means in their power. Responses varied in enthusiasm but on 31 December 1901 a conference took place at Helena, Montana, of governors and attorney-generals of the States involved and a resolution was passed approving 'any proper and suitable proceeding which may be instituted in any court having jurisdiction by the sovereign State of Minnesota, or any other State affected thereby, designated, designed and intended to speedily and finally test and determine the validity of such consolidation or threatened consolidation. And further, we unanimously protest against any combination or consolidation which restricts or stifles free competition in the trade or commerce of the country'.[2] On 20 December 1901 the federal Interstate Commerce Commission had adopted a resolution calling for an investigation into 'consolidations and combinations of carriers' including the 'community of interest' plan.[3]

Meanwhile the St. Paul *Globe* had on 22 December 1901 published a statement by J. J. Hill setting forth the circumstances in which the holding company had come into being. Originally (and some such device had been in his mind long before the Northern Pacific 'corner' precipitated affairs) it stemmed from the desire of several long-standing shareholders, whose ages ranged from 70 to 86, to combine their individual holdings in corporate form in order to

[1] Adler, op. cit. vol. 1, p. 110.

[2] Balthasar H. Meyer, *A History of the Northern Securities Case* in *Bulletin of the University of Wisconsin*, Madison, Wisconsin, 1906, pp. 242–3.

[3] Pyle, op. cit. vol. 2, p. 169. The 'community of interest' plan was the railroads' answer to the prohibition of pooling (see Robert E. Riegel, *The Story of the Western Railroads*, New York, 1926, p. 304).

secure permanent protection for their interests and a continuation of the policy and management which had done so much for the development of the North West and elsewhere. It had then become necessary, in order to prevent the Northern Pacific from passing under the control of the Union Pacific interests, and with it the joint control of the Burlington, to pay off the $75 millions of Northern Pacific Preferred stock. The enormous amount of cash required for this purpose, from a comparatively small number of men, made it necessary for them to act together in a large and permanent manner through the medium of a corporation, and the Northern Securities Company afforded them the means of accomplishing this object. 'The Northern Securities Company is organized to deal in high-class securities; to hold the same for the benefit of its shareholders, and to advance the interests of the corporations whose securities it owns. Its powers do not include the operations of railways, banking, or mining, nor the buying and selling of securities or properties of others on commission; it is purely an investment company . . .'[1]

In the belief that their legal position was absolutely watertight, Hill and his friends proceeded with the detailed arrangement of their affairs, although it was not long before injunctions were being taken out against the new company. Towards the end of 1901 Hill sent Mount Stephen a six-year railroad operation forecast; on 28 December Farrer told Ellis he would forward this for his perusal if it seemed to merit this. He had some reservations about it, and wrote to Ellis on New Year's Day 1902 (Mount Stephen was to give Ellis the document):

. . . Considering how little he or we have been able to foresee in the past it seems to me little use making forecasts for six years ahead, especially when material conditions, such as the question of Rates, have varied in the past sufficiently to upset all calculations made in previous years. You will notice that in his estimates, he makes no provision for capital expenditure.

I sent Lord Mount Stephen a table prepared in this office of comparative figures of many of the Western Roads,—I understand he has handed it on to you—Will you return it to me when you have finished with it— The figures giving the capitalization, as determined by the market price of the shares, are interesting; as also the comparison of the C.B. & Q.'s train miles used to carry ton miles earnings. There would appear to be

[1] Kennan, op. cit. vol. 1, pp. 328–9.

vast room for savings in this direction—We have not been able to include the Union and Southern Pacific figures, as their Reports are not yet to hand. We have a message this morning from New York saying that the conversion of Northern Pacific Debentures into Northern Pacific stock is temporarily postponed pending a decision on these injunctions, but our correspondents believe that the delay will be temporary only.

In fact, the legal processes which proliferated around the Northern Securities Company—a perfect carnival of lawsuits as Pyle termed it—dragged on for three years. To pursue in detail the various stages would result in this narrative becoming quite unbalanced; it is proposed therefore to confine this account as far as possible to the reactions of Hill's London friends and particularly to the problems which faced Lord Mount Stephen in that he had based large charitable donations on a source which stood at times in considerable jeopardy.

On 29 January 1902 Gaspard Farrer reported to Hill that so far in England the exchange of Great Northern into Northern Securities seemed to have been small, but it was possible that many holders had done the transaction through their own bankers 'while many may be temporarily deterred pending the decision in the litigation'. The English public was chiefly interested then in 'Kaffirs', but 'while they continue selling most of their U.S. holdings there has been quite a disposition to inquire for Northern Securities shares and since the close of the year we i.e. Lefevres and Barings together have placed some 12,000 shares including an order for 6,000 odd received from the Boss for one of his Royal friends. I believe that once this legal question is settled there would be quite a little buying here . . .' They had had an inquiry from brokers as to the possibility of making a market for them in London, but had thought it better to discourage them for the moment. 'No doubt in any such operation many of the shares would find their way back to New York on an advance but some would remain. The shares would be well advertised and the advertisement bear fruit in time. In case we think it wise to move we will communicate with you but I felt confident you would not wish any action to be taken till the legal status of the company was assured. Meantime we are daily putting away the Burlington joint Bonds and must have absorbed several millions: they seem to be dirt cheap and fit for the widow and orphan . . .' Was there any chance of Hill coming over?

Mount Stephen had offered Gaspard his river again that year but the latter was doubtful. He had just joined Baring Brothers, and had inhibitions which on 19 March he explained to John Sterling:

> No one could have been nicer than John, and all my Baring partners in wishing and even insisting on my going out to fish: nevertheless I am more than doubtful: three weeks at Metis, the minimum for which one would hope to stay, entails a 6 weeks' absence at least or 8 weeks if I go west to see Hill as I ought—and this is a lot out of a 12 month if I am to give reasonable attention to work here [Lefevres] and at No. 8 [Bishopsgate]: moreover I have been preaching at the latter shop that there is altogether too much absence and holiday—as there is—However you may be sure I would dearly like to come and will cable you as soon as I have finally decided. To escape coronation festivities is an added inducement if such were wanted.

In the event he remained in London, feeling deprived. He wrote to Louis Hill on 17 July: 'Sterling writes me enthusiastic accounts of his holiday at Metis, where the weather has been bad and rainy, and the river too high, but nevertheless a good bag has been made, and owing to the high water all fish have given the best of sport . . .' Louis knew what pleased Gaspard even more than fishing records, and the latter acknowledged what he had sent: 'Tabulated figures, which as you no doubt appreciated when you sent them, are just the kind of statistic that appeals to me. Thanks also for the crop Reports: it is a year now since my last visit to America and the longer the absence the more you seem to be living in a far country, so that any news is gratefully received . . .' After the report on Lord Strathcona's coronation year activities quoted above on page 164, he went on: 'Lord Salisbury's resignation caused no surprise. He has long wished to go, and recently broke down painfully in the House of Lords, forgetting his cue, so that it had become evident he was past serious work. Balfour's succession to the Premiership has been welcomed cordially by everyone, including Chamberlain, but Chamberlain will be the leading spirit in the Cabinet and all the more powerful for not being nominally the leader. The probabilities are that he will remain at the Colonial Office, and Hicks Beach's place be filled up by one of the younger members of the Cabinet . . .' Less than a year later, Joseph Chamberlain was to launch the Tariff Reform campaign which was to dominate British politics for the next three years, bringing down the Balfour Government; Lord Mount Stephen was to contribute £10,000 to it in the cause of Imperial Preference.

Gaspard continued his recital of events with a stock market review—business fairly active in all departments except American: 'Northern Securities shares change hands very occasionally, and there is certainly no disposition to sell, which is the more remarkable as nearly every other American stock has been sold freely and passed out of the possession of English people . . .' Lord Mount Stephen had left London for Brocket for the summer: 'He is remarkably well, and as full of go as ever he was'. Gaspard had given up hope of getting out that year, 'but I hope to come next spring and go over the Road, either before or after the fishing'. On 20 August 1902 Farrer reported to John Sterling: '. . . Lord Mount Stephen is passing through Town today to spend a short time with Charlie Ellis at Haslemere where the latter has made himself a home and a garden of unique interest. He is a great gardener and in correspondence with all the best gardeners all over the world . . .'

Acknowledging Sterling's letter of 6 August, Farrer was relieved to find that he was still confident of the outcome of the Northern Securities litigation: '. . . I do not see that it matters very much what the decision is in the long run, but the immediate trouble of an adverse decision, the explanations to ignorant clients, the prospect of which appals me . . .' A few weeks earlier he had sent Sterling a Press cutting of an interview stemming from President Theodore Roosevelt's action in having the legality of the Northern Securities Company tested in the Federal courts by the Attorney General, Philander C. Knox.[1] He asked Sterling: 'What grounds has Woodlock for his statement of the general legal opinion in America on the question of Knox's case? Is he correct? I have a letter from Grover [Great Northern counsel] very confident in the opposite sense—and though of course one recognizes the difference between legal opinion and a Court's decision, I had hitherto understood that Mr. Hill had justification for his views in the opinion of serious lawyers'. He was then obliged to write to one of his clients that Northern Securities, priced at 108 in New York, with dividends at 4 per cent with the prospect of some increase in the course of a year or so, had a lawsuit pending, 'which if decided against the Company will alter its constitution, though it cannot take away from the shareholders the property which they own. I am entirely satisfied with my investment and intend to hold it, but I should have thought

---

[1] On 14 September 1901 Theodore Roosevelt had succeeded to the Presidency on the assassination of President McKinley.

for your purpose a Bond of the Company would have been a more satisfactory investment, such as, for instance, St. Paul, Minneapolis and Manitoba Sterling 4's or Northern Pacific 3% General Mortgage Bonds ... or Northern Securities Shares, which are freely dealt in in New York . . .' To a lady in Wiltshire he wrote: '. . . As to Northern Securities, all I know about them is favourable, but as you ask my advice, I must tell you plainly that no profit, however great, would induce me to risk my entire means and consequently independence in one property. I hope therefore if we effect a sale of your London United Tramways you will be content to reinvest the money in some security in this country yielding a fair but safe rate of interest. I might point out that in case Northern Securities shares increase in value, as we all believe they will, your holding now is sufficiently large to secure for you a marked addition to the value of your property'. On 4 September 1902 Farrer wrote to Charles Ellis of active operations in New York in Northern Securities: the price the previous day had touched 117.

Meanwhile Mount Stephen, before leaving London, had written to his god-daughter, Frances Wolseley, on 27 June from Carlton House Terrace:

My dear Frances,

There is no need for any apology for writing to me about anything you are interested in. I am delighted with your letter showing as it does an understanding mind about matters of which ladies, in general, are rather vague.

About the Amalgamated shares. There is a big fight going on in the U.S. among the copper producers which I am hopeful will end in a victory for the Amalgamated, but in War as your father will tell you there is much in good luck. "Now the best laid plans of mice and men gang aft awry". Seeing the uncertainty hanging over the Company, I have made up my mind, to take you out of the Copper business and will take over your shares and give you Northern Securities Company shares for them, on the basis of what the Copper shares cost. I have a lot of these copper shares and a few more or less makes no difference to me, no matter when and what the outcome may be. Let me know how many shares you have, and I will on hearing from you write again and tell you what to do, to get the business through. I quite expected, in 1900, that the dividends would be raised from 8% to 10%, and am, of course, disgusted that it should have dropped to 2% per annum.

Yours always,

Mount Stephen

Frances noted in her autobiographical manuscript: 'Again in July I had very clear instructions from this kind and generous godfather what to do, and he exchanged my poor copper shares for 80 Northern Securities shares. He added: "Some day I hope these 80 shares will be worth double the money originally paid for the copper shares"'.[1] Later that year, her godfather increased her holding to 200.

MOUNT STEPHEN AND THE KING'S FUND

On the accession of King Edward VII, the new Prince of Wales (later to be King George V) became President of King Edward's Hospital Fund for London. This organization, founded in 1897 on the occasion of Queen Victoria's Diamond Jubilee, to channel charitable giving into a central fund which would then distribute it according to need among the various London hospitals, was originally named the Prince of Wales's Hospital Fund, and throughout the lifetime of Lord Mount Stephen, who was to be its largest benefactor, the current Prince of Wales was to be closely associated with it.[2] From 1899 to 1901 Mount Stephen had contributed a relatively modest £1,000 a year: in Coronation year, he and Lord Strathcona first gave £500 each to a special Coronation Fund, intended to stimulate the public's response to a not-too-popular appeal. The basic needs of the sick poor did not catch the imagination either of the wealthy who preferred to support a particular project which would be associated with them personally, or of the less well-off who had attachments to particular hospitals. To Mount Stephen, who with Lord Strathcona had already endowed the Royal Victoria Hospital in Montreal, had provided a cottage hospital in his boyhood home of Dufftown,[3] and was supporting the Aberdeen Royal Infirmary, the King's Fund represented the ideal in hospital giving for the London situation. Lord Strathcona, who was giving generously to his own list of projects, was persuaded once more into a joint gesture, vainly intended partly to encourage similar action in others of like means: on 24 November 1902 it was announced that they had each given £200,000 to the King's Fund. This meant £20,000 a year, or nearly half of what the Fund then aimed at getting on investment account, as opposed to incoming

---

[1] PVW 120/603. See p. 224 below, footnote 1.
[2] See Heather Gilbert, *King Edward's Hospital Fund for London : the first 25 years*, in *Social and Economic Administration*, Basil Blackwell, Oxford, vol. viii, no. 1, Spring 1974. The early records of the King's Fund are in London County Record Office (reference A/KE). [3] See Gilbert, vol. 1, p. 188.

annual contributions. The investment, in this case, was in the Northern Securities Company. It was a magnificent advertisement. Only one other prominent benefactor of the Fund followed their example: Samuel Lewis, a money-lender, had died in 1901 leaving £250,000 to the Fund subject to his wife's life interest in the capital. His widow handed over this income (£10,000 a year) as well as promising £2,500 a year on her own account, and when she died in 1906 left to the Fund, in addition, half the residue of the estate, in all over half a million pounds.

Mount Stephen's and Strathcona's gifts had been known to the Fund's officers earlier in 1902 and the Prince of Wales in September wrote each a personal letter of thanks, to which Mount Stephen responded on the 5th:

Pray accept my warmest thanks for your Royal Highness's most kind, though far too complimentary letter, which I received last night.

It is a great pleasure to me to know that you think I have been of some use to you in your efforts to make the King's Hospital Fund a more efficient aid to the London Hospitals than it has yet been, but if you will allow me to say so it is *entirely* due to the *tact* and good judgment with which you used my proposed contribution to the Fund, now nearly a year ago, that the Fund has benefitted by Lord Strathcona's contribution; no one else could have done what you have done; this is only the plain truth; I was on the point of writing to your Royal Highness when your letter came, to say that now the "cat was out of the bag" and the way open for me to speak privately of the claims of the King's Hospital Fund to any one likely to help in the work yet remaining to be done, that I should at once set about trying to do what I could to make up the £15,000 to £20,000 a year still required to complete the £50,000 a year we set out to secure . . . I may say here that I am quite hopeful Mr. Morgan will give us a substantial contribution, and I have already a promise of £100,000 from an old friend whose name I am not yet at liberty to mention: I am writing to Mr. Carnegie today . . .

I am sure Lord Strathcona will be greatly pleased to receive your letter: I have not had a scrap from him since I put him into relation with the lawyer, though I had a huge Haunch of Venison from him two days ago, from Glencoe, which shows that he has forgiven me for anything I may have done to relieve him of a little of his surplus money . . .

He added a postscript: 'We desire to share in the feeling of relief and happiness with which your Royal Highnesses must regard the restoration of the King to perfect health'.[1]

[1] RA GV C273/12.

The Duke of York's conversation with Lord Strathcona had taken place in Montreal in the course of his world tour with the Duchess in 1901. The latter wrote to Lord Mount Stephen from Ottawa on 22 September to acknowledge the gift of a 'lovely silver fox boa' and continued:

We had a very pleasant stay at Montreal and the Strathconas were most kind. The Duke will have told you in his letter of the success of his conversation with Ld. Strathcona and the Duke feels deeply grateful to you both for your great generosity, he is simply delighted at the thought of the Hospital Fund getting on in this splendid way. We had the pleasure of meeting both your sisters at Montreal and Mrs. Meighen told me of her visit to you at Brocket last July. I am charmed with Canada and am much looking forward to the trip to the North West in the beautiful train built for us. I wish you and Gian had been here for our visit . . .[1]

The Duchess had written to Gian from Sydney, Australia, on 1 June 1901, anxious about the latter's health, 'glad to know that you are really feeling better, the one thing to set you up would be to go to Canada, and we are still hoping that Lord Mount Stephen will soften his heart and give us the great pleasure of meeting you and him there which would be quite delightful . . .' She had ended the letter: 'With many messages from us both to you and Lord Mount Stephen and hoping to meet in Canada!'[2] but Gian, who was longing to go, was to be disappointed. Not until she was widowed did she achieve her ambition to visit the country which had meant so much to her husband. She wrote to the Duchess from Brocket on 27 September—they had just bought the Duke of Grafton's house in London, 17 Carlton House Terrace, 'which gives me a great deal of work as it is in a terrible state at present—Mr. Bertram assures me it will be lovely when finished'—looking forward to witnessing their Royal Highnesses' triumphal return to London in November, and to having them at Brocket in December: 'We have been watching every movement of your Royal Highnesses in the papers, and now we picture you on our! Railway, and only hope the weather will be lovely that you may see all that wonderful country at its best . . .'[3]

NORTHERN SECURITIES: IN THE COURTS

Soon the round of litigation which was to place in jeopardy this so-welcome charitable gesture was to begin. Briefly, the first stages

[1] RA GV CC44/196.　　　[2] RA GV CC44/195.　　　[3] RA GV CC47/69.

were as follows: the Interstate Commerce Commission, at its general session in Washington, D.C. on 20 December 1901, affirming its duty to enquire into the operations of all common carriers, particularly any consolidations and methods of association, ordered an inquiry which began on 8 January 1902 in Chicago. Its findings were to form part of the testimony in the Northern Securities case. On 7 January 1902 the Attorney General of the State of Minnesota moved in the Supreme Court of the United States for leave to file a bill of complaint against the Northern Securities Company. This was refused on 24 February 1902 on the technicality that a minority of shareholders were not represented as parties to the suit, whereupon the Minnesota Attorney General, Douglas, brought suit in the State Court, citing the Sherman Anti-trust Act and maintaining that the State, as a shipper, could take the case to the U.S. Circuit Court, where it was tried. A simultaneous similar move by the State of Washington made some initial progress but came to nothing. Meanwhile the United States Attorney General, Knox, had on 19 February 1902 given his opinion (referred to in Farrer's letter to Sterling) that the 'merger', being the virtual consolidation of two competing continental lines, therefore creating a monopoly, violated the provisions of the Sherman Act, and President Theodore Roosevelt therefore directed that action be taken to have the question judicially determined. Accordingly on 10 March 1902 the United States commenced suit in the U.S. Circuit Court at St. Paul against the Northern Securities, Great Northern and Northern Pacific Companies. This sat at St. Paul from October to December 1902. There were therefore two separate cases in the Circuit Court: the special trial court with four judges—Caldwell, Sanborn, Thayer and Van Devanter—sitting under a special Act of Congress deciding the federal government case, and the regular circuit court under Judge Lochren deciding the State of Minnesota case.[1] A worried J. P. Morgan asked the President whether his new U.S. Steel Corporation was to be next on the list for this treatment, but was reassured; Nemesis caught up with him in 1911.

In March 1902 James J. Hill wrote to his trusted friend D. Willis James, a partner in Phelps, Dodge and Company and a large shareholder in Great Northern:

We are fully prepared for anything we have to meet, and in this case the question is simply, was there a conspiracy between the shareholders of

[1] Meyer, op. cit. pp. 243–58. Pyle, op. cit. vol. 2, pp. 169–70.

the NP and the GN shareholders to form the Securities Company for the purpose of restraining or restricting interstate commerce? You and our other GN friends know that the Securities Company was not a conspiracy . . . The company was formed by the holders of one fourth of the shares and the option was left to all others to decide for themselves individually whether they would join in the new company or not . . . All of our counsel feel that our case will be easily won and that in the end we will have the advantage of having our charter rights confirmed by the Supreme Court. In fact, our action will show that we prevented the UP interests from holding the NP, and through it the joint control of the Burlington restraining and practically destroying the trade of the North West and of the whole country, as it concerns the Oriental trade . . . It really seems hard, when we look back on what we have done, and know that we have led all Western companies in opening the country, and carrying at the lowest rates, that we should be compelled to fight for our lives against the political adventurers who have never done anything but pose and draw a salary'.[1]

Jacob Schiff, while writing to a member of Congress that he welcomed the prompt action of the President, since 'if the creation of the Northern Securities Company is contrary to law, it is much better for all concerned that this should be ascertained at an early period . . .' nevertheless was distinctly alarmed. Although the Northern Securities Company itself could no doubt be dissolved without grave consequences, he feared a disorganization of the entire railroad and industrial affairs of the country: 'there is not one important railroad which does not control competing lines, directly or indirectly, through stock holdings'. He hurried off to see the President himself in Washington, returning to repeat his views in writing on 6 April 1902:

. . . I hope, Mr. President, you will feel assured that I have no other motives, in the bringing of my views before you, than such as come from the concern I believe I am justified in feeling, as to the distress and suffering which may possibly be brought upon the country by the conditions which I fear must result from a judicial affirmation of the claims made by the Attorney General in his bills of complaint against the Northern Securities Company. No one can have a more intense desire than I that your Administration should result in great credit to yourself and in every possible benefit to the country, nor would I wish that anything be permitted to be done in any endeavour to correct the situation which would not entirely safeguard the dignity of the Government'.[2]

---

[1] Pyle, op. cit. vol. 2, pp. 170–2.   [2] Adler, op. cit. vol. 1, pp. 111–12.

The relatively new factor of the oriental through trade, which had stimulated the competition between railroads hitherto geared to serve the interests of the north west and accentuated the need to comb the country to the south and east for products to exchange for the tea, silk, and other exports of China and Japan (hence the usefulness of the C.B.Q. network) emphasized the truth of Meyer's observation on the 'impossible doctrine of protection of the public by railway competition'.[1]

On 7 March 1903 Gaspard Farrer wrote to Hill: 'The news of your sailing came as a pleasant surprise, as I feared that something would occur to detain you in America. I need hardly tell you how immensely we are looking forward to seeing you again. It seems years since we last had a chat together'. Farrer had booked rooms for Hill and his daughter and Hill's secretary at the Carlton Hotel. 'Lord Mount Stephen joins me in every expression of welcome'. There followed a busy two weeks, of which he finally got down to writing an account to John Sterling on 20 March; acknowledging first 'many letters' from the latter:

... I hope you will not think that during this long silence my letters to you have been going, as on that fatal occasion, to our friend James S. [Stillman][2] The fact of the matter is that I have been busy lately, and Hill's and Shaughnessy's arrival have thrown me back in all my correspondence. I went up to Liverpool to meet the 'Celtic' and found those two Railway magnates in good form, particularly Shaughnessy, [now President of Canadian Pacific] who told me that Hill had been quite worn out when they sailed from New York, but had picked up wonderfully on the voyage. Both Lord Mount Stephen and myself have had many talks with the former, and we are hoping before he leaves us to get some idea of his future policy and requirements. He is perhaps more discursive than ever, and extraordinarily unsatisfactory in frankness. He does not seem to be able to face telling one what his requirements are likely to be, though one knows as a certainty there must be another side to the position which he is always bringing forward, viz., the difficulty of getting rid of his cash earnings. In spite of all this, which is incidental to his character, I should say that he has never been more hopeful of the future of his properties, and more certain that there will be a speedy realisation of the profitable times which he foresees. He has gone to Paris this morning but will be back again next week, and sails on the 4th ...

[1] Quoted in Kennan, op. cit. p. 339.
[2] See Chapter IX, p. 355.

As to the fishing, Farrer was sorely tempted by Sterling's invitation, and while advancing the same arguments against so long an absence from work as a visit to Metis would entail, concluded 'However I am quite determined to come, unless anything unforeseen prevents me, and accept your invitation with very great pleasure. The Captain is in London for a few days just now, and would have liked dearly to accompany me, but unfortunately that is out of the question for this year'. Eddie Hunter-Blair was ill. 'I took him to see Lord Mount Stephen and had a very pleasant chat. He is, as usual, full of you and your plans, and told Lord Mount Stephen yesterday: "Sterling was the only man of whom he never got tired" '. Gaspard promised to write again the following week about Metis, referring also to Sterling's new house in New York 'which I am longing to see. The Captain contemplates writing a pamphlet entitled "The Millionaire and his Marble Halls"'.

There was some further correspondence about Metis, Gaspard writing on 8 May 1903:

As to your own guests at Metis, ask whomever you like—Rockefeller, Rogers, and every Amalgamated officer if you please, and unless we can get what we want out of them, we will send them to the Mill Pool whenever the water is in flood with instructions to the canoemen as to what to do . . .

He referred to the current difficulties of the Amalgamated Copper Company in which, through Sterling's recommendation, both he and Mount Stephen had invested and which had just passed its dividend. This deviation from the sound advice invariably expected from Sterling made irresistible the impulse to tease his old friend. 'The fact is', Gaspard was later to tell Mount Stephen, '(Sterling) is a little too near to the inside to get a proper perspective without being sufficiently inside to see through H. H. R[ogers] spectacles'.[1] Rogers was later to be Vice-President of Standard Oil; an ambitious young man, he had, as Stillman's biographer Burr wrote: 'traveled a long way since that anniversary of his marriage when he carried home to his wife a new rocking-chair, bearing it in his arms for a couple of miles on a hot highway, because he had no money left to pay the

---

[1] H. H. Rogers had been the leader in the 1899 Amalgamated Copper syndicate which took over the Anaconda Copper Company of Butte, Montana, under the auspices of the National City Bank, backed by Standard Oil. Adverse public reaction followed (see Burr, op. cit. pp. 141–3. For early history of Anaconda see Adler, op. cit. vol. 1, pp. 155–7 and Pyle, op. cit. vol. 2, pp. 205–8).

freight'.[1] The following year Farrer was to report to Sterling his attempt to prise some information out of James Stillman, whose Standard Oil colleagues were endeavouring to settle copper problems in Montana: 'I asked J. S. point blank whether he had anything to say about them, and he replied "no"—then with some shame-facedness added "I believe our people are going to win out and that an end will be put to some of the troubles we have had in the past"—I suppose such a general statement was as much as one could expect from that Sphinx-like person'.

But to return to Metis and the plans for 1903: Gaspard assured Sterling:

Seriously, Lord Mount Stephen has no wish but that you should ask whatever friends are most congenial, and I need hardly add that any friends of yours will be most welcome to me. I am making arrangements to send out my rods and clothes to Turnbull, and will pick them up in Montreal on my way through. I have no desire whatever to go across to St. John River, and I may say that so far I have not been invited, nor do I expect or deserve to be after my behaviour last year. It looks to me from your letters as if you intended that I should go. Let me tell you that if I do, it will only be in your company, so you had better prepare to face the yacht, the launch, and other amenities that the trip will involve —I have avoided writing anything to Mr. Hill about the date of my coming, or indeed of my coming at all, and am in hopes that he will not even know I am out. I should be very glad if you could get Jimmy [?Stillman] with us.

Mr. Hill has written me two letters about the decision, and one to Lord Mount Stephen, but in none of them does he make any mention of an alternative plan in case the Supreme Court upholds the present judgment. He seems very confident that he will obtain some modification on appeal, but even with material modification it appears to me that existing plans must be a good deal upset. I quite think that the solution foreshadowed in your letter of the 28th seems a reasonable one on which to work . . .

CONFLICTING JUDGMENTS

On 9 April 1903 the four judges sitting in the Circuit Court trying the federal case had decided against the Northern Securities Company, finding that it accomplished the object which Congress had declared illegal. Judge Thayer wrote the decision and the other

[1] Burr, op. cit. pp. 106–7.

three concurred.[1] Meyer was to write that from the point of view of history, the Northern Securities Company was the logical culmination of a long series of events as old as the railway itself, in which the inherent tendencies towards combination had been in perpetual conflict with laws assuring natural competition. In that conflict the forms of co-operative effort and combination had been metamorphosed into new shapes to avoid the ban which the law had placed upon the old. These new forms, wrote Meyer, have generally been slightly in advance of the law. Wrote Thayer: 'the Securities Company accomplishes the object ... perhaps more effectually than other forms of combination generally known in 1890 when the Anti-trust Law was passed'. He went on to say that although the motives might have been wholly laudable and unselfish, that the combination was formed by the individual defendants to protect great interests which had been committed to their charge, or that the combination was the initial and the necessary step in the accomplishment of great designs—'it may be that such a virtual consolidation of parallel and competing lines of railroad as has been effected, taking a broad view of the situation, is beneficial to the public rather than harmful . . .'—the only question before the court was whether or not it constituted a combination *having power* to 'suppress competition between two or more competing and parallel lines of railroad engaged in interstate commerce'.

The judgment in the State case given in August 1903—Judge Lochren—found that the mere possession of power did not warrant the assumption that such power would be used criminally. Meyer points out that, historically, the most interesting argument for the defence related to the development of railway combinations and the evolution of the holding company. It was contended that the consolidation of competing lines had been common knowledge before 1890, when the Anti-trust Law was passed, and that if Congress had intended to prohibit such in future the law would have given direct and definite expression to such a prohibition. Hence Congress did not intend to forbid, and did not forbid, 'the natural processes of unification which are brought about under modern methods of lease, consolidation, merger, community of interest, or ownership of stock'. The Northern Securities Company, moreover, was not a railroad but an investment or holding company.

---

[1] Meyer, op. cit. pp. 258–73. Pyle, op. cit. vol. 2, pp. 172–3, also Noyes, *Forty Years of American Finance*, pp. 347–8.

Nevertheless, the judgment in the federal case was followed by an injunction to dissolve the Northern Securities Company; it was enjoined from voting its stock, acquiring additional stock, paying dividends or exercising corporate control, but was permitted to return stock to holders who had received it in exchange for railway shares. The Company appealed to the Supreme Court of the United States.

Jacob Schiff wrote complacently on 13 April 1903 to Samuel Rea of the Pennsylvania Railroad that the results of the adverse decision in the federal case would be very far-reaching, but he was not unduly pessimistic; 'we shall, no doubt, henceforth find a great deal of unwillingness to embark in new affairs, but that is no misfortune, for promotion has been frightfully overdone . . . and in this respect perhaps the Northern Securities decision may prove a blessing in disguise'.[1]

Gaspard Farrer began again his appalling task of educating the ignorant investor. On 14 April 1903 he wrote in much the same sense to three of these about the decision given against the legality of the constitution of Northern Securities which had, and would perhaps for some little time, temporarily affect the *market* value of the shares. The intrinsic values of the properties were of course unaltered. He enclosed to each a cutting from that morning's *Standard* which explained the situation. To 'the Admiral'—who was not so much ignorant as blindly loyal—he called the *Standard's* telegram a 'pithy summing up of the position as it stands today' adding that the decision of the court was 'as vexatious as unexpected'. He continued the general explanation:

. . . I think you understand that the Northern Securities Company is in the nature of a Trustee Company, holding the shares of the two Railways —the Northern Pacific and the Great Northern. The decision of the Court is in effect to say that it is illegal to form a Company for such a purpose and it is possible that eventually the Northern Securities Company will have to be dissolved and the shares of the two Railway Companies distributed to the present holders of Northern Securities Shares.

I have not the smallest hesitation in saying that the Railway properties as measured by the price of Northern Securities shares today, viz., about 98 London, are remarkably cheap for anyone who is able to pay for his shares and hold them for permanent investment. The decision of the Supreme Court cannot be given for some time to come, and there will

[1] Adler op. cit. vol. 1, p. 112.

probably be ups and downs in the market before then, but I have no fear of the outcome of the properties themselves in the long run.

One of Farrer's addressees was comptroller to one of Mount Stephen's 'Royals'.

To John Sterling Farrer wrote on 29 April, acknowledging his of the 14th: '... We are very much interested in your opinion of the decision, ... Whatever the result is in the Court of Appeal, I think possibly the check given to speculation by the present decision will have been no bad thing for the country as a whole, but it is unpleasant that we should be the ones to have to swallow the medicine'. This was an echo of Schiff, but also explained Gaspard's unwillingness to go out of his way to see Hill that Spring. To his letter of 8 May regarding the latter, he added: 'We have just received Mr. Hill's Northern Securities circular, and are rather surprised at its issue. The figures are too general to be of any practical use. I can only imagine that his object in publishing them was for the benefit of the Law Courts and not for his shareholders, i.e. to shew that the Northern Securities was in fact nothing but a distributing Company. The figures of the circular obviously do not show the strength of the position, which lies in the figures of the properties themselves'.

Farrer had been anxious not even to visit New York on his way to Metis—he was sailing at the end of May—but in the end he accepted Sterling's pressing invitation to stay with him there on arrival, and in fact spent two more days in New York before sailing for home. Otherwise, he wrote to Edward Tuck in Paris on 25 July, his visit was one purely of pleasure, and he did not go west:

... Mr. Hill paid me a visit at Metis on the way to his river, but both he and I had many guests, and we had little opportunity for serious business talk. He is however in excellent spirits, and full of confidence as usual. I wish he was as full of cash as of confidence,—but you know his habits in this respect, and I expect he is incorrigible. The Burlington borrowing the other day on short notes was not a pleasant feature, and one cannot but suspect that the Great Northern is even worse off than the Burlington so far as cash is concerned. However I have no doubt he will manage to get along somehow or another ... It is quite certain that Mr. Hill cannot issue fresh stock while this decision is hanging over us, and if he requires money, he will have to borrow it on Bonds or short notes, nor in my judgment would it be prudent to increase his dividend ...[1]

---

[1] The court decision forbidding payment of dividends was not yet in effect pending the result of the appeal.

Gaspard concluded: 'Returning to your enquiry about Northern Securities stock held in this country, I may say that about one-fifth of the entire capital is now owned in Europe, and the amount held here is constantly increasing. We know ourselves of between 5,000 and 10,000 shares purchased recently on the decline, and our clients are still buying. You must recollect that though Hill claims that but 7 per cent of the stock is on the Street, that 7 per cent now represents a total of $28 million, so no wonder Stock is always easily obtainable, especially in times like these. The holdings which my friends and I have do not give me a moment's uneasiness'.

VII

Northern Securities: victim of circumstance

MOUNT STEPHEN AND HIS GOD-DAUGHTER

IN 1903 Field Marshal Viscount Wolseley published the only two volumes of his memoirs ever completed: *The Story of a Soldier's Life*. The dedication ran as follows: 'To the Right Honourable Lord Mount Stephen—I dedicate these volumes of varied experiences to you who for forty years have given me your unvarying friendship'. Writing from their new country home at Glynde in Sussex to his wife who was at her 'grace-and-favour' apartments in Hampton Court Palace, Garnet had wanted her advice about this: 'I have just thought it might be well to dedicate my book to Mount Stephen. He might buy several copies and at any rate might possibly feel flattered by the attention of one of his *very* oldest friends . . .' This was on 2 June 1903; the following day he had Louisa's answer: '. . . I think the dedication to Lord Mount Stephen an excellent idea and he is such a trusty real friend he deserves it . . .'[1] The financial aspect of the work was very much on Garnet's mind. He had written on 18 May of his negotiations with the publishers, and calculated that if the latter paid him £5000 outright, 'That would be an addition to your income for ever of £150 per annum and for Frances after you . . .'[2] Four volumes were planned; the first two only got as far as the Ashanti expedition. It seemed that the manuscript of these was already circulating among his friends: Lady Dorothy Nevill, whose *Reminiscences*, published in 1906, painted a frank picture of English society as it had deteriorated during her long lifetime, had read it. Mount Stephen wrote to his god-daughter on 24 December 1902: '.. Tell your father that Old Dolly Nevill writes to me that she had just finished reading his book, and felt as if she had lost a friend, "it so interested me" she adds'.[3]

---

[1] W/P 32. LW/P 29.   [2] W/P 32.   [3] PVW 120/610.

Following his retirement Wolseley had, with Mount Stephen's approval, accepted a directorship with Sir Donald Currie's Union Castle Line,[1] and for some time made regular visits to town to attend meetings, but this routine gradually faltered. His lapses were spasmodic over the next few years; there was further neck trouble and he complained at intervals to his wife about his failing memory: '. . . I wonder if loss of memory can be *tackled* by any sort of treatment?' he queried on 26 November 1903.[2] But always he referred to it as if it were a new development, which must at all costs be concealed from others. He appeared to be unaware that it had been remarked long before his retirement. This lack of awareness did not yet embrace the problem of his daughter: '. . . What shall I give Frances for Xmas?' he appealed to Louisa on 18 December 1903 during one of his trips to town. 'Don't you think if both you and I together gave her ten pounds it would be the most acceptable present we could give her—I wish we could present her with a sensible and suitable mate. That would be the best Xmas Box she could obtain . . .'[3]

It is time, since Frances' relations with her godfather were becoming closer, to provide some more background to this aspect of the Mount Stephen story. Frances' earliest recollection of her godfather was of being taken to see him by her German governess, and coming away with a sealed envelope (not to be opened until she got home) which excited only Miss Pannebakker. The £50 cheque which it contained opened a bank account from which Frances eventually bought her first hunter. She was not, on this visit, put through the Shorter Catechism as her mother had teasingly prophesied. When Frances was about eleven—about 1883—and staying with Lady Arthur Russell at Shere, Louisa wrote 'There is a parcel waiting for you from Mrs. Stephen and it has something very pretty in it'. At fourteen Frances set out with Lady Stephen to choose two books at Bumpus which they then took to Mr. T. J. Cobden-Sanderson to be specially bound. To their great discomfiture he deplored their choice as being unworthy of his art and chose two others; these, in exquisitely-tooled calf and gilt, with the two sets of initials 'G.S'. and 'F.W.' are now in the Hove collection. They must have been among the earliest examples of the bookbinder's work: the chance conversation with Mrs. William Morris in 1883 which led to this '41 years old and intellectual rolling stone

[1] W/P 30.   [2] W/P 32.   [3] Ibid.

par excellence', Thomas James Cobden-Sanderson, taking up the craft is said to be too well known to bear repetition.[1] Even writing with hindsight, Frances remained slightly cross that the afterwards world-famous bookbinder should have rejected the 'well-printed and handsome' books she had chosen as 'too bulky in size and especially in thickness for his slender fingers to manipulate successfully' and 'being only a binder, and scarcely then a booklover, selected the poor edition of Tennyson that I possess, gorgeously clothed in his binding' and a Shakespeare.[2] As the years went on, her godfather's gifts took other forms: silver-backed brushes, a miniature, a brooch. The earliest letter in the Hove collection from Lord Mount Stephen, dated 12 October 1898, warns Frances to take care when out hunting: '. . . remember it is nearly always the good swimmer that gets drowned'.[3] His later management of her investments, and his kindly guidance in her difficult family relations were to make him an increasingly important figure in her life. His letters to her are of more lasting value in that they often reflect events of which other evidence is scanty, whether of a business or a social nature. That of 18 May 1900 (referred to on p. 161 concerning his gift invested in Amalgamated Copper shares) included the news: 'Gian and I are well, having almost recovered from our unexpected visit to Windsor on Monday . . . We go to London on Monday, and shall be there in attendance on Mr. Jim Hill, of the Great Northern Railway, who goes back to America on June 1st . . . My love to your mother, and tell her the Gt. Nor. is most prosperous'.

At Farmhouse, Glynde, in 1903 Frances had taken to helping the gardener, and when in that year he left, Lady Wolseley engaged a lady who had advertised herself as a widow in distressed circumstances as gardener. Louisa then got the idea, from recent experiments elsewhere, of having students to learn gardening under this lady, two arriving in March. It is hard to say why Frances, in her

---

[1] *Times Literary Supplement*, 11 June 1970, review of Frederick B. Adams Jr. (Compiler): *Bookbindings by T. J. Cobden-Sanderson*, An Exhibition at the Pierpont Morgan Library, Spiral Press.
[2] PVW 118/176-7. It was typical of Frances that in her retrospective Diary, p. 124 (incorporated in her memoirs PVW 119) she gives a quite different account: she, twelve years old, the bookbinder 'a regular craftsman of the middle ages . . . keen as a knife upon carrying out beautiful work and his wife, who I believe has since become one of the most active of the suffragettes . . .' Besides the miserable Tennyson, this version puts 'one of the Italian painters'. 'The bindings had that curious indented back which is characteristic of his work and the high polish which is a secret of the art, that he has not betrayed to others . . .'
[3] PVW 119/475.

autobiographical manuscript, should describe this innovation as 'one of those wonderful fancies evolved by my mother and fraught with amusement for her'.[1] The results admittedly bordered on the ludicrous at times but the idea was one which Frances herself was about to pursue with varying degrees of success. When Louisa wrote to Garnet on 16 March: 'Two pupils have arrived . . . another comes shortly. It will be a Horticultural College soon . . .' neither she nor her daughter realized that before long Frances would be founding her own college of gardening and have her own land at Glynde. One of the gems of Garnet's letters to his wife is a pen-and-ink portrait of one of Frances' early head gardeners, a 'portly and manly' figure in Edwardian costume.[2] But although Garnet wrote satirically of gardeners 'in hats and feathers' flitting about the garden—' "flit" is not a good word' he admitted of the above-mentioned head gardener—he conceded 'Frances manages her gardens well'.[3] Louisa also wrote of 'great garden improvements'[4] and it was she who suggested in 1904 that Frances should design a prospectus for the school and enlist some prominent gardeners such as William Robinson and Gertrude Jekyll as patrons. As usual Frances took up the suggestion. The present writer cannot recall any occasion, on any subject, on which Frances did not follow up a line of action suggested by a correspondent, with the sole exception of an assurance by Lord Curzon that although peeresses in their own right might not sit in the House of Lords she was quite entitled to subscribe to a war memorial there.[5]

NORTHERN SECURITIES: FARRER LOOKS AHEAD

As the next stage in Frances' relations with her godfather anticipates developments in the Northern Securities affair it is necessary now to revert to that topic. The central part of Farrer's letter to Tuck of 25 July 1903 manifested his reaction to what became known as the 'rich men's panic' of that year in the United States:[6]

. . . On the general American situation I do not take the gloomy view which seems prevalent. They are suffering from an acute stomach-ache at present. For two years past the American public has not been buying

---

[1] PVW 120/621.   [2] W/P 34.   [3] W/P 33, W/P 34.
[4] W/P 31.   [5] PVW 120/662–5.
[6] See also Noyes, *Forty Years of American Finance*, pp. 308–13 and Adler on *Schiff*, vol. I, pp. 177–8.

securities, while leading Houses there have been printing them as fast as the presses could work, and the trouble now is they are all short of cash—all, that is, in financial centres, but this will right itself in time, though the process is unpleasant while it lasts. Already Europe is taking large quantities of their best securities, and it looks as if standard stocks have got to a level at which the Public there are buying as well as the Public here. I have no shadow of doubt but that in two years time we shall be reselling to America securities now being bought, and at very largely increased prices. The greatest danger ahead is the situation in Industrial Securities. It is quite plain that neither the public in America nor here will buy them at any price, and I can see no help for that situation but that the nominal capitals of these companies should be squeezed down to such a level that the late owners and recent sellers of the businesses should think it worth their while to repurchase. In other words, that there should be a transfer of ownership from the present Wall Street holders back to those who created and understand the business. Nothing strikes one more in opening a New York paper than to see the long list of American Industrial Companies, of which I, who am not accustomed to see American papers, had never even heard. Every business in America seems to have been turned into a Joint Stock Company and capitalised after the manner of the Steel Trust . . .

So much for Gaspard's visit 'purely of pleasure'. By September he again had on his mind the relatively small number of shareholders, this time of the Northern Securities Company, instead of merely of the Great Northern. Writing to Mount Stephen on the 2nd, he asked for the list which Hill had brought over in the Spring, that he might compare it with one he had just received from New York: 'I may say that the total number of shareholders is 2,333, as compared with 2,192 on May 4th of this year, altogether too small a number for so big a concern'. To Louis Hill he wrote on 4 September: '. . . I am confident that we ought to direct our efforts towards increasing the number of our shareholders—twenty times the present number would be none too many for the capital of the Company and its financial position would be enormously strengthened in consequence'. He had noticed that there had been less expansion lately in traffic, but told Louis this was probably a good thing—they needed quiet times to take stock and 'find out whether your foundations are sufficiently solid to bear the superstructure . . .' Lord Revelstoke was contemplating a visit to the United States and Farrer wondered whether a meeting with James J. Hill was possible. (Gaspard was uneasy because Barings' relations with the Union Pacific looked like becoming closer, and he was anxious that Revelstoke should speak frankly to Hill on the subject.)[1] He himself felt out of date regarding developments in St. Paul, he told Louis, and must come out before long. He wrote, too, to J. N. Hill on 15 September hoping that he might travel back with Lord Revelstoke: Mount Stephen and he were very anxious to see him (James Norman was now in the Northern Securities office in New York) and Gaspard's golfing holiday 'literally depends on your coming. I would take you round all the best links in England, and Scotland, & could promise you a royal time'. In a letter to Mount Stephen of 19 November 1903 he enclosed the latest list of shareholders, having had placed against the names in black ink their holding as at 3 August, and having also marked new holders. The change was not great but in the right direction, and 'is quite interesting in certain cases'. He had written on 30 September to a correspondent in Montreal: '... We are feeling much more cheerful about the Northern Securities case and are not altogether without hope that the decision may be entirely reversed in the Supreme Court'.

Farrer's prophecy to Tuck regarding Hill's possible need of ready money had its sequel in his letter to Charles Ellis of 11 November 1903:

The advance to the Great Northern Railway Company will be £1.5 million to represent which Barings will issue £1.5 million Certificates similar in form to those issued in the case of the Argentine Government advance recently repaid.

The certificates will be dated 1 December 1903, will bear interest at 5% payable half-yearly, and will be due in two years say 1 December 1905. They will be secured by the deposit with B.B & Co. of

(1) £1,500,000 GN notes

(2) £2,000,000 St. P. M. & M. 4% Pacific Extension 1st Mortgage Bonds being part of the mortgage for £6,000,000 of which £3,000,000 are already outstanding in the hands of the public and quoted on the London Stock Exchange.

Mr. Hill writes that he spent last year $15 million on capital account of which approximately half was provided by surplus income, and the other half by temporary bills ... which the present advance will repay.

The price at which we can offer the certificates will be 99½ and the

[1] Gaspard Farrer Letter Books, Farrer to Mount Stephen, 3 October 1903.

yield therefore 5¼ per cent including redemption. If you care for them I will reserve for you whatever you require.

We have said nothing of this business at present to any one but Lord Mount Stephen and I must ask you to keep the matter to yourself for a few days.

He wrote in the same terms two days later to Beverley MacInnes, Mount Stephen's secretary, adding that the certificates were in denominations of £100; the security was excellent 'being the IOU of the Great Northern, plus St. P. M. & M. Bonds to the extent of £2 million sterling, to cover an advance of £1·5 million leaving a margin of 33 per cent'.

THE KING'S FUND: ANOTHER DONATION

In November 1903 Farrer was in Scotland, whether or not accompanied by James Norman Hill; this emerges from his correspondence with James Cole, Mount Stephen's former butler, who was about to leave for Australia with his wife to serve Lord and Lady Northcote in the same capacity. On 19 January 1904 the *Montreal Star* reported that the Mount Stephens were lending Brocket Hall for the honeymoon of Princess Alice of Albany and Prince Alexander George of Teck, younger brother of the Princess of Wales, later as the Earl of Athlone to be Governor-General of Canada. Prince Alge, as he was known, had been invited to Brocket along with his sister on the latter's return with the Prince of Wales from their world tour. Princess Alice, in the Reminiscences entitled *For My Grandchildren*, describes Brocket as 'a most adorable place'. She had been somewhat surprised, but touched and impressed, on leaving Windsor Castle after the wedding on 10 February 1904 'amidst the usual shower of rice' when Uncle Bertie—King Edward VII—had said: 'Remember, always go to church wherever you are'. Accordingly, on the following Sunday they attended divine service at the small church of Lemsford, but 'were covered with confusion when the hymn chosen had that refrain "Therefore give us love"!'[1]

Mount Stephen's new year greetings to the Prince of Wales had come with the disclosure of a new and characteristic idea for the benefit of the King's Fund: he would give a further £100,000 on

---

[1] London, 1966, p. 16. Princess Alice was the only daughter of Prince Leopold who died in 1884 when she was a year old. See above chap. I, p. 2, Queen Victoria to Sir George Stephen.

condition that three others should do likewise within the next two months. He was hoping to get one friend to follow suit—that this was the same friend who had been mentioned earlier becomes clear—and if this were achieved he was confident that the Prince would be able again to persuade Lord Strathcona.[1] He reported to the Prince on 6 January 1904 that having written to his friend reminding him of his promise of 1902 the latter had replied repeating his promise and his 'high approval of the object we are aiming at, but it seems to be almost impossible for him to overcome his disinclination to let the *money go*, although it is of no use to him, & he would not be a bit the poorer if he gave you the £200,000 tomorrow'.[2] On 17 January Mount Stephen had to admit defeat, at least for the moment:

I have had my friend in London since Wednesday but I regret to say, while most friendly and favourable towards increasing the endowment of the King's Hospital Fund & says he will some day, before long, carry out his intention to subscribe £100,000 or perhaps £200,000 to the capital of the Fund but is not ready to do so just yet &c &c &c. The fact is that he is unable to conquer his natural disinclination to "pairt" with the money.

Having pressed him to act now at this opportune time as much as I dare, I think it will be politic to let him alone for a little while.[3]

The identity of his friend is never disclosed: the fact that Hill did not appear to have visited London at that time reduces the possibility that it was he; it may have been Charles Ellis, and if so the hesitation would have been quite characteristic. The recent appeal to shore up the Great Northern would hardly have diminished his reluctance. From a letter written by Mount Stephen to Sir Arthur Bigge on 16 October 1908 on the subject of possible contributions to the King's Fund, it would seem that he also had John S. Kennedy in mind:

I hope "little Andy" (Carnegie) will have seen the inclosed from yesterday's Daily Telegraph; it would help him to make up his mind to do, what I am hoping to see him do, some day, for the King's Fund, namely to send the President five million dollars (£1,000,000 stg.) U.S. 5% Steel Bonds. He got about 200 million for his interest in the Steel Co: & would never miss this 5 million.

When I first knew Kennedy in 1878, he considered himself a *very rich* man having by 20 years hard work accumulated $500,000. He was agent

[1] RA GV C273/25.   [2] RA GV C273/26.
[3] RA GV C273/27.

for the Dutch Bondholders from whom I bought the Bankrupt St. Paul & Pacific Railway, which became the St. Paul Minn. & Manitoba Railway in 1879 & years afterwards the Gt. Northern; Kennedy was very useful to me. To reward him I *gave* him 1/5 interest, making him equal to Hill, Kittson, Smith & myself & that is how he became the Scotch Millionaire. He & Hill both joined the syndicate which undertook to build the C.P.R. in 1880, of which I was the reluctant head, & after things began to look black & nobody had a good word to say about the C.P.R. they both (Hill & Kennedy) sold out their shares and deserted me. They are no doubt very sorry for themselves today.

Why I am telling you all this ancient history I don't know. Forgive me![1]

Mount Stephen had clearly been brooding on the seeming ingratitude of one or both of these men.

At first Mount Stephen had suggested that the Prince of Wales might make a personal approach to the five or six men who were likely to respond, then, writing to Sir Arthur Bigge, the Prince's secretary, on 22 February 1904, and recognizing that because of the Prince's connection with several London hospitals it might be difficult for him to press the claims of the King's Fund, he proposed that he should furnish the Prince with an unsigned letter outlining his anonymous offer. This could be used when he addressed the Fund's General Council at its March meeting. The letter also revised Mount Stephen's offer: he was now prepared to give a third, instead of a quarter of the total, and his offer would remain in force until 31 December 1904.[2] Moreover, while not attaching any other conditions, Mount Stephen expressed the hope that no portion of the funds subscribed for the relief of the sick poor would be diverted to the purposes of medical education. This somewhat controversial matter was later referred to a special committee which upheld Mount Stephen's view.[3] Meanwhile the Executive Committee made three vain appeals in the Press. Writing to Sir Arthur Bigge on 4 April 1904, Mount Stephen referred to this, adding: 'If two or three men could be found *able* and *willing* to put their hand into their pocket our object would be gained; the sum required is too large for the general public'.[4] Once again he was over-optimistic; December came with no other donor materializing. Writing to

---

[1] RA GV C273/74. Carnegie had given the Fund £100,000 in 1907.
[2] RA GV C 273/28 and 29.
[3] A/KE/2/2. See also A/KE/2/6, and A/KE/27/2.
[4] RA GV C273/33.

Bigge on the 16th that he was 'disappointed but not defeated', Mount Stephen asked him to find out quietly from the Secretary of the Fund the amount by which the income from investments that year had fallen short of the goal of £50,000, adding: 'Pardon my troubling you with this little matter but I do not want those city magnates to be gossiping & speculating as to what my object was if I applied to them direct for this information, which you can get without attracting notice'.[1] On 21 December he told the Prince that if there was no response by the 31st he himself would give the Fund £200,000 worth of Argentine Government Bonds yielding £11,000 per annum. On 1 January 1905 he wrote more fully:

I am very sorry to learn that the anonymous offer to contribute the necessary capital to provide one third of the annual sum required, say £14,000, to make the fixed income of the King's Hospital Fund up to £50,000 a year, has lapsed, in consequence of the inadequacy of the response to the appeal made by Your Royal Highness now nearly a year ago.

Having for many years past taken a great interest in all that concerns the Sick-Poor, and having from its foundation regarded the King's Fund as an ideal organization for the distribution of the gifts and subscriptions of all those who like myself have no personal interest in any particular Hospital or Convalescent Home, it is therefore a great pleasure to me to be able to send Your Royal Highness, inclosed in this, an order for the delivery to your order, as President of the Fund, of £100,000 Argentine Government Funding Bonds & £100,000 Buenos Ayres Water Works Bonds. These Bonds yield an annual income of £11,000 a year, leaving £3,000 a year still to be provided for, affording a great opportunity for some one both willing and able to do a beneficent act in aid of the most deserving of all our Charities.

I am sorry to see that the distribution this year is only £80,000, just a little over half the sum aimed at on the foundation of the Fund. I sincerely hope that the distribution will go on increasing from year to year until the £150,000 originally aimed at has been reached.[2]

Mount Stephen's decision to give Argentine securities instead of the usual railway bonds was significant.

NORTHERN SECURITIES: DISSOLUTION ORDERED

On 14 March 1904 the Supreme Court of the United States had upheld the decision of the four judges who had tried the case in the

[1] RA GV C273/43. [2] RA W64/13a.

Circuit Court and ordered the dissolution of the Northern Securities Company. It was a close thing: four of the Supreme Court judges thought the formation of the Company to be within the law: four thought it was not. The ninth, Judge Brewer, sustained the opinion that the power to restrain trade, even though not exercised, was unlawful; he dissented from the larger application of such principles, on the ground that 'the broad and sweeping language of the opinion of the court might tend to unsettle legitimate business enterprises and stifle or retard wholesome business activities . . .' He held that such a device as the holding company might 'be extended until a single corporation whose stock was owned by three or four parties would be in practical control . . . of the whole transportation system of the country'. The appeal was therefore dismissed.[1] This did not end the litigation: there remained to be settled the manner of redistribution of the Great Northern and Northern Pacific shares which had been turned in by holders at the beginning. The Union Pacific interests expected to receive back intact the large holding of Northern Pacific which they had accumulated in 1901; others, including Hill, considered that the most equitable way was to do it on a *pro rata* basis, to which Harriman at one point evidently agreed,[2] then resisted to the extent of bringing another lawsuit.

The Supreme Court's decision had 'set the cat among the pigeons' on Wall Street. John Sterling relayed to Mount Stephen something of the atmosphere in New York, of the comings and goings of the different parties as a meeting was arranged on 16 March at Hill's office there.[3] He wrote on the 18th:

Day before yesterday Mr. Harriman telephoned around, that he was obliged to go to an Illinois Central meeting, and wished to know if I could not attend a consultation at 11.30, at Mr. Hill's office, in reference to the Northern Securities decision; that he could not go himself but that Judge Lovett [the new Counsel for the Southern Pacific, formerly connected with one of the railroad companies in Texas] would represent him, but that he wanted me to go on his behalf also. I telephoned him back, that the conference would probably last all day, as there was much talking to be done, and my judgment of these preliminary talks was that nothing ever was accomplished, that I was certain to hear about the matter before it went very far, &c, &c. He said that Mr. Kennedy, Col. Lamont, Col. Clough [Vice-President, N.S.], and everybody else would be there,

[1] Noyes, op. cit. pp. 348–9. Pyle on *Hill*, vol. 2, pp. 173–4. Adler on *Schiff*, vol. 1, pp. 112–13.
[2] Pyle, op. cit. vol. 2, pp. 178–9. See p. 250 below.
[3] RA GV C273/31.

and he thought it would be a good thing if I could go too. But I begged off, for, as a matter of fact, I did not want to go at his instance. Mr. Hill afterwards telephoned around, but I happened to be out when the telephone came.

Yesterday morning Mr. Hill came himself, and we had a long talk about matters. I found him in a very different state of mind than I really had anticipated. I thought he would be breathing slaughter against everybody, but, on the contrary, I found him cool and collected, and really very much relieved in his mind. Notwithstanding all this, I venture to say, he will never forgive the Supreme Court, and will be especially severe (when he can find the proper occasion) on Justice Brewer.

I supposed that, as a matter of pride, he would insist upon the Northern Securities Company being kept alive to such an extent, that it would continue to hold the Northern Pacific Stock, but thought he would distribute the Great Northern, and form with it and the Burlington a new Company. On the contrary, I found that he was not only willing, but was insistent upon absolutely dissolving the Northern Securities Company and never hearing of it any more. This was quite a relief . . .

Sterling then outlined the plan as Hill had presented it to the meeting the previous day, when discussion of it had been adjourned to the 17th. He concluded: 'I told Mr. Hill that I would write you a few lines to tell you the pith of what he had stated, and he said that he hoped I would, as he might be too pushed to write you, although he intended to do so the very first moment he had the opportunity'. An enigmatic note from Mount Stephen to Sir Arthur Bigge on 7 April saying: 'Here is a *lively* criticism on the Judges of the Supreme Court which may amuse H.R.H. to read'[1] has unfortunately become separated from its enclosure, but it was almost certainly attached to a letter from James J. Hill.

Sterling wrote a second letter on 18 March reporting the results of the second meeting which Col. Clough had called to explain to him.[2] Meanwhile Judge Lovett had told Harriman what Hill proposed; Harriman at once dissented, and Lovett did not attend the second meeting.[3] On 22 March Hill issued a circular to Northern Securities shareholders conveying the resolution passed by the Board of Directors; he referred in passing to the beneficial effects which in his opinion the company had wrought by increasing commerce and reducing rates, and stated that the company had been organized with the utmost economy and in the full

---

[1] RA GV C273/40.   [2] RA GV C273/30.
[3] Kennan on *Harriman*, vol. I, p. 389.

belief that it did not violate any law of the United States. Now it was necessary to reduce the capital stock of the company and distribute to its shareholders the shares of the two constituent companies. A meeting of stockholders was announced for 21 April 1904 at the company's office in Hoboken, New Jersey. Prompt action was necessary to deal with the question of dividends.[1]

Col. Clough had called back at Sterling's office to ask him to get Mount Stephen to sign a proxy voting form and send it out by first mail. His earlier explanation to Sterling about what the stockholders were to be asked to ratify was as follows:

... 99% of the stock of the Securities Company shall be retired at once, by delivery to the holders thereof of Northern Pacific and Great Northern Stock. Every 100 shares of the Northern Securities Company Stock so retired will receive $3,925 par value of NP Stock and $3,017 par value of GN Preferred Stock. This is equivalent to 39 shares of NP Stock plus $27 scrip, and 30 shares of GN Stock plus $17 scrip. These, figured out at the respective prices at which they were originally taken over by the Northern Securities Company, namely 115% for NP and 180% for GN, makes a valuation of $9,946.65 in these securities for each 100 shares of Northern Securities Stock.

The present outstanding Stock of the NS Company is $395,400,000. It is to be reduced by this process to 99%, which is $391,446,000. This will leave outstanding $3,954,000.

The object of making this large retirement is so that the Court will not have any jurisdiction over any specially large amount of Stock. This 1% of unretired Stock will be paid hereafter. There are either other assets in the treasury of the NS Company or else there are assets which have been taken over for the benefit of the GN and the NP respectively...

On 23 March 1904 Gaspard Farrer was informing sundry correspondents that he was leaving England for two months; he was in fact sailing for America. Mount Stephen meanwhile was trying to keep the Prince of Wales *au fait* with developments. It cannot be said that the latter seemed unduly worried about the rather precarious position of the bulk of the King's Fund's capital: it was enough that Lord Mount Stephen was keeping an eye upon it. Unfortunately not all of the enclosures mentioned in the latter's letters to Sir Arthur Bigge are now available, having presumably been passed on. On 4 April Mount Stephen wrote that Hill had

---

[1] Meyer on *Northern Securities*, pp. 290-1.

cabled stressing the importance of English friends sending their proxies early in order to avoid the delay of having to adjourn the meeting (of April 21).[1] Mount Stephen added: 'I quite agree with you when you say that Nor: Sec: shares are things to get and keep, even if one has to beg, borrow or steal in order to get them. All this will be evident by and bye . . .' His letter of 6 April was more disturbing:

> The cable from St. Paul in Monday's Times was a surprise to me; I at once cabled Hill asking him what it meant & I now enclose a copy of his answer; all my previous cables said both parties harmonious and on good terms. John Revelstoke's partner, Gaspard Farrer, is now in New York— he cabled yesterday . . .[2]

The Reuters cable from St. Paul of 3 April, published in *The Times* of the 4th, was as follows:

> A petition dealing with the liquidation of the Northern Securities Company, signed by Mr. E. H. Harriman and Mr. Winslow Pierce, acting as trustees for the Oregon Short Line, has been filed in the U.S. Circuit Court here. The petition asks the Court to direct the Northern Securities Company to return to the original shareholders the Northern Pacific stock exchanged by them for Northern Securities stock at the time of the formation of that company, and to prevent a *pro rata* distribution of Great Northern and Northern Pacific stock among the shareholders according to the amount of their present holdings in Northern Securities, as planned by the directors of the company. The petition is returnable on the 12th instant.

Mount Stephen did not mention that a report from New York printed by *The Times* on the same day under *Foreign Markets* observed: '. . . The uncertain attitude of the Harriman interests towards the Northern Securities situation induces caution . . . Today about 1,000 shares of Northern Pacific stock changed hands on the kerb at from 134 to 136, closing 136 bid, and about 1,000 shares of Great Northern at $166\frac{1}{2}$ to 171, closing 171 bid'.

Hill's cable read: 'Notice of application to the Court reached me Sunday morning and was only published here this (Monday) morning. Information to enable Times publication could only come from the desire of the opposition to create confusion and delays on your side. Our counsel *seven* Lawyers unanimous that

[1] RA GV C273/33.   [2] RA GV C273/37.

application can have no effect beyond possible delay'.[1] Mount Stephen continued his letter to Bigge:

> This strategic move on the part of the Harriman crowd has no doubt been taken to force Hill to give them better terms than they are entitled to in the interest of their own roads U.P. &c. &c. &c. The application comes before the St. Paul court on the 12th. when I *hope* it will be dismissed, but one can never be sure what a court will do; I am glad to see the interest HRH takes in the case. The inclosed cutting from today's Financial News will perhaps interest him though it was written on 26th March it gives a fair account of the whole position.
>
> I have already told you how important it is that all the proxies should be in New York for the meeting of 21st. I should think the court at St. Paul would say on 12th. that the mode of liquidation is a matter to be settled by the majority of the Nor: Sec: shareholders, but we'll see.

REDISTRIBUTION PLAN: FURTHER LITIGATION: HARRIMAN IN LONDON

The following day, 7 April 1904, Mount Stephen wrote again, more briefly, to Bigge: 'By way of keeping alive your interest in the squabble I send you inclosed a copy of a cable just received from Farrer . . . which coming from him means a (? lot) & is most satisfactory. I hope this fuss will soon "blow out". In any case we have the property & it can't be taken from us & it is worth a great deal more money than the present market price of the Nor: Sec: shares'.[2] Farrer had said: 'Believe Hill will come out on top with prestige among banking and investing classes here such as we have never thought possible'.

What had happened was that on 2 April E. H. Harriman and Winslow S. Pierce, counsel for the Oregon Short Line Railway Company, and the O.S.L. Company, as purchasers of the Northern Pacific stock in 1901, had petitioned the four circuit judges against the *pro rata* distribution of Northern Securities stock. Their petition was turned down, whereupon Harriman brought suit in the U.S. Circuit Court in the State of New Jersey for an injunction to prevent the *pro rata* distribution. The Court issued a temporary restraining order whereupon Harriman circularised the share-holders of the Northern Securities Company in advance of the meeting of 21st April informing them of this and claiming that the shares of Northern Pacific capital stock which he had turned in to

---

[1] RA GV C273/34.   [2] RA GV C273/38.

the N.S. Company in November 1901 (over $37 million of common stock and $41 million preferred, plus 'the common stock into which the said preferred stock has been converted') belonged to the Oregon Short Line Company; Northern Securities had merely been the custodian, and had therefore no right to redistribute.[1] The hearing was set for 25 April in Trenton, New Jersey,[2] but the processes of law postponed this until 20–23 May; the preliminary injunction (to restrain the Company from distributing the securities) was granted on 15 July 1904 whereupon Hill appealed.[3] Meanwhile at the meeting on 21 April there was an overwhelming vote in favour of Hill's plan, the Harriman interests being of course at a disadvantage. Pending the result of the latter's injunction, however, nothing further could be done. Mount Stephen told Bigge on 11 May that it was unlikely that the dividend would be paid before the last week of the month.[4] A circular to the Northern Securities Company shareholders on 11 June said dividends were still delayed but assured them that cash had been set apart for this purpose with Trustees, and dividends would follow immediately when redistribution was permitted.[5] The Investment Ledger of the King's Fund for 1905 shows that during this period of suspension the dividends on the Fund's holdings were advanced by Lord Mount Stephen himself.

On the day after Judge Bradford granted the preliminary injunction in the New Jersey court, Gaspard Farrer wrote both to 'the Admiral' and to Lord Roberts in the same sense. He enclosed a copy of a message received that morning from Hill explaining the 'position in which Judge Bradford's decision, announced in this morning's papers, leaves the question at issue. In effect, he declines the responsibility of giving a judgment, and leaves the matter for the decision of the Supreme Court [in fact, Circuit Court of Appeals], where the case will come on for hearing in September, —meanwhile, immediate steps are being taken to enable the vidend to be paid. As you are aware, the money required for this has been placed in the hands of Trustees, and as soon as an Order of the Court can be obtained, it will no doubt be distributed to the shareholders'. Pyle quotes a letter written by Hill that summer:

---

[1] Meyer, op. cit. p. 291. Kennan, op. cit. vol. 1, pp. 389–90.
[2] Meyer, op. cit. pp. 295–7.
[3] Ibid. pp. 298–9.   [4] RA GV C273/42.
[5] Meyer, op. cit. p. 340, Appendix 8.

... The present lawsuit is brought, as the parties admit here, not because of any wrong done them, but because they think they have everything to gain and nothing to lose, 'as Mr. Hill will protect their stock as well as that of everybody else, as long as he is in charge'. This, however, is cold comfort. If they desire to continue holding their stock we can have no objection and will treat theirs as well as we do our own, but we cannot allow them to impair or destroy our property. You have but little idea of the difficulties I have had to deal with and get along with during the last two years. You know that I never would be connected with a property that was run for the benefit of those in the saddle and not for that of the shareholders . . .[1]

In August 1904 E. H. Harriman descended upon London, England, fitting in also a visit to Aix-les-Bains. On the 17th Farrer wrote to Lord Revelstoke, also holidaying at Aix: '. . . Harriman arrives on Monday, and has arranged to see Stephen before he sails'. He added: 'For your own information I may say that we have just heard that Hill will shortly advance to share-holders the belated May and August dividends. I should have preferred to have obtained leave from the Courts for the Company to pay them, but suppose they found this impracticable'. Farrer pursued the subject in his letter to Lord Revelstoke of 22 August: '. . . Harriman has arrived and saw Mount Stephen this morning, and I am to see him this p.m. We have nothing to propose to him from Hill, and have satisfied ourselves that the present is not a time when we can interfere in the squabble with any chance of bringing about more amicable relations between the two. Whenever the issue now before the Courts is decided a settlement may be possible, but neither Harriman nor Hill will be satisfied until the Courts have given judgment on the question of the redistribution of the Northern Securities assets . . .'

Farrer saw Harriman both before and after the latter had been at Aix, and Harriman was afterwards to remark to John Sterling on what he detected to be a slight coolness in Farrer's demeanour on the second occasion as compared with the first. This Gaspard was to deny, but at the same time he had been himself surprised at the favourable impression made on him by Harriman at their first meeting. Farrer was to write at great length, particularly to John Sterling, about his reactions to this nervous-, almost shifty-looking little man who was also the giant of the Union Pacific. He was not

[1] Pyle, op. cit. vol. 2, pp. 179–80.

quite what he had expected, yet Farrer was not at all sure whether or not to believe in what he had been led to expect. There was the matter of an alleged agreement between Hill and Harriman concerning the Burlington about which Farrer had written to Hill on 13 July, copying the letter to Sterling. To anticipate events a little, it may be well to quote now what Farrer wrote in this connection to Sterling on 27 December 1904: '. . . You remember that on the 13th July I sent you a copy of my letter to Mr. Hill in which reference is made to an Agreement alleged to be deposited with Morgans regarding Harriman's having an equal voice in the control of the Burlington. As to this, Mr. Hill now writes to me:

Jim told me something about some Burlington Agreement which he ['Harriman' is inserted in Farrer's hand] claimed to yourself and the Boss; I never made any such Agreement with him. The only foundation for any such claim was before the Northern Securities was formed and before they sold their N.P. stock Morgan's people said they had a joint voice in Burlington matters through a joint representation in the Board of the Company.

James Norman Hill and Farrer had together seen Harriman in America that spring. Farrer continued:

We think it is evident, looking to Harriman's claims and Hill's admissions, that there was some kind of an Agreement or verbal understanding between the two as to the Burlington Road, which may or may not have been one of the conditions of the transfer of Harriman's NP shares; [see above pages 206 and 212] we cannot help thinking there has been some genuine misunderstanding between the two. Surely the sensible plan, if we get a decision in our favour, would be for Hill to go either directly or through a third person to Harriman and endeavour, *forgetting about the past*, to settle on a policy of peace which would be dead fair to both and to which both could agree . . .

But to return to Harriman's visit: on 23 August 1904 Farrer acknowledged Sterling's letters of the 9th and 12th, the latter replying to specific questions: 'most interesting. The essence of the Metropolitan Agreement, stripped of the technicalities of the Lease and the Voting Trust which after all were merely machinery for carrying it into effect, seems to have been an *equal* division of power in Burlington management between Hill and Harriman; thus confirming Harriman's contention . . .' He went on:

Harriman sails tomorrow in the "Baltic". Lord Mount Stephen saw

him yesterday morning and I in the afternoon; we have not had an opportunity of consulting with each other since our visits, but we had previously
agreed to tell Harriman that we could do nothing towards a settlement
at the moment or hold out hopes of any until the method of the redistribution of the NS assets had first been decided by the Courts.
Harriman obviously and sincerely believes he will win, and hopes he
will win for everyone's sake, ours as well as his own; for if he is beaten
he intends to go tooth and nail for J J H's scalp. He tells me he was
certain of Bradford's decision, and had he not been certain would never
have come abroad: surely an unfortunate admission! As there is only
one way by which he could be certain—by knowing—and I should hate to
think that that was true. I believe your own judgment as to the ultimate
result differs from Harriman's, and from a commonsense layman's idea one
can hardly imagine that the Law would deny the legality of the Northern
Securities Company's holdings, and subsequently render a decision that
would hand over the majority of the NP shares to another rival, parallel
and competing Road; however, it is useless to prophesy; but for us all
it is an uncomfortable position to have to uphold Hill when we are
morally certain that he has failed to keep his agreements; we know that
Hill has never yet kept an agreement with his neighbours in the North,
and must reluctantly conclude that Harriman was right in saying that he
will never keep an inconvenient agreement at all unless there is the
power to enforce it against him. Moreover we do not for one moment
believe, even if he wins his case, that he will be able to carry out his
ambitious schemes for the future in the face of Harriman's opposition.

Meantime I cannot think that Harriman's present course of endeavouring to detach Hill's following by petty worrying in the matter of dividends is wise; it is certain to anger Hill's larger shareholders, and to set
public opinion in Hill's favour; moreover, one would imagine it to be a
dangerous policy to be using the Courts and the delays of the law to wear
down an opponent; if one were a judge there is nothing one would resent
more.

Harriman sailed on 24 August, and the next day Mount Stephen
and Farrer had a long discussion together, comparing notes about
their individual interviews with him. This was briefly reported to
Sterling by Farrer on 25 August; repeating Harriman's assumption
that he would win his case, Farrer had suggested, he said, to Harriman that there was an alternative: '... without expressing any
opinion as to the ultimate decision my view of the drift of the
suit, so far as it had at present progressed, did not agree with his;
it seemed to me in favour of Hill rather than of the Union Pacific
interests. Harriman at this broke out with the only signs of temper

during the interview, and was violent in his threats of the course he should adopt in that event. Lord Mount Stephen reads this, together with Harriman's present action, as meaning that they are far from confident of winning their suit, in fact believes they will lose, and I am bound to say that this interpretation seems to correspond with their acts in now endeavouring to delay and worry Hill's shareholders'. Nevertheless Farrer concluded his letter: 'We like Harriman better the more we see of him; in matters of policy, negotiation and general dealing with his fellow-creatures he is far broader than J. J. H. and we cannot help feeling in our heart of hearts that in his present dispute he has probably a genuine grievance'.

That day Gaspard had had the more difficult task of writing to James J. Hill. This probably explains the brevity of his letter to Sterling.

Mr. Harriman sailed yesterday on the "Baltic". On his return from Aix to London I saw him once for about half an hour. Lord Mount Stephen had one interview of similar length, about which he will no doubt write to you. So far as mine was concerned, I have really nothing to add to what I wrote to you in July. The more I see of Mr. Harriman the more I like him, and the more I deplore that you and he cannot come together. He has not a tithe of your grasp of transportation matters, and does not pretend to have, but in many other ways is monstrously able, and each of you would be of untold assistance to the other were you working with confidence and in harmony with each other; in fact unless you and he are together I can see no outfit that will at all be able to balance or cope with the particular interests of his moneyed associates. I beg that you will remember that there are not only all the mischief makers in Wall Street working to keep you apart, but also officials of the respective systems who from mere zeal and with the best of intentions in the world are continually pouring poison into your ears: complaints identical in substance and almost identical in words, which you write to me of his officials, he makes to me of yours. I cannot but think that in all this fight perspective has been lost, and that the concessions which each would have to make to the other in an amicable settlement involve giving up far less than is at present sacrificed by these unfortunate differences.

We do not believe that even if you win your suit, as we believe you will, it will be possible for you to carry out the programme you outlined to me in the Spring in the face of Harriman's continued opposition; but even if you did, how could you expect to permanently retain an undivided control of the system: the better you make it the more anxious they will be to acquire it, and in the end, if they persist, certainly have the power to succeed.

We do not suppose you would ever consent to a settlement now, but if you win your suit we do sincerely trust you will be able to make such arrangements as will deprive Harriman of any possible ground for complaint, and put an end to this squabbling in public.

This may be an appropriate point at which to quote from a letter (referred to in note 2, p. 240) written by Hill that year (1904) and which mentioned Harriman's initial agreement to the *pro rata* plan of redistribution: '. . . Mr. Harriman was the first director of the Northern Securities Company to whom I went after the decision of the Supreme Court to consult as to how we should dissolve the company, and he immediately said the only thing we could do was a pro rata distribution. This he repeated on several occasions for four or five days, and at the end of that time came to my rooms to tell me that he was afraid he could not carry it out, and the next day he wrote me a personal letter to the same effect, after he had assured me that we would have their full co-operation; and, in the meantime, having had his own counsel present with the Northern Securities counsel in consultation as to the legal steps to be taken, and his counsel agreed fully and said that it was the only legal and moral course that could be pursued under the circumstances. Within ten days from that time they brought the present suit, giving as the reason that "We knew, of course, that Mr. Hill wanted the control of the Northern Pacific, and it would be a great property in his hands, but we wanted to get control of it if we could . . ." In which case the Great Northern would be hemmed in along the northern boundary without any outlet anywhere except on terms to be made for it . . .'[1]

It would not be entirely quoting out of context, moreover, to extract one or two snippets from the annual supplement which *The Statist* was shortly to publish on American railways, pointing out first, however, that on 1 October 1904 Gaspard Farrer had written to E. T. Nichols, of the Northern Securities office in New York: '. . . Mr. Paish, one of its sub-editors, left this week in the "Majestic" for a tour of the US, and it might be quite worth your while to endeavour to see him; he is sure to call at your office. You will find him intelligent and a very nice fellow'. It was not, as will be recalled, Farrer's first contact with *The Statist*. Publishing just

[1] Ibid. p. 179.

after the Supreme Court had given its decision the following March (1905) the section dealing with the Northern Pacific opined: '... But whether this decision will finally settle matters is doubtful. If Mr. Harriman does not further contest the distribution of the assets in the proportions proposed it will mean that Mr. Morgan will continue to control the Northern Pacific Company. The latter contingency would mean that the Northern Pacific and the Great Northern will continue to work together in harmony, and that the Burlington will be controlled in their joint interest. There is, however, another contingency which cannot be ignored. Not only is the Union Pacific affected by the acquisition of the Burlington by the Northern Pacific and the Great Northern, but the Chicago, Milwaukee and St. Paul line is also understood to feel aggrieved, and reports are current that the Milwaukee intends to extend its system to the Pacific. In the interests of all concerned a satisfactory solution of the difficulty is greatly to be desired ... The Northern Pacific is a very valuable property. Most of our readers are doubtless aware that the line extends from St. Paul, in Minnesota, and from Ashland and Duluth, on Lake Superior, to the Pacific coast, and that it enjoys a very large grain and lumber traffic, while it has a considerable tonnage of coal and other minerals ...' The paper listed four circumstances which had contributed to the N.P.'s improved earnings and profits in recent years: the 1896 reorganization of its finances; the quick adoption of the 'statistical and other methods which Mr. Hill had introduced on the neighbouring Great Northern property, and, as a result, great economies ... in handling the traffic'; the rapid development of the States served; 'Lastly, with harmony between the Northern Pacific and the Great Northern, there has been no violent drop in rates, although considerable reductions have been made for the purpose of stimulating traffic, as the growth in density has permitted freight to be handled with greater economy ...'

All these considerations were in the minds of those concerned on both sides of the Atlantic. The 'Milwaukee' (sometimes also referred to, confusingly, as the 'St. Paul') came under the financial control of William Rockefeller of the 'Standard Oil group'—which included James Stillman. What Gaspard Farrer was to call its 'wicked, predatory and totally unnecessary extension to the coast'[1] was not

---

[1] Gaspard Farrer Letter Books, Farrer to Howard Elliott, President of Northern Pacific, 30 January 1924. See also Adler, op. cit. vol. i, p. 150 and Burr on *Stillman*, pp. 110 and 141.

achieved until 1909. Again, relations were complicated to a certain extent by Farrer's personal liking for Will Rockefeller. As for James Stillman, he had been in London during August 1904, not quite maintaining but not altogether abandoning his Sphinx-like demeanour. Gaspard wrote to Sterling on 10 September after Stillman had departed on the "Oceanic" the previous week following discussions on possible arrangements between the 'Northern' lines and the 'Milwaukee' and Chicago and North Western:

... Stillman will be with you on Monday and give you the latest news of us. He has been more than nice personally as a companion outside business and so far as business is concerned says, and I believe really feels, he is more at home in our office and with John and myself— particularly with John—than anyone else in this country. He came very near to unbosoming himself on business matters several times—much nearer than he has ever been before, but obviously never quite managed to get out all he had on his mind. John likes him personally, and likes talking to him—thinks he could work with him, and we are both confident that had we made the least advance Stillman would have welcomed us. The matter has given us the gravest consideration and I am in doubts as to whether you will consider we have come to the right decision. It is perhaps mine and Lord Mount Stephen's rather than John's, and is to the effect that we had better be guided by the experience of all others who have dealt with that particular crowd rather than be influenced by the friendly disposition which J. S. himself feels or pretends to feel. I doubt whether in any close alliance we could maintain our independence, and were we to enter into such should only find after a time that we were being used and had the wrong end of the stick. So at present matters remain *in statu quo* with much personal friendship on both sides and I hope some confidence on Stillman's part in our business ability and unquestionably professions on his part that he will put everything he can in our way—but nothing beyond that, and we have made no mention whatsoever of our New York end ...

Farrer had written on 12 August 1904 to Lord Revelstoke at Aix: '. . . I do not myself see the connection between joint control of the Burlington and the extension of the St. Paul and North West to the coast, but I suppose Stillman thinks, with an equal voice with Hill in the policy of the Burlington, he could compel the N.P. and G.N. to make traffic arrangements with the St. Paul and North West which would be satisfactory to the latter Roads'.

To refer again to *The Statist's* section on the Northern Pacific, the writer put forward a solution to the impasse which he said 'was generally favoured by those not directly concerned in the settlement . . . that the Great Northern should be permitted to acquire complete control of the Burlington, that the Union Pacific should be assisted to secure control of the Chicago and North Western [Marvin Hughitt's line; he had been associated in the reorganization of the Union Pacific. See above Chapter IV, p. 135] and that the Milwaukee should be given control of the Northern Pacific. Such a solution would appear to make for the general good. It would obviate the construction of a new Pacific line, and it would strengthen the existing companies, at the same time that the public interest would be safeguarded by the existence of three independent and powerful railroads between Chicago and the Pacific coast . . .'

Meanwhile, Gaspard Farrer's August correspondence has by no means yet been exhausted. On 26 August he turned his attention to James Norman Hill whom he was relying on more and more as a 'go-between'. He reminded him that he was expected in England in October: 'I shall never forgive you if you fail to come' and continued:

Harriman left in the middle of this week; I saw a certain amount of him during his stay here, and the favourable impression which he created on us both during our trip this spring has deepened on further acquaintance. It is a great pity that your father and he cannot come together; your father has had to deal with all sorts and conditions of men in his life and with most has managed to get on with success. Lord Mount Stephen and I are convinced that Harriman is far more reasonable than the majority of business people with whom one has to come in contact, far more reasonable than his Standard Oil associates, and is in many respects the complement of your father in ability, I mean, as able and wise in his particular line as your father has proved himself in his own special business. You may be sure that sooner or later the two will have to come together, it is merely a question of time. The trouble is that each lacks confidence in the other, and it is unfortunately the business of mischief makers and zealous officials to foster suspicions.

We do not believe that Harriman in his heart of hearts thinks well of his own law case, though he professes supreme confidence; but we have no doubt that even if he loses he will be sufficiently powerful to thwart us in carrying out our schemes for the future, and has the metal behind him to secure control of our properties in the long run if he and his moneyed associates so determine.

In his letter to Sterling of 10 September 1904 about Stillman's visit, Farrer had stressed the importance of James Norman Hill's keeping in touch with his father's English friends:

When I was last in America Jimmy Hill arranged to come over here this autumn with a view of seeing Lord Mount Stephen and myself and spending some weeks with me going round the golf courses. I have just cabled him to know when he is sailing, and sincerely hope that if you get a chance of seeing him you will urge him to come. I would like to see him for his own sake and so as to keep in touch with him, and think it very desirable, both in his own and his father's interests, that he should come in order to see Lord Mount Stephen.

Probably letters from Brocket have already posted you as to our friend's mental attitude on the Northern Securities case. From daily letters to me it is only too evident that he is getting out of heart and out of patience with Hill, and unless J. J. H. manages his affairs better in the future it is clear to me that he will lose the support of his oldest and best friend here. As you know well, Lord Mount Stephen likes people to be successful, and the one sin he cannot forgive is failure in this respect. He very rightly considers that for the last two or three years Hill has muddled his affairs, and from want of temper and want of foresight and want of fair dealing with his neighbours has brought difficulties on himself and his partners from which he will only be able to extricate himself now by concessions which should have been made from the start. Nothing can be clearer to us than that even if Hill is successful in his law suit he will never be able to carry out the programme which he outlined to you and to me last Spring in the face of Harriman's opposition. If he wins in November he will be in a better position to treat, and that is the utmost we can now hope.

On 27 August 1904 Farrer had written to Mount Stephen elaborating on a telegram despatched to Brocket earlier that day announcing the presence in London of George F. Baker of the First National Bank of New York: '. . . I very much hope you will manage to see him, the more so as he has obviously great fears of Harriman having captured London: I told him laughingly that I was not half so afraid of Harriman capturing us as of Stillman capturing him: this made him sit up. He seems to me much more reasonable and fair-minded than most of those with whom we have talked, but at the same time he owns that he dislikes Harriman and doubts his being straightforward . . .' He added a postscript: 'You will remember that Baker is on Hill's executive committee so that one has to be a bit careful about mistakes of the past'. Baker had been one of the group who had planned the Northern Securities Company, and also of that which had participated in the negotiations leading to the Burlington purchase.[1] Four years later he was to

---

[1] Pyle, op. cit. vol. 2, p. 164. Overton on *Burlington*, p. 258.

work with Harriman on the rescue of the Erie, an operation which, according to Kennan, raised Harriman in popular estimation.[1]

Farrer's last August letter, written on the 30th, was to Harriman himself; it was written by hand and mailed to the Hon. Hugo Baring, New York, to be sent to Harriman's private address:

A line to thank you for your kindness to me personally and for the trouble you took to explain to Lord Mount Stephen and re-explain to me your differences with Mr. Hill from your point of view. From all sides London the Continent and N.Y. we hear that you have "captured" Mr. Hill's English friends so I hope that you also feel some satisfaction from our intercourse and that your time and efforts have not been wasted.

The moment for a settlement may not yet have come but whenever it does I hope it may be with a personal confidence between you and Mr. Hill as heads of separate systems closer than you have ever yet contemplated. I do not see any other outfit capable of preserving for Western roads their independence as sellers of transportation before those who already their largest customers are fast becoming their largest proprietors as well.

NORTHERN SECURITIES: PLAN TO ADVANCE DIVIDENDS

Hill was still worried about the non-payment of dividends, and evolved a scheme which only added to the tribulations of Gaspard Farrer and to the further frustration of Mount Stephen. Farrer wrote to the latter on 3 September 1904:

The following from Hill this morning: "In case we do not secure permission from Court to distribute to shareholders surplus cash if I borrowed $2,000,000 and advance without interest $2.25 per share on all holdings up to 2,000 shares for each holder taking security for such advance a deposit of three shares for each 100 advanced upon to be paid from the distribution of cash assets when made under decision of Court, how would such arrangements be received in London and Paris?"

I think you will agree with me that the deposit of 3 shares as collateral for the advance is impracticable. In practically all cases shares in London are represented by ten share certificates, and the trouble and expense involved in splitting would render the transaction impossible, besides I doubt whether the ordinary shareholder would understand why he should have to pledge any part of his shares in order to obtain a dividend which he would naturally consider as his right. My own impression now

[1] Kennan, op. cit. vol. 2, p. 318.

is that Hill had better leave the matter alone unless he can obtain an order from the Court. What would you say to his giving us and Tuck permission to approach the smaller shareholders individually with the offer of an advance without interest on their note of hand, engaging to repay the sum advanced as soon as they are in receipt of the dividend; it would not be reasonable that Hill or we Bankers should take any pecuniary risk, and I should think that the Northern Securities Company might have assumed that. There would be few if any cases where trouble would arise. Please let me know your views that I may reply to Mr. Hill.

Farrer wrote in similar terms to Edward Tuck in Paris on 5 September, asking what he thought of Hill's proposal and stating his own views. He added: 'I understand that a fresh effort is now being made through the late Attorney General Knox to endeavour to obtain permission from the Courts to pay dividends ...' On 7 September he relayed to Mount Stephen two messages from Hill: 'The first in point of time reads, "Would it be more convenient to have amount advance stamped on certificates?" The second reads, "Thanks. My object was to ascertain definitely what your cable settles. Alternative is to stamp certificates with amount paid. Expect to take latter course if dividend not permitted by Court which we should know within two or three days". This second message is satisfactory and looks as if Hill's vision was becoming clearer as to the necessities of the case. We have also a message from Tuck saying that he takes the same view as we do ... I return you Tuck's letter which shows excellent good sense'. He then wrote to Tuck acknowledging the letter sent to Mount Stephen and reporting the latest from Hill. He added: 'How do you like your position of Banker to the Paris shareholders of the Northern Securities? Our excellent friend at Brocket, who has been most unwillingly exalted to that same honour in London, becomes daily more savage. It is to be hoped that you can take your honour with more philosophy, and thank heaven for this additional opportunity of extending your well-known and unfailing good nature'.

Writing to Hugo Baring of Baring Magoun in New York,[1] acknowledging cables concerning Northern Securities, Farrer on 17 September complained: 'Hill is exceptionally tiresome and vacillating. If the Company is unable to pay dividends, or distribute its assets by way of dividend, it would almost seem better

[1] After the Barings crisis of 1890 the New York office was reorganized as Baring, Magoun & Co. In 1906 it became Baring & Co., and in 1908 reverted to Kidder Peabody & Co, a branch of the Boston firm.

to do nothing. The "soup kitchen ticket" plan, as a friend of mine calls it, of advancing a dole to the smaller shareholders, would be viewed with but very moderate satisfaction on this side ...' He repeated his misgivings to Tuck on 1 October: '... We are doubtful as to whether it will do any good on this side, though there may be individual cases which one could approach privately with a view to giving them relief. One of the difficulties which I foresee is that the plan will create two classes of stocks, i.e. the stamped and unstamped stock, a contingency which, as you will appreciate, is very undesirable'. Before long Gaspard was dealing with just the type of case he had envisaged; on 18 October he was writing to 'the Admiral', Lord Clanwilliam: 'Lady Clanwilliam asks if she should accept Mr. Hill's offer of the advance; she states that she does not need it. Under the circumstances I have advised her to do nothing. There is a suit pending which should be decided in the Courts in the next few weeks, which will clear up a good many points; meantime there is no reason for accepting the advance unless for the sake of getting the money *now*. She will certainly receive it from the Company in the form of dividends in the course of time. In case anything occurs to alter my view I will not fail to communicate with her'. At a later stage—on 6 May 1905—Gaspard was to write to Hill: '... You would be amused at some of the letters we have been receiving. Quite a number of holders had never discovered that they had not had dividends and one lady most indignant at the trouble we are now giving her in order to obtain her past rights'. He told Sterling on 29 October 1904, enclosing a copy of a circular sent to holders, that the number who had accepted was 'infinitesimal, I think about 7,000 shares in all'. In November he was helping Mount Stephen through the mechanics of advancing dividends privately to the King's Fund.

Meanwhile Farrer continued to weigh up the respective characters and attributes of Harriman and Hill. On 24 September 1904 he wrote again to Sterling:

Lord Mount Stephen has shown me two letters received from you with a reference to myself. First as to *Harriman*, let me say that if I appeared more reserved to him on his return from the Continent, it was unconsciously on my part. I like Harriman, but cannot reconcile his professions with his acts. He *professes* to desire harmony with Hill, and *takes action* (granted for the benefit of his own UP interests) which we can only construe as most inimical to the Northern Securities Company. He *professes* supreme confidence in the strength of his case at law: he *does* everything possible to postpone a final decision.

Under these circumstances it is hardly to be wondered at that I do not care to wear my heart too much on my sleeve, and more especially as my own small experience only accords with the character which seems to prevail generally among those who have known him for years past, and, as I gather from an epithet in your letter to Lord Mount Stephen, with yourself as well. At the same time, Harriman interests me: I like talking to him, and he seems to me in many ways quite the biggest of those financial magnates in your country whose acquaintance I have had the privilege of making. It seems such a pity that he and Hill cannot work together, as one is really the complement of the other: Hill admirable in matters of transportation, and Harriman in matters of policy and finance . . .

ILLNESS OF LADY MOUNT STEPHEN

On the day the above letter was written, Mount Stephen had other worries. Gaspard ended it: 'Lady Mount Stephen is in the surgeon's hands this morning, and I am just off to learn the result of the operation'. In the letter to Sterling of 25 August in which he had discoursed at length on his and Mount Stephen's interviews with Harriman, Gaspard had gone on to talk of 'Lady Gian's' continued progress, as though she had been ill for some time, and of the doctors' favourable prognosis for the operation. Gaspard was troubled less about the actual operation than about the fact that one of Gian's lungs had earlier been damaged. 'I am satisfied she has no business to remain in England during the winter months, and, as you will understand, it is difficult to get him to move away from home, and really rather hard on him at his time of life to be obliged to go, but I have no doubt whatever but that he ought to go, at least during January, February and March'. Writing to Robert Meighen, Mount Stephen's brother-in-law in Montreal, on the affairs of the Canada North West Land Company on 30 August, Farrer said: 'Lady Mount Stephen is going on as well as could be expected; I am sorry for both her and him that they should have the anxiety of the operation before them, though the doctors seem to say that she is a good subject for it. I have very little doubt that she will be very much stronger when it is over than she has been before'. On 3 October he was able to tell John Sterling: 'Lady Gian is mending as fast as can be, and will be up in a day or so, and perhaps down at Brocket by the end of the week . . .' To Robert Meighen he wrote on the 6th: 'Lady Mount Stephen is practically convalescent; she has had an extraordinarily rapid recovery, which his Lordship attributes in part to her being so excellent a patient and to "doing everything she is told". I take pleasure in reminding him that that is an attitude which he can hardly expect to continue on her recovery, in fact she will have a long leeway of disobedience to make up'. The last bulletin, to Robert Meighen on 1 November 1904, reported Lady Mount Stephen's complete recovery, she 'was out shooting yesterday, and, I understand, shot quite a number of pheasants'.

—AND OF JAMES NORMAN HILL

The next invalid to cause Farrer some concern was James Norman Hill. In his letter to Tuck of 1 October 1904 he noted that 'Jimmy' was in mid-Atlantic and would be arriving next week; to Sterling he wrote on 3 October that he was to arrive 'on Wednesday and we shall be anxious to hear what he has to say. I am expecting to take him off to Scotland for a week or ten days'. This meant golf at North Berwick. On 14 October, however, Farrer told Sterling that although James Norman had been in England for ten days he had not, until that morning, showed any signs of caring to move to Scotland. He was suffering 'quite severe attacks of neuralgic headache and rheumatism'—with no apparent cause—which would come on and leave equally suddenly. A single round of golf seemed to tire him completely. Gaspard had got him to see a doctor and was awaiting the verdict. Gaspard was a 'good deal disturbed'; although there seemed no grounds for uneasiness regarding J. N.'s general health, 'the prospect of his taking an active part in the management of Northern Securities property seems to me fading away. Hitherto I have always refused to give up the idea that he would some day take a prominent part in the direction, though I fancy you yourself have long ago dismissed any such idea; I am for the first time beginning to see that your views of him are correct. It is a thousand pities, as he is far honester than his father, in many ways broader, and full of good sense, but he does not seem to have the physical health or persistency of character to get on the treadmill and stay there. I have not written a word to his people about his rheumatism, so please keep the matter to yourself . . .'

On 18 October Farrer mentioned to Robert Winsor, of the

Boston firm of Kidder, Peabody, that he was leaving town next day for two weeks in Scotland. The Scottish trip was not a success; he told Sterling on 29 October that this was because of James Norman's neuralgia, which had been practically incessant since his leaving New York. 'He was obviously in great suffering for several days while we were with my sister, and I consequently determined that the best thing was to get him back to town as soon as possible. He now proposes to abandon his visit to Paris and sail today. I confess it will be a relief to me to get him off my hands. Tuck has come over from Paris to see him and is staying with me'. On 1 November Gaspard wrote to James J. Hill about his son:

I wrote at length last Saturday to Mrs. Hill with regard to Jim's health. His continual headaches must have been most wearying to him and entirely spoilt any pleasure for him in his visit here. I sincerely trust that on his return to New York he will put himself in the hands of some *first rate* physician, who could watch the case from week to week until the cause of trouble was ascertained and a remedy found.

I grieve so for the worry this will be to Mrs. Hill and yourself. I am sure you will be patient with him.

The last sentence would appear to be unnecessary except from one who was *au fait* with the situation. Gaspard wrote next day to Sterling rehearsing again J. N.'s symptoms but coming to no conclusion. The doctor had said he should see Sir William Osler, then at the Johns Hopkins Clinic at Baltimore, but the latter was just about to leave Baltimore for Oxford. Although his younger brother Louis had married in 1901—with the abundant approval of all—James Norman was then still a bachelor. On 16 November 1904, writing on other matters to James J. Hill, Gaspard added: 'I am hoping any day now to hear news of Jim. In spite of his feeling poorly during his visit here, he made the best possible impression on those of your old friends whom he saw, and I am satisfied they would be as willing to extend their confidence to him as have your old and principal friends in New York'.

PLAIN MESSAGES FROM LONDON

In the letter to Tuck reporting James Norman's imminent arrival (1 October 1904) Gaspard asked: 'Can you trace the recent buying of Northern Securities? Here we are told it is New York buying, and in New York we are informed that it is London: I am fairly puzzled. J. J. H. cables me this morning asking for information, but makes no mention of the reported agreement with Mr. Harriman'.

Two days later Farrer was telling Sterling: 'We are very much excited over the rise in Northern Securities, and are quite unable to trace the source from which the buying comes. Apparently J. J. H. is equally concerned, as he has been cabling us on the subject, and informs us this morning that "some friends in New York are adding to their holdings", which we imagine interpreted means that he has got nervous himself, and is buying to prevent others increasing their holdings without paying through the nose. I cannot help thinking that permanent holders here will be disposed to sell if in the course of a few weeks they do not receive their dividends, or an intimation that litigation is to cease. As to the latter point, Hill cables definitely that no arrangement with Harriman is contemplated or possible. Harriman, when he was here, told us that he considered Northern Securities Shares cheap, and that it looked as if he might be compelled to add to his holdings. We shall be surprised if Mr. Hill has not some hard lessons yet to learn . . .'

Farrer's faith in Harriman as a financial operator was to be shaken too before long. On 2 November 1904 he wrote to Sterling: '. . . We are much amused at the way Harriman has been hoisted by his own want of foresight in the matter of the Oregon Short Line Bonds; it is the more amusing as I fancy the largest holders of the Bonds were people connected with Northern Securities, and it is they, therefore, who will have made most of the money by the redemption of the Bonds at 102½. The fact that Harriman goes to the heavy expense of repayment does not look as if he intended easily to submit to a settlement of his differences with Hill . . .'

Regarding the mysterious buying of Northern Securities stock, Farrer wrote to Mount Stephen on 14 November enclosing a message received that morning from Hill, and his firm's reply; he added: 'It is not a bad thing to find that he is on tender hooks [*sic*] as regards Harriman's possible absorption of Northern Securities stock. So far as I can see, he must make up his mind to the possibility of raids now and for all time if he wishes to continue his policy of the free lance . . .' Referring to an earlier letter to Mount Stephen of 10 November, in which he relayed a message just received from Baring Magoun of New York to the effect that the Northern Securities case had come on for hearing in the Courts the previous day, but observed that they did not state whether the case was being considered on its merits, Farrer now added: 'We are still in ignorance as to whether the case has been considered on its merits'.[1]

On 16 November Farrer wrote to Hill acknowledging sundry cables:

You report that your lawyers are satisfied with the progress of the case, but do not say whether it has been tried on its merits; however, I suppose it has been in view of your cable.

If judgment is given in your favour, both Lord Mount Stephen and I sincerely trust you will see your way to come to some amicable arrangement with your neighbours; no amount of profit is worth the worry which these last few years must have entailed upon you, and this at a time of your life when you ought in fairness to yourself and to your wife to be taking things more easily . . .

He went on to discuss something that was obviously on Hill's mind: the possibility of the large-scale purchasing in London of options on Northern Securities stock. Farrer thought this unlikely, if only because nine-tenths of the stock in England was held by permanent investors, 'mostly private people, who have never even heard of an option and do not know what it means . . .'

To Sterling he wrote on the same day in rather different terms:

. . . Hill cables that he expects the decision next month, that his lawyers are well pleased with the progress of the case. This, of course, means absolutely nothing, and we are anxiously waiting to hear from you your opinion of affairs; we do not yet even know whether the case has been tried on its merits: I suppose so, however. If the case goes against Hill, I cannot help thinking a good many people here will sell out, they are sick to death of litigation. If it should go in Hill's favour, we sincerely trust you will use your influence with Hill to induce him to come to some arrangement with Harriman. No amount of profit is worth the worry and vexation of the last few years which this quarreling has entailed, and which both Lord Mount Stephen and I are satisfied might have been avoided if Hill, Kennedy & Company had exercised a reasonable amount of temper and consideration for our neighbours.

Hill was still cabling about options, and again, on 22 November, Farrer returned a reassuring reply, but took the occasion to point

---

[1] 'On its merits', i.e. having regard to the right or wrong of the case, apart from questions of procedure. The case then before the courts was Hill's appeal against the injunction forbidding *pro rata* distribution.

the moral once more: '... I do not believe your neighbours have in this case been in the market, but they will never cease their demands to secure what they believe is their due until they have obtained it, either through settlement with yourself, through the Law Courts, or in a last resort through acquiring control of the properties you direct'. On 30 November 1904 Gaspard gathered all the recent threads into a report to Edward Tuck in Paris:

... Hill cables tolerably frequently, obviously much exercised at any move in the market, fearing that our U.P. friends may be on the warpath. I do not think they have been in the market—as a matter of fact, but we are not altogether sorry to find Mr. Hill in this state of nervous anxiety, it will make him more docile and shew him the necessity of coming to a settlement when the points now at issue before the Courts have been decided.

In a recent letter from a friend in New York occurs the following sentence:—"The trial of the case itself, as you know, has not yet taken place. Mr. Hill claims that the trial will involve no question not raised in the appeal from the injunction order. Harriman, however, claims otherwise".

From this it appears that the merits of the case have not been tried, which is rather disappointing to me ...

If I have any news from Hill of interest I will be sure and send it on to you. Mr. Hill accounts for the rise in Great Northern by the advance in all Steel properties and the greater value given to all Iron Properties in Minnesota. It is pretty plain from the G.N. Report that the moment Hill is free to move financially he will issue a further $25 million G.N. stock to his stockholders; at least this was my interpretation of the sentences in the Report.

Meanwhile Farrer had been in correspondence with E. T. Nichols, the Great Northern's man in New York; Hill was now anxious to retrieve any available shares of St. Paul, Minneapolis and Manitoba. It was ascertained that there were two French holders, and Farrer wrote to Tuck on 9 December asking whether he knew them and could approach them: '... I am ashamed to trouble you in the matter, but know that you would be glad to help Mr. Hill in any way you could'. On the same day he himself approached the comptroller of one of the royal households with the same proposition. Tuck responded willingly, and Farrer told him on 12 December:

... We expect a decision on the 15th, and are confidentially informed from a source on which we rely (not Mr. Hill) that it will be favourable for us, though how far this is guess work or how far based on knowledge I cannot say. Nor can we predict what steps our friend Harriman may take subsequently. Hill cables us in obvious anxiety lest holders here, in case of a distribution, may sell their Northern Pacific shares; this he is most anxious to prevent. I am cabling him today to tell him that in case the decision is in our favour I should consider there is danger of holders here selling at the present level of prices, in the event of the decision not being followed by a general settlement with Harriman disposing of all litigation and all attempts to raid our stock. I do not believe the ordinary holder will be content to continue holding if he sees further vistas of litigation or the necessity arises for devices for tying up the stock. I should imagine that your friends in Paris will have pretty much the same feelings on the matter; in fact anything for a quiet life, especially when it can be obtained plus a large profit, which at present quotations practically every holder can secure.

He explained further to Tuck on 13 December that Hill was worried lest, when a distribution of Northern Securities shares was made, holders should sell their Northern Pacific quota but retain their Great Northern. Naturally enough Hill hoped they would retain both, letting him keep control of both roads. Gaspard was 'quite unmoved' at the idea that, with the N.P. in Harriman's hands, the G.N. would then be comparatively valueless, but he saw no future for Hill's schemes without the acquiescence of the Harriman group. He sent Tuck, for his own information only, the latest and most forthright cable messages he had yet sent Hill; including the one referred to in the letter above, but the more forceful because in the meantime Mount Stephen had apparently been adhering too closely for his taste to the 'stand-without-hitching' philosophy. The whole exchange was on 14 December 1904 communicated to John Sterling in New York:

On Saturday last [9 December] Lord Mount Stephen received two messages from Mr. Hill, one of which reported that he expected a favourable decision in the course of this week and was anxious that we should use our best endeavors to prevent his following here selling their N.P. shares, to which they would be entitled on a distribution. Lord Mount Stephen replied that he need not fear immediate sales, but after consultation with me, I cabled on the 12th December as follows:—

"Have seen Lord Mount Stephen. We earnestly hope decision if favourable to us will be followed by settlement of all issues with your neighbours. We think there is danger of many holders here preferring a quiet life and the profit of present prices to prospects of further litigation or the necessity of devices for tying up stock". To which Mr. Hill replied:—

"Contention of opponents is ownership of control N.P. which favourable decision definitely settles our favour, making settlement other questions quite simple; important, however, remember with N.P. in hands opponents with joint control Burlington our only safe course would be to sell them G.N. also. Personally I care more for our faithful friends than for myself, and would regret see their interests sacrificed after winning lawsuit. Northern Securities actually worth over 180 if we carry our plans into effect. Let us be patient".

We have taken further counsel together here and with Tuck, and today cabled him in the following terms:—

" If favourable decision promptly followed by treaty peace, people here would not sell their holdings either Company, probably increase, but if litigation and fighting continues, we fear many oldest friends will sell out both Companies. Estevan. Farrer."

Farrer had added a separate brief cable on his own account: "Thanks message. Have nothing to add to last paragraph my letter 22 November. Farrer". He explained this reference to Sterling (as quoted on p. 262); he did not believe the U.P. had been buying Northern Securities, but was sure they would not rest until they had got what they wanted by some means. He then repeated to Sterling the cable he had sent him at the same time:

"Lord Mount Stephen and I cable J. J. Hill as follows:— 'If the decision is our favour followed by more litigation and fighting, satisfied many of oldest (our) friends here and Paris will sell out both companies'. Refer to my letter 16 November. Farrer". [See p. 262]

Farrer concluded the letter to Sterling:

The above will, I think, explain themselves to you, and our state of mind over here. It must be as evident to Mr. Hill as it is to us that a decision of this case, however favourable to us, does not definitely settle the questions at issue between him and Harriman. We do not believe it makes the settlement of those questions "simple", nor that Mr. Hill will be in a position to "carry his plans into effect" without at least the tacit acquiescence of Harriman. Are we taking too pessimistic a view of our situation? I fancy not; and that you will agree, and always have agreed, with these views. In fact, that Mr. Hill cannot in these days build Railways and run them irrespective of his neighbours and in disregard of their wishes. However this may be, we doubt our ability to keep his European holders together in case this decision is followed by further litigation and fighting. Every one can now see a large profit on his holdings, and is sick to death of squabbling which results in the withholding of dividends, and which he has a shrewd suspicion is continued to satisfy the personal ambitions and pique of those in command. I sincerely hope that you, Baker, Lamont and others of Mr. Hill's friends, on whose good judgment and fairmindedness one can count, will find opportunities to bring this unfortunate squabble to an end.

He added an afterthought: 'In the second of Hill's original messages to Lord Mount Stephen he mentioned that the three Companies had cash on hand $44 million. Can you account for this? The Northern Securities dividend in suspense plus their ordinary working cash balance might together amount to from $15 million to $20 million, but we cannot understand how the balance has accumulated, unless it is the result of a recent Burlington Bond sale ... earmarked for Bonds about to mature'. This last point Sterling investigated and was able to assure Farrer that the large cash balance in hand was the result of earnings only.[1]

The gist of the exchange was sent to Tuck on 15 December, with Farrer's comment: '(Hill) will not like it, but it is much better that he should be prepared for what we believe likely to occur, and we are satisfied it will not be wise for him to rely on some of his old followers in the way he can on such people as yourself and ourselves, who even if we did not agree with him would go far in his support by reason of our long personal friendship and business association'. He did not, however, copy to Tuck the handwritten letter he sent that day to Hill, although a copy went to John Sterling with the instruction: 'Please destroy':

Your recent messages to Lord MS urging holders to retain their NP's when distribution has taken place determined us to tell you frankly the feelings of your following here and the action they are likely to take under the alternatives of peace or further war.

On the co-operation of Ld. MS, Ld. Strathcona and myself you can surely count for any reasonable policy whether we go with you in it wholehearted or not,—but many others who have neither a life's business association or personal friendship to weigh with them are in our opinion likely to break away from us and sell unless a permanent peace is in sight, and we cannot blame them. We have been in communication with Tuck who coincides with the view so far as Paris holders are concerned.

Now as to your cable to me, I wish we could agree with you that a

[1] Gaspard Farrer Letter Books, Farrer to Sterling 13 January 1905, acknowledging Sterling's letter.

decision in our favour definitely settled the question of control. We do not, nor do we think that you will be able to "carry your plans into effect" in the teeth of opposition from your largest shareholder.

But this is controversy—we can only trust that when the momentous hour arrives for deciding your policy you will be guided by that right judgment in all things which has due respect both to your own and to your neighbours' rights. You are building up an organization for all time—for a time when it will no longer be able to look to your brains and strenuous devotion for help.

An appeal on the grounds of your own personal comfort is I know useless but I do sincerely trust my dear Mr. Hill that a settlement may be possible which will bring relief and comparative rest to your life. You have made money for your followers beyond the dreams of avarice and in this case I believe that such a settlement as we should wish for you will be best for them also. I do not believe that a position of our road among its neighbours (of which you have often spoken) of being "independent of them all" is possible in these days or even desirable if it was.

This letter will reach you close upon Xmas day—Please give Mrs. Hill my best wishes for her, for you, and for you all—I shall never forget the Xmas I spent with you in St. Paul or the many kindnesses which I have received at your hands.

Six days before the above letter was written—9 December, the day that Mount Stephen had received the message to which he had replied with such prompt optimism—Hill had written to Farrer. Acknowledging it on Christmas Eve, Gaspard spoke of this letter as being 'much appreciated: that you should care to write to me in such a strain is evidence of your regard and this you know I value highly'. Hill's letter had arrived that morning; since writing it Hill had had Farrer's and Mount Stephen's cables but not the former's letter of 15 December. The diplomatic Gaspard continued:

Your claims about your own work cover but a part of the truth; with my imperfect knowledge I can add largely to the table—you have indeed made partners of your shareholders and have given them unsparingly—and quixotically—your brains and life's work without asking or receiving any compensation.

But much as you have done for us all you have done as much only in another form for the good name and fame of American corporate management. Wherever Great Northern shares are held or known your name is known too and as synonymous with all that is upright—there surely can be no fairer prouder record.

Just one line as to our attitude here. I say our for I believe the Boss agrees. When Harriman took action against you you had no alternative but to fight and if the daily expected decision is adverse I would fight again to the end. But given a decision in our favour I would endeavour to settle with Harriman on a policy which would insure future peace. How otherwise can we expect his assent to a transfer of the Northern Pacific interest in the Burlington to the Great Northern or with his existing big stake in our properties expect him to resist adding to his holdings. As your largest shareholder and permanent neighbour both in the middle and far north-west it surely must be wise to come to a settlement if any reasonable concession can obtain it, and whether this concession is to the UP, to the St. Paul, or to Harriman's pride.

Perhaps you are right about his character. You must often have dealt successfully with as difficult a man as he: to us here he spoke fairly and we liked him personally—but we have no interest in his properties and shall take none so long as he is at war with you—our interests and our loyalty are to you, and we have no intention of loosening the ties and friendship of a lifetime.

This letter also was apparently copied to John Sterling. Farrer's to the latter of 27 December gives some idea of the drift of Hill's:

My letters of the 14th and 15th and copy of my letter to Mr. Hill enclosed will, I think, have relieved his mind and yours, as I can see both from letters received from him and from yours of December 14th that you have been a good deal exercised. We cannot understand why Mr. Hill should have chosen to read into our joint message meanings that were not there expressed and that were never intended. He has been cabling me on several occasions lately as to the market in London, who were the buyers and who the sellers, who was giving option money and who taking it, showing anxiety as to what was going on here; and not unnaturally. Under the circumstances the least we could do was to warn him of the probable or possible attitude which many holders here would be likely to take in case litigation was continued after the now expected decision. The warnings we have had from holders here have been quite numerous. It is possible when the time comes we can by our own action induce them to continue following us and Mr. Hill, but I am sure you will understand there are many on whom we have no hold whatsoever, and many others towards whom we should not be inclined to take the responsibility of urging them to continue holding if they showed a strong disposition to sell . . .

Here Gaspard interjected the section quoted above (page 247) about an alleged agreement with Harriman about the Burlington, possibly as a condition of his turning in the U.P.'s Northern Pacific shares when the Northern Securities Company was being formed.

He then referred to another recent letter from Hill, dated 13 December, 'ten pages closely written in his own hand: it is too long to trouble you with, and it really only deals with his past relations to his shareholders and the management of the properties entrusted to him . . .' It seems possible that here there has been some confusion of dates and that Farrer was writing of Hill's letter of 9 December, or that the one letter was in fact dated the 13th, written on receipt of Farrer's cable of the 12th incorporating Mount Stephen's latest views. At all events Farrer concluded his letter of 27 December to Sterling: 'The Boss has just been here, and we agree in thinking that our joint message will have done Hill no harm, even if it did excite him for the moment. When we personally, as distinct from our friends, intend to terminate our partnership with Mr. Hill, we shall inform him of the fact and in the most direct way'.

Although Gaspard did not 'trouble' Sterling with Hill's latest letter it seems he lent it to that other very much interested party, Charles Ellis at Haslemere. He sent him also a copy of a message just received—this on 31 December—from 'a friend in New York' —presumably Sterling—as well as an extract from a recent letter from Hill to Mount Stephen concerning the comparative cost of iron ore in Minnesota and in the Southern United States: 'If the figures are correct', he commented, 'and Hill has anything like the 500 million tons to which he lays claim, there ought to be pickings for Great Northern shareholders some of these days'. Adverting to the current litigation, he observed: 'As to Johnson's argument, it is difficult to judge the value of one counsel's argument without seeing that of his opponent, but I agree with you in thinking that Harriman will have difficulty in getting over his previous affidavit. Did not the whole argument strike you as singularly unpolished? I have always heard Johnson spoken of as being at the top of the tree, but his speech and manner struck me as being that of an uncultivated mind, and the manner of delivery not that which would appeal to a judge in this country'.

COURT DECISION: HARRIMAN RENEWS LITIGATION

On the last day of this anxious year of 1904 Farrer wrote to John Sterling:

Mount Stephen writes me this morning that he has just dispatched a ten page letter to Mr. Hill, so that by the time this reaches you, Hill will be in as full possession of our views as it is possible to make him. It is hardly worth again referring to Mr. Hill's fears that we were going to sell out our stock at such a juncture as this; I need hardly tell you that such an idea never crossed our minds. We thought, and still think, however, that a number of people would sell if after a favourable decision litigation is renewed. We were anxious, too, in sending our message to Mr. Hill, to put in a counter weight to the combative advice which Mr. Hill is apt to get from Kennedy and Clough. Mr. Hill writes me that he is constantly in communication with you, and never takes a step without your advice. I only hope this is true, as both Mount Stephen and I would then be quite satisfied as to the course adopted ...

On 3 January 1905 the circuit court of appeals decided in favour of Hill and the Northern Securities Company, thus reversing the injunctional order of 18 August 1904.[1] Gaspard lost no time in expressing to James Norman Hill 'my fervent hope that you will keep in touch with Harriman and maintain your friendship with him. A settlement of the questions at issue between him and your father is bound to come in time and it looks as if the time were approaching now, and a settlement will be as easy again if Harriman has confidence in and friendship with yourself. We are quite sure here that half the difficulty is caused by the unfortunate suspicions that have arisen, and we are equally confident that the only way to treat a man like Harriman is to lay your cards on the table and make it difficult, and almost impossible, for him to be otherwise than frank and straightforward with you'. As though to pledge their support in this daunting task, Gaspard added to this letter of 3 January 1905: 'Some few weeks ago Mount Stephen and I sent your father a joint message as to the course we considered many holders here were likely to adopt in the event of a favourable decision being followed by fresh litigation. Your father seems to have interpreted this as meaning that Mount Stephen and I were intending to sell out; not a very complimentary interpretation to us. He may rest satisfied that when we intend to sell we shall inform him in the most direct way; meantime he has obviously been so disturbed by our message that we have been spending our days since inditing him epistles to say that though neither a wife nor a mother we will never desert Mr. Micawber'.

In December 1904 Ernest Cassel had returned from a visit to the United States, according to Gaspard Farrer 'a most rampant

[1] Meyer, op. cit. p. 299.

bull on everything American'. He seemed, Farrer had told Sterling in his letter of 31 December, to have been immensely impressed with Harriman: 'says he is a man with whom he could work . . .' In Bishopsgate Street they were not taking the financier too seriously. Farrer wrote to Sterling on 13 January 1905:

. . . John [Lord Revelstoke] had a long talk yesterday with Cassel regarding his trip to the US and asked him point blank as to the Harriman Hill dispute. He replied that Harriman had as far back as the time of his (Cassel's) departure for America given up all hope of ever winning the suit or being allowed to appeal to the Supreme Court; expressed himself as content with the increment of value on his investment, and gave Cassel the impression (or at least Cassel gave John the impression) that he would bother his head no more in the matter. This is quite important if true, but I should myself have doubts as to whether Harriman would ever sit down content whatever he professed, and unless some concession is made either to his Roads or his vanity I can hardly believe he will consent to the sale of the NP interest in the Burlington without raising further trouble in Court. Indeed, this particular point is one that has always presented great difficulties to my mind. If an independent Director of the NP, I should find it hard to persuade myself in the interests of that Company that any compensation from the GNR was sufficient for the sacrifice; and I could well understand that if the question was raised in Court a Judge would decide that NP Directors interested in GN were not the proper persons to place a value on the NP share in the Burlington.

But still nothing seemed to happen. Lady Wolseley wrote to her husband on 19 January 1905: '. . . Godpapa's letter about N. Secs. is encouraging. He always talks of a "*melon*" to cut . . .'[1]

Then on 23 January Farrer wrote to Edward Tuck: '. . . Our own people in New York cable us that Harriman's appeal to the Supreme Court is expected today and that Mr. Hill and his friends seem to be confident that the Court will not consider it . . .' Hill had cabled also to the effect that about 100,000 shares had recently gone into the hands of 'strong personal friends and to New England' and Farrer told Tuck: 'We had quite expected a number of people here to sell their shares after the decision and some few have, but others have bought and I should think on the balance there are as many held here as ever'. Gaspard was feeling cheerful enough next day to twit his old friend Charles Hosmer, agent of the

[1] LW/P 31.

Commercial Cable Company and now a CPR director—whom he regarded rather as a merchant venturer—about the fortune he was reputedly making: '. . . If I have a regret it is that you are not in Northern Securities, but perhaps that was too much to expect of one so bound up with CPR . . . All your old friends here are well and more prosperous than they had ever anticipated from the compulsory saving they have been obliged to make through our friend Harriman's action. Harriman little understood what lessons of thrift he was about to inculcate among the following of his opponent . . .' On 30 January 1905 Harriman obtained a writ of certiorari in the Supreme Court of the United States.[1]

Gaspard Farrer wrote a letter of explanation to his father on 1 February:

Enclosed is a copy of the last decision of the Courts on the merits of the Hill Harriman case. The writ 'a certiorari', whatever that means, granted on Monday to Mr. Harriman is on appeal from the decision to the Supreme Court. That this appeal would be allowed our lawyers have informed us was inevitable, and they state further that in their opinion it was to our interest that the final decision should be given by the highest Court of Appeal. This appeal comes forward for hearing on the 20th February, and we hope a decision will be given shortly afterwards. Mr. Hill's counsel are entirely confident of the result. Harriman threatens further litigation, but this Mr. Hill's lawyers do not seem to fear, and they are of opinion that in case the Supreme Court ratifies the decision of the Court below, no matter what further litigation Harriman is able to bring forward, the Court will then grant permission to Mr. Hill to distribute so much of the Northern Securities assets as represents the past and unpaid dividend.

I can quite understand that this litigation and postponement of income is vexing to you. At the same time we really think the end is now in sight . . . Personally, I will not under any circumstances sell *my* shares pending the close of this litigation, and until we are able to see clearly our way in the future and get the chance to reap the fruits of past patience . . .

THE KING'S FUND: FINANCE COMMITTEE

In Farrer's letter to Sterling of 13 January he had treated with some levity Mount Stephen's New Year gift to the King's Hospital Fund of £200,000 worth of Argentine Bonds (above p. 239). 'The

[1] Meyer, op. cit. p. 299.

Boss', he wrote, 'has had cartloads of begging letters as a result of his gift to the Hospitals, letters coming not only from this country but from all parts of the world, Ellis's dry comment being "serves him well right". The gift has proved a great puff for Argentine Government securities, with which we here in Bishopsgate Street should have been glad to dispense. The country's securities are becoming much too popular. It is bad for any man or country to get money too easily, and fatal for a Latin-American republic'. In his letter to Hosmer on the 24th he struck an even more facetious note: '. . . Lord Mount Stephen is full of go and as young as ever he was; he is down this week for a few days staying at Windsor much to his disgust, but his friends tell him it serves him well right for contributing another £200,000 to the King's Hospital Fund . . .' adding later to this sentence: 'I have just heard he has got the GCVO, poor man!'

The decoration was not bestowed without some persuasion. The Prince of Wales wrote from County Galway to the Princess on 26 January: 'I am glad you saw the Mount Stephens. I see Papa duly invested him with the GCVO. I quite understand his explanation with regard to his originally refusing it'.[1]

Writing to the Prince of Wales's secretary, Sir Arthur Bigge, on 1 March 1905, Mount Stephen enclosed a cutting from the *Financial News* regarding his choice of Argentine Bonds as a gift for the King's Fund.[2] When the gift was first announced, the paper had published a comment 'from a well-informed correspondent, who suggested that there was room for some doubt whether these securities were of the class which such a body as the King's Hospital Trust ought to hold'. This was apparently not solely a reference to current Trust Law, which required Trusts to invest only in certain approved securities, but a specific attack on Argentine securities as such. The correspondent admitted that, invested in trustee securities, Lord Mount Stephen's gift might well, at a maximum of $3\frac{1}{4}$ per cent, yield only £6,500 instead of £11,000 a year; but what, he asked, of the small investor who might thereby be persuaded that this was a safe investment for himself? A 6 per cent investment inevitably involved a certain amount of risk 'and . . . the risk in Argentines is that a revolution may any morning put prices down 20 points'. This had evoked heated reaction from the Republic.

---

[1] RA GV CC3/144.
[2] RA GV C273/46 and 47,

The Review of the River Plate, quoted in the same Press cutting, declared:

> Revolutions are today a thing of the past, and there is no more fear of one breaking out than there is of a war with England. Of course, we desire it to be understood that we do not refer to an occasional unpleasantness in an upper province. These, however, do not affect the nation, and are nothing more or less than street brawls. The Republic is every day becoming more firmly established, and those who have faith in its future are acquiring as much of its securities as they can hold.

Mount Stephen's comment to Bigge was: 'I wish we could get £300,000 more of these doubtful bonds . . .' When making such a gift, it was his custom always to calculate the annual income which it would provide; when later he found that in this case the 'city magnates' who directed the King's Fund's finances had switched most of his Argentine securities, he set out to campaign for a separate Finance Committee for the Fund. The first item in the Fund's original Investment Ledger of Non-Trustee securities is a 'family tree' setting out exactly what happened to Mount Stephen's gift of Argentine Bonds, tracing reinvestments and quoting folio numbers in the Ledger showing the position as at 1 January 1908. This is clearly a copy of information asked for by Mount Stephen himself, and the 'tree' shows the extent to which the original gift had suffered. He felt that the Fund lacked the financial expertise in transatlantic markets demanded by the preponderance of such investments in its portfolio; the present Trustees were more likely to plump for an English railway company or the Metropolitan Water Board in preference to counterparts in the United States or Argentina.

While declining to serve on a Finance Committee himself, Mount Stephen was prepared to nominate its members: Mr. Hugh Colin Smith, lately Governor of the Bank of England, Lord Rothschild, Treasurer of the Fund, Lord Revelstoke, Sir Ernest Cassel and Mr. Robert Fleming; he was particularly anxious to have Fleming. The Prince of Wales and his secretary had a somewhat agonised discussion, both as to who would chair this team and as to how they would react to one another; wrote the latter: '. . . The dear old man went on to say that he will give further securities . . . as soon as ever the Hill arrangement is come to but he does not want to see this capital dealt with by men who he openly says do

Northern Securities: pro rata redistribution approved   275

not understand the business! I know Your Royal Highness quite recognizes that he ought to have a considerable say about the finance of the Fund . . .' Bigge ended his letter of 11 September 1906:

> This is a terribly long story but I have endeavoured to plainly explain what are the views of the best friend the Fund is ever likely to have. He has the strongest faith in the Fund as the one way of working the Hospitals & saving them from Municipal control—But he says there ought to be no alteration in its constitution—*no charter: no representative control, no restrictions as to investing securities.* The money is given to the Prince of Wales and he appoints whoever he chooses to administer it.[1]

The new Finance Committee met for the first time on 1 November 1906; there was at first some confusion as to its specific duties, but once these were clearly defined as embracing all matters dealing with finance including the investment of all moneys, the recommendation of the total amount for annual distribution and the expenditure of any money other than this, the results as visualized by Mount Stephen began to be seen. It proved necessary, however, to apply for an Act of Incorporation for the Fund—this became law in July 1907—in order to achieve the independence of action which Mount Stephen so much desired.[2] In 1908 the latter gave a further block of Great Northern Railroad shares, providing an annual income of £7,000, sufficient to bring his total contribution to the King's Fund up to £30,000 a year.[3] Bigge wrote to the Prince of Wales:

> . . . This he says is all he can do in his lifetime for the Fund. Dear old man! It really is splendid of him—But he wants to try and make this additional gift a lever to extract more out of the old fox! and I shall have to tackle him again . . .

The 'old fox' was Lord Strathcona.

NORTHERN SECURITIES: *PRO RATA* REDISTRIBUTION APPROVED

On 13 February 1905 Lord Mount Stephen wrote cheerfully to Sir Arthur Bigge:

> You will, I am sure, be sick of seeing my handwriting, but I think the inclosed may interest Their Royal Highnesses. You see, while Nor:

[1] RA GV C273/60, 62 and 63.   [2] A/KE/2/2.
[3] RA GV C273/67, 68, and 69.

Sec: shares continue to be quoted 153/154 in London, Gt. Northern shares have risen some 20 points during the past week & are now quoted at 279 in London, which means that the Gt. Nor: shares which were taken into the Nor: Sec: Co. on its formation 3 years ago at *180* are now worth *280* & are not unlikely to go to 300 by the time they come to be given back to us Nor: Sec: shareholders; I should not be surprised if this upward move in Gt. Nor: had the effect of raising the price of Nor: Sec: shares another 10 or 20 points, but it is always dangerous to prophesy.

I hope and believe we shall have a decision in our favour this month, but be that as it may, we are bound "to come out on top" in the end. The *property* is there & it is ours & no one, no court can take it from us & what is more it is increasing in value every day.[1]

An equally optimistic James J. Hill had on 2 February cabled Gaspard Farrer: 'For construction about 300 miles new Road will sell million Pacific Extension 4's, if you care bid at price and accrued interest payable here based on dollar value expressed in Bond, will be glad hear from you before approaching others'. Retailing this to John Sterling on the 7th, Farrer said they had in fact put in a bid, but suspected that Hill 'was playing his old tricks of which we have had experience on a former occasion, as you may perhaps remember . . .' and that the Bonds were already sold. This was in fact the case; on the 10th a message of thanks from Hill reported 'a better market in New York'. Gaspard told Sterling: 'I know you will be interested in this story; Hill's behaviour is again as extraordinarily characteristic of the man, one's not surprised that Harriman is suspicious of him and finds him difficult to deal with'. Nevertheless the suave Gaspard wrote with complete equanimity to Hill on 22 February 1905, acknowledging several letters and saying they were not surprised that 'New York Bankers were in a position to outbid us'. He continued:

With regard to the Nor. Sec. Shares, quite a number change hands here daily, most of the buying being of a speculative character and not such as we either have initiated or should encourage. I am glad to hear from you this morning that you see no evidence of the Harriman party accumulating stock. I do not think that any of our close friends have sold, though these friends have others, whom we know less intimately or only know of, some of whom undoubtedly have been tempted out by the rise in price . . .

I do hope that in the course of the next few days a decision favourable to yourself may be given and that the worst of your anxieties may be over.

[1] RA GV C273/44.

If later on you felt at leisure to come over I need hardly say how welcome you will be.

On 26 February Lady Wolseley, to whom Garnet had by now turned over all his worldly goods (his solicitor, Gaspard's brother Frank Farrer, had, she said, been afraid that Louisa might refuse to lend him his uniform in the event of war) wrote to her husband: 'Lord Mount Stephen advises me to keep the £900 at Cox till "Northern Sec" turns up as it will be useful then he says he thinks we may hear of N.Sec: settlement any day now ...'[1] On 1 and 2 March the Court hearings were in progress. On the 3rd a rather disgruntled Gaspard told Sterling that, contrary to what the Boss had told him, he would not be free to come out to Metis, certainly not until end-June or mid-July; he was up to the eyes in Argentine business ... 'Then again if I could come out and if—with a big I— Mr. Hill again invited me to his river, I could not go to Metis and refuse him after my conduct two successive years in the past. So you see I can do nothing but plead "non possumus" '.

On 6 March 1905 the Supreme Court of the United States affirmed the decree of the circuit court of appeals: Hill had won.[2] Mount Stephen wrote to Bigge on 12 March: '... I hope we shall hear this week that steps have been taken to carry out the distribution of the assets of the Nor: Sec: Co'.[3] On the 17th he was forwarding him a letter from New York explaining why this was being delayed.[4] Gaspard on the 28th was quoting to Sterling a letter from Stillman: ' "now that the Northern Securities litigation is over" thus confirming Harriman's statement to Lord Strathcona. We only hope it is over'. On 2 April Mount Stephen told Bigge: '... I am confident the income from Nor: Sec: Shares will be greater than I have estimated ...' On the 14th Farrer reported to Sterling that Mount Stephen was 'in the most extraordinary form, walking about everywhere in the West End and prophesying that Nor. Sec. will touch 200 tomorrow morning, and I am bound to say so far they are doing their best to justify him ...' Then came Hill's cable on 15 April:

Our opponents are selling their Nor. Sec. shares in London. Investors here are buying largely. Indications are that our three roads' income over and above all fixed charges will exceed fifty million dollars for year

[1] LW/P 31. LW/P 27.
[2] Meyer, op. cit. pp. 299–304.
[3] RA GV C273/51.   [4] RA GV C273/52.

ending 30th June next. Our friends who hold on will have no cause for regret.

To this Mount Stephen replied: 'Glad they are selling out. People here more inclined to buy than sell'.

REPORTS THAT HARRIMAN SELLING OUT

On 18 April the London agents, Barings and Morgans, received authorization to accept Northern Securities shares for transmission to New York to be exchanged *pro rata* for Great Northern and Northern Pacific. Next day Hill cabled Harriman's latest move:

They have sent in for transfer all but eight thousand shares. They put large selling orders on market this morning & price dropped 15 points for a few minutes when it recovered and buying is apparently by good investors. The stock is ultimately worth over 200 *without* the Iron ore property based on earnings.

Forwarding copies of Hill's cables to Sir Arthur Bigge on 19 April 'which explain the cause of the slump' Mount Stephen added: 'They seem to have put their whole 820,000 shares on the market. I hope Hill is correct when he says they have sold all but 8000 shares. I am glad they have sold out and that we are rid of them . . .' Adding an instruction about the exchange of the King's Fund shares, Mount Stephen finished: 'It will be better to leave the "old fox" alone until after the Nor: Sec: business is out of the way & he has got his railway shares back in his possession'.[1] Farrer wrote to Lord Revelstoke in Paris on 24 April: '. . . Hill cables that Harriman has continued selling and that his own friends have added materially to their holdings on the slump, but have done nothing to organise support for the market. It is rather curious that Unions [U.P.] should have shared in the fall; that Company will realise an enormous profit if it eventually disposes of its entire Nor. Sec. holdings as we hope it will, and there would seem, therefore, to be reason for the shares rising instead of falling . . .' Two days later Farrer relayed to Lord Revelstoke Hill's latest cable: 'Strong reason to believe UP conclude they are not safe in holding any shares parallel competing Roads under recent opinion Supreme Court. Our investing friends quietly buying without advancing market. Everything looks favourable for us here and in West'. But to Tuck

[1] RA GV C273/57, 58 and 59.

that day Farrer aired his doubts: '. . . If Harriman is really selling, one is only surprised the fall has not been greater. I am rather afraid that Mr. Hill's wish is father to his thought . . . I shall refuse to believe that UP interests are afraid of holding Nor. Sec. shares until I know it as a fact. In my opinion the news is almost too good to be true. What a comfort it would be if we knew for certain that UP interests had cleared out of every share they possessed. But 820,000 shares will need some marketing . . .'

The seeds of doubt sown in Farrer's mind took root and cropped up at intervals amid the aftermath of the Court decision. Mount Stephen and he were anxious to know what Hill was now doing to ensure future control of Great Northern and Northern Pacific—if indeed some such precaution were necessary in view of the Harriman rumours. Farrer asked Tuck on 26 April, and Nichols on the 28th if they had any news; on the latter date he wrote again to Tuck: 'I am rather doubtful about Germany going back into NP at the present level of price, and as you say 80 millions of stock at 175 will need a deal of marketing . . .' On 29 April he addressed all the questions that were troubling him to James Norman Hill: that of future control, of U.P. sales of Northern Securities and who was to absorb these . . .: 'I see you have dropped (Harriman) off the Board of the Nor. Sec. Coy.; presumably you had good reason for the step, though in principle, as you know, I regret it . . .' There were rumours of a bonus issue to G.N. shareholders of some iron ore stock, and of the possible sale to the G.N. of the N.P.'s share in the Burlington: 'You may remember that this is a measure we discussed last year, and to which I look forward with some dread, though I would like to see it consummated. I shall be agreeably surprised if Harriman consents . . . I cannot in my own mind reconcile the sale as in the best interests of NP . . .' Gaspard shuddered at the thought of possible further litigation. On 17 May 1905 Farrer mentioned to James J. Hill that he had written to his son but had had no reply; he then asked Hill direct about his future plans for 'securing control beyond peradventure' of G.N. and N.P. On the same day he appealed again to Tuck for news.

IRON ORE CERTIFICATES: BONUS FOR THE FAITHFUL

Meanwhile on 2 May he had written once more to James Norman Hill, since in a letter to Mount Stephen J. J. Hill had at least divulged plans for a distribution to G.N. shareholders of iron ore stock, share for share. This Gaspard seized upon as an opportunity for some well-chosen words to be addressed to the shareholders and to the general public, pointing out that the mines had been acquired by those responsible for the management of the railway company in their individual capacity and held by them in trust for the shareholders until the time was ripe for distribution: a unique gesture. A 'plain but careful statement of facts' was all that was required: 'we and others like us can point the moral and adorn the tale'. He ended by harping on a familiar string: 'If Harriman is really selling his shares, we shall need a far wider clientele than heretofore, and the present seems a good opportunity for obtaining it . . .' He pointed out to Tuck on 4 May how they could each use a well-worded circular to underline the difference between the G.N. management and that of the Equitable Insurance Company with which Harriman was connected, and which was then the subject of much adverse publicity (although he told Hugo Baring, in this connection, 'I am sorry our friend Harriman is scorched').

From the first an important factor in the acquisition of the ore lands was to ensure that Hill's railroads got the transportation of the ore from mine to smelter. On 27 January 1899 Hill personally bought the Wright and Davis railroad and about 25,000 acres of land on the Mesabi Range. The railroad—the Duluth, Mississippi and Northern—was sold on 1 May 1899 to the G.N.'s Eastern Railroad of Minnesota. (The Duluth and Winnipeg, from the ore fields to Duluth, where the smelter was, had already been bought by the Great Northern on 2 June 1897 and then merged with the Eastern Minnesota: see above p. 120) Hill had clearly intended from the first that the ore lands should pass to the G.N., since he had taken the trouble to forestall anti-trust action (against holders of railroad concerns plus mining lands) by forming on 25 July 1899 the Lake Superior Company Ltd. with which the lands were placed in trust on 20 October 1899. Later, after more ore lands had been acquired, all were transferred on 7 December 1906 to the Great Northern Iron Ore Properties trust, the trustees being Hill's three sons, Louis, James Norman and Walter, with E. T. Nichols, and "certificates of beneficial interest" which could then be bought and sold on the market were issued and distributed to holders of Great Northern. Neither Hill nor the U.S. Steel Corporation, which was to lease the ore lands, could be certain of the actual amount and quality of the ores, but both believed it to be very large. At the time of purchase only the Mahoning mine was in production.[1]

HILL–HARRIMAN AGREEMENT

On 5 May Farrer wrote to Daniel Lamont of the Northern Pacific: '... We shall be intensely interested here to see whether Harriman continues selling his UP holding in Northern Securities; there seems no good object in his retaining them, but whether he retains them or not, I know you, as a man of peace, will rejoice if an amicable understanding can be reached between his interests and ours, when and wherever they clash ...' He was so sure that Harriman was not, in fact, selling all his Northern Securities holding that, as he told Tuck on 4 May, 'I should not be surprised if sooner or later we are asked to help buy out the UP's interest in Nor. Sec., but I do not believe any steps have been taken so far in that direction ...' When he repeated this, however, to John Sterling on 9 May he added: 'It is the kind of business that George Baker, Clark Dodge and others would undertake, and we have some reason for believing that they have it in contemplation; ... as you have rightly said in your letter to Lord Mount Stephen, we have no particular object in helping our neighbours to realize at the highest possible figure ...' He was still curious as to why, if Harriman were flooding the market, the price of Hill's securities had been maintained. But he was glad to have from Lamont—who within six weeks was to be dead—a cable which immediately on 25 May 1905 he passed on to Tuck: 'Agreed with Harriman for joint construction disputed territory in Idaho, only matter pending'. Farrer added: 'We have confirmation of it from other sources; it is satisfactory to hear that the only point at issue [with the Union Pacific] has now been settled, but I do not suppose it will be long before other and perhaps more difficult questions arise between those two ambitious and jealous magnates'.

Farrer wrote to Hugo Baring in New York on 7 June 1905:

... The agreement between Hill and Harriman is very satisfactory; they have sent me copies of it, and so far as I can judge there is no reason why

[1] See William Watts Folwell, *History of Minnesota*, St. Paul, 1926, 4 vols., vol. 4, chap. 1. Pyle, op. cit. vol. 2, pp. 189–230. King Edward's Hospital Fund Investment Ledger December 1906 giving full details of agreement 7 December 1906 between Great Northern and Lake Superior Companies. Louis W. Hill was founding President and remained chairman until 1945 and a trustee until his death in 1948 (1971 Annual Report Louis W. and Maud Hill Family Foundation, St. Paul).

this settlement should not have taken place years ago, indeed, no reason why there should ever have been a squabble at all. But the fact is the trouble lay in the control of the Burlington and nothing else, and once that was settled by the Court there was no reason for Harriman continuing to show his teeth. Hill seems confident that Harriman has been selling some of the UP holdings in Nor. Sec. but his opinion is not apparently shared by everyone in New York, as I hear Bob Bacon [of J. P. Morgan's] among others does not believe that any shares have been sold. If you hear anything to confirm or refute Hill's views we shall be interested.

On 13 June Farrer was able to tell Tuck that he had had a long communication from Hill 'dealing almost entirely with the past and the policy which he took up in eliminating UP interests from his Board and subsequently settling with Harriman on the points in dispute . . .' As to the future, the predominant interest was the possible lease to Morgan's U.S. Steel Corporation of the G.N.'s iron ore complex. Hill confirmed that earnings from the three Roads that year would exceed $50,000,000, of which 7 per cent dividends on G.N. and N.P. would only divide $19,600,000. The previous week Lady Wolseley had written to Garnet: 'Mount Stephen . . . says we ought to have all our Dividends from America by now . . . he expects that during the current year our income from these railroads will be *doubled* . . .'[1]

Alongside these material preoccupations of early 1905 Gaspard had been much concerned about the illness—it was tuberculosis—of Mrs. James J. Hill, for whom he entertained the most affectionate regard. Hill was keeping Mount Stephen informed and by 26 April Farrer could report to Tuck that she was 'mending'. He wrote to Hill on 6 May: 'A line to tell you how sincerely we rejoice with you and you all at the better accounts of Mrs. Hill and the prospect of her complete restoration to good health. She is the light of your life and your house and beloved by all your friends who know her . . .' He wrote again to Hill on 17 May:

Your letter about Mrs. Hill reached me just after I had posted a note to you. Your news is most comforting and you may be sure you have my sympathy in all you write about her constancy and courage—in simplicity and strength of character I do not know her equal and the cords with which she binds her friends to her are none the less strong for being silken. Please give her my love and tell her how much I rejoice to think she is regaining her health for her sake, for yours, and selfishly for mine . . .

[1] LW/P 31.

His letter to Tuck of 8 June betrayed renewed anxiety and on the 13th he told him: '... I do not much like (Hill's) account of Mrs. Hill, in actual words he writes hopefully and assures me that the Doctors report there is nothing to prevent her recovering completely, but she is obviously very weak still and I fear her health will be a source of anxiety to him for some time to come'. In October of that year Gaspard had a letter from Mrs. Hill's daughter Charlotte Slade—once the little girl who had promised to play her violin to him—and wrote to Sterling on the 5th that this gave but a fair account of her mother; he was afraid it would be a long time before Mrs. Hill recovered her strength—'if ever'.

In his letter to Sterling of 5 October 1905 Farrer said he had been informed of the impending issue of $25 million G.N. stock to shareholders at par. Harriman's biographer Kennan records that the U.P. allotment was taken up, increasing that holding by 37,444 shares.[1] Kennan further writes that in the remarkable boom in the market for railroad securities in late 1905 and early 1906— especially for Hill's stock—(N.P. selling at up to $232.50 and G.N. to $348) Harriman disposed of nearly all his N.P. and G.N. shares at prices which gave the Union Pacific a net profit of about $58 million. This is confirmed in a letter of 10 February 1913 from Farrer to Sterling, his source being the U.P.'s annual report for that period.

[1] Kennan, op. cit. vol. I, p. 395.

VIII

Transatlantic uncertainties

FARRER KEEPS IN TOUCH

'I grieve daily more and more my inability to come out this year for the fishing'; Gaspard Farrer had written in his letter of 14 April 1905 to John Sterling, 'nothing would please me better than to be able to come out and feel I need not be back for six months, in fact that I could loaf down at the fishing and stay there as long as one found it amusing'. In an earlier letter of 28 March he had told Sterling: 'I am more than ever determined to shake off all my bonds in a few years' time and leave others younger and more capable to do the work here'. Now he continued with news of 'the Captain', always associated in his mind with holidays at Metis:

Poor Eddie Blair has been having a bad time—three severe operations since December, but he is now practically right again, and we hope he will have no further trouble. A letter from him this morning asks when you are coming over. "Tell Sterling", he writes, "that we have had a burglar alarm here in Scotland and every window on the ground floor has been fitted with shutters and iron bars; tell him, too, that I will provide him with revolvers that will shoot, or won't, according to his fancy, and will do my best to provide him with such society as he is accustomed to down the Bay; tell him he must come".

Seriously, are you coming this year? Will you come if I come out to fetch you? I think you must make up your mind that the Boss will never go out; he seems less and less disposed to move every year. Shaughnessy is now here and has been giving us glowing accounts of Canadian Pacific prospects, and developments to be in the North West. I think if anything would tempt the Boss to make the trip besides the pleasure of seeing his friends it would be the pleasure of seeing that Western country again. Lady Gian is dying to go, but I doubt if he will be persuaded. If once our New York matters are settled, and two big conversion loans . . . out of the way, I could sail at any time, and will gladly come to escort you over, if that would be any inducement to help in making up your mind.

But Sterling was not to be persuaded, nor was Mount Stephen.
Writing to Tuck on 28 April Gaspard concluded: '. . . Mrs. Tuck
. . . will have to get together with Lady Mount Stephen and settle
on taking the trip . . . It is quite plain to me that both she and Mrs.
Tuck make their respective husbands a deal too comfortable at
home!' He added: 'Lord and Lady Mount Stephen are in great
trouble over the death of their dog Chang'. (He was able to tell
Sterling on 23 January 1906: '. . . Both he and she are by this time
wrapped up in the new dog, who, like another noted character,
swells visibly before one's eyes as a result of incessant cake and
bread and butter'.)

At least one of the Metis friends crossed the Atlantic that year:
the stout cotton-merchant, J. O. Bloss, dined with Gaspard one
evening in August before going on to Aix. The latter told Sterling
on the 16th: 'He seemed in excellent form and his shadow had
certainly not grown less'. Towards the end of the previous year two
American lady friends of Sterling had been in London, Gaspard
writing to him on 2 November 1904 that he had just seen them off
at the station: '. . . We have entered into a triple alliance, offensive
and defensive, to bring about your transportation to this side of
the Atlantic; sooner or later you have got to come . . .' On 5
October 1905 they were apparently back; Farrer wrote that Miss
Agnew had telephoned, and he had called and got news of him
'moreover told from a somewhat different point of view than that
of Blossie. You must be sure and let me know if I can do anything
here for either of your womenkind. Lord Mount Stephen is quite
indignant that you did not tell him they were over here . . .'

In Farrer's letter-books there is a gap from October 1905 to
January 1906. When the correspondence resumes Hill was just coming
to terms with the U.S. Steel Corporation for the lease of the iron
ore lands which he had acquired on his own account and was now
transferring to the railroad company.[1] Farrer relayed to Tuck on
5 February 1906 a message from Hill that he had practically
settled 'on a basis, as I understand, of 80 cents freight, 85 cents
royalty, the latter increasing 3 cents and 4 mills per year, with a
minimum output after 6 years of 9 million tons annually. He does
not say what the output is to be for the first 6 years, and that after

---

[1] Mount Stephen's niece Elsie Reford recalled that on hearing of the lease he cabled
Hill: 'Very bad news'. It seems he would have favoured working the mines themselves
but Hill was anxious to separate railroad and mining activities.

all is a point which interests you and me a deal more than what is going to happen when we have "got our wings on" . . .' To Hill he wrote the following day: '. . . The distribution will be a magnificent evidence of your works of supererogation on behalf of your shareholders'.

Regarding James Norman Hill, Farrer had told Tuck on 15 June 1905: '. . . I gather Jimmie is taking a more active part in supervising the management of both Burlington and NP, and I am pleased to hear of this as his abilities are too good to be wasted in playing golf and loafing'. On 6 February 1906 Farrer wrote directly to James Norman:

Lord Mount Stephen has shown me your letter to him about the NP which is most interesting and has done more to establish my faith in justification of the present prices of NP stock than any amount of estimates as to the value or its future earnings. When the work to which you refer is complete you will have a magnificent machine for economical production, and you should be able to defy all competition and wax fat whatever the fate of your present and prospective neighbours! You mention the asset of the CB & Q. During your father's visit [in late 1905] he never ceased talking of his desire to take that asset over on behalf of the GN and amalgamate GN and CB & Q Roads. What a chance for you and me if you will but be stiff in the back! Think of the glorious possibilities when we get our fingers once round the old gentleman's neck! Was ever so obvious an opportunity for our rapid road to fortune! You might tell him my ideas and break gently to him what he has to expect . . .

That this light-hearted letter was tailored for young James is confirmed in Gaspard's comment to Sterling on 27 February, when he was discussing Hill's future plans as outlined to them in England: '. . . The scheme would suit my own book admirably if it can be carried out without leading to future trouble. But this I doubt. I doubt the wisdom of concentrating control of one-third of the mileage of the railways in the U.S. in so limited an amount of stock as $200,000,000 and inevitably, therefore, in so limited an amount of hands . . . Do you not think that in the present temper of the people of the United States such schemes will lead to interference by the State? So far from thinking Hill and his family would be in a stronger position, my belief is that they would be in a weaker one; and we have less to fear from the remote possibility of raids by Harriman or others than we have from criticisms by the people as a whole and consequent interference by the Government'. Another 'tailored' letter was addressed by Gaspard on 8 March 1906 to E. H. Harriman himself; released from his undertaking to Hill not to do so while the Northern Securities difficulties were unresolved, Farrer had himself made an investment in Union Pacific (as, indeed, Mount Stephen was to do) and told Harriman: 'You have hitherto known me in the role so often assumed by Englishmen in your hospitable country, that of the "deadhead" and "free luncher". Today I am writing in an even more formidable character as one of your "d - - d shareholders"; and a hungry one at that—content with 6%—not a bit! "L'appétit vient en mangeant". I was about to write to you to express a pious hope that, if UP still retained its GN and a bonus of Iron Ore Stock was distributed, that that in turn might reach the pockets of UP shareholders . . .' He had just, however, received a balance sheet which 'if it has any foundation in fact' promised plans 'much more comprehensive, and . . . so much the more acceptable to your shareholders . . .' In August 1906 the UP dividend was increased from 6 to 10 per cent.

MOUNT STEPHEN AND HIS GOD-DAUGHTER

In July 1905 Garnet Wolseley and his daughter Frances were with the Mount Stephens at Brocket. Lord Cowper, the owner, had just died and Mount Stephen was negotiating a new 21-year lease with the heir, although the old lease still had eight years to run. Garnet wrote to his wife on the 30th:

> Our party consists of Rowdy Lane and his wife and of—Hang it I forget his name, the tall once goodlooking now stout and goodlooking man who used to be always with the Duke of Connaught . . .
> Frances has just come into my room and tells me that Mount Stephen informed her he has added to her possessions so that in future her fortune *from him* will be £500 per annum. I am very glad of this. *So when you and I are potted, she will be quite able to live comfortably as an old maid.* In fact, would not, all things considered be a bad catch for many a wifeless man of forty or fifty years of age! I suppose she will eventually have at least £2,000 per annum . . .[1]

(In the event, Frances was all but cut out of her mother's Will.) The next day, back in town, Garnet had to write and apologise to Louisa

[1] W/P 34.

for having forgotten to keep a luncheon appointment with her: 'I humbly ask your pardon but I now begin to feel nervous about going anywhere by myself for I can remember nothing . . .' Even in this state his talent for a picturesque phrase did not desert him; he wrote to her in November: 'I am now but an idler upon earth and like a topless hat that has no rim to it'.[1]

Thenceforward much of the Wolseley story is contained in the papers of the daughter Frances, and always in the background is the figure of her godfather, full of kindly concern for all of them, retaining the confidence of each. As Frances began to shape her own career in horticulture she became more and more estranged from her parents. As other people at odds with one another correspond only through their solicitors, so the Wolseleys communicated through Lord Mount Stephen; even if letters did pass direct he would be given a copy, and often Frances would ask his advice before replying to one of her parents' more querulous accusations. When communication broke down completely it was Mount Stephen who kept Frances informed about her parents. They continued to visit him and Louisa to write, so that he could assure Frances that she need not worry about them, they were completely self-sufficient, and much as he regretted the estrangement, which he always hoped might be happily resolved, there was nothing she could do except remain open to any overtures from them. That he did not similarly keep the parents informed about their daughter is evident from Louisa's letter to Garnet of 7 May 1911: '. . . I had a nice letter from Lord Mt. Stephen to whom I had written. He never *mentions* F.—I wonder if he ever sees her . . .'[2] It is possible that by keeping them ignorant he hoped to encourage some overture; his willingness to divert their disapproval from Frances to himself by taking responsibility for her line of action was frustrated; neither Garnet nor Louisa, while Garnet lived, would think ill of him.

By 1906 Mount Stephen's gifts to Frances gave her a total share capital of £16,000, or over £750 a year, 'which is', her godfather told her, 'better than a poke in the eye with a sharp stick'.[3] With this behind her, and with a loan, which became a gift, of £500 from the Misses Lawrence, sisters of Sir Trevor Lawrence, President of the Royal Horticultural Society, and old family friends generally referred to as the Good Ladies, Frances in 1906 built her own house on land she had rented adjoining Farmhouse, Glynde, to enlarge

[1] Ibid.   [2] LW/P35.   [3] PVW 120/662–5.

her gardening activities. The original idea was to house her head gardener there (Frances early realized that she herself could not manage without expert help) but to keep two rooms for her own use in case of need. There had been some unpleasantness in the winter of 1905–6 when her mother shut up Farmhouse to go up to London and then abroad leaving Frances to go into lodgings. Garnet had been unhappy over this and had hoped Louisa might be able to arrange for a servant to keep Farmhouse open for Frances, or for Frances to join them abroad: 'Don't let us run further apart from her than she wants'.[1] By this time the Lawrences had no inhibitions about taking Frances' part against her mother while insisting that Garnet, whom they revered, was not responsible for his actions. The building project rather alarmed Mount Stephen. He wrote in July 1906 in answer to Frances:

... Do I understand that your friend has made you a present of the money she has advanced you, or is it only a loan to be repaid? I hope you don't mind my asking these questions, as I should be very sorry if you have been persuaded to go into debt for the money to build the cottage. I am always afraid of debt ...

It was on seeing this letter that the Lawrences turned their loan into a gift, so that Frances was able to reassure her godfather, who then wrote in 7 August: '... I have such an absurd horror of debt, that it is quite a relief to me to know that you are not in it'. He went on: 'From what you say about Glynde, I fancy it is an ideal place for your father to spend the latter days of his life, and your gardening operations there must be a great interest to you both'.[2]

This question of where Garnet ought to live became an acute cause of contention between Frances and her mother, reaching a climax in 1908 when Louisa decided to give up Farmhouse entirely, thus depriving Frances of some gardening facilities such as glass-houses on which her college depended, in order to live in future between Hampton Court Palace, Mentone in the south of France, and a rented London house. Louisa thought her husband ought to winter abroad; Frances was sure he preferred to be at Glynde. Garnet's own pronouncements tended to be inconsistent; as a general principle, so long as his wife was with him he was happy anywhere; he loved Glynde when the sun shone: it was the sort of place he had dreamed of retiring to—a mellow old English home,

[1] W/P 35.
[2] PVW 120/683.

not too large—but he did not much care to be left alone there with Frances. They had been left alone there together in 1904, when he had written to Louisa: 'She strictly performs her duties as if they were laid down in Kings Regulations and Orders for the Army, but not a glimmer of interest or affection is thrown into the "game" '. The following year in the same circumstances he wrote of Frances as 'dutiful but not affectionate . . . as well expect an elephant to knit . . . Frances is like a machine-made companion as far as I am concerned. I meet her at meals, I know she is "*somewhere about*", . . . and when I "put a penny in the slot" she answers the call made upon her'. In 1904 he had, unwillingly but valiantly, accompanied Frances to stay at the Press baron Lord Glenesk's villa at Cannes, in pursuance of a Glenesk family plan to marry Frances to the heir, Oliver Borthwick, and had written to Louisa:

. . . Oh how I should enjoy this place if you and I had a house on the sea at some distance from the mob! I should certainly spend all my winters here and so avoid all the fogs and dreariness of November, the cold and festivities of December, the fogs of January and February and the bitter winds of March. But then one should have a house here and that would be beyond our means . . . I would much prefer the Farmhouse and its winds and cold fogs and rains with you to all this splendour of colouring and clear sky and balmy and seductive weather . . .[1]

The building of Frances' house at Ragged Lands was the watershed from which her relations with her parents began to go rapidly downhill, and not necessarily because it looked like a gesture of independence. Had the house itself not been of an undistinguished contemporary style even her mother might have felt differently about it; in her opinion it was a hovel. Frances describes, not without humour, one of the two visits in ten years which her mother paid her there, and how the only object to soothe Louisa's troubled eye was an ancient oak table. Her mother was so struck with it that the collector in her very nearly overcame the outraged parent. 'The rest of my house she looked at with compassion'.[2] Although Garnet's lapses of memory were becoming more and more marked, it does not appear that his conclusions about Frances were other than the result of his own quite acute observation. Apologising to Louisa in 1906 for the erasures in his letter he wrote: '. . . while I scribble with my hand, my brain is thinking of Frances and of how much

[1] W/P 33.
[2] PVW 120/749.

she loses in being coldhearted, especially to you. But I suppose she can't help it. I make it, therefore, a point to think as little and as seldom of her as I can . . . I have long long ago given up any hope of seeing any affectionate interest in us or our doings grow up in her. She has none to bestow on anyone and men are clever enough to find that out'. Yet it was clear that he found it difficult to dismiss the subject. In February 1907, aboard Sir Donald Currie's yacht, he kept asking Louisa: 'How is the "enigma"? Where is she and what is she doing? . . . How is our Sphinx? Have you heard from her of late, and if so, from what locality'?[1] Louisa went through a similar process of veering from disappointed affection to hopeless distaste. 'I wish she had the *devil* in her, if she could only be a little affectionate. Don't you?' she wrote to Garnet in 1904.[2]

In 1906 to 1907 Frances wrote to her godfather for advice about taking up rights issues of the Great Northern and Northern Pacific. It was clear that her expenditure at Ragged Lands had eaten into her resources (her account in her memoirs of her travels abroad that year made it plain that she was feeling aggrievedly impoverished) and subsequent correspondence suggests that Mount Stephen gave her £1,000 outright, explaining how she could repay the balance to her bank by selling old shares.[3] Frances told Mount Stephen that she had discussed with her mother the question of her continuing with the gardening college after Farmhouse was given up, and that her mother entirely approved, adding that it was clear that her parents were more relieved than otherwise when she was not with them. She went on to criticise the new doctor who had advised that Garnet should leave Glynde (she had been accused of collusion with the old one) evoking the following reply, written on 20 July 1907:

. . . I had not heard of your mother's intention to let Farm House and to live hereafter between the Palace and Mentone, but if she has decided on that course the only thing for you to do is acquiesce. The inconvenience to you of losing the Farm House garden will soon pass away. The extra expense to which you will be put in living with your maid at the cottage need not be a serious inconvenience, and it can easily be provided for by the sale, by and bye, of some of your shares, either Great Northern or Northern Pacific, whichever be decided when the time comes.

I should have hesitated to give you this advice, were I not convinced

[1] W/P 35–36.
[2] LW/P 30.
[3] PVW 120/686–7, 691–2, 718–20, 752.

that it will be better for all concerned if you have a little home of your own, and only go to them when they want you. Meantime you should try and be as considerate as possible with your mother, giving in to her in every way, and showing her how deeply you share her feelings of anxiety about your father. Do not hesitate to write whenever you think I can be of service to you. Always your affectionate godfather . . .

'I should think he is aware how matters are', wrote Miss Louey Lawrence to Frances, on being shown this letter, and she offered to help when the payments on the Northern Pacific issue became due. Mount Stephen was obviously not prepared to encourage extravagance; he had already expressed the opinion that her parents ought to make Frances a regular allowance, sufficient for her to live independently. When Louisa sent him a copy of the letter she wrote to Frances on 24 July 1907 (both she and her daughter were then under the roof of Farmhouse) asking her daughter to put it in writing that she wished to live separately, in which case her mother would consider giving her an allowance in lieu of her keep and that of her maid, Mount Stephen saw Lady Wolseley and after discussion it was agreed that Frances should have £150 a year. Mount Stephen then wrote to Frances suggesting that if she agreed with him that she ought to be independent she should write a very affectionate letter to her mother saying that she had decided to act on her godfather's advice: 'If this plan is carried out, you will be your own mistress entirely, living your own life and managing your own affairs, and will always be ready to go to them, whenever they may want you and invite you to come'.[1] On 28 September he told Frances: '. . . I have good news of your father and mother. They seem to be very happy together and not to want anyone with them. They are everything to each other, which, under the circumstances, is a great blessing . . .'[2]

DEATH OF CHARLES ELLIS

On 27 March 1906 Gaspard Farrer wrote to Thomas Baring in New York (their branch there, formerly Baring Magoun, was now known as Baring & Co.): '. . . I am grieved over Charles Ellis; he is down at Haslemere, refuses to see anyone and refuses now even to have his letters read to him. I greatly fear we shall never see him again; he has obviously given up all hope of himself. We cannot

[1] PVW 120/735-7. [2] PVW 120/751.

make out exactly what his trouble is, but besides that of which you know I fear there are complications. The nurse writes that he is rapidly getting weaker'. To Sterling on 4 April Farrer wrote at greater length, obviously much moved and feeling a need to compose an obituary of someone who might well never get another:

We went yesterday to attend the funeral of poor Charles Ellis. Though I do not think you knew him personally you must have heard so much about him that I know you will like to have the last news there is to give. There were very few people there: the Boss; Iveson; Yorke, husband of Lady Lilian whom you may remember in the old days at Causapscal; Lord Desart one of the executors; Alfred Egerton, the Duke of Connaught's man; Lord Emlyn, husband of one of his heirs; Freddie Bentinck, a cousin and an executor; Mrs. Evelyn Ellis, a sister-in-law, and her two children. He was buried at Frensham. Though only 40 miles from town the trains are abominable; we took two hours to get down there and two hours to get back. Arrangements had been made to give us lunch at the house and we felt therefore compelled to go there, though personally I would far sooner have gone straight to the church and back again. The place itself was absolutely made by him, every square yard had his own individual stamp upon it. There is no place like it in England; only 90 acres in all and every inch of it planted with some tree or shrub or flower under his own supervision, plants gathered from all over the world. It was sad to be there without him and to feel that no one can ever look after the place with the same knowledge and care and affection as he did.

As you probably know, he was not on very good terms with his relations; all the family are as queer as ever they can be and part of the queerness seems to take the form of disliking those whom they should like the best. He has left some rather inconsiderable legacies to members of his family and their children and the bulk of his property to three girls of John Thynne, John Thynne and his wife being among his oldest and best friends. Each girl will get about £1,000,000. The eldest who gets the place as well is the wife of Lord Emlyn, the second married Lord Hindlip, the third is still a child.

I am afraid the Boss will feel his loss badly. I think Charlie Ellis really liked him better than anyone else, and though they did not see a great deal of each other owing to one living at Haslemere and the other at Brocket, they wrote constantly, and I have no doubt that Charlie Ellis thought more of Lord Mount Stephen than of anyone else. He was certainly the most individualistic character whom I have ever met and in spite of his strong prejudices and dislikes attracted by the force of his character the affection of a large number of friends . . .

NEW GREAT NORTHERN ISSUE

At least that year Gaspard had the consolation of a visit to Metis. Writing to Hill on 4 May 1906 in a relaxed mood—the London shareholders were 'all right. I have never known them worry so little over a fall in the stock market. The Boss himself gets worried by some of his west end friends, but you need not disturb yourself about them. They will not sell ... Looking to the large amounts which by your reckoning must have been sold by the UP, I am only surprised that the fall has not been greater ...' —he concluded: 'I expect to be out in June and hope to see you and Mrs. Hill then; please give her my kind regards'. He saw Hill both on the St. John River and in St. Paul. Arriving back in London at the end of July he wrote to Hill on 4 August:

... I found Lord Mount Stephen very flourishing on my return though rather disappointed that I could bring him no more definite news as to your affairs than I had when I started from London. I have, however, assured him that you are as anxious to move as he can be, and that he and his friends will have no reason to regret their patience. Lord Mount Stephen was somewhat astonished to find me returning in the unwonted garb of the rampant bull. I meant to come back pessimistic, but the facts seemed too strong for me. I only regret that I could be of no assistance to you. It was evident to me that the points for decision involved issues of politics and law quite as much as finance, and that no one who was not closely in touch with both the first issues could give an opinion worth recording ...

Farrer had found the United States in the throes of Government investigations: it was the year of the Interstate Commerce Commission's enquiry into the consolidation and combination of carriers generally known as the Carriers Investigation, and of the adoption of the Hepburn Act, increasing the I.C.C.'s authority and extending railroad regulation. He had told Hill in May that he had been looking forward to the autumn, and autumn demands for money, with 'considerable apprehension' but felt the recent check to speculation and business generally had made the position much safer. The events of that autumn, leading to the 'rich man's panic' of 1907 and what James Stillman's biographer Burr called 'the end of an era'[1] in American stock market history postponed Hill's plans longer than Farrer had expected. Writing to Lord Mount Stephen

[1] Burr on *Stillman*, p. 239.

on 5 November 1906 regarding a friend's investments, he listed a number of possibles '—or if shares too speculative he might wait for Hill's Debenture Stock . . .' He went on: 'The U.S. owes so much short money to Europe that I cannot help thinking there will have to be a good deal of liquidation (and lower prices &c.) in New York during the next three months and I don't feel as if I would care to buy *shares* for myself at the present moment . . .' To another friend Farrer wrote directly on 10 December: 'Owing to dear money in New York, Great Northern shares are unfortunately somewhat lower now than when you purchased them. It seems a pity to sell them at a loss. Would you like us to pay for them on the chance of being able to sell them at better prices after the turn of the year?'

When on 18 December 1906 Frances Wolseley sought Mount Stephen's advice on her investments (p. 291 above) her godfather replied next day:

. . . Take your Iron Ore Certificates to Cox & Co. for safe keeping and try to forget that you have them. The longer you keep them the better you will like them. Then as to the new Gt. Nor. shares offered at par, go to Cox & Co. and sign an application for all the new shares you are entitled to. When the instalments fall due, you can if necessary sell old Gt. Nor. shares to pay them. And as to Nor. Pacific new shares, do exactly the same thing when you receive their circular . . .

He wrote further on 3 February 1907: '. . . The Great Northern shares will not be issued before the 25th. This delay is caused by legal proceedings in the Minnesota courts . . .' In that year the I.C.C. turned its attention to the Harriman lines and Farrer told an acquaintance that it was 'likely to be the storm centre for some time to come' although he rightly predicted that his correspondent would not lose on U.P. in the long run.

By the end of that year Farrer was fairly complacent about the Great Northern. He wrote to R. I. Farrington, the second Vice-President, on 6 December that he was glad to see he had been engaged in consolidating all the various companies owned and operated by the company, 'and I hope it may lead to a presentation of the Company's accounts for the future in a form better suited to the limited comprehension of the uninitiated layman . . .' He told Robert Fleming on the 10th that although it was not easy to make out all the figures in the G.N. Report, he believed them to be accurate, and even doubted whether the entire capitalization, when current construction was completed, would work out at as high a figure as that quoted. By 30 December 1908 he was telling Farrington that the G.N. balance sheet—which he had been studying over the Christmas holiday—was an enormous improvement on its predecessors; after a detailed analysis which included a few criticisms, he assured him that 'otherwise it couldn't be clearer'.

PROBLEMS OF CHARITY

On 16 November 1904, just before the gift of Argentine Bonds to the King's Fund, Gaspard Farrer had written to John Sterling: 'Lord Mount Stephen will probably have written to you about his personal affairs. He is again being haunted with the dread of having too much money, and is worrying to divest himself of his worldly goods; I tell him he will end in the workhouse'. The problem had already been taxing Mount Stephen to the extent that before his first large donation to the Fund he had consulted such an unlikely source of counsel as Professor Goldwin Smith, then living in Toronto.[1] The latter wrote to him on 22 May 1901: 'I have not been unmindful of the question you asked me to help you in solving . . .' He had consulted 'a good authority on the subject' who had suggested 'a club-house for working men which he said would keep them from objectionable places in which they now hold their meetings'. Smith himself could not help thinking that 'healthy lodgings for the poor, in place of the filthy dens in which they fester, are about as beneficent as anything that can be devised. In the way of libraries, Carnegie is doing all that is needed, perhaps more . . . A good block of lodgings for the poor would be not only useful, but to some extent monumental, which I think a consideration, if secondary, not to be despised . . .'

This might well have appealed to Mount Stephen, in view of his own early experience in London. Times had changed, however, and his reaction to someone who informed him that boys in his native land were no longer going barefoot had been: 'Then I only hope they will run as far with shoes as without'.

Goldwin Smith wrote further on 1 February 1902, recommending to Mount Stephen the Duke of Newcastle's Education Commission Report of 1861 to show 'to what misdirection and

---

[1] Haultain on *Goldwin Smith*, pp. 372, 378, 381, 388.

abuse pecuniary bequests for charity are liable after the death of the founder. You will perhaps be led to be cautious in instituting such things as old-age pensions, or pensions of any kind. A fine building for a public purpose is not liable to misdirection or abuse. It preserves the memory of the founder and preaches munificence to posterity ...' He went on: 'In providing endowments for Scotch Ministers you run the risk of having your benefaction swept away by theological revolution ...' going on to cite a quite erroneous view of a Darwinian theory. 'To help the existing Ministers, if they are worthy and depressed in circumstances is of course quite right and safe. So is to subscribe to a hospital or to add to its endowment ...' Again on 4 March 1902 he wrote: '... You say you do not care to be a founder ... But I think monuments of beneficence are good and pleasant things for society. They link the generations together and preach regard for humanity ...' But on 2 October, hearing the news of Mount Stephen's and Strathcona's gift to the King's Fund, Goldwin Smith was thoroughly approving: 'I can only clap my hands at your munificence, which is undoubtedly well bestowed ...'

Begging letters inevitably became a feature of Mount Stephen's life. But to one source of appeal he was never deaf; he wrote on 18 March 1907 to the Princess of Wales:

I have received the paper on the proposed Illustrated Lectures on the Colonies for use in the schools of the United Kingdom which Your Royal Highness has just sent me; I am all in favour of our boys and girls being thoroughly drilled in the geography of the Empire at school & think the proposed method of teaching them to *understand* what the Empire means is very good. The difficulty to be overcome arises from the fact that already the children attending our elementary schools have far too many subjects to learn with the result that they (most of them) *learn* nothing 'forget it all in three months after they have left school'. I am a great believer in the *Three R's*. Children drilled in them *thoroughly*, can easily do all the rest for themselves. "Cram" is not education. But all this, Madam, you know better than I do & I beg your forgiveness for boring you with my views on elementary education. I dare say I am a bit of (a) "crank" on the question.

I enclose a cheque for £500 & should like it to be an *anonymous* contribution. If it were to become public I should be driven out of the country by begging letters ...[1]

[1] RA GV CC47/131.

The Princess of Wales—afterwards Queen Mary—shared with Gian Mount Stephen a passionate interest in what might be loosely termed antiques, objects of interest and beauty, heirlooms of the past and of the future, particularly those associated with royal family history. Both kept a watch on the salerooms—the snag being that as Queen Mary sent a representative to bid for her, Gian could not be sure that she was not bidding against her royal friend. Some of these articles were exchanged as gifts; some of Gian's purchases were brought rather surreptitiously into use in her home as her husband tended to tease her about her extravagance. Dame Nellie Melba, the Australian opera singer, recalled such occasions at Brocket: '. . . at dinner, as soon as the soup was served, he would put on a mock frown and say: "Gian, I have not seen these plates before. You have been buying more rubbish. What is the meaning of it?" '[1] In December 1907 the Prince and Princess of Wales were to join, as they had done before, the annual duck-shooting at Brocket; on 24 November Princess Mary wrote from York Cottage:

We now find that our son's holidays begin on Wednesday Dec[r] 18th so I am writing to ask you whether it would be possible for you kindly to put him up for that night at Brocket? It would be so kind of you if you would manage it & any tiny room wld. do. We feel terribly indiscreet at asking this favour but when we arranged the Brocket visit with you, we did not know about David's coming so soon. We hope to stay with you till Thursday afternoon (19th) & leave *after* shooting . . . We are much looking forward to our visit & hope the ducks will be plentiful. Would you like me to bring my motor as I did last year, that is if you can put it up?

I hope you & dear "George" (how cheeky & familiar this sounds) are well.

Writing her 'bread-and-butter' letter after this visit the Princess observed that 'David' had been 'so pleased'.[2]

Just as in 1904 Mount Stephen's uneasiness on the subject of financing medical education had contributed to the setting up of a committee of enquiry, so a letter of his in 1908 led eventually to the appointment of a committee in 1910 to look into alleged abuse of hospital out-patient departments. On 28 May 1908 he wrote to Sir Arthur Bigge:

[1] Nellie Melba, *Melodies and Memories*, London, 1925, p. 268. Not all her recollections were accurate. Frances Wolseley wrote that Lady Mount Stephen, on reading Melba's account of a Carlton House Terrace dinner party where Lord Roberts, who could not bear cats, insisted (correctly) that there was one in the room, declared that this had not happened at her house.
[2] RA GV CC44/202 and 203.

This morning's mail has brought me a perfect avalanche of begging letters (mostly) among them the inclosed which I am sending to you as a member of the Council of the King's Fund. There is I think much truth in what the writer says! I hope you & your colleagues may be able in time to remedy the abuse of the London Hospitals by Out Patients. I suspect all the London Hospitals are, more or less, to blame . . .[1]

The abuse complained of was that people tended to resort to out-patient departments who either could afford to go to a doctor, were covered by Friendly Societies which would have met a doctors' fee, or who were less in need of medical attention than of some more social type of care. Mount Stephen's concern was intensified by the factor that at the time his gift of some £26,000 was being partly devoted to the building of an out-patient department and casualty block at Aberdeen Royal Infirmary. When the committee was announced on 14 December 1910 by the Duke of Teck (who had succeeded as President of the Fund on the accession of King George V to the Throne) one of the members was Mount Stephen's son-in-law, Lord Northcote, now in retirement.[2] Northcote had been appointed a Charity Commissioner in 1891, and as Governor of Bombay from 1899–1904 he had done much to improve hospital facilities in that famine- and plague-ridden presidency. The report was delayed to take account of the 1911 National Insurance Act, and action was further postponed by the outbreak of the 1914–18 War, but the chief solution to the problem consisted in the extension of the Almoner system.

AMERICAN CONTACTS

Farrer paid a flying visit to New York at the beginning of 1908, seeing J. J. Hill there; he was to return later for the fishing. His letter to Louis Hill of 18 February was a searching inquisition into the prospects of the Great Northern Iron Ore Properties. He had told Lady Clanwilliam on 30 September 1907 that the first dividend on the Iron Ore Certificates had now been paid 'and though small is always something to the good . . .' (The Admiral had died on 4 August.) In 1909 he was writing cautiously to investors who had found themselves possessed of these unfamiliar securities; he was clearly becoming resigned to results later rather than sooner. His letter book for 1908 is incomplete (and none are available for 1909

[1] RA GV C273/73.   [2] A/KE/2/4.

and 1910) but the Metis fishing records[1] show that Gaspard was there from mid-June to early July with Sterling, Bloss and William Rockefeller, and landed some noble fish including several 32–pounders.

Mount Stephen had never met Will Rockefeller; an occasion had nearly arisen in London in 1905. Farrer wrote to Sterling on 9 May of that year while the 'Milwaukee's' extension to the Pacific was under consideration:

... I discussed (your letter) with Lord Mount Stephen, who is satisfied that no good could result from his meeting Mr. Rockefeller so far as a settlement of the Railway interests in the North West are concerned. Lord Mount Stephen does not know the situation there sufficiently to discuss it, and still less to commit Mr. Hill to any line of policy. Moreover, he is of opinion that if any settlement is to be reached with people like Mr. Rockefeller and Mr. Stillman, the advance must come from them in the first instance, and that were you to send Mr. Rockefeller a line of introduction to Lord Mount Stephen, the former might consider it as an approach from the Hill party to induce him to come to terms, in fact that Mr. Hill was anxious for a settlement.

As a matter of fact, we have no definite knowledge here in London that there is anything to settle. In case the Milwaukee and St. Paul extends to the Coast, the probabilities are that a favourable opportunity for settling difficulties will occur before it reaches its destination. That, at least I believe, has always been Mr. Hill's opinion.

I believe, notwithstanding all Lord Mount Stephen has said of Mr. Rockefeller, that he would in his heart of hearts rather like to meet him; not, however, to discuss the North West Railroad situation, but in a general way as one capable and successful business man has pleasure in meeting another equally capable and equally successful ...

They were to see more of James Stillman in the next few years; now virtually retired and living mostly in Paris, the New York banker seemed sometimes at a loss for occupation and took to haunting Bishopsgate. On 23 October 1908 E. H. Harriman wrote to Stillman from Arden, his country home in New York State, full of holiday news of his young children, and after a burst of activity spending 'lazy days here in which I do nothing but loaf'. He ranged over the field of their common interests: he was in no doubt but that Taft would win the coming election, after which 'everything will continue just as it is now with a little more sentimental activity.

[1] These records are in the possession of Mr. Eric Reford.

The greatest menace from which we need protection is the plethora of money the world over. Unemployed money is an instrument of mischief greater perhaps than unemployed labour. You should look to it that your bank doesn't get drawn into syndicates for new construction which will be destructive in a measure of the properties in which the bank itself or its proprietors may be interested . . . I was glad to get a glimpse of your doings and rumors of Lord Mount Stephen's continued good will; he is exceptionally endowed with fair-mindedness and common sense. Most other foreigners only look to the dividends paid without knowing anything of the difficulties or giving them a thought . . .' Referring no doubt to his recent successful stand against the I.C.C., he wrote: 'The feeling or sentiment in the West has changed absolutely. The communities should [*sic*] not do enough for us and all are willing that we should have charge of all the Railroads in sight, whether competing or not so long as we had them and for improvements, &c . . .'[1]

CANADA NORTH WEST LAND COMPANY

In 1909 Mount Stephen broke his personal connection with the Canada North West Land Company. The transfer of the Company to Canada (see chapter 1, pp. 33–40) had by no means solved all its problems, and the Farrer letter books for the next thirty years contained plaintive evidence of this. On 28 August 1894 Van Horne told Mount Stephen:

We hope to be able to close up the Canada North West Land Office in Winnipeg very soon now. There has been a good deal of work growing out of the change in the organization in which Mr. Scarth was necessary, and we have besides had the hope that he would fall into the Governorship; but we will not wait for that any longer, now that we are about able to spare him.[2]

On 8 February 1898 he replied to a query from Mount Stephen: 'You ask about the Canada North West Land Company. Its expenses are almost nil and for 1898 it should make a good showing in sales. I think its upward turn has come too and I have no doubt at all of its profitable outcome'.[3] This was over-optimistic. During a visit to Montreal in 1900 Farrer had discussed the Company's

[1] Burr, op. cit. p. 241.
[2] Van Horne—Stephen Letter Book 1894–8 (PAC), pp. 21–25.
[3] Ibid. pp. 172–6.

future with Mount Stephen's brother-in-law Robert Meighen, President of the Lake of the Woods Milling Company, apparently in the hope that Meighen might be persuaded to extend his business talents to this unsatisfactory protégé of past and present C.P.R. directors. Farrer wrote to Meighen on 8 October 1901:

... I have had many discussions with Lord Mount Stephen on the subject, and as he has written to you fully, I will not worry you afresh with the steps we here should advise but will only add my hopes to his that you may be able to take the business up. It would certainly make a great difference to my confidence in the Company's future if firstly *you* made the selection of a paid officer to do the work on the ground in the North West, and secondly, were willing to supervise this officer's work, and assist him with advice ... I am satisfied that the risk of investing in the Company is small, and the prospect of profit very considerable, especially in view of this year's harvest and the gradual filling up of the country ...

He went on to say that Meighen could count on almost unanimous support from shareholders in the United Kingdom; Mount Stephen's and Strathcona's holdings alone would give him a clear majority, while in Canada the C.P.R. with another large holding could probably also be counted on for support. He concluded:

... I ought to add that when the transition from London to Canada was made, sales were non-existent, expenses were heavy, tax questions were threatening, and the till empty. The C.P.R. people at our request came forward, took up the burden of management, and without a stiver of pay from that day to this, have brought the Company round to its present sound state, so that every consideration is due to them on personal grounds, and no change could be attempted except in consultation with them and with their approval ...

Having received a favourable response from Robert Meighen, Farrer wrote again on 26 October 1901 mentioning a point that he was to stress a good deal: the need for revaluation of the Company's lands. Another of his anxieties was that land should be sold for cash, and not paid for in shares of the Company: this he pressed in a letter of 6 December 1901 to R. B. Angus—one of Gaspard's diplomatic approaches, recognising the part the C.P.R. had played —and also when writing on 28 November to Charles Ellis, one of the patient English shareholders. His letter to Angus of 14 March 1902 showed that they differed as to whether the Land Company

ought to be in competition with C.P.R. land sales; Farrer held that
when the railway lands contiguous to theirs were out of the market,
the Land Company would then get double the price they could have
got on a competitive basis. To this letter he added: 'I hear you are
building yourself a lovely house in the country. You always seem
to me to have ordered your life just right, retaining sufficient work
to be of interest, and sufficient leisure for interests other than those
of the daily treadmill'. Mr. Angus's house was at Senneville,
Montreal. An art-lover and antiquarian, he was to maintain his
business interests to an advanced age, becoming president of the
Bank of Montreal at the age of 79 (1910–1913) and remaining a
director of Canadian Pacific until his death at Senneville in 1922.[1]

Farrer's next preoccupation was the repayment of the Preferred
shares. He wrote rather prematurely to John Sterling on 20 August
1902: '. . . Have you noticed that the poor old Canada North West
Land Co. is at last reviving, and holders who invested their money
in it 20 years ago and have been without dividends ever since, have
at last the opportunity of getting their money back . . .' On 6
November 1902 he wrote to Ellis about getting his proxy in support
of an application to the Canadian Parliament for powers to pay back
the Preference shareholders *pro rata* as lands were sold; a similar
letter went to 'Papa'. He had told Ellis on 4 September: '. . . You
may recollect that land sales were fairly active from '80–'82 and then
a complete cessation for 15 or 16 years. The same thing may happen
again, so that though one may look for an eventual return of $75
per Deferred Share, that cannot be viewed as their present value. Of
course, with reasonable luck, the sales from now onwards should
average a higher price than $5 an acre, in fact keep on increasing
in price as the land diminishes . . .' In 1903 Mount Stephen and
Farrer were still agonising over how some return might be made to
the long-suffering shareholders; Farrer wrote both to the C.P.R.
President T. G. Shaughnessy and to E. B. Osler in Toronto who
had a long connection with the Company communicating their
views, and discussed these with Meighen in England. Farrer kept
repeating that a land company was essentially one in liquidation;
regular dividends were not expected: 'It is not the character of the
share'. But by 1904 the Company's cash assets were sufficient, he
thought, to extinguish the Preferred shares, and on 6 February he

[1] The author has not been permitted to examine the R. B. Angus papers in the Public
Archives of Canada.

told Meighen that he could wish the retirement accelerated. He deprecated advances to settlers, telling Meighen on 14 March that the Company was not in the mortgage investment business. Later that year he was buying Deferred shares for Mount Stephen as they were being put on the London market, telling Meighen on 18 November that if he felt it incumbent on him to pay a dividend on the Deferred he hoped it would be 'one of small proportions'. He would prefer the Company to continue the reduction of the Preferred capital until it were entirely repaid.

On 12 July 1905 Farrer wrote to Meighen: '. . . Lord Mount Stephen tells me that you have sent him excellent reports of harvest prospects, our land sales indicate that immigration and demand for farms is constantly increasing, and we hope to hear from you before long that financial arrangements have been made for the repayment of outstanding preferred shares'. His acute ear had registered that another land company was getting up to $8.50 an acre, and on 16 October he commented to Meighen that he was all in favour of holding land for higher prices. He could understand Meighen's astonishment when the latter found that his own officials were selling lands below the recommended price, he wrote on 27 February 1906, but by 1 April, when the final repayment of Preferred shares gave him a preponderant interest, he forecast that Meighen would be able to get his own way entirely: 'Your patience hitherto has seemed to us almost unlimited. Personally I should long ago have taken matters into my own hand and found a big hole for officials who acted contrary to my wishes . . .' By March 1906 the Company was selling its land at a minimum of $10 an acre, and in April the Preferred shares were finally repaid, although even now Farrer began to worry lest the Company had had to borrow for the purpose. On 25 July 1907 he congratulated Meighen on an excellent report; Mount Stephen and he were satisfied that this was due to Meighen's insistence on holding for higher prices and not selling to speculators at less than the original cost. On 23 December 1909 Mount Stephen himself wrote to Meighen from Brocket:

Referring to what you say in your letter of 2nd. about Sir Thos. Shaughnessy's visit to this side & my shares in the N.W. Land Co. I have not seen Sir Thos. yet but am hoping to see him either here or in London after he returns from Paris. In regard to my Nor West Land Shares (*8123*) I have decided to sell the whole to you for the sum of $43,285 *58*. These figures are taken from Mr. Turnbull's last July

LORD NORTHCOTE
(from *Review of Reviews*, 1904)

statement; so that in regard to the N.W.L. Co. you will be free to do what you like as the largest shareholder of the Company . . .[1]

Two years later, on Meighen's death, his son Frank took over his responsibilities, with continued advice from Mount Stephen, although war service was to intervene. Farrer also, on behalf of Lefevres, kept his interest in the Land Company, revising his theories to suit the changing times. By 1923, when the Company's taxes threatened to swallow its income, his final advice was to reduce the price of the land and 'clear the lot'.

MOUNT STEPHEN AND THE WOLSELEYS

In August 1908 Garnet Wolseley was again aboard Sir Donald Currie's yacht; this time the *Iolaire* was cruising in the Hebrides. On the 26th he wrote to Louisa at Hampton Court Palace: '. . . I *forget*?! whether this is 1908 or 1909, but I favour the former . . .' Mount Stephen's old friend and Wolseley's late colleague General Sir John McNeill, latterly senior Equerry to Queen Victoria, had for some years owned the island of Colonsay. Gaspard Farrer had written to J. J. Hill on 4 August 1899: '. . . There seems a prospect of Sir John getting rid of Colonsay; a great relief to him if he succeeds' (in fact it was acquired by Lord Strathcona). Now McNeill who had died in 1904 was very much on Garnet's mind, although the name of his island continued to escape him; at one point he was convinced it was Scalpay, where the yacht had called because this was Currie's island, and Garnet felt resentful that Currie should now be there instead. He rambled on through several letters about the man whom he had often criticized in his lifetime: 'poor fellow, I often think of him and his curiously jerky manner; a good soul & a brave, determined Soldier who laughed at danger . . . I hope he is in Heaven but I can only think of him as I knew him here full of life, energy & good nature & goodwill towards all men & women . . . I hope I shall be "told off" to serve alongside of him in Heaven . . . I hope I may serve shoulder to shoulder in Heaven with John McNeill . . . Was it Colonsay or Scalpa? . . . poor John McNeill is always in my mind—"*all round*" he was a right good fellow & an excellent fighting soldier . . . Colonsay or Scalpa—I forget which it is or was called in his day . . .' And

[1] This letter is in the possession of Mr. Eric Reford.

suddenly, in mid-stream: '... Do you ever hear news of the old maid of Glynde?...'[1]

A year later, on 18 August 1909, he was writing from the London house in Gore Street: ' " Here I am again" dressing for another show. This time to receive the little nigger from Persia. Having done so I shall be free until dinner when I have to dine at a State Banquet at Buckingham Palace in his honour. I do not yet know if I shall be again required this week to dance attendance upon him'. This curious fantasy must have gone back to 1889 when the Shah visited London during Wolseley's earlier spell at the War Office.

Mount Stephen had written to Frances on 19 January 1908: '... I don't think you need worry about your father and mother at Mentone. They are evidently enjoying themselves and prefer being alone by their two selves, being all the world to each other ...' He was glad to hear how well her plans were going at Ragged Lands and was looking forward to her first book *Gardening for Women* which came out that year. Gian had promised to get him a copy, when 'I will tell you honestly what I think of it'. He added: 'I have had a nasty cold in my head, but am now nearly alright again.'[2] On 10 June 1908 Mount Stephen wrote to ask whether Frances would like to take up the lease of Farmhouse on her own account: it still had eleven years to run. She replied that she now preferred to remain in her own cottage and her godfather agreed with her decision.[3] She was still keeping up a not very happy correspondence with her parents and sent Mount Stephen a letter she had had from her father, to whom she had apparently suggested that she visit them at Hampton Court. Mount Stephen wrote on 13 June:

I return your father's letter. I do not see that you can do anything but respect his expressed wishes by only going to them when you are invited. Your mother complained to me of what she called your "breezy acquaintance *manner*" "without heart" on the occasion of your last visit. So long as she is dominated by this feeling it will, I think, be better for you to say nothing and obediently respect her wishes to be left alone with your Father. Perhaps *time* will remove the strained relations between you when you understand each other better.

When your mother writes to you be prompt in replying & in terms becoming a daughter. What your mother seems to crave from you is a warmer expression of your love and affection for them. She perhaps forgets

[1] W/P 37.
[2] PVW 120/757.
[3] PVW 120/764.

that many people have great love and affection but little power of express-ing it. None of us are made exactly alike.
I still hope *time* will change all this & remove all misunderstandings.[1]

Frances accordingly wrote in dutiful terms to her father, ending: 'I hope you will however still continue to let me hear from you as I do very much care to know, and I shall tell you my doings, dull as they may be, in case you care to hear of them'. Her letter cannot have been well received, as on 24 June Mount Stephen wrote:

I think you should go on writing to your mother but *not* to your Father ... and let her use her own judgment whether to communicate it to your Father or not. Your mother is in an excited state of mind over your Father and is much to be pitied, but I am in hopes *time* will do much to restore matters between you to their natural condition.

I suggest when you write to her that you should tell her you think it better you should not trouble your Father with letters.

On 11 July Mount Stephen asked Frances to let him know the position of her Bank account: 'I want as soon as it can be done, to see you out of debt & free from all bother about money'. On 24 July he wrote: 'I am today writing to my agent in New York to transfer into your name 27 shares Gt. Nor. which I happen to have & for which I have no particular use, and to buy for you 5 more shares so as to make up your holding of Gt. Nor. to the round 200 ...' He calculated that her income would then be £950, including her parents' £150 allowance. Not surprisingly, he obviously assumed that this amounted to being comfortably off. Louisa came down to Glynde that month to oversee the removal from Farmhouse and wrote scathing letters to Garnet about Frances and her establishment: '... She is most *persistent* in her visits here, but as they are of the driest nature they oppress me extremely while they last, and fill me with sorrow when they are over. I am glad that you too are not exposed to them as they would leave you sad and weary ...'[2] Garnet wrote on 11 July from Hampton Court: '... I never wish to see her again and am glad she has not settled down near Hampton Court. Have I made a Will? I know I did so *once upon a time*, but is it in existence? I hope I have not mentioned F. in it for I should like that whatever she might get from us, should be for you to bequeath to her. I can never in my heart

---

[1] PVW 137.   [2] LW/P 34.

pardon her disgraceful treatment of a mother who has always been so good to her'.[1] Louisa spent a day with the Mount Stephens at Brocket in September 1908 and wrote to Garnet: 'He was most kind and genial and so was she. He told me F.'s income now is £950 a year *with* our £150. She really has no excuse for making poor mouths, and bringing discredit on us'. Recently a gift of a dress from the Lawrences had provoked Garnet to prophesy that soon his daughter would be on the parish coal list.

An attempt later in 1908 by her parents to make Frances respond to an appeal for financial aid from her old governess was met with a quite definite negative reaction from Mount Stephen: Miss Pannebakker was no business woman (as Garnet had pointed out to Louisa some years earlier) and any such aid would be money thrown away; if the Wolseleys chose to subsidise the governess's school, which was a failure, that was their affair. He took responsibility for Frances' stand and advised her on 16 January 1909 to stop writing to either of them for a time: 'Perhaps your silence may soften them . . .'[2] He had meanwhile returned to Frances her cheque for £50 sent in payment of a loan, saying: 'I hope you will accept (it) as a Christmas present from your old Godfather'.[3] In April 1909 Frances went to Italy with her Sussex friend Mary Campion, but became ill there and returned to London. A specialist diagnosed nothing radically wrong. In June her godfather wrote to Ragged Lands hoping that she was better and enclosing a letter he had had from Louisa: '. . . You can see how hurt she is at not hearing from you. Please return her letter to me and say nothing to *her* or to *anyone* of my having sent it to you to read. I am very sorry for your mother. You can see how much she loves you in her heart . . .' This was misguidedly dealt with by Mary Campion who was at Frances' request opening and answering her mail, the London doctor having ordered complete quiet and no form of worry. She wrote to Mount Stephen a somewhat incoherent letter explaining that Frances had asked her to write both to Lady Wolseley and to Lady Mount Stephen but that she had forgotten to post the letters. Louisa had offered both her London house and the Hampton Court apartments (where she was then in residence). Mount Stephen wrote again on 23 July 1909 quizzing Frances about her doctor:

[1] W/P 37.
[2] PVW 139.
[3] PVW 120/779.

'Those queries will show you that I am not much of a believer in Doctors and medicine . . . Fresh air and plenty of it, with good food and no worries will do more for you than Doctors . . . I have torn up your Mother's letter. I am glad you keep her informed as to your progress. She is and cannot help being anxious about you'.

On Frances' thirty-seventh birthday, 15 September 1909, there came from her mother 'Our little gift for today, with *much* love, to a good daughter'. Yet in October her father composed, and in November lodged with his new solicitor, a memorandum recording Frances' 'desertion of us, her parents' to be produced should Louisa need to contradict any contrary version by Frances.[1] On Christmas Eve Mount Stephen wrote to thank Frances for her gift and continued:

I was glad to see your handwriting again. In your last letter to me you were forbidden to either write or read letters . . . Gian and I spent an afternoon with your Father and Mother at Gore Street and we were glad to find them both looking so well and bright. I have been laid up for the last two weeks with an attack of Bronchitis but am now all right again . . .

In December 1909 the Prince and Princess of Wales were again at Brocket: 'the only drawback being the absence of our dear and kind host', wrote the Princess afterwards on 17 December. 'I hope that our good friend Sir James gave a continued satisfactory report'.[2] Sir James Reid was Mount Stephen's chief medical man during his last years.

Frances heard nothing from her mother between April and September 1910, and her birthday gift to her father in June was returned. On 17 September Frances replied to her mother's letter in a somewhat solemn manner, assuring her that her feelings towards them both were as warm as ever. The death of King Edward VII in that year led, in the words of Frances' memoirs, to the 'cessation of much social movement'. In July she had been asked to organize a conference of women gardeners in connection with the Japanese–British Exhibition; Lady Mount Stephen undertook to attend the associated farming conference provided she was not called on to make a speech. These gave an impetus, Frances wrote, to public interest in women's work in land cultivation.[3] Mount

[1] PVW 139.   [2] RA GV CC33/205.
[3] PVW 139.

Stephen wrote to Frances on 7 November 1910, having lately heard from her mother. He had, he said, written to Lady Wolseley

... begging her to give up *worrying* about you and the unhappy estrangement between her and you, pointing out that your having made your home at Glynde was finally settled by her as the best thing for both, a decision in which I *heartily* agreed. In fact there was nothing else to be done. Your poor mother has worked herself up into a state of nerves that is bad for her, and correspondence only does her harm ... It is all too sad for words, but you must try bear it in silence.

He added a postscript 'I ought to have written before but I have been a little under the weather for the last ten days—am all right now'. He was then 81. Frances replied by return: '... I can never thank you enough for all your great kindness and help in advising me. I do not at all like having to bother you so often—although your letters and good counsel are such a comfort to me—for I feel I am not only taking up your time but also causing you pain and worry ...'[1]

THE RECIPROCITY DEBATE

On 9 February 1911 Gaspard Farrer was writing both to E. T. Nichols of the Great Northern and to Howard Elliott of the Northern Pacific on the subject of what he loosely termed the Reciprocity Treaty between the United States and Canada. It seemed to him that if carried through it ought to be of benefit to Great Northern interests and to many enterprises in the North West on both sides of the border, although some individual interests such as fruit growers in British Columbia would inevitably suffer. 'I hope it may safely pass' he told Nichols; being a Government measure, and Sir Wilfrid Laurier's party in so strong a majority, he wrote to Elliott, he had little doubt of its being carried in Canada. He was unable to judge President Taft's difficulties, but 'on general principles one would judge that a lowering of the tariff wall must be beneficial for both countries taken as a whole ... *Prima facie* one would think that an arrangement which secured for the Canadians a market of 90 million people must be more in their favour than one which secured the U.S. a market of 7 millions ...' In fact, the Americans had entered discussions with more enthusiasm than the Canadians,

[1] PVW 139.

and it was the latter who insisted that there should be no Anglo-American treaty, but that each country should introduce concurrent legislation.[1] In the United States the agreement was approved in July 1911; in Canada it became the issue in an election in which Laurier's Liberals were defeated by Robert Borden's Conservative Party.

Farrer had written to Robert Meighen on 28 February: 'With Reciprocity in sight and Canada on the verge of becoming part of the United States (pace Mrs. Reford) we must look for compensation to our feelings by getting a U.S. price for our lands! . . .' Meighen's daughter, Elsie, who had married Robert W. Reford of the Montreal shipping company, was, like her father, an outspoken opponent of reciprocity, apparently sharing with many Canadians the opinion that it was 'yet another assault by the Laurier government against the imperial connection, a long step on the road toward commercial and eventually political union with the United States'.[2] One can imagine her lively discussions on the subject with her uncle when she visited the Mount Stephens that spring. On 22 March Gaspard observed to Sterling '. . . Van Horne is here and I am dining with Fleming tonight to meet him.[3] He appears to be rabid on the subject of the Reciprocity Treaty; so also is Meighen from whom I have received many pages of invective against the short-sighted policy of our English Government. I suppose, however, the Treaty is likely to go through . . .' To Meighen he wrote on 25 March that Lord Mount Stephen 'treats your alarm about Reciprocity with considerable philosophy; like myself he believes the Canadian is every bit as good as the American and rather better, and is confident that Canada will not be annexed to the U.S. until she wishes to be, and if she wishes, no treaties or trade relations would prevent that unfortunate occurrence . . .' On 21 April Farrer told Meighen: '. . . I gather the treaty is now likely to go through, but this will not prevent its repeal if in the course of time Laurier's party go out and other views prevail . . .' The September election in Canada disposed of the question for the moment although the Borden government 'took pains to assure the United States that the result . . . did not mean the beginning of an era of hostility in Canadian–American relations'.[4]

[1] See Robert Craig Brown and Ramsay Cook, *Canada 1896–1921. A Nation Transformed*, Toronto, 1974, pp. 179–85.　　　　　[2] Ibid. p. 180.
[3] Van Horne had by then left Canada for Cuba.
[4] Brown and Cook, op. cit. pp. 203–4.

IRON ORE CERTIFICATES: HILL UNCOMMUNICATIVE

In his letter to Nichols of 9 February 1911 Gaspard had said that he was disappointed at hearing nothing of Mr. Hill coming to Europe; he had hoped he would have been able to spare time this spring. He had written cryptically to Mount Stephen the previous 17 November of a letter from Hill which he enclosed '. . . which is quite interesting. I shall say nothing of its contents for fear his imagination may have again got away with him'. He told Sterling on 17 February 1911 that he had heard nothing from the Hills for a long time, and again on 3 March—his firm having to his relief just avoided handling a 'Milwaukee' issue in London which 'would have given the coup de grace to our friendly relations with Hill; if indeed they can still be called friendly.—I have not for a long time heard from him or the sons and Nichols, who used to write to me constantly and of his own accord, has since the summer practically ceased corresponding and has avoided answering the one or two questions which I have put to him'. He went on:

I am quite certain that Nichols' behaviour is not on his own initiative and that he is acting under orders. I may tell you that soon after my return last summer I wrote to Nichols asking him for the New York Stock Exchange papers relating to the quotation of Ore Certificates to enable us to obtain a quotation here, and got no reply; so some months after sent him a copy of the letter. He then answered that he had never received my first letter, but did not send me the papers. I am sure Nichols was speaking the truth and have no doubt whatever that my letter arrived in Nichols' holidays, was opened by Terhune, given to Mr. Hill who quietly pocketed it and said nothing, and I suppose gave orders that the papers were not to be sent. Why, Heaven only knows. I have discussed this matter with our friend at No. 17 [Carlton House Terrace]. He says truly enough that Hill has never known how to treat his friends with decency and consequently never keeps them, and I confess to being tired of trying to do anything for him; still I should have been and always shall be sorry to undertake any business that would seem to him inimical to his interests.

Turning to a more congenial topic he concluded: 'The Boss has been giving me your very nice messages about the fishing, indeed I should like to go if I can manage to get away . . . June would be as good a month for me to be absent as any, as with Coronation festivities on here there would probably be but little business stirring . . .'

Farrer had business in New York and Boston that year and could probably spare only a week or ten days for Metis; he was also engaged on a new venture of which he had written in February although the plans were not yet settled: he was building two new houses for himself, one at Sandwich, his favourite golfing resort, the other at No. 7 St. James's Square in London. His architect was Edwin Lutyens, who in fact departed before Gaspard's houses were finished to achieve one of his most famous monuments (next perhaps to the Cenotaph): the new Viceregal Lodge and administrative buildings in New Delhi.

Gaspard was already living with his two brothers on the opposite side of St. James's Square and wrote on 10 March to J. O. Bloss, who was actually thinking of coming over *for* the Coronation of King George V and Queen Mary, that he must come and stay and see the Procession from his windows. This would mean that 'Blossie' would miss Metis, but 'on the latter score you will have to make your peace with J. W. as best you can. *I* shall not forgive you, but if you finally decided to come the course I suggest is the only one which you would be allowed to take ...' His brother Harry would be there and 'you will have to make the best of a family party of sisters and their children who will certainly invade us for the purpose of watching the Procession ... I am afraid my house does not afford a suite of apartments with baths and all the rest of it with which you provide me in New York ...' The new houses were to remedy this. He told Sterling on 15 March that he had issued this invitation to 'Blossie' if he came for the Coronation. 'I would gladly go three thousand miles to avoid it', was Gaspard's feeling 'but luckily have the inducement of a visit to you at Metis as an added incentive'. Lord Mount Stephen had more mixed feelings about the occasion. He had been asked if he would carry the Banner of Canada in the Abbey, and although assured by Sir Arthur Bigge that this task was not onerous he replied on 16 March with obviously sincere regret that he ought not to accept lest when the time came he should not be able: '... I would have loved to carry Canada's Banner in the Coronation procession ...'[1] So far as Bloss was concerned, in the event he elected to go to Metis, but came to London in September.

On 27 March 1911 Farrer repeated to Nichols a cable in which he had queried a report that Mr and Mrs. Hill were sailing for

[1] RA GV Coronation Record Box B/268 and 270.

Genoa; he was sorry this was not true. But two days later he was reporting to Sterling a letter in which Hill offered to take him to the Pacific coast: 'I should like to go there . . .' He acknowledged Hill's letter on the 31st:

. . . I was delighted to hear from you and to find you writing in good spirits—thank you also for your invitation to the fishing. I have promised to go to Sterling at Metis and am already in disgrace with him for cutting my visit there short as I am bound to leave for home before the end of June. I am afraid therefore that a visit to the St. John is out of the question much as I should have enjoyed it had I more time at my disposal. As to your second proposition of a visit to the coast that too I should enjoy and if when I get out I find you are really going I shall be delighted if you will take me with you. My present intention is to sail either May 13 or May 20.

I cordially agree that the business position in the U.S. is constantly getting sounder; also that it will be the better in the long run if your people will (be) content to go slow for another year especially in view of decisions, tariff revisions and next year's election. But will they be so content? If the crop outlook this spring is good it will be hard to restrain them as it seems to me.

The Boss read your letter and figures with much interest and wishes me particularly to remember him to you—he is finding locomotion rather a difficulty now and a difficulty therefore in keeping warm out of doors during the winter, but in other respects he is very well; nothing pleases him so much as to hear of what is doing in the north west and of the prosperity of your roads . . . .

If Mrs. Hill is with you [in New York] please give her my best regards. I look forward to seeing her.

On the same day he wrote to Arthur Gwinner of the Deutsche Bank acknowledging a copy of his annual report which he had sent on to Lord Mount Stephen, and saying that he hoped to go over the Northern Pacific when in America. (Farrer also took the opportunity of his middle western visit to see something of the Burlington, spending two days in Chicago and making the acquaintance of the first Vice-President Darius Miller and his wife.)

Farrer had told Sterling on 17 February: 'I had a letter from Stillman, quite optimistic for him, indeed more optimistic than he has been since immediately after the 1907 panic . . .' Lord Revelstoke apparently received a different impression of the banker's demeanour. On 10 March Farrer reported to Sterling that Stillman was seeking election to the St. James's Club in London, but Gaspard had 'found he was in the hands of a man whose advocacy is sufficient to ensure the Archangel Gabriel's being pilled. In his place I have got T. B. [?Thomas Baring] to propose him and the Boss to second him and Harry Northcote to support him, so I hope he may get through all right, but I thought it as well that the Committee of the Club should realize that Stillman did belong to the best Clubs in New York ... One can never be sure in a London Club as to how far any stranger's candidature will be acceptable'. On the 15th he was able to tell Sterling that his friend had been elected: 'The Boss was in a considerable fuss about it; happily most London Clubs are now so comparatively short of members that election has in almost all cases been handed over to committees of the Clubs ...' There was therefore less danger of 'irresponsible pilling'[1] than used to be the case. He civilly expressed the hope that they might see Stillman in London before long. Within a few days Stillman was indeed there, divulging nothing, trying to persuade Gaspard to postpone his sailing until 20 May while the latter wanted Stillman to sail with him on the 13th. Gaspard evidently gave in, as he was writing to John Turnbull in Montreal only on 12 May that he was sending his trunk and rods to him as usual: 'They contain only my personal effects and half a pound of tobacco'.

The fishing at Metis was disappointing that year, neither did Farrer get much satisfaction from J. J. Hill, either in New York or during ten days in St. Paul. What he particularly wanted to find out was the prospects for the Iron Ore Certificates, about which he had been corresponding before leaving with Tuck in Paris, puzzling over the statistics that found their way into the Press. He wrote from Metis to James Norman Hill at the Northern Pacific office in New York, who was obviously not in sympathy with his father over iron ore, prefacing his queries about the ore situation and about the N.P. with his usual light remarks: he had seen J. N. on his way to Metis but proposed to return by the St. Lawrence route to avoid the heat of New York. He hoped J. N. would come over next year when he would be able to put him up 'at my chateau in London, and take you for a change of air at the weekend to my chateau at Sandwich'. He hoped the St. John River was not also experiencing the scarcity of fish they had suffered at Metis.

The main news of Farrer's visit was given on his return in letters

---

[1] Current slang for 'blackballing'.

to Tuck (20 July) and to one of the private investors in G.N. and therefore in Iron Ore Properties in London (11 July)—the latter rather more cautious. He told Tuck he had found Hill in New York, and was rather shocked at his appearance; he had lost so much weight, and was a bad colour. Mrs. Hill explained that this was owing to loss of teeth, and that he wouldn't go to the dentist for a 'new set of store teeth' and therefore had difficulty in eating. Later, while Gaspard was in St. Paul, 'he seemed to pick up a lot and was in excellent spirits'. He went on:

I satisfied myself that both Roads were in good physical condition, better certainly than they have ever been and GN probably rather the better of the two. Crop conditions when I left at the end of June were all that could be desired and I should hope that nothing has occurred since to materially change harvest prospects. Hill is obviously keeping a firm hand on the treasury and will not allow a dollar more than is absolutely necessary to be spent until he sees his way clearer ahead. Last year's bad harvest has kept traffic at a low ebb and St. Paul and Soo competition have made inroads on the smaller traffic that remained; business, however, was picking up slightly when I left St. Paul. The Bond sale of the new mortgage took place during my stay there and added to Mr. Hill's content.

We paid a visit to the [Iron Ore] Range and I returned without being the slightest bit the wiser upon the only point about which you and I and other Certificate holders are seriously concerned, viz,: our future dividends. I gathered, however, we should be lucky if we got this year a dollar and a half as we did last year; certainly the Trustees did not expect to distribute any more at the time I left. At the same time it is very apparent that Mr. Hill is being constantly attacked on the subject and is very sensitive, and I gather that if any means could be found to expedite payments to certain holders he would be very glad to have them adopted. I wish I could have given you some news of specific interest, but I obtained none from Hill or anyone else, and I fancy the fact was there was nothing to be said. Mr. Hill was obviously confident of being able to continue his railway dividends and most unwilling to commit himself further. He takes a pessimistic view of the industrial situation in America, where he thinks the productive capacity has been increased out of all proportion to the country's consuming requirements, and owing to high cost of production export is well nigh impossible. I ought to add that Hill's pessimism seemed shared by most of the really big men to whom I talked, not pessimism that there was anything unsound in the situation, but rather a disbelief that there would be any revival of business. Most factories, as you know, are working half time or thereabouts, and with tariff revision and Presidential election ahead of us it is difficult to see how there is to be any great change in those conditions, unless perhaps some small spurt if a good harvest is gathered . . .

Gaspard had come away more hopeful, however, for the longer term, especially as the general attitude towards railroad corporations was—as Harriman had said—becoming more reasonable. (That year nevertheless saw the Federal Government suing the U.S. Steel Corporation under the anti-trust laws—unsuccessfully.) To his London friend Gaspard wrote that Hill had had nothing to say about Ore Certificates and there was no prospect of an increase in the dividend for the present year. 'The lack of information supplied to certain holders is from no wish to hold back information on the part of the Trustees, but the probability of their distributing dividends depends not upon themselves but upon the operations of the U.S. Steel Company, and their operations again on general conditions in the United States . . .'

To Mount Stephen Gaspard reported in person. He told Sterling on 15 July: '. . . I spent one evening this week at Brocket and had a long gossip with the Boss over my trip and all that I learnt on your side. He was greatly disappointed at our bad luck in the fishing, but I was able to assure him that we had enjoyed ourselves none the less'. The previous day he had heard by cable of the death of Robert Meighen, and mentioned this to Sterling: '. . . I expect the Boss will feel it very much both on his sister's account and on his own. He had got to rely on Meighen for anything he wanted done in Canada. I am glad to think I so recently spent those few days with him, and he then certainly was in the best of spirits and apparently of health. I shall miss him much . . .' Meighen had of course been living in the former Mount Stephen house in Drummond Street, very worthily maintaining the hospitable traditions of this compact but exquisitely built mansion which Gaspard had known of old. It now passed to his son Frank.

The late-season fishers evidently did better that year. On 2 August Farrer wrote to Hill: '. . . You must have had a glorious time fishing; I hope it did you all the good in the world. Your own score was tremendous', while on the 4th he told Bloss: 'The Boss has a cable from Metis reporting that Mrs. Reford and Lady Sybil Grey killed five and twenty fish last week . . .' The discussion was still continuing in December: on the first of that month Farrer sent Sterling an extract from a letter of Mrs. Reford's to Mount Stephen, adding: 'His theory of the scarcity of fish last (season) is that they had gone past us and got up above the dam and into the deep hole under the falls; I can hardly believe that this is the case. But it is curious that no fish are ever seen above the dam until spawning time, or are ever seen getting over or attempting to get over the falls at the mill . . .'

DEATH OF LORD NORTHCOTE

Meanwhile there came another gap in the diminishing Mount Stephen circle. On 9 August 1911 Mount Stephen was in Town for the House of Lords debate on the Parliament Bill; Gaspard wrote to Sterling before dining at 17 Carlton House Terrace: '. . . He has been very much upset over Meighen's death and is a good deal worried about Harry [Northcote]. I do not know what is the matter with him, but he seems to have had a collapse in the digestive apparatus and I hear is the shadow of his former self . . .' Harry was at their country home at Eastwell in Hampshire where he died on 29 September. No comprehensive appraisal has yet been made of the public career of the first and last Lord Northcote. J. A. S. Grenville in his book: *Lord Salisbury and Foreign Policy. The Close of the Nineteenth Century*[1] quotes a few thought-provoking letters from Salisbury to the new Governor of Bombay, the son of his old friend and colleague, Stafford Northcote, Earl of Iddesleigh, who had so tragically died in Salisbury's office shortly after being dropped from the Cabinet following criticism by Lord Randolph Churchill.[2] In David Dilks' *Curzon in India*[3] it seems that after some initial doubts the Viceroy came to hold a very high opinion of Northcote. Events in Australia during the latter's subsequent Governor-Generalship there, in the early days of the federation, were not such as to bring him into the public eye. The *Review of Reviews* of 20 January 1904, on the occasion of his appointment, published an anonymous 'Character Sketch' of which the opening paragraphs suggest why he remains a peripheral figure:

Lord Northcote is one of those men of whom all the world speaks well, and in Lady Northcote he has a wife whose praise is equally wide-

---

[1] London, 1964.
[2] See Earl of Oxford and Asquith, *Fifty Years of Parliament*, London, 1926, 2 vols., vol. 1, pp. 165-6.
[3] Vol. 1, *Achievement*, London, 1969.

spread. If he cannot make a success of the role of Australian Governor-General, the post itself had better be abolished. For Lord Northcote, so far as the public knows, has never made a mistake in his life. He has no enemies, and all who know him are his friends. He is a genuine, quiet, thorough-good-sort kind of a man, loyal and true, with a clear judgmatical head on his shoulders, and no nonsense about him, no bounce, and no "side".

He is neither pushful like Mr. Chamberlain, nor self-assertive like others who may be left unnamed. He has stuck to his work, and done his duty in whatever rank in life it has pleased Providence to place him. As he has been in Britain and in Bombay, so he will be in Australia. He is the very antithesis of Lord Curzon, whose restless energy and intense consciousness of his superiority is hardly tolerable even in India, and would be absolutely intolerable in Australia. He is not a German bureaucrat like Lord Milner, who knows that he knows so much better than other people as to be an irritation even when he is right and a positive peril when, as sometimes happens, he is wrong. He is not an extravagant man. He will not find his allowance inadequate. He is no prancing proconsul. Neither is he a great actor who is forever posing as the central figure on the political stage. He is plain born and bred English country gentleman, whose word is as good as his bond, who inspires affection and commands confidence. He is, therefore, so far as it is possible for the British public to conceive the situation at the Antipodes, the ideal Governor-General for Australia.

"I like drab men best", said Mr. Morley to me on one occasion when I was descanting upon the fascination of the Russian Bayard, General Skobeloff. Lord Northcote is a drab man after Mr. Morley's own heart. He has it not in him to be guilty of a raging indiscretion. He keeps on the even tenor of his way, straying neither to the left hand nor to the right. He gets on no one's nerves. He is a steady stager, a hard worker and a conscientious administrator. During his long career in official positions, and in the House of Commons, he never made a speech which burnt its way into the popular mind, or did anything picturesque or particularly heroical. He is as incapable of converting his official position into a pedestal for self-display as he is of petty intrigue or personal meanness. As Governor-General, the Australian Ministers will find in him an unobtrusive councillor and an experienced friend. He will be no figure head, for he is too sensible to be ignored, but he will make no dictator, for he has in him the soul of a constitutional sovereign whose power rests upon influence and not upon authority.

He was born so, for he is the true son of his father...[1]

[1] See also Proceedings of the Royal Colonial Institute, vol. xl, 1908-9. Dinner to Lord Northcote, ex-Governor General of Australia at Hotel Metropole 19 January 1909.

JAMES STILLMAN

On 22 August 1911 Farrer wrote to Lord Revelstoke: '...
Stillman dropped in this morning and spent a couple of hours here,
rather to our vexation. He has plainly nothing to do and does not
know how to occupy his time. He is very pessimistic about business
in the U.S. on account of both Government agitation and labour
troubles; he thinks that labour there is sure to emulate labour at
home ...' Britain was then suffering both rail and dock strikes.
This Jeremiah dined with Gaspard the following evening 'in
tremendous spirits and decidedly triumphant at his prognostications
having proved correct', Gaspard told Sterling on 25 August. In
September Stillman was back in London planning a motor tour of
the West Country. 'He comes and sits in our office', Farrer told
Sterling on the 6th, 'much as he does in your house at home; I
hope he does not find us very uncivil, but we really ... cannot give
up the whole day to him, but I am glad he comes and always
delighted to see him ...' He was Sterling's friend, and clearly
Gaspard would so much have preferred to persuade the latter over
the sea to Bishopsgate. The U.S. Government had turned to
investigating the National City Bank's Security Company ... 'very
vexatious, but I suppose the real broad question is not as to whether
that Company is legal or not, but whether in the existing state of
feeling in the U.S. it is wise for any corporation or set of men to
parade their power before the public and be constantly taking
measures which will obviously increase it ...' On 10 November
Gaspard wrote that Stillman had turned up again the previous day
'in very good spirits apparently about everything but the market; on
this he was most decided and direct, more so than I have ever known
him before, stating and reiterating that in his opinion the time had
not arrived to invest money and that he should keep his in cash...'
They discussed Kuhn, Loeb's contrary view and Gaspard added his
own opinion: 'That we can have any return of active business with
expansion of Railways, industries, etc., I do not believe, until
political affairs are much more settled and there seems no prospect
of this for a year to come. But I also think that the fundamental
business conditions are good and healthy and that prices have been
on the low side'. He added the latest news from the City: 'While
we were still talking the market commenced to move up and has
for the last 12 hours been booming with every conceivable tale

being circulated to encourage a rise; among others that this suit against the Steel Corporation will be forthwith abandoned. Indeed, this morning in a stockbroker's eyes there is not a cloud upon the sky, and those who have had the courage of their opinions during the last few weeks have a fine opportunity to reap their reward . . .' Stillman 'turned up last night', Farrer told Sterling on 1 December, 'not very fit, had been motoring in a cold wind which had caught him on the chest . . . but he seemed very cheerful in spirits. I fancy he goes back to Paris today'. Writing to Stillman himself, back in Paris, on 13 December, Gaspard added a sly postscript: 'Canada continues her prodigal course. £7,000,000 yesterday for Canadian Northern,[1] £5,000,000 this morning for C.P.R. If only Canada would consent to annex the U.S. Lovett [of the Union Pacific] may yet be able to borrow his money at 4%'.

A more welcome visitor, both on his own account and also on Sterling's, was J. O. Bloss. On 6 September 1911 Gaspard told Sterling: '. . . Blossie turned up this week in very good spirits . . . We have arranged together that our alliance should be offensive as well as defensive; we are determined that we will no longer be ground down by your iron heel. It is a thousand pities you are not here also . . .' and on the 11th: '. . . Blossie has been down with me at Sandwich and was made to do more sightseeing in the 24 hours he was there than he has ever done before in his life. We fairly hustled him about. He returned to town with me last night to spend a week in bed'. On 26 September Gaspard wrote: '. . . What luck Blossie had in not having been on the "Olympic"; I hope you will tell him what I write and cheer him up'. The s.s. *Olympic* had been disabled: Tuck and his wife had been aboard, and George Baker had been due to join it at Queenstown. Farrer told Sterling on 11 September: '. . . I had a nice visit from George Baker in a genial and optimistic mood, though coming down to hard facts the best he had to say of his country was a repetition of the old advice given by Junius Morgan to J. P., never to be a bear on his country's securities. He did not seem to me well posted about the Steel Company's recent explorations of Hill's ore lands but mentioned that he wished his railroad properties gave him as little concern as did the ore properties . . .' Baker was the largest single shareholder in the First National Bank of New York of which he was President,

---

[1] Brown and Cook, op. cit. traces the history of the Canadian Northern from its 'Mackenzie and Mann' era to its nationalisation in 1917.

21

and which had had an equal share with William Rockefeller and James Stillman (there were many other participants) in the Morgan syndicate which had launched the Steel Corporation.

THE YOUNGER GENERATION

Mount Stephen wrote from Brocket on 30 June 1911 to William R. MacInnes, Vice-President of Traffic, C.P.R., and a brother of his former secretary Beverley:

... I was very sorry at missing you and Mr. Baker when you called at Carlton House Terrace; I should have enjoyed seeing you & having a talk with you over bygone days &c. It is not easy for me to think of you except as a child before you came over to school. Those *early* impressions seem to become brighter the older I grow, but that is not uncommon in the case of old men ...

I am delighted to see the great prosperity of the C.P.R., the once-despised "wild cat scheme" which the London Stock Exchange refused a quotation for its shares.[1]

On 8 November 1911 Gaspard reported to Sterling: '... I hear young George Baker is in this country with his bride ... I am very much interested in his marriage, and cannot remember your ever having mentioned it to me ...' He continued to make a point of cultivating the acquaintance of the younger generation. Mount Stephen enjoyed visits from his Canadian nephews and nieces: that year not only the fishing enthusiast Elsie Reford had been over but also her brother Frank Meighen, Gaspard writing cryptically to Robert Meighen on 25 March that Frank seemed to be taking back with him a 'whole troupe of young ladies of the ballet! I hear that happily Mrs. Adami is to be on board so I hope she will keep an eye upon him ...' Frank's cousin Mary Cantlie, daughter of Mount Stephen's sister Eleonora, had married Dr. George Adami, later to be Vice-Chancellor of the University of Liverpool. More seriously Farrer wrote to Frank on 12 September 1911 that Mr. Thomas Skinner, founder of the Stock Exchange Yearbook and for long connected with Mount Stephen's Canadian interests, was just leaving for Canada and hoped to see Frank in Montreal: 'I sincerely trust you may make friends with him; he is a thorough good fellow, very straight, very reliable, and for your guidance very sensitive and very rightly proud of the part he has had in establishing the [C.P.R.] Company's credit in this country'.

[1] This letter is in the possession of Mr. Eric Reford.

IRON ORE: FUTURE UNCERTAIN

August crop reports from the north west that year had been unfavourable although Farrer told Tuck on the 19th: 'I am not so far at all concerned about either NP or GN dividends, but in these days of strike manias which are contagious it requires a bold man to prophesy . . .' By harvest—as so often happened, either for better or worse—the outlook was entirely different, and cheering reports came in both from Hill and from Howard Elliott of the N.P. One imponderable remained; writing to Sterling on 25 August Farrer mentioned having heard from a friend in the City that 'if the attacks on the U.S. Steel Company continue and are concentrated on their possession of the raw material the Company might think it prudent to take advantage of their option to abandon the lease in the hopes of quieting public opinion. I do not think he knew anything whatever from reliable Steel Coy. sources and personally, though I should regret any changes in the existing status, I should not worry at having to resume possession of the property. The only real worry to my mind would be if on further exploration the ore was found not to be there in the quantities expected . . .' He repeated to Sterling on 5 October that he had heard vaguely about the possible abandonment of the lease of Hill's ore lands by the U.S. Steel Company, 'but had never taken much stock in the statement. It would no doubt be a serious worry to Hill to have to begin over again to find buyers for his ore, but if the ore is there in the long run holders of the certificates might feel sure they would come out . . .' The rumours persisted; Farrer wrote to Lord Revelstoke on 19 October: '. . . The news about Ore Lands is not cheerful reading. Enclosed is a cutting from the "Daily Telegraph" which seems to have the best account. I have not thought it worth while to cable and make enquiries; the property itself will not run away'. The following day he told him there was still no news from Hill but another cable in the *Telegraph*. 'You may take it as a fact that the Finance Committee of the Steel Corporation have recommended the abandonment of the lease together with various other steps, all with a view to complying with the Sherman law, or at least with the attitude of the Government at Washington. No doubt their recommendation will be confirmed by the full Board. The newspapers are of course all astray in saying that the lease was unprofitable for the Steel Co. except in the limited sense that up to date they have had to pay rentals and have not been in a position to take out ore to recoup themselves ...' A month ago Farrer had had the figure from Louis Hill for ore shipments to the end of August; he had told Sterling on 26 September that shipments from the Hill docks seemed to have increased a million tons on the year 'though the shipments at all docks have decreased 9 million tons, the total at his docks being 6 million. Not bad work considering how short the season has been; it looks as if they would come near to shipping the 10 million they had anticipated. I only wish we could see some result of their work in dividends on Ore certificates'. He had written also to Louis on the 27th.: '... I presume that your increase is partly the result of the Steel lease and that the Steel Company are obtaining their supplies from your lands rather than their own ...' He concluded his letter to Revelstoke:

... The abandonment of the lease will be a worry and trouble for Hill as he will have to make other arrangements, and as for the Certificate holders they lose as solvent and responsible a tenant as the U.S. can produce, but the property remains and other buyers can no doubt be found. The actual business of mining is a simple one, there should be no trouble about that; marketing is a different matter, but there are so many steel consumers in the U.S. outside the Steel Corporation that I should feel entirely confident of satisfactory arrangements being made ...

He did not mention the question of royalties, those *locusta migratoria* which, multiplying year by year, were to descend upon and ravage each wagon load of ore, and even, according to the terms of the lease, upon empty wagons if the minimum quantity for any year were not mined and shipped. It was agreed at the time that the price was high but the Steel Corporation had reserved the right to cancel the lease in 1915, on two years' notice being given.[1] To one of the Certificate holders Farrer wrote on 26 October reassuring him that although there seemed little doubt that the lease would be relinquished 'in that event the property will be returned to the Trustees with a large amount of development work already carried out ... the Trustees seem to have no doubts but that a profitable market for the ore can be found without difficulty ...' He professed 'no concern whatever as to the value of the property'.

[1] For general information see Folwell on *Minnesota*, vol. 4, chapter 1, and Kenneth Warren, *The American Steel Industry* 1850–1970, A Geographical Interpretation, Oxford, 1973. Also Grace Lee Nute (ed.): *Mesabi Pioneer*, Reminiscences of Edmund J. Longyear, St. Paul, 1951, pp. 61–62.

On 27 October 1911 Farrer was writing to Hill acknowledging a letter of the 13th concerning a Brazilian metallurgical venture with associated railroad which his firm were exploring, and noting that Hill was in fairly good spirits about G.N. prospects. The annual report, too, had just arrived. The official notice of cancellation of the Ore lease and the simultaneous news that morning of the U.S. Government's prosecution of the Steel Corporation were relegated to a postscript. On the 31st, giving another Certificate holder a very non-committal view of the philosophy which seemed to guide the U.S. Supreme Court, he concluded: 'As to the Ore lease whether it transgressed the law is a moot point; in any case the lease was made "coram populo" and nobody either on the Steel Co.'s side or on Mr. Hill's dreamed that it would ever be considered illegal'. Louis Hill was keeping Farrer supplied with statistics of the physical movements of ore to the ports and the latter wrote to him on 3 November:

In view of the Steel Coy.'s recent decision to terminate the lease, I should imagine this increase is likely to expand further during the next few years while the lease still runs. I am sorry for the work and worry the loss of so responsible a tenant will entail upon you personally; but I have always felt that the position of the Trustees under the lease, vis-à-vis holders of Ore Certificates, has been uncomfortable and would sooner or later have led to trouble. I hope the opportunity will now arise for establishing these relations on a basis that will be more satisfactory for you as well as for the beneficiaries.

He wrote in similar terms on 7 November to E. T. Nichols in New York (albeit with the preface: 'no doubt when the future policy is more settled some one of you will be good enough to let me have a line to tell me the position'). He repeated that it was 'a nuisance losing so good a tenant, but I shall be surprised if Mr. Hill does not in some way or another manage to come out satisfactorily ...' To Hill, also in New York, he wrote on 17 November acknowledging his of the 3rd (with 'so good an account of G.N. operations'):

... Then as to the Ore Certificates: I have realised from the first that their value depended on the quantity of ore contents, as to which there obviously must be some degree of guessing till the stuff is actually dug out. The cancellation of the lease gave me concern on your and the Trustees' account, and on that only, as it will undoubtedly involve you in a considerable additional degree of work and worry, and for this I am sincerely sorry. It will be a great triumph if you are eventually able to prove that the Steel Corporation have made a serious blunder in their recent pusillanimous action; so far it certainly has not brought them immunity from prosecution. If later when you see the situation clearer you would ask Nichols to send me a line as to the position, or could find time to write yourself, I should be grateful. I would give a good deal to have a talk with you over the situation generally. I have been wondering whether I could find time to run out for a few days about Xmas or the New Year, but I am afraid it looks as if I should be too busy here . . .

Farrer, getting ever more avid for information, opined on 1 December to Sterling that as Tuck had, he believed, 50,000 Ore Certificates, 'he has sufficient interest to keep him busy trying to extract what information Hill and the Trustees in America possess. I understand Hill professes that there will be no difficulty in finding a market for his ores, that he has had several applications already and could sell a large parcel for delivery in 1915 at $1.50 profit.[1] . . .' To Tuck himself he wrote on 13 December 1911 that cables from London to New York asking the cause of a recent fall in price had 'elicited answers to the effect that it was caused by no intrinsic reasons but by statements of the Trustees that no dividends would be payable until 1915 . . .' For this Gaspard blamed Nichols who, he thought, had been speaking out of turn. He was perturbed that certain leading brokers in London were proposing to write to New York demanding firm information: 'I think it probable that unless a response in the way of information is forthcoming within a reasonable time, there will be a tendency for these same firms' (comprising 'practically everyone who has for many years past supported for themselves and their clients the Hill securities') 'to advise their clients to dispose of their Hill holdings'.

He wrote of this to Sterling next day: '. . . Stockbrokers have been quite ugly about it. We have refused in any way to join in the movement they were projecting but finally consented to forward a letter to the Trustees provided it was first submitted to us for approval. I took care therefore that every word was eliminated to which exception could be taken . . .' He told Tuck on 19 December that he was writing to Hill to tell him it was a case for the soft answer and he had no doubt that though at first Hill would be much annoyed about the protest, 'he will on consideration see how advisable it is to be considerate with his clientèle here. You are

[1] Presumably $1.50 profit per ton of ore: the Steel Corporation lease was based on 59 per cent of metal per ton of dried ore.

perfectly right in saying that everything in connection with Ore Certificates has hitherto brought nothing but discredit upon Hill; it is really very bad luck upon him in many ways, but partly, indeed I may say largely, his own fault . . .' He had just had a letter from Hill, written on the 6th, 'a good deal of it abuse of the Steel Coy. which I am sorry to see and will not repeat', but containing some facts which Gaspard passed on to Tuck on a confidential basis: they included some estimates, as a result of the Steel Corporation's drilling operations, concerning possible production up to 1915 and the whole vast potential of the property. What was still problematical, even if these figures were accepted, was the amount of development still required to realize this. Gaspard wondered if by some means the Trustees could initiate a prospecting programme before the actual expiry of the lease. His letter to Hill on 20 December 1911 was in Gaspard's usual style on such occasions: congratulatory as to the ore estimates, regretful that the London brokers had not exercised more patience—but recommending the "soft answer"—passing then to his Brazilian interests, and ending with a postscript: 'All possible good wishes to you and yours for Xmas and the New Year. I wish there was a chance of our seeing you on this side'.

Almost immediately an adverse rumour began circulating both in London and New York regarding the quality of the ore being mined, and Farrer passed on his account to Hill on 22 December 'in case the Trustees may like to deal with the question in their forthcoming report . . .' He relayed it also to Tuck that day, discounting it as the inevitable concomitant of the heavy fall in Stock Exchange value: 'Hill certainly told me during my visit to the States last summer that the quality had been coming out better than they expected . . .' His third and most circumlocutory letter of 22 December was to the immediate source in London (staying at Brown's Hotel) of the rumour, to whom he had already communicated his doubts over its authenticity. Acknowledging a further note he admitted that his own sources were 'not those which would be most anxious to proclaim the poverty of the ore'. The "crab" about the Ore Certificates was, he had always thought, the fact that those connected with the Steel Corporation had not, so far as he could see, been buyers of the Certificates: 'I have frequently tried to ascertain what the Steel people really thought of the property but have never been able to get a direct opinion . . .'

Nevertheless certain financiers with a foot in both camps and seeing the statistics of each had expressed entire confidence in the Ore Certificates. His own faith in the value of the Ore properties remained undiminished, 'but if you ask me my reasons, I am bound to add that they are based on faith in Mr. Hill and not on outside expert opinion . . .' From a later letter of 1 January 1912 it appears that Farrer had convinced his correspondent.

Inevitably, Farrer took up the matter with John Sterling. On 23 December 1911 he acknowledged the latter's letter of the 15th:

. . . Of course George Clark [of Clark, Dodge] is right and there should have been publicity of accounts; the Trustees might well have protected themselves from any too optimistic conclusions being drawn from the figures by qualifying footnotes. I am very much against publishing anything that would involve the property in greater taxation; it would have been amply sufficient for the Trustees to have confined their remarks to the bare statement that quantities and quality so far as exploration had gone were satisfactory, provided such to be the case. I do not think there is any doubt but that Hill will now have to submit to greater frankness. He has taken a tremendous responsibility on his own shoulders by the statements he has made personally, and for which up to date the Trustees have given no sort of confirmation . . .

He mentioned the rumours regarding the quality of the ore, enclosing a letter on the subject and quoting 'sundry articles that have been appearing in the "Iron Age", an American publication, in which it is stated that the Steel Co. was glad of the political excuse for abandoning a lease which was altogether too burdensome in its terms'. He repeated his disquiet that he could see no evidence of the Steel people having bought the Certificates—he seemed not to count George Baker, whose Bank had been in the Steel syndicate and who personally held the Certificates—observing that as they had been carrying out the exploration, they ought to know most. He continued:

. . . However, in spite of all these bear points, I am not discouraged; the only poor man whom I have put into the Certificates I have bought out again, so that my responsibilities are limited to my own pocket, and that of my Lefevre firm. Probably the earlier estimates which Hill sent us when the lease was first concluded were too optimistic, but I am still pigheaded enough to believe the old man will prove more right than his present day critics. When George Baker was here in the summer he assured me that his holdings gave him not the slightest concern, and I know from other sources that he has added largely to his own holdings since, and presumably he ought to see something of the property from the Steel Corporation side. You may be interested to hear that Hill wrote recently to me that the ore proved to date was 400,000,000 tons and this outside 200,000,000 in the Mahoning Mines; he further repeated the statement that he would have no difficulty in marketing in large quantities at $1.50 per ton profit in excess of all charges; further that as the Steel Corporation would hand back the mines in a condition to ship 6,000,000 tons yearly he could see no cause for anxiety. Personally I have felt for some time past that Ore Certificates in spite of obvious disabilities were a better property to hold than Railroad shares: I see no reason to change my mind. The Boss is of course mad about the matter and madder with Hill than ever before—very unfortunate; perhaps it is just as well that the Atlantic separates them.

IX

Shortened perspectives

CHRISTMAS at Brocket in 1911 was a quiet one, only Gaspard Farrer joining the Mount Stephens, '. . . very pleased to be with them and I think they were glad to have me', he told Sterling on 6 January 1912. 'Both of them in very good form, but he is certainly much less able to get about every six months. I was shocked to see the difficulty he had in getting into a low carriage. They are coming to town on Monday next . . .' Alice had been at Eastwell over Christmas, where Gaspard's brother Frank, of the Farrer law firm, was helping to deal with her affairs: 'she is rather overwhelmed by her Australian mail, over two thousand letters—it seems incredible . . .' She thought of keeping on Eastwell although Gaspard wondered if she realized the worry that a large place would entail. For the moment, however, she was planning a quiet holiday on the Riviera, staying for two or three months with Lady Jersey. Gaspard had been a trifle critical of Harry Northcote's Will: the residue had gone to the Jersey family whom he calculated to be the richest people in the country. The second son, Arthur Villiers, was to become closely associated with him in business, following an introduction by Lord Mount Stephen. Gaspard's Christmas offering to Sterling had been a case of Cox's Orange Pippins; he had written in November: '. . . In looks and size they are not to be compared with your western apple, but I think I may say of apples as Jorrocks did of his young woman: "looks not so much an object if the shekels be forthcoming", and if the flavour is forthcoming in the apple I care little about its having a full figure or a pink cheek . . .'

Sterling meanwhile was faced with a new experience: just before Christmas he had announced the engagement of his ward, a lady apparently not in her first youth, and known to Gaspard, who responded in his letter of 6 January:

. . . I cannot tell you how much pleasure this has given me both for Miss

Trowbridge's own sake and for your own. After these many years under your charge it must be an untold happiness and relief to you to feel that she will soon have a husband to look after her for the future ... I have sent her a cable and a note and am trying to find her a wedding gift. What fun it would be to be able to be present at her wedding! I wish I could come out and see you acting the heavy father at the ceremony and presiding over the wedding breakfast afterwards. I am very glad to think you like her young man; it is just as well by the way that he is not so very young, but as you say, just a suitable age for her ...

The wedding was to be on 10 February, and on 27 January Gaspard proudly told Sterling that he had selected an old silver cake basket for his ward 'made six years before the Declaration of Independence, and therefore while you or your forebears were still British subjects. It is quite a pretty one and I hope will have reached her before now'. He was very much put out when it transpired that Mount Stephen had also chosen a cake basket, 'as I told him previously' (he complained to Sterling on 27 February) 'that that had been my choice, indeed my basket had already been sent off. I suppose he forgot when he went to choose his present ...' This was not the only confusion to arise over Miss Trowbridge's wedding presents: on 5 March Farrer acknowledged Sterling's letter of 20 February: 'We have been chuckling a good deal over that necklace; please tell Blossie that I think all the more of you for having got that hundred thousand dollars in the newspapers without ever having spent it ...'

In his letter of 27 February 1912 Gaspard had gone on to say: 'You will have learned of Lord Strathcona's illness. I fancy it has been quite serious—as indeed any such illness must be for a man of his age—probably the most serious illness he has had for many years. The Boss has also had quite a bad cold, happily only in the head and throat, but with his tendency to chest weakness one is always nervous; however, I think he is happily nervous himself and willing to take good care ...'

In the spring of 1912 Elsie Reford was over from Canada and Gaspard reported to Sterling on 4 April: 'She told me she was shocked to see how rapidly the Boss is aging, how much indeed he has aged since she was here before Christmas. I cannot help thinking, as of course I wish, that this is her imagination rather than the fact. He certainly gets much deafer and much less willing to move about and his interests are becoming more and more confined, but he seems to me just as cheery and breezy about such matters as do interest him as ever he was . . .' Mrs. Reford's two sons, Bruce and Eric, were then at school in England; she was that day taking them over to the continent for their Easter holidays.

A new factor was beginning to enter into Farrer's business prognostications: to Howard Elliott of the Northern Pacific he had written on 23 December 1911:

> We are closing the year here with a great deal of labour unrest, but business is being run full speed ahead and no doubt the demand for labour partly accounts for the readiness with which greater demands are being constantly made on the employer. Politically we are feeling rather more comfortable; I do not myself believe there is the remotest chance of England being the aggressor as against Germany. The people of this country do not want war and have no grievance against Germany other than the cost to which the increase of their navy puts us. The danger, as it seems to me, lies entirely in the temper of the German people. Their Government I believe to be sensible enough . . .

Writing on 17 February to John F. Stevens, Hill's former Chief Engineer, he mentioned an impending coal strike, but saw some hope of better relations with Germany: '. . . Whatever the outcome of a war with Germany might be, the result to merchants and bankers would have been most utterly disastrous . . .' By 5 March the coal strike was in progress and Farrer was telling Sterling: 'How curious it will be if the continued growth is checked and perhaps even the eventual dissolution of the big corporations takes place through the impossible demands of labour; I do not think it had occurred to anyone that that was the most threatening quarter of all . . .'

For some time Farrer had not heard from either James Norman or Louis Hill, but at the turn of the year came news of both. In a letter to Sterling of 23 December he had said: 'I am amused to hear that Jim after absenting himself for three years from his duties on the Northern Pacific Railroad, has risen from his bed in the hospital and against all the doctors' and family advice insisted on making a tour of inspection in mid-winter; possibly three weeks on his back with surgeons hovering round him has quickened his conscience'. To J. N. himself he wrote on 27 March 1912 care of the N.P. office in New York, acknowledging a note from Del Monte, California. He was glad to hear that J. N. was feeling so fit again —better than for twenty years—and hoped that his golf had undergone a similar resurgence:

You talk about seeing me soon; I hope this may mean you are coming over here ... You promise to write me about the business outlook. I almost hesitate to write the words Ore Certificates, for I imagine you must have been even more worried about them than we have here; still if you have any news as to the Trustees' policy and prospects I should be interested to hear ... Your Report was no doubt designedly very conservative not to say pessimistic in tone and I think you were obviously wise in so making it, but I could not help laughing at your father's counterblast before the Stanley Commission almost the day after its appearance. He certainly is splendidly unrepentant and in spite of the evidence before one I still cling to the hope that he may be more nearly right than the facts today seem to warrant. I remember that you never shared his optimism ...

He thanked J. N. for 'what you write about my father; few people enjoyed their life more than he did, and almost to the end. I am sending you enclosed an article that appears in today's "Times" with reference to him'.

Writing to Edward Tuck on 27 December 1911, Gaspard mentioned a report in that morning's papers of the resignation of Louis Hill, accompanied by his denial, adding: 'I have always felt some doubts as to his being able to summon courage to break it to his father that he intended to resign. Perhaps these newspaper reports will help him to the avowal ...' Two years earlier Louis had apparently confided to Farrer that he thought of withdrawing from the Great Northern on his fortieth birthday. Referring to this in a letter of 19 March 1912, but making no mention of the recent report, Gaspard observed that if he did carry out this intention 'it will be a satisfaction to you to feel that you have carried through the old machine successfully in bad times and left it in good shape'. In the event, Louis carried on, succeeding his father that year as chairman of the board of directors. James Norman, on the contrary, gradually loosened his hold on railroading and became interested in Texas Oil.

IRON ORE CERTIFICATES: FAITH AND HOPE

In his letter to Louis of 19 March 1912 Gaspard acknowledged two letters of 28 February and 6 March and pronounced as 'encouraging' the probable ore movement forecasts: 'I have always been an optimist on the eventual outcome of the property and even your "report" failed to quench my faith; I still believe that your excellent parent will prove much nearer right than his critics of today, though I have always understood you did not fully share his views ...' Commenting on the 'very satisfactory' statistics of Great Northern earnings he went on to express his astonishment at the volume of business all over the United States 'and cannot help thinking that if such volume exists when times are admittedly bad, it will take very little to give the Railroads all the business they can handle ...' The Iron Ore Properties "report" Gaspard had awaited and eventually received with his customary apprehension and exasperation, followed by detailed analysis and questioning of Nichols. As a result of much cabling to New York he had in fact been sent an advance copy and also a 'letter of explanation'. These, he had hoped, would really explain, but—he told Tuck on 1 February—'I am almost past hoping for anything in the way of lucid statement with regard to this property', adding the postscript 'Why should the report need a letter of explanation'. On 13 February he acknowledged a letter from Tuck, who would by then have seen both the published report and a copy of the letter of explanation: 'I notice you date it "the Lord's Day" and end it "hurriedly" and so have concluded that you spent the rest of the day on your knees praying for a dividend on Ore Certificates. I hope your prayer will be heard ...' His own faith in Hill still held. He could even tell Tuck on 13 March: '... Lady Mount Stephen tells me she has a letter from Mrs. Tuck very depressed on the subject of Ore Certificates. Looking to the Report, the price, and the lack of dividends I can well understand this, but I do not share her feelings; I believe holders will come out all right with a little patience, and I hope Mrs. Tuck will take all the better care of herself so that she may live to enjoy the benefits of her patience aforesaid'.

In a letter of 19 March 1912 to C. H. Labouchere of Hope and Company, Amsterdam, Farrer for the first time, it seems, brought up the question of royalties on the iron ore. He was quoting from another letter which he had recently seen from an interested party: ' "Of the 500,000,000 tons, therefore, which the Holders of the Certificates may once have flattered themselves that they had leased to the Steel Corporation, only one-fifth is on freehold land; all the remainder involves an annual obligation to pay royalties, and as regards about 100,000,000 tons, an obligation which excludes any prospect of direct profit". I do not think the situation could be more pithily expressed'. Part of a letter which Farrer was to write to Tuck on 6 October 1932 has been quoted above on page 64; going through some old papers then, Farrer sent Tuck 'communications from J. J. H. re Ore Certificates, which, together with our experience of the man for many years, seems some justification for my, alas mistaken, optimism about the investment. I ought to have made further enquiry and from independent sources. It will ever remain a mystery how our friend ignored that our ores were subject to heavy royalty and ignored the clause in the Steel contract enabling that Company to cancel the lease . . .' In 1912 Farrer repeated his then conviction that '. . . notwithstanding all criticisms that it would seem one could fairly make, I still retain my faith in the ultimate value of the certificates which is in other words a faith that the old gentleman in St. Paul will in the long run prove nearer right than his critics'. To Tuck he wrote on 28 March: '. . . I have no doubt whatever that J. J. H. will move heaven and earth to get that ore property on a remunerative basis; his counterblast before the Stanley Commission to the pessimistic Report of the Trustees seemed evidence to me that he was pretty mad at the tenor of the Report itself, and quite unrepentant about his original statement of the value of the property'. 'Like you', he wrote to Sterling on 4 April, 'I feel in my bones that some day these Certificates will sell on a very much higher level than they do today . . .' adding, however: 'Even if future facts warrant his past statistics, that will not absolve (Hill) from his omission to disclose the adverse circumstances connected with the property . . .' Farrer was to miss Metis that year owing to his Brazilian preoccupations—although he made a business trip to the United States in November—and told Sterling: 'As the fishing time approaches I am feeling sadder and sadder at being unable to join you . . .'

DEATH OF GARNET WOLSELEY

In May 1911 Frances Wolseley, acting on a suggestion of her father's old friend Sir Henry Bulwer, who was keeping him company at Mentone while Louisa took her regular cure at Vichy, wrote to her mother—via her godfather—proposing that she join them when her mother returned. On her being rebuffed, Mount Stephen advised Frances not to force herself upon them. Of Garnet he wrote: 'I was afraid he would miss your mother while she was away at Vichy, but he evidently does not think of anyone or anything out of sight, which is a great blessing'.[1] Nothing could have been further from the truth. Garnet wrote constantly to Louisa, torn between wanting her to complete her cure and wanting her with him. His cheerful nature was sadly tried by the companions she had, he realized, thoughtfully provided for him and of whom he wanted none. 'We have a nice little man with a red face staying here now. I cannot for the moment recollect his name, though I have known him many years', he told her on 30 April.[2] In a letter merely dated 'May 1911' he wrote:

My dearest, dearest Loo,
    Without you, life here is a species of dullness that I hope may be peculiar to this climate. I try to write of events long past, but in the midst of some picture I have drawn upon my sensitive brain I suddenly see your face, and at once all the rest of my brain picture fades away and I see you only.
    The next time that it becomes necessary to leave me here, I beg that you will make no effort to supply me with companions. With me, it is you or else no-one. I hate making conversation for people I do not care even the irreligious "Damn" . . .[3]

He never mentioned Frances.

On 8 June 1912 Mount Stephen acknowledged Frances' birthday greeting, being particularly interested in some photographs of her gardeners:

I have never seen women using the *spade*. In old days in Scotland the men and boys only used it. The '*howe*' [hoe] and '*heuck*' [hook, or sickle] were the women's tools. In your photo the women look quite *handy* with their spades . . . I am a confirmed believer in the doctrine that *work* is the true religion for both men and women, and I often wish that the *love* of work was more generally felt by our youth of both sexes than it is.[4]

He wrote on 1 November 1912: 'Your Father and Mother called on us in London last Wednesday for ten minutes, both looking well. They are off to Mentone on the 7th'.[5] This was Garnet's last visit to the friend who had not varied now for fifty years.

The following March, on a visit to London, Frances read the news of her father's death at Mentone on a sandwichman's board

[1] PVW 139.   [2] W/P 39.   [3] W/P 39.
[4] PVW 139.   [5] Ibid.

in Knightsbridge. This explained a message of sympathy she had just received from Sir Anthony Weldon who, unknown to the War Office, had been designated to arrange the funeral at St. Paul's Cathedral. Lady Wolseley had indeed written to Frances on 20 March: '... I realise that he is going from me. I do not wish you to hear this casually but from me ...'[1] but not knowing Frances' address in town had addressed the letter to Glynde to be forwarded. In answer to the latter's telegram Louisa wired: 'Am not strong enough for funeral. Will you attend and come here afterwards'.[2] She had 'as was her wont ... made all the arrangements, even at the distance of Mentone'.[3] Frances was to take the leading part, and Garnet's brother George, 'whom she always disliked ... (was to be) kept in the background'. Frances—now the Viscountess Wolseley— accordingly attended St. Paul's as chief mourner, accompanied by Gian Mount Stephen. Of the funeral Frances afterwards wrote:

We were all driven there in a dense fog by Lady Mount Stephen, the soldiers everywhere lining the streets. Two carriages she provided, as I took with me also Miss Campion, and a huge wreath made by Miss More at Glynde; and the latter came too, to look after it, until such time as I was to place it on the coffin ...

The next day I was able to rest, and then with the early hours of the following one kind Lady Mount Stephen came again for me and took me to the station where I was speeded off to the Riviera with my faithful old maid Elgar. As they waved goodbyes I could read a look of some anxiety on the face of Lady Mount Stephen, for she knew that they were not easy days before me.[4]

Her godfather had however written on 26 March: '... I am glad your mother has asked you to come out to her at Menton after the funeral ...'[5]

Frances' visit to Mentone was indeed an uneasy one, during which she was treated more as a guest than as a daughter. With her mother was Sir Coleridge Grove, Garnet's former Military Secretary, previously briefed by the Misses Lawrence as to Frances' viewpoint, receiving in turn Lady Wolseley's confidences.[6] Yet when Frances left on 10 April Louisa wrote: 'I thought of you journeying through the night. The little tokens and acts of affection in your

---

[1] Ibid. [2] PVW 120/838. [3] PVW 120/841.
[4] Pegram, *The Wolseley Heritage*, pp. 199–203. Elsa More was the current 'fore-woman' of the gardening college.
[5] PVW 139. [6] PVW 120/847 and 854.

last half hour here did me good and strengthened my hope for the future. Ever, my dear child, Your Mother, who has you always in remembrance'.[1] Mount Stephen wrote to Frances on 16 April 1913: 'I was real glad to get your letter and to know from yourself that you thought "*on the whole*" your visit to Mentone was a success. I have a letter from your mother dated the 8th in which she speaks very nicely about your visit and your "reconciliation" &c.'[2] Louisa now took up permanent residence at Hampton Court Palace, whilst Frances pursued her career in Sussex. In July 1913 she was admitted to the Worshipful Company of Gardeners, the third woman to have this distinction. In October she was given the freedom of the City of London, of which her father had been made a freeman in 1874. Louisa was quick to ascribe these honours to the circumstance of Frances being her father's daughter. Mount Stephen wrote on 1 October: '. . . I hope she will *forgive* you for dining with the Lord Mayor . . .' a reference to a banquet for the Worshipful Company of Fruiterers, at which event Frances had been quick to note that in the City the Lady Mayoress had precedence.

FIN DE SIÈCLE

Gaspard Farrer wrote to Sterling on 1 April 1913: '. . . Lord Mount Stephen has been greatly depressed over Wolseley's death and, except Harry's, has felt it more than the loss of anyone since Charlie Ellis died'. He was glad that Mrs. Reford was with him, although he forecast her displeasure at the postponement of their fishing date that year to mid-June. (Her party would then be liable to miss the best of the season). Gaspard had hoped to sail on 14 May, giving him time for a trip to the Pacific coast, but in the event could only get away on the 31st, joining Sterling in Montreal on 15 June. He wrote complacently on 6 May 1913 to Howard Elliott: '. . . Happily for the moment the Balkan situation seems clearing up, and it seems certain now that we shall not have any further war, or at least any serious complication amongst the bigger Powers of Europe. That is a very satisfactory feature, even more satisfactory to my mind, is the continued better relations between Germany and ourselves . . .' His house at Sandwich was now ready for occupation and he was slightly put out at having to spend one of the last Sundays in May at Brocket to meet the Tucks who were over on a

[1] PVW 139. [2] Ibid.

visit from Paris; 'I hate missing my week end at Sandwich where the gardens are beginning to look charming', he told Sterling on the 17th.

They had 'an excellent season's fishing' however, he told Beverley MacInnes, now living in Toronto, on 29 August; 'not quite as many fish as we have sometimes killed but very sporting fish from start to finish. I believe Mrs. Reford has had very good luck since'. Lord Mount Stephen had been very pleased with a visit recently paid him by the latter's mother, his sister Elsie Meighen. He was now looking forward to the visit of her son Frank with his bride. James Stillman had been with them at Metis that year, busy with his camera, although Gaspard, writing later to J. O. Bloss, was rather scathing about the results: 'I suppose they are as good as photographs taken in that kind of way can be made, but anything more unsatisfactory for the purpose of giving one an idea of the place I could hardly conceive. It is hard enough to recognise the places, even when one is so familiar with them as we are . . .' Of his return to England via the St. Lawrence Gaspard told Bloss: 'the sea (was) like a mill pond, which I told Sterling. I did not add that we were twelve hours motionless in a thick fog surrounded by ice. That Northern route is certainly not one I should choose for a nervous person'.

He had written to Sterling on 23 July 1913: '. . . I spent Monday night at Brocket, and found them very well, but Lord Mount Stephen even more incapable of walking than when I left, but his spirits are excellent. He showed me Mrs. Reford's cable reporting her first week's score of 41: it certainly is a wonderful record'. On 11 August he wrote to Tuck in apologetic vein: '. . . The fact is I really gained no news whatsoever of our properties during my visit. I was in New York only a week and did not see Mr. Hill there. He called for a moment at Metis on his way down to his own river to see if I could go with him, but this I could not arrange'; (there had, in fact, been much heart-searching over this since Gaspard had received an invitation from Hill early in May: he had then passed the onus of a decision on to Sterling, or at least had postponed making one until they met) 'and he did not stop long enough to give me any chance of prosecuting enquiries. Jim I saw only for a moment; he seemed bullish on Ore Certificates, but the price then was below 30 . . .' Hill, he heard, was taking the same tone. James Norman, suffering again from rheumatism, had from

February to April been on the Riviera, staying with Stillman at Cannes; Tuck had reported seeing him there and that he was 'bullish about Ore Certificates' then, forecasting a small additional dividend.[1] At that time Gaspard had told Tuck that he had almost forgotten the existence of his Ore Certificates, and wrote to E. T. Nichols on 27 March (awaiting the Report of the Ore Trustees) that 'holders must have become resigned, as we have not been worried about them to anything like the extent recently that we were in former years ...' Getting more impatient by 18 April, however, he told Nichols: '... We have been persecuted with enquiries as to why (the Report) has not made its appearance'. This was later explained by the illness of the official preparing it, coupled with the proposal, in view of the Steel Corporation's decision to relinquish the lease, to include in the Report a map showing the situation on the Range.[2]

When in New York, Farrer had also seen Darius Miller, whose management of the Burlington he much admired. He wrote to Miller on 27 August that he had sent his recent letter to Mount Stephen 'who is delighted with it'. Farrer still corresponded assiduously with Howard Elliott of the Northern Pacific—about which he was less happy—and after October 1913 with his successor J. M. Hannaford, explaining that many people in England, potentially permanent investors, looked to his firm for guidance. When he heard in late October 1913 that the Hills were selling out their large holdings he rather hoped that the result would be a more vigorously independent financial policy. He suspected that the Great Northern, partly in self-defence against such competitors as the Milwaukee, was spreading its tentacles to the detriment of the Northern Pacific. Prospects for business in general were not bright at the end of 1913, but he was able to write enthusiastically to J. J. Hill on 5 November about both Great Northern and Northern Pacific Reports just received. Of the G.N.'s new construction he declared: 'Anyone who had been buried from the world for the past six years coming back to read the Report, would hardly suspect that hostile Legislatures, Interstate Commissions, labour troubles and an exacting public were rampant through the land, and it is rather refreshing in these days to find anyone moving ahead

[1] Gaspard Farrer Letter Books, Farrer to Sterling, 26 February 1913; Farrer to Stillman, 15 April 1913; Farrer to Tuck, 6 February and 28 February 1913.
[2] Ibid. Farrer to Tuck, 23 April 1913.

with faith in the future apparently unshaken . . . I should very much like to have a talk with you about the future, and unless you come over this winter I shall arrange to go out early next spring in the hopes of being able to spend some time with you . . .'

One event of 1913 merits passing mention in this chronicle. On 2 August Farrer wrote to R. D. Morrison of the Canadian Pacific office in London that on his return from Canada he had found the business connected with the repayment of the C.P.R. First Mortgage Bonds and the issue of Debenture Stock completed for the time being. 'That an operation involving so much detail has been put through with facility has been due in large measure to the prompt attention and accurate work of your office . . .' This harked back to the first official connection of Barings with the C.P.R.: to the crucial bond issue which in 1885 had saved the railway (vol. 1, p. 179).

Farrer's letter to Sterling of 18 November 1913 has, in retrospect, an air of *fin de siècle*. In contrast to the 'wonderful summer and autumn . . . hardly a day yet on which a great coat has been wanted' he wrote of 'distress among the stockbroking community'. He himself had been chained to his desk since his return from Canada, seeing little of his Sandwich house. His town house, on which plasterers' and painters' strikes had held up progress, was almost finished: Lutyens, before leaving for India, had 'practically finished my library and I hope in a week or so to be able to get my books into it; it will be a lovely room . . .' He had seen Lutyens' drawings for the new Government buildings at Delhi 'perfectly magnificent. I thought them most original. They want a motto for the entrance and he has suggested "Govern them and lift them up for ever;" I cannot conceive anything happier . . .' He continued on a sadder note: '. . . You will be grieved for Lord Strathcona over his wife's death. I fancy, poor thing, that the end must have been a release for her and for them all; her mind had entirely gone . . .' He had spent the last Sunday but one with Alice Northcote, 'the first time I had been in the house, rather more liveable than I had expected but both gardens and park depressing in their size and magnificence. I cannot understand how she can tolerate being there, as she has to be so much alone'. His brother Frank and two sisters, with 'the Captain', Eddie Hunter Blair, were embarking on a three months' trip to the West Indies and Panama; 'I have tried to persuade them to return via Cuba and New York and drop in upon you en route—I can imagine your horror at the prospect of this female invasion!! I fancy however that would be too extended a trip and that they have already taken their passage in a steamer returning from Trinidad'. He ended: 'Is Blossie still contemplating a winter trip to Egypt?'

James Stillman continued to hover between Paris and London but, Gaspard wrote to Sterling on 4 December 1913, showed 'no disposition whatever to return to his native land'. On his October visit he was 'in conversation . . . bluer than he was when we three were together at Metis, and that is saying a good deal . . .' He dined with Gaspard in December and 'talked with me for half an hour after dinner and apparently most confidentially, but there were others in the room and he so lowered his voice that I practically did not hear a single word of what he said. I gathered, however, and John confirms, that he is rather less pessimistic than he has hitherto been about U.S. affairs, in fact almost ready to turn the corner . . .' On 13 September Gaspard had told Sterling that he trusted the opinion of Stillman—remote from affairs—more than that of people close to affairs. Stillman had been particularly friendly during his December visit, he wrote to Sterling on 1 January 1914, and when he said he intended returning to London in a few days Gaspard had asked him to stay at his house. 'He thought for a moment and then said in that peculiarly hard tone which he can assume: "no, certainly not". For an instant I felt it was like a slap in the face, but then remembering who he was I laughed to myself to think how thoroughly characteristic. He certainly cannot count graciousness of manner among his virtues. I am glad to find however he was pleased at the invitation . . .'

On that New Year's Day 1914 Gaspard told Sterling: 'Strictly between ourselves I have told John of my intention to get out of business. I propose to give up to the younger partners the major portion of my interest in the business as from this 1st of January, with a view to departing altogether whenever the financial sun is again high in the heavens. It is high time younger men took up the work . . . I am off today to the top of a Swiss Alp . . .' He wrote enthusiastically to Stillman on 12 January of the Swiss Alp, Andermatt: 'my first experience of winter sports, though my part was that of spectator and general picker up of the pieces of my more youthful and enterprising companions . . .' He had since his return been to Berlin and back, on business. There was no sign of uneasiness there, he told Robert Winsor of Boston on 16 January, except regarding the political situation in the Near East. Paris remained uncomfortable. To Sterling he wrote on 21 January of a complete *volte face* in London: a marked fall in the value of money and a rise in the value of first class securities.

On the same day he wrote to Darius Miller of the Burlington: '... I have ventured to send your figures to Lord Mount Stephen who is still keenly interested in everything American, and of course especially in the North West and the properties over which Mr. Hill presides. I enclose you his letter to me; please give it to Mrs. Miller and if she allows you to read it you may, otherwise not'. Regarding the Great Northern, Farrer had told E. T. Nichols on 18 April 1913: '... It is very satisfactory to hear of the increase in your number of G.N. shareholders; a widely-distributed share list is the best protection a Railway can have and must constitute its surest reserve in time of troubles. My own feeling is that at the moment the "rights" business has been somewhat overdone, but that of course is due to the shareholders and public generally feeling that railroad property is not the property it was. I wish I could share your feeling that the days of railway persecution are coming to an end; ...' On 20 February 1914 he exploded upon Sterling: '... The Great Northern fresh issue of stock came to us as a complete surprise and a very unwelcome one; it is hardly decent considering that the last instalment of the last assessment has only just been paid. I feel confident shareholders here will sell their rights to a man. We have heard nothing from or of Hill since meeting him at Metis with you last summer!' This last was not quite accurate, although Hill's letter to him of 28 July had dwelt on the 'very satisfactory' G.N. earnings and was still 'bullish' about Ore Certificates, leaving unsaid most of what Farrer wanted to hear.

The inevitable happened: four days later he was writing to Sterling: 'When I wrote you last week I said I had not heard from Mr. Hill for months. Now I have a long apology from him, in the course of which he mentions incidentally the birth of another grandchild; he does not mention Jimmy so I suppose it must be one of the sisters: do let me know which of them it is ...' Hill did not appear to be worried by either the new (Underwood) tariff (which besides introducing a measure of free trade provided for a small graduated tax on incomes, for revenue purposes) or the Banking law (in 1913 the Federal Reserve System instituted a central banking organization)—'quite the reverse'. The only positive information concerned Hill's proposal to distribute more in G.N. dividends in future rather than put money back into the Road 'which as he truly says the shareholders never see again but have the pleasure instead of paying taxes on the increased value thereby imparted to their property. I confess I should regard his proposals in a more serious light if he were not at the moment applying to his shareholders for more money. Much as I like J J H, I confess that there have been incidents in his career of late that have made me more suspicious of him than I used to be. He does not mention the subject of Ore Certificates or Northern Pacific. I shall try and come out early this spring so as to be able to spend a few weeks with him'.

Acknowledging Hill's letter on 25 March, Gaspard expressed his pleasure at hearing from him and his disappointment that Hill was not coming to England: this was shared by 'the Boss' who 'would have loved to have you here, even if your visit had been of the shortest'. Perhaps he would come next year. Meanwhile Gaspard was to be at Metis with Sterling in mid-June and hoped to arrive perhaps a month beforehand, so that he might be able to see Hill and other friends and perhaps take a trip West. He had not been to the coast for many years. He then broached the subject that was in his mind:

Cables from New York have been constantly repeating of late that your old scheme of G.N.-Burlington amalgamation was imminent. As you know it has never appealed to me, partly from fear of the effect on Northern Pacific's interest, partly timidity at the size of the scheme, but mainly I suppose as a result of insufficient knowledge. However I know the scheme has always appealed to you and, if you have made up your mind to bring it about, you may rest assured my prejudices will be put aside, and I will do what little I can here to help it through . . .

'None of us here in London have a word of Hill's intentions', he wrote to Tuck on 26 March 1914 'and he obviously either has none or does not wish us to know, for an 8-page letter written in his own hand to me arrived on the same day as the cabled news of his fresh issue of stock, though the letter itself contained no mention of it . . .' To both Tuck and Sterling Gaspard confided his fear that the Northern Pacific Board would be persuaded to 'sacrifice their birthright in the Burlington equity for a mess of pottage'.

On 12 March 1914 Farrer had written to Tuck surveying the world's stock markets (only London and Berlin were causing no anxiety) and concluding: 'But the fact is I am too old and hide-bound to absorb modern practices in finance and it is high time I retired; I shall be glad to be gone . . .' On the 17th he was telling Robert Winsor: '. . . There is to be an increase in the Russian army following an increase in that of Germany last year, and in consequence a violent campaign in the German Press against Russia, but our own Foreign Office do not believe in trouble, and John who is just back from Petersburg is of the same opinion'. The Irish Question was again to the fore: '. . . I believe we would have Consols at 80, if a way of settling peaceably with Ulster could once be found'. He had told Tuck: 'Lord and Lady Mount Stephen are in very good form and are in London at the present time'. Gian's activities on this visit are reflected in a letter from Queen Mary of 12 March:

Buckingham Palace

Dearest Gian

You are really much too kind & generous. I am simply delighted with the charming little family souvenirs of all sorts & kinds you have been good enough to send me and thank you with all my heart. The charming little George IV pocket book & the frame with the commemoration of the Pᶜᵉ. & Pˢˢ: of Wales' marriage I shall give to my eldest son as I am doing all I can to encourage his collecting family things. The Sussex cut glass is a beauty—The miniature by Horace Hone is of George IV. The head of George III (brooch) is also interesting. The Print of Queen Charlotte is a beauty. The enamel of my Grandfather has given great pleasure to my daughter who is delighted to have it. So you see everything you sent is much appreciated.

Christies' books I gratefully accept as they will be of much use to me for reference. It was such a pleasure showing you my rooms on Sunday as you are so very appreciative of detail & worthy of all the beautiful objects which are ever a constant joy to me. It always seems strange to me that there can be people to whom these things mean & say nothing to them. I confess I pity them as they miss much in life—Once more heartfelt thanks—

Ever yʳ devoted & affect:

Mary[1]

Gaspard Farrer, meanwhile, was making a determined start to his retirement. At the end of March he was off to Germany for ten days' holiday, spending two days in Dresden 'over pictures and china

[1] RA GV CC44/213.

and three in Vienna over pictures and sight seeing generally . . .' he wrote afterwards to Sterling on 9 April. He planned to sail for America on 9 May, spend a week in New York and Boston, then go west to St. Paul and probably to the coast, joining Sterling in Montreal on 14 June—unless the latter would join him in the trip to the Pacific, which Gaspard would much prefer: 'Do come, if you can, or rather if you will, for I know you can if you will'. He even proposed to Stillman that he should join in the American trip: 'It certainly is ridiculous at my age to spend my few remaining years worrying in the City, when there is so much to see and enjoy elsewhere . . .' In America too Gaspard would meet up with Barings' latest recruit, young Patrick Shaw-Stewart, cast in the traditional mould: Eton, Oxford—Fellow of All Souls—who was broadening his experience (and keeping out of social temptations: late nights were bad for business) among their transatlantic connections. Gaspard wrote him on 15 April, having just enjoyed a glorious Eastertide of brilliant sunshine: 'My 20' × 30' garden at Sandwich is ablaze with daffodils, tulips, anemone apennina and anemone fulgens . . .' (this was but part of a three-acre estate). On 28 April he wrote to James Norman Hill, now deep in Texas Oil, looking forward to seeing him and his wife, and on the 30th to J. M. Hannaford of the N. P., anticipating a quiet financial summer, especially if there were a General Election.

From Metis he wrote first on 17 June to Darius Miller of the C.B.Q.: after leaving him in Chicago he had spent four days in St. Paul and had then gone west with J. J. Hill as far as Glacier Park, whence Hill had returned home while Gaspard continued on to Seattle and Vancouver, coming east again by Canadian Pacific, 'a most interesting trip' he told Miller. Hill was looking particularly well and was in great spirits, although he realized that business was likely to be difficult for some time to come. He was 'full of your praises and the enormous relief to him of having the Burlington Road under your charge'. With them at Metis was Mr. McRoberts of the National City Bank. 'I wish you were here too and we would show you what a vacation really is. At present you have not the slightest conception, moreover I should like to see whether you should continue to smile on losing the biggest salmon on record'.

On the 19th he wrote to Frank Meighen on New Brunswick Railway business and reporting on the river: 'We started in fairly well with the fishing, but after the first two days the weather has turned very hot with a strong wind from the South, and we have scarcely seen a fish in the last few days. I doubt whether there are many in the river so far . . .' But Metis afforded other delights, quite apart from fishing and congenial companionship. On 1 December 1914, in a postscript to Sterling, Gaspard was to relate: 'Lady Peterson of Montreal whom I met at Lady J's told me she could never get any dainty provisions in June—they were all ordered by a millionaire New Yorker for shipment to Metis! and she had to be content with the leavings! I denied all responsibility and referred her to you'. Reporting back to Alfred Mildmay at Barings on 17 June he said: '. . . Please tell John my friends here, who ought to be well informed, see no reasons for J[ames] S[tillman]'s greater confidence as to business prospects in the U.S. The one cheering feature is the excellent crop prospects. Winter wheat . . . will be the biggest crop the country has ever had . . .'

Gaspard was incapable of 'loafing' for long. On 26 June he was writing to Hill's son-in-law George Slade, husband of the violin-playing Charlotte, Vice-President of the N.P. at St. Paul, for some blank Operating Sheets and one monthly one filled in, for the railways in which his English clients were interested. He added: 'My trip to the coast and back was extraordinarily interesting, and to me perhaps especially the return journey as I had not been over the Canadian Pacific Railway for the past twenty years. They have certainly got a most magnificent road, especially between Winnipeg and the Lakes . . .' The unwonted flow of letters from Metis continued. On 22 June 1914 Gaspard told Lord Revelstoke: 'The more I hear McRoberts and Sterling discussing the situation in the U.S. the less optimistic I feel. Both are of course identified with the old order of things . . . but McRoberts is a comparatively young man and quite prepared to be receptive of new ideas . . . He does not see how Railroads can continue to develop and believes national-ization to be inevitable . . .'

In mid-July 1914 Gaspard was back in London, and reporting on the 21st to Robert Winsor in Boston: '. . . I find everyone here in very good spirits and many of them soon to disperse for their holidays. Business unfortunately at a low ebb and political affairs both at home and in the Near East in too disturbed a state to make anyone even wish for greater activity'. On 27 July he was telling Cecil Baring, holidaying on Lambay Island: '. . . We have had a letter from the Germans in reply to ours stating that they could not contemplate any association with us in a funding operation for the present, and indeed since receipt of their letter it has become apparent that the Near Eastern question is too serious for anyone to think of entering into fresh engagements . . .'

BRITAIN AT WAR

Gaspard Farrer's letter of 7 August 1914 to Robert Winsor of Kidder, Peabody in Boston, giving a blow-by-blow account of the events in the City of London that preceded the outbreak of war with Germany on the 4th belongs by rights to the Barings story. The war had come 'like a bolt from the blue'; '. . . our whole machinery of credit had temporarily broken down and we were face to face with a general collapse, and no J. P. Morgan among us to take the lead and make others get together and follow . . .' He finished:

. . . But how trivial all these worries of personal finance are compared to the overwhelming anxiety for our Fleet, for those who are fighting in it and for all their belongings. We shall surely learn that there are other things in this life worth more, much more than worldly possessions. We have been grateful for sympathy shown us by many American visitors.

Another letter he wrote that day was to young Arthur Villiers . . . he was right to resign his post . . . especially as the firm was of German origin: 'I agree with you that it is a bitter thing to be fighting Germans, among whom we have so many friends and for whom as a nation we have sincere respect, but it is right to draw a distinction between the German Government and the German nation, and I reserve my bitterness of feeling for the former . . .'— rather a *volte face* since his 1911 letter to Howard Elliott (above p. 332). Villiers was soon in uniform and 'at the front' with the British Expeditionary Force, but survived to become a partner in Barings.

Replying in lighter vein on 14 August 1914 to a letter of Sterling's obviously written just before war broke out and asking him to commit himself in writing about next year at Metis, Gaspard wrote:

. . . Knowing that you would wish to have the matter really copper fastened I delayed doing so until I could ascertain from Counsel the proper stamp to put upon the contract, and now all this tragedy has arisen and we have learned by sad experience that *no* contract is worth the paper it is written on. Why, this time twelve months I may be languishing in prison in Berlin or stony broke and sweeping a crossing; so you must content yourself without the written contract that you know to be valueless and remember that I am in the frame of mind of never wishing to enter into any contract of any sort again.

It has really been a trying three weeks, though the Government's recent action as regards bills has relieved the great anxiety so far as we are concerned. We are all here, all fit, and as cheerful as we can be, and after all how trivial our little city worries are compared to our anxieties about the war and all those immediately engaged in it. We are everlastingly grateful for the sympathy of the American people. Will you tell Blossie that I received his letter and if his friends turn up here I shall be delighted to do anything I can to assist them. The one service all require is a passage home and in that we are, alas, powerless to help![1]

The following day he was telling Michael Gavin, another Hill son-in-law, marooned with his family in a Surrey hotel, that it was useless to ask steamship companies to keep rooms at his option: if he decided on a date Gaspard would hand this on to Morgan Grenfell to get the soonest passage available. This was successfully achieved. On 25 August he assured E. T. Nichols in New York that he would do his best for his friend. As to the Great Northern instalment due on the latest issue, he wrote that people had paid up fairly well considering the times, and they had passed on the money without delay; 'we are none the less obliged to you, however, for the consideration you have shown us in the matter. We were somewhat exercised as to the rate at which we should accept payment but eventually settled it at the rate at which we were getting remittances from America at the moment in gold'. This was to be the tone of many letters throughout the next four years: the patient nurturing of personal relations was bearing fruit of an unwonted variety; contacts even with the German-orientated firms of the U.S. remained civilised; like the French wine trade, in time of war business went on, although an ever-increasing measure of Government intervention became inevitable, both as to the temporary turning-in of American securities to the Treasury and, eventually, as to the direction of American railroads. For Gaspard Farrer the vision of retirement receded. In addition to his former concerns he now had to take account of wartime restrictions and difficulties, bear with

---

[1] The reference to 'sweeping a crossing' was to the still-extant London institution of road crossing-sweepers in the days of horse-transport, when paths at certain intersections would be kept clear for pedestrians.

the frustrations of dealing with Government departments and sit on a number of Government-inspired committees.

'I was at Brocket on Sunday', he wrote to Sterling on 1 September 1914, 'and did not think the Boss looking well. He is very much upset about the war and is having some trouble through want of circulation in the feet; I do not like this symptom at all, but perhaps it will pass away so you had better not allude to it in writing to him . . .' On 5 August Queen Mary had acknowledged Gian's offer of help in some form of war work.[1] James Pope-Hennessy quotes from the Queen's Diary for that day: 'Set to work to make plans to help the existing Organisations with offers of clothing & money etc.' He goes on to describe the process by which Queen Mary's Needlework Guild—threatening to defeat its own ends by accentuating distress and unemployment in the clothing trade—was superseded by the Queen's Work for Women Fund, administered by the all-party women's Central Committee for Women's Training and Employment.[2]

In Paris the Tucks were working with the American Red Cross; on 28 September 1914 Gaspard told Tuck: '. . . Stillman who has just arrived from New York has been complaining that Americans are much more excited over the war than we are . . .' The ship on which he came had been crowded with Englishmen from all parts of the world coming home to fight and Stillman believed that before long a number of Americans would be trying to join if they could. During September and October the banker dithered between England and Scotland, reconsidered a plan to go to Paris, rejected another to return over the mined waters of the Atlantic to the United States. He found to his irritation that he was no longer allowed to send thither coded cables. Robert Bacon of J.P. Morgan's, Farrer told Sterling on 7 October, had just returned from Paris and the allied lines, very worked up about the war. The Admiralty had been besieged by offers of neutral shipping, including the Great Northern's *Minnesota* which even Gaspard could not dispose of. Patrick Shaw-Stewart and thirty others from Barings' staff had enlisted; already four out of five of Gaspard's cousins at the Front had been killed. The house at Sandwich had been lent to the Colonel commanding the Territorial regiment there 'and any two friends of his whom he liked to bring'. Gaspard communicated to Sterling on 22 October his dismay when the friends turned out to be the

[1] RA GV CC44/215. [2] Pp. 490-5.

Adjutant and the Adjutant's wife: 'I have not dared to go near the place since. Now I hear the regiment is off to India on Sunday and I am desperately anxious to know whether Mrs. Adjutant goes too or whether she intends to remain in possession; if so what am I to do; was ever such a predicament for a poor man. Meantime I am sorry to say Lady Mount Stephen, Alice Northcote and other of my lady friends, instead of sympathising with me in my troubles are making merry over the matter. They tell me it will take a woman to get her out so I have begged them to come and assist ...'

He had been at Brocket on Sunday: Mount Stephen was becoming increasingly lame and would not willingly walk even a hundred yards away from the house. Frank Meighen was with the Canadian contingent on Salisbury Plain, he told Sterling on 30 October 1914: 'It gives me the shivers to think of Frank Meighen being a Lieutenant-Colonel in command of a regiment of men; I can hardly suppose he knows anything more about the job than you or I ...' Already the loss of life was terrible although [General Sir John] French was said to be full of confidence ... Farrer overlooked the fact that since 1891 Frank Meighen had been in the militia; he had helped organize the 1st Regiment Canadian Grenadier Guards and had just formed the 37th Battalion for service overseas. George Cantlie too was on active service. He had joined the Black Watch (Royal Highland Regiment) of Canada in 1885 when barely eighteen. Mount Stephen had written to him at Winnipeg on 6 September 1909 (he foresaw for him a 'very busy Fall in the C.P.R. from all the accounts of the crops that reach this side'): '... I was interested in the photo of your invasion of the U.S. You and your Highlanders have a very martial look in the picture ...' George had been in England when war broke out—his first visit with his wife, whom Mount Stephen had long wished to meet. He had returned to Canada to raise the 42nd Battalion, which as Colonel he then took over to England and into action in France. To the end of his long life Cantlie remained devoted to the Regiment, becoming its honorary Colonel; railroading for him never had the same appeal.

Writing on 29 December to Frank Meighen who had sent him his Lake of the Woods Milling Company Report, which Gaspard always liked to compare with the Pillsbury Washburn one, the latter commented on its excellent showing: 'Of course dear wheat means difficulties for milling ... I am afraid you must have had an uncomfortable Christmas time; Salisbury Plain is not an ideal place in the midst of rain and wind such as we have had lately'. In February 1915 Frank, with the Canadian contingent, was in France.

In his position Farrer was ever conscious of the attitudes both of the American Government and of individuals there.[1] In a letter to Bloss of 10 November 1914 he feared that the U.K. action regarding shipments to neutrals might seem highhanded and even illegal to U.S. shippers; to Hill, who through him had sent a donation towards Belgian refugees, he wrote on 1 December acknowledging a letter of 11 November and his sympathy regarding the war; Gaspard had no doubt but that 90 per cent of Americans were with the U.K. It was difficult to believe that 'the many very nice and capable Germans whom you and I both know could be whole-hearted in the German policy of offence'. Meanwhile the Great Northern Report was satisfactory: 'I sent down your letter to the Boss, who bids me send you his warm regards'. He had advised Robert Winsor on 13 November against letting his son Bob come on a visit just then; he did not wish to worry Mrs. Winsor, or intend to convey that conditions were serious, or likely to be . . . 'Personally I have never myself believed either in Zeppelins or invasion, and I should think the time of year is unpropitious for either of these adventures . . . I believe, however, those who are competent to judge have always thought a raid a possibility . . .' James Stillman was still hovering: on 1 December 1914 Gaspard told Sterling he talked of going to the seat of War . . . to the Riviera . . . to Torquay; Gaspard believed he would stay in London or go to New York. On 11 December he wrote that Stillman had left for Paris for a few days. 'He has become exasperatingly slow in his old age and seems quite unable to dispense with all those ways and airs of mystery which entirely preclude his getting anyone's confidence. Indeed, if we did not know him so well and feel in the bottom of our hearts that he wishes to be friendly, we should be filled with suspicion. However I guess he is too old to change his ways now . . .' His postscript stated: 'J. S. has taken a passage for New York per *Lusitania* 16 December'.

Farrer's letters became a medley of war finance and the family anxieties of his and Mount Stephen's circle. '. . . . I saw Lady Strathcona a fortnight ago after an interval of some two years', he

---

[1] Patrick Devlin's *Too Proud to Fight : Woodrow Wilson's Neutrality*, London, 1974, provides an excellent commentary on the subject.

FRANCES GARNET, VISCOUNTESS WOLSELEY
with two lime-pit workers in her Sussex garden
(*in the Hove collection*)

told Sterling on 1 December 1914. 'She has grown a good deal older in appearance and gray but she seemed in pretty good form and much relieved that the report of her son's being wounded proved to be incorrect. She made many enquiries after you and spoke of her regret at having been unable to get out to visit you this year'. Lord Strathcona had not long survived his wife's death and his daughter, familiarly known as Maggie Smith, had inherited the title. She had married in 1888 Robert Jared Bliss Howard, M.D., F.R.C.S., of Montreal. Gaspard met her again in the street in late April 1915: 'She tells me she has one boy at the front and two more preparing to go out . . .'

FRANCES WOLSELEY: WOMEN ON THE LAND

Soon after the outbreak of war Frances Wolseley decided to give up her gardening college but was persuaded by her forewoman, Elsa More, a former student, to let her carry it on, the latter to have the land and glasshouses rent free with other perquisites and a salary of £200 a year for at least three years. Frances was to continue living—alone—at her house there and be available for advice. She consulted her godfather, who accepted her estimate of the situation and raised no objection since she spoke well of Miss More.[1] He probably remained unaware of the crises of temperament which ultimately ensued, and these are no part of the Mount Stephen story. In his letter of 21 September 1914 he wrote, having in mind it seems Louisa's growing objections to certain commercial aspects of the gardening college:

I note all you say about your mother and am not sanguine that the new arrangement will make any permanent change in her attitude towards you but I sincerely hope I may be mistaken. It seems impossible for her (to) see any good in you or in anything you do, to me an *incomprehensible* state of mind on the part of a mother towards her daughter. But there it is and you must bear it as best you can never forgetting that she is your mother and not quite responsible for all she does and says to you, a sore trial for you to bear. She has quite stopped writing to me about anything. She evidently thinks I am to blame for not siding with her in her attitude towards you.

That I should not mind if I could have the happiness to see her changed towards you.

All well here. Gian is busy slaughtering poor little partridges and

[1] PVW 120/899–902.

regretting they are not Germans. When are you coming to see us here? It seems ages since we had a peep at you.[1]

Relieved, on the whole, at having turned over the frequently vexatious responsibilities of the college—now to be run on strictly military lines—Frances turned more to writing and to voluntary work in connection with women's work in horticulture and agriculture, as well as to supporting the new Women's Institute movement. She was still very much a woman of her class and time, very conscious of her new status in society, but with a very limited sphere of influence. A short spell in a paid post taught her that this invalidated any claim to deference, and all concerned appeared relieved when she relinquished the small salary in order to serve on the county War Agricultural Committee. Yet she was genuinely interested in her country pursuits and wrote in her memoirs the heartfelt comment: 'It is always my privilege, on the afternoon of Sundays, to find myself once again the sole owner of my garden . . .' Similarly 'Upon Bank holiday, a general holiday is given . . . the Captain [Miss More] clad in mufti tells me that she is about to leave for Eastbourne, after which she makes me a military salute, as if I were the Commander-in-Chief at the very least. The ensign upon the roof garden is consequently lowered, and peace reigns for the rest of the day . . .'[3]

Mount Stephen continued to advise her about her investments. On 28 October 1914 he wrote: 'This morning I sent you a little memo. regarding your finances which I hope you may be able to "*take in*".' Discouraging her from responding to some war-work overture about which she had consulted him, he went on: 'She is a tiresome woman and you should I think . . . tell her that you are fully occupied and have no time (to) take up new schemes of any kind, no matter how good and useful they might be . . .' He saw no indication of 'this horrid war' ending nor could he predict what 'those crazy Germans may try to do. They are desperate and ready to try anything and we must meet them as best we can until they are conquered and made harmless. Have you read Von Bernhardi's book? Read it and tell me what you think of it, also what you think of Prof. Cramb's book'.[4]

[1] PVW 139.   [2] PVW 121/928.   [3] PVW 121/931.

[4] PVW 139. Friedrich Adam Julius von Bernhardi, author of *Germany and the next war* (20th impression London, 1914) had followed this with *Britain as Germany's vassal*, London, 1914. Professor J. A. Cramb's *Germany and England* was published in 1914.

FARRER'S WAR REPORTAGE

Writing to Tuck on 21 December 1914 Gaspard Farrer commented: 'there may of course come a time when the continent and England commence to liquidate their American holdings in earnest, not by wish but of necessity'. He added that the Government was in good spirits about the war 'but the real optimists are the soldiers who have lately been coming back for a few days holiday ...' Deprived of the so-carefully planned life of leisure in his town and seaside houses Gaspard could still find recreation in writing to John Sterling. He had actually spent Christmas at Sandwich, now 'comparatively deserted' by the military, before describing to him on New Year's Day 1915 the still-normal passing of the old year in London: 'As I went to my room last night and threw open the windows the clocks were striking twelve and steam whistles and foghorns commenced to blow, reminding me of the New Year's Eve I spent with you. All possible happiness to you for 1915, to you and Blossie also. I do not know what there is to wish for you, but may destitute old ladies increase in number and Texas Company dividends in amount; may Blossie's smile continue to broaden and farm deficits continue to shrink; may your letters continue to remain forgotten and unposted on your desk and your poor young lady continue to keep her head on her shoulders'.[1] Three days later the teasing continued:

Once upon a time when Merry Edward VII was King, a letter of mine to you was unfortunately addressed to Jimmy Stillman. Your consequent explosion of unparliamentary language is still ringing in my ears.

Recently I have heard rumours of how the mail department is conducted in your office.

Now this morning comes a note from the Manager of the London Joint Stock Bank enclosing confirmation of our recent Argentine cable correspondence with the [National] City Bank, and sent by the City Bank to him in error.

It is twelve o'clock, as black as night; it has been raining for a month, is raining again this morning, a thick, drizzling, penetrating rain; every joint in my body is aching with rheumatism; I sigh for the days of shaving when razors were handy and could joyfully welcome a Zeppelin bomb;

[1] Sterling was President and trustee of the Mirian Osborn Memorial Home Association, providing care for aged, indigent gentlewomen. Farrer was to write to Sterling on 24 December 1917: 'How are the farming operations getting on? I suppose improvements have practically come to an end. The chicken and dairy farm ought to be a mine of wealth for you ...'

but I confess this little incident makes me smile, smile in front and behind, all over, so that neither Blossie nor the Cheshire Cat could compete. Why not have sent them direct to the London City and Midland Bank while they were about it? No wonder Jimmy's footsteps are dogged by the police if his correspondence gets sent broadcast in this way. Of course, knowing what goes on in your office, I am not surprised at what goes on in *your* Bank.

My dear old man, you really have given me intense pleasure, and I may add the whole incident does not matter a twopenny damn.

In February James Stillman was 'in sunny Italy': Gaspard told him on the 19th: '. . . I have a letter from Sterling this week written immediately after the Germans' proclamation about the war zone, which has added the final touch to his holy horror of seafaring; he concludes with a "Thank the Lord I am not in the passenger business" '. Germany had declared that the safety of neutral vessels in the waters around Great Britain could not be guaranteed.[1] At San Remo Stillman became ill and Gaspard, knowing that he was 'very nervous about his health and I expect will be entirely prostrated by this trouble', set about enquiring about doctors within reach who could be recommended. Communicating this information to Stillman on 7 April 1915, he wrote that Lord Mount Stephen desired him to send his sympathy and hoped for a speedy recovery. 'The Boss thinks he is probably more frightened than hurt and I hope this is correct'; Gaspard told Sterling on 29 April 1915 'there is no doubt he was very frightened . . .' From Lugano in Switzerland Stillman wrote on 22 April that he felt so much better he even contemplated going to Metis for the fishing. Farrer was indeed startled to receive in June a cable from Stillman from Metis (the *Lusitania* had gone down in May 1915) but this turned out to be from the son, James A. Stillman, to whom he wrote on 27 July: '. . . it seemed to be in harmony with your Father's somewhat mysterious movements that he should suddenly turn up at Metis while all his friends were expecting him to be still in Switzerland . . .'

After the death of Lord Roberts while visiting the B.E.F. in France in 1914 Gaspard, an executor, wrote to Sterling on 2 February 1915 that Mount Stephen and he were taking over his holding of Ore Certificates at par: '. . . not exactly a profitable transaction for us, but I suppose it will be all the same a hundred

[1] See Devlin, op. cit. Chapter VII.

years hence, and it will make a great difference to the ease with which the family's affairs can be settled'. In spite of what Gaspard termed 'a falling off in his powers of locomotion', Mount Stephen was still taking a keen interest in what was going on, in fact seemed to have taken on a new lease of life just because so much was going on; '. . . the Boss shows me your letters to him from time to time', Gaspard told Sterling on 4 March 1915; '. . . recent decisions of the Interstate Commerce Commission have been slightly more favourable to the Railroads . . . The Boss is in town and particularly well, much better I think than he has been for several years past . . .' Did Sterling still think that U.S. business showed no improvement? Mrs. Reford was over from Canada to see her boys, he told Tuck on 15 April; one had joined the army, the other had his school holidays. 'Your sister arrived on Sunday with her husband', he had just written to Frank Meighen, 'and I gather rather disappointed that her ship was not torpedoed on the way over'. To James Norman Hill he wrote on 29 April: 'Lord Mount Stephen is in town, very well but anxious over his nephew Meighen, who is commanding one of the Battalions of the Canadian contingent and has been in the thick of the recent fighting [in the Ypres salient]; happily however he has escaped unharmed so far . . .' 'The Boss says very little but I am sure has been greatly disturbed about him . . .' he told Sterling. To Frank himself Gaspard wrote on 14 May 1915:

. . . We have all been thrilled with the heroic fight which the Canadians put up; you must indeed be proud of your men and feel that you are recompensed for the hard work you have gone through since August . . . I can assure you all English folk are as proud of the Canadian Contingent as any Canadian can be. You can imagine how thankful we are that you yourself have got through safely.

Your uncle and aunt went down to Brocket yesterday, permanently for the summer he thinks, but I expect they will be constantly up in town . . .

Gaspard's wartime letters early adopted the phraseology that has become associated with the Great War. So far, in spite of the appalling casualty lists (people were 'behaving magnificently' over their losses) and of the Treasury-ridden life of the City where financial restrictions were gradually becoming tighter, life continued to be extraordinarily normal. In the lull before the German Spring offensive of 1915 Gaspard golfed again at Sandwich and was having redecorated the now-dry walls at No. 7 St. James's Square. Other friends were strangely employed at times: one spent 'every other night on the top of some high building manoeuvring searchlights'. He continued to act as interpreter between Americans and British; after the appearance in *The Spectator* of an article by St. Loe Strachey he told Robert Winsor on 29 March 1915: 'People here, and the better informed the more it is the case, thoroughly realise the friendliness of the disposition of the American people both in what they do and what they have forborne to do, and further understand that your Government could not have done other than they have done . . .' On 20 April he wrote a long letter to J. J. Hill: 'It is long since I have written to you . . .' He had, however, been following Hill's addresses and speeches . . . the burning question being the uncertainty over the price of wheat in all the circumstances prevailing. Of Germany he wrote: '. . . is it not inconceivable that so practical, capable and sensible a race should have gone so far astray. They really have not a friend now left in the world so utterly have they lost their heads; while prior to the war they had almost conquered the world throughout in peaceful pursuits'. There continued in London small purchases of American Bonds by 'those who like to have their investments with 3,000 miles of sea between its location and the seat of war'. He concluded: 'Your friends here are well and frequently ask me after you. It was a great disappointment that you were unable to pay us a visit, but it was manifestly out of the question this year . . .'

Writing to James Norman Hill on 29 April 1915 'I was glad to hear that you still existed . . .' he went on: 'I quite agree with you about U.S. Railroads: the limitation of the money to be made in them stares one in the face. As to Ore Certificates, you are no doubt right in thinking them dear at 40, yet I have not sold a share and do not think I shall. Partly sentiment, partly pigheadedness, partly a dislike of jobbing, but mostly an incorrigible faith in the old gentleman, all make me most unwilling to part with a single share: I should lie awake at nights if I did. Then again we have been busy here, occupied with the firm's affairs and with the War, and I seem to have neither time nor interest for a gamble'. He ended: 'Please remember me to the old gentleman when next you see him . . . I simply dare not look forward but I hope we may meet in happier times'.

On 7 May 1915, unaware of the sinking that day of the *Lusitania*, he was telling Colonel W. P. Clough of the Northern Pacific in New York: '. . . Today we are all burning with indignation over the use of poisonous gases and the description of the horrible torture which they inflict. It is a comfort to us to know that we have the sympathy of the people of the United States and that they will be as horrified at the Germans' inhumanities as we are ...' With his usual concern for the families of his business friends he went on to ask what had become of Mrs. Darius Miller; the bright and morning star of the Burlington had died the previous year. By 10 November 1916 Farrer was writing to George B. Harris, veteran and President of the C.B.Q.: '... In the deaths of Mr. Hill, Darius Miller, and Colonel Clough, you must have lost three very close friends, and, as I know, three as good men as one could wish to have as friends'.

Frank Meighen continued to forward to him from France statistics of Canadian firms in which both were interested. In the letter of 14 May to Frank quoted above he had added:

... Lord Haldane's remarks [Lord Chancellor, a former Secretary of State for War] in the House of Lords last night are interpreted as meaning that conscription is near at hand, and I believe the educated classes in the country will welcome it. President Wilson's attitude and utterances have their comic side: the Americans themselves must be perfectly mad at the way he has behaved; it will be interesting to see how he gets out of his difficulties, for his Note to Germany [of 13 May] which appears in this morning's papers apparently engulfs him to an even greater extent than before in case the Germans refuse to heed him. I feel convinced that nothing would induce him to fight ...[1]

Back in April Farrer had written to J. O. Bloss that it was impossible to accept Sterling's invitation to Metis that year, adding: 'You will no doubt have seen the King's letter[2] which appears in this morning's papers on the drink question, and I trust you and J. W. will think of me with sympathy as your pony cocktails slip down your throats before dinner ...' There was some consolation for the loss of Metis in a pleasant, if not uneventful, Whitsuntide at Sandwich. He told Sterling on 26 May: 'The garden there is an old orchard, very much like some of those New England orchards at the back of your place and Blossie's house ... blossom and hundreds of red and yellow tulips ...' But he wrote sadly of the loss in France of two cousins and of his greater grief at that of

[1] Ibid. especially p. 292.
[2] King George V renounced all alcoholic drinks in the royal residences. James Pope Hennessy comments (*Queen Mary*, p. 508): 'It was an example which was not followed by the country at large, but it added to the general fatigue of life in the Royal establishments'.

Denys Stephenson, a Clanwilliam connection, 'who was almost like a son to me' and had spent the last ten days of his life in England with Gaspard in London. On the morning of Whitsunday a German Taube 'came right over the house flying at an enormous height up, and the week before several Taubes and Zeppelins had visited Ramsgate and Deal and dropped bombs . . .' The war was coming nearer. On 11 June he wrote to Sterling hoping to catch him at Metis 'as without my restraining and retaining influence I feel that you are liable to cut your holiday short and hurry back unduly to your beloved Wall Street . . .' He sent remembrances to all the party 'and to my friends at Metis, Annett, Coffin, Miller etc.'. These were the canoemen from Gaspé, descendants of Jerseymen, who turned up year after year.

In June 1915 the C.P.R. President, Sir Thomas Shaughnessy, was in London on business but in poor health, Farrer told Sterling on the 11th: '. . . One can only hope he has in his organisation provided for a successor. His place will be hard to fill, as there is no one left who can take it who has also grown up with the organisation and knows it from the start . . . My own impression is that the C.P.R., as indeed all Canadian affairs, have a hard time ahead of them'.

On 7 July 1915 Gaspard wrote to Mount Stephen who had been forwarding Sterling's cables from Metis and had now written enclosing a 'really capital letter' from him 'which makes me regret the more having missed a year out there with him. Blossie seems to have much the same kind of misfortunes every year on that motor trip'; (the previous year he had had car trouble on the journey from New York) 'I wonder he is not tired of it. It would be much simpler either to send the car up with the chauffeur or perhaps better still to hire one from Quebec and have it sent down by train. Sterling does not say where he fished every morning but I suspect at the Bridge and in the Rock Pool only, while obviously the bulk of the fish were up above: hence his poor score during the early weeks . . .' (Mount Stephen later sent Gaspard Sterling's complete fishing record.) He went on to discuss recent developments in regard to payments of American debts; although Britain seemed more happily placed than France or Russia, he quoted Henry P. Davison of Morgan's as saying that 'even one so pro-English as George Baker had been shaking his head and asking how any country could stand an expenditure of three million sterling per

diem and remain solvent . . .' This heralded the beginning of the
idea of raising a loan by the collection in Britain of American
securities which would be deposited as collateral. At this point
Farrer did not think this was yet warranted, but had written to ask
for Sterling's views. A restriction of purchases in America in future
would help, he thought: 'I expect the Government in their hurry to
make up for our general unpreparedness has ordered right and left
in the U.S., in many cases where the same things might have been
just as well bought here at home'. With this view he later found that
Robert Fleming concurred.[1] He thought the current War Loan
would be well subscribed 'but the question is what is well. I should
think five hundred millions very good indeed . . .' Two days later,
repeating his views to Sterling, he remarked: 'but when one comes
to hundreds of millions one feels quite at sea and without experience
to guide one . . .' The sum subscribed turned out to be £570
million.

The melancholy news had just come—cabled by Sterling to
Mount Stephen—of the death at Hill's St. John River home of
Samuel Thorne, an old associate who had, *inter alia*, been in at the
planning of the Northern Securities Company. Hill wrote to Farrer
with details, the latter copying the letter to Tuck on 26 July. The
day before he suffered a heart attack Thorne had 'caught five fish,
one of which weighed 28 lbs and in the evening was quite well and
pleased with his "big fish".' Hill went on: 'Lord Mount Stephen,
Angus and myself are about all that are left of the old guard'.
Gaspard added: 'Alas, I am afraid that is true'. On 7 June 1915
Mount Stephen wrote from Brocket to Frances Wolseley:

> Many thanks for your letter which I read on my 87th birthday (Sat-
> urday). I am perfectly well but cannot help feeling that I must be getting
> to the end of my birthday "tether", and not caring very much when I
> reach it. This horrid war in which we are entangled makes life hardly
> worth living.
> Is there any chance of our being able to persuade you to come down
> here and see us for a few days if you can spare the time. Gian has many
> things in her garden she would like to show you and to make you jealous
> of if she could.[2]

Acknowledging a letter from Robert Winsor on 13 July 1915
Gaspard wrote: '. . . Your postscript touches a point on which I

[1] Gaspard Farrer Letter Books, Farrer to Lord Revelstoke, 6 August 1915.
[2] PVW 138.

have often thought of late; that there will be a great transfer of wealth and business from us to you seems to me inevitable, but that surely should be a matter to which we can be resigned with good grace, at least I hope so . . .' He realized that now there was 'another winter campaign ahead', but told Hill on the 15th that people in Britain were 'more and more determined to face the sacrifices that a continuance of the war involves . . .' For him at this juncture this meant adding to his responsibilities membership of a commission of enquiry. He told Tuck on 26 July 1915: 'It is absolutely ridiculous my taking part . . . as the subject is one about which I know nothing whatever, but these are times when one does not like to refuse. I should very much doubt myself whether much economy is possible without passing a sponge over the legislation of the last ten years . . .' Writing to Winsor on 11 August on the happier topic of his son Sandy's engagement he commented that the American Press seemed to have already decided that the Allies were beaten. 'Such a contingency has not even occurred to any Englishman: I suppose it is the advantage of being stupid, and I hope we shall long continue in ignorance of our being beaten, even at the risk of continuing stupid as well . . .' This referred to alleged German propaganda being planted in the American newspapers.

There is a gap in the Farrer letter-books from August 1915 until June 1916, apart from the odd letter in September, January and February. Gaspard's last recorded word for 1915 was a letter of 2 September to one of the young Clanwilliams, serving in the Royal Navy, and was on the subject of Ore Certificates. From the dividend point of view there was no doubt but that these were selling at their full value. Six months ago he had been advised by a 'New York friend' who followed them closely to sell out at 36 on these grounds. He was not prepared to dissuade Captain Meade, yet it was a mining property not decreasing in value—value which would not affect prices until the Company was actively mining and selling. If business revived in the U.S. this would come quickly. His conclusion was: don't sell at present prices if you can afford to wait.

X

Ingathering

A VISIT TO BROCKET

In February 1916 Frances Wolseley's *In a College Garden* was published by John Murray, and was, she herself writes, on the whole well-reviewed. Mount Stephen sent her *The Scotsman's* verdict, which he said was worth reading.[1] He did not apparently commit himself further. Both in her preface and in the text Frances betrayed much of her belief in class-distinction; she hoped that the chance of emancipation brought by the war would be eagerly grasped by women who had until then learned those 'traditions of discipline, order, and *esprit de corps*' which generations of Public School or regimental life had taught to men, only from their brothers. Her attitudes would probably have passed almost un-challenged by her readers. She believed that gardening as a career was for upper-class women; her correspondence, perhaps percep-tively, shows that she thought that the working-class woman with a husband at the Front would certainly not—receiving an allowance—take to gardening as a patriotic duty, nor did men apparently welcome them on the land. She felt sufficiently encouraged to proceed with *Women and the Land*, to be published by Chatto and Windus; this was perhaps the book acknowledged at Christmas that year by the Misses Lawrence, although they had of course read it, having got it from Mudie's Library directly it came out.[2]

Frances' attitude to her godfather was undergoing a subtle change, best illustrated perhaps by comparing two visits she paid, one on 10 August 1915 to a friend in Sussex, the other on 17 October 1916 to the Mount Stephens at Brocket. Of the former she wrote: 'I bicycled over to Firle Place to visit a friend of mine, Leila, Viscountess Gage. There, I found the usual wartime dimin-

[1] PVW 121/951.
[2] PVW 140.

ished household, as footmen and odd man were all away fighting and only a thin delicate looking young man came to the door and took long even to do that simple task. Her Ladyship was in old garments, but still managed to have a glittering silver tea pot on her table . . .'[1] and of the second:

. . . I went down to Hertfordshire to visit my dear, kind godfather . . . It is always a pleasure to see him but I grieve to say that although well in health, he shows signs of unfitness in following the rapidly changing phases of our nation's life. It is only natural at his advanced age, and perhaps his wife is wise in keeping up the establishment at Brocket, as far as she can, in the style of luxurious comfort of pre-war days. Certainly her own clothes, old and shabby, do not betray personal luxury, but in the matter of tall men-servants, the ceaseless procession of varied scones, biscuits and cakes, that are handed round wastefully, and many other unnecessaries of a large house, one is constantly finding oneself inwardly grieved. Perhaps as Fate has given me but a tiny house and limited means, which permit of my supporting myself alone, giving me no opportunity of helping others, I am rather a hard critic. Anyhow, the excessive luxury hurt me, and I was glad for once to get away, for the great prancing horses, the liveried coachman, and all the paraphernalia that one had hoped to see no more, jarred terribly upon me. When I got out of the train at Glynde, it was with some difficulty that I could see my way through the inky blackness of the night . . . "Will life always be wartime with us?" I asked myself . . . although I have stolen a march upon others and have played in a sense at war, and lived in a small house with only two maids and no carriage to drive in, for ten years already, it does not make one quite reconciled to the prospect.[2]

Asked to comment on this picture of Brocket in wartime, Elsie Reford's younger son Eric wrote on 19 September 1969: 'I can only say that when, as a small boy, I went over from my Preparatory School at Lockers Park to visit them, I was not struck by this in any way, and as far as the food was concerned, I was not impressed by any great lavishness. It is true that once when I went to stay at 17 Carlton House Terrace, but I think that was before 1914, I was vastly impressed with a bath being brought into my bedroom by two footmen and, of course, I well remember that there was always a footman sitting at the door in a wicker chair with a high back, ready to open it during calling hours'.

[1] PVW 121/931.
[9] PVW 121/1002.

DEATH OF HILL: MOUNT STEPHEN MAKES HIS WILL

The Farrer letters resume again some two weeks after the death on 29 May 1916 of James J. Hill, too late for immediate reactions, but in the following months there are several comments on the event and on its concomitants. It was a shock to all his friends in England, who had known him since the summer of 1880—before Hill became an American citizen—Farrer wrote on 2 August to the President of the Northern Pacific, J. M. Hannaford (Mount Stephen's acquaintance, of course, went back further); they had had 'no previous warning of there being anything amiss'. He went on:

Apart from the personal qualities that one got to know of life in his own home, I always thought that in business nothing was more to his credit than his power to reconcile himself and adapt his ways to new conditions. The regime under which all his early years of life were spent had quite passed away and after the uncontrolled power which in those times was placed in the hands of the Railway President, it must have been hard to recognise and co-operate with the superior powers which public opinion and the Law has set up of recent years . . .

Some rather high-flown phrases which followed did not accord with past pronouncements. More natural and undoubtedly affectionate was his comment to Tuck on 10 August 1916: '. . . I am sure our poor friend would be much more interested in after life in purgatory, with plenty of scope for his talent of construction and reorganization, than as a first class angel with his wings on, as he used to say himself, in Paradise'.

Mount Stephen's early reaction was to remake his Will; Hill had left none, thereby causing many difficulties. Farrer was soon in correspondence with Sterling, an executor, although the final document was not drawn up until 23 November. Disregarding the watertight legal terminology, which considerably lengthened it, it was a relatively simple affair; already Mount Stephen had set up numerous Trusts for the benefit of relatives, to which had since been added the charitable instruments already recorded. On two points Gaspard ventured to offer advice. Mount Stephen had decided—rightly, Farrer thought, having in mind perhaps the occasional problems which still cropped up over the 1884 Annie Charlotte Stephen Trust—that his estate should be wound up quickly: 'You would be cognisant of the conditions then prevailing and will be in a better position to judge what is wise and according to your wishes than anyone else'. He went on: 'do you not think that the leaving of a decision, in which Sterling and [John] Turnbull [Montreal] must acquiesce, on the merits of charitable objects in this country, would place them in a difficulty? So much for your actual question'; (this in a letter of 9 November 1916) 'but as you have raised the subject, would you consider again your emigration bequests? The two big public objects of charity with which your life has been connected are the Hospital Fund here and the Victoria Hospital in Montreal. Both Harry and I feel [Henry Farrer, solicitor] that no better use can be made of property than by devoting it to hospital charities. Conditions surrounding emigration and the institutions which conduct it are much more liable to change, and I have often wondered whether so large a sum as you have left in this direction will be properly spent . . .' In the event the Will included a bequest of ten thousand pounds to Dr. Barnardo's fund for the emigration of children to Canada, two thousand pounds to the Royal Victoria Hospital and the residue—after family and staff bequests and annuities—to the King's Fund. It was clear that Mount Stephen still held his affairs in his own hands and made his own decisions: this was shortly to be illustrated in— as Gaspard made it—an amusing incident. Meanwhile the latter assured Sterling on 31 July 1916: '. . . I was at Brocket last week and thought the Boss remarkably well. He has a nurse for massage and probably as a result is much more active than last year. He is quite willing to walk down to the garden twice a day; a quarter to half a mile each way; a distance which he would not have dreamt of attempting a year ago . . .' Mrs. Reford had just left for Canada intending to go straight down to Metis. Stillman too, after helping Tuck with some charitable works in France, had been in London (Gaspard told Sterling on 26 June) and was returning to America via New York, seeming to Gaspard in better form than for many a long day, 'full of chat'. The other Farrer brothers, Frank and Harry, had however thought him much aged since they last saw him. Later, on 9 September, Gaspard told Sterling he thought Stillman would be wiser to stay in America until the war was over: 'moreover I believe his presence in New York will do more to forward the cause of the Allies than anything he could do in Europe'. Needless to say the banker did nothing of the kind, returning the following February just as the submarine warfare was being resumed.

LENDING DOLLAR SECURITIES

But to go back to June 1916: the main preoccupations were those resulting from the British Government's invitation, through McKenna the Chancellor of the Exchequer, to holders of American and Canadian securities to lend or sell these to the Government to supplement the payment in gold of Britain's debts to the United States. For Gaspard, who was by now also deep in committee work —two of his four committees reported that year—it was almost like the days of Northern Securities again as he wrote around to his circle of investing friends advising each as to which securities they should or could lend; minimum amounts acceptable had been set and the same conditions did not apply to all. '. . . It is a poor business to exchange these solid values for powder and shot', wrote Gaspard to Hannaford on 2 August, 'but if necessary we must be willing to pawn our shirts to win and I am thankful to say I believe we are . . .' The scheme was not yet compulsory, although the alternative was a swingeing tax on dividends. There was a good response; Mount Stephen, in his enthusiasm, evidently overstepped the mark and offered securities that were under the jurisdiction of the Annie Charlotte Stephen Trustees—including the sternly meticulous John W. Sterling. Farrer wrote to the latter on 9 September:

I have sent a serious answer to your very serious letter re Annie Charlotte Stephen affairs, so you must forgive me if I now add that the situation has caused me an infinity of merriment. You dear old straight-laced, puritanical, wayback New England Covenanter. I would not have you for a Trustee for anything in the world, with never a chance of breaking through the Trust. But do tell me, if our breezy Brocket friend in a fit of light hearted patriotism chooses to offer to lend investments which he has not got, why should it matter to you? You might as well lie awake at night if he offered to lend Windsor Castle or Westminster Abbey . . .

In the end the A.C.S. Trust Ore Certificates were successfully registered under the British Government's 'B' scheme whereas later other holders had theirs requisitioned. In the same vein, recalling that the germ of the scheme had first been sown by Henry P. Davison, Gaspard wrote to Tuck on 19 October 1916: '. . . Most of the Morgan firm seem to be in London at the present moment. I am thinking of suggesting embargoing them and offering them as collateral for the next loan'.

He himself had already lent his American railway securities, and on 14 December 1916 wrote to the National Debt Office offering his Great Northern Ore Certificates ($650,000 worth at current market value) on loan to the Treasury 'without consideration provided I retained a power of sale'. The Certificates were in New York and endorsed, and could be delivered immediately. By 8 February 1917 he was writing to E. T. Nichols: '. . . Our Government has recently requisitioned the Certificates from the holders so mine are up the spout. However, I hope to see them back again some day and meanwhile eke out a simple livelihood—something less than six ounces of meat per day—from the distributions you make from time to time'. He had repeated to Tuck the previous June that he saw no reason to change his views about the Ore Certificates, views founded on Hill's faith in their ultimate value: '. . . it is quite certain that his death cannot alter the value of such ore contents as the properties contain . . .' Thanking Nichols on 13 October 1916 for a *New York Times* article of September headed *Steel Trade faces a famine in Ore* he observed: 'You will not be surprised to hear that I was able to read it with unruffled equanimity . . .' and went on to quote the subsequent confirmatory remarks on their recent arrival in London of 'certain American gentlemen whom we have reason to know are among those in your country best conversant with the availability of steel products in America . . .'—no doubt those referred to above in his letter to Tuck.

Lord Revelstoke had in 1915 become Chairman of the King's Fund's Finance Committee. At a meeting on 28 June 1915 they considered the question of buying $4\frac{1}{2}$ per cent War Loan and for this purpose decided to try to sell a considerable quantity of their American securities. At the time this involved physically shipping them to America along with sealed blank transfers. In the event they were sold the following year to the British Treasury under the new scheme and the proceeds were invested in 5 per cent Exchequer Bonds. At the same time (May 1916) further large blocks of the same securities shared a like fate and by the end of that summer their entire holdings—except Ore Certificates—had been transmuted into Exchequer Bonds or Treasury Bills. In the last transaction Northern Pacific shares realized a loss of £39,890 on £185,584 worth although those of the Great Northern showed an appreciation of £22,698—both on average book value. The Fund's Seal Register records in January 1917 the resolution of the Finance Committee to deposit the Fund's shares in Great Northern (U.S.A.) Iron Ore Properties with His Majesty's Treasury under Scheme B. (Under both A and B securities could be requisitioned, but under B only at scheduled prices plus 5 per cent thereon.)

In his letter to Sterling of 9 September 1916, Gaspard said he had heard from Mrs. Hill: '. . . I fear from the letter she must be terribly broken down. What a gap these two years since my last visit have made among my railway friends, Hill, Van Horne, Miller and Clough all gone . . .' Writing to Tuck on 10 August 1916 Gaspard had very much hoped—and he knew Tuck would agree although they shared some reservations about him as a railway-man—that Louis should 'have every chance given him to prove his capacity as Head of the Road. I have for many years preferred NP to GN for fear of the disorganization that might occur on Mr. Hill's death, though I quite realise the GN is strategically the better property of the two and can always be operated more cheaply . . .' To Louis he wrote on 9 October 1916 acknowledging the Great Northern Report—'fairly comforting' in view of the shortness of the crop. They could not expect, he said, a repetition of 1914 and 1915 conditions but no doubt ore traffic would help to com-pensate: 'Perhaps the day is not so far off when Ore Certificates will prove their value, though when that day comes I am sure we shall all be wishing that your father had been there to see it . . .' Passing to politics, Gaspard hoped Woodrow Wilson would not win the next election: he had 'little use for professors in either politics or business' (he had been suffering on one of his committees from John Maynard Keynes). He ended the letter: 'You have—and have long had—a big load to carry. No one will be better pleased than I at every success you attain'. He told Tuck on 14 March 1917, on receipt of a circular letter from Louis, that he was glad to see the latter had 'made a beginning of attempting to concil-iate his father's old friends, but it is somewhat late in the day and I am afraid he will find it is a deal easier to lose his father's friends than to make fresh ones . . .' He was to write again to Tuck on the subject of Hill's railroads and their future on 9 October 1917, having just seen in a New York paper a list of Hill's assets: 'I can hardly believe the list complete and have not got it by me at the present time, but it included $24 million as the value of his Bank shares, and $7 million as the value of his Railway shares, and $7 million as the value of his Railway Bonds, the total $60 million. Among the Railway shares were 50,000 GN and 10,000 NP, and besides these there were 50,000 Ore shares ... Altogether the list as reported was one to make his foreign associates shiver down the back, at least that is how it struck me. No doubt he had become disgruntled about railroad property as an investment, and his training unfitted him for believing there would be any virtue in an Interstate Commission with its plenary and irresponsible powers ...'

TOTAL WAR

Gaspard was still keeping open house at 7 St. James's Square for the younger generation of friends on leave from the Front or over from America; among the latter was Phil Winsor 'who distributed impartially and openhandedly, the umbrellas of all three brothers in taxicabs over London'—all being recovered by Hardman, the butler. Patrick Shaw-Stewart had been awarded the Croix de Guerre in Salonica, he told Sterling on 15 November 1916, 'where the lions attacked the transport animals of Xerxes' army of invasion, he says ...'

On 10 November 1916 Queen Mary wrote to Lady Mount Stephen with whom she had just exchanged objects of vertu. Her Majesty continued: 'What a pity your "dear George" has got a cold in his head. I only pray it will not go down to his chest. I so agree with him that the length of this horrible war is most depressing ...' She added a postscript: 'Please thank "dear George" for his kind message and give him my love'.[1] The Queen wrote again on 20 February 1917 after the further exchange of interesting gifts: ' ... It was such a pleasure to us seeing you both last Sunday and to find "dear George" so well & unchanged which for *88* is *very* remarkable. Au revoir next week ...'[2] Frances Wolseley described, in a memoir written about 1936, the visit of two younger members of the Royal Family to Brocket in her godfather's time: there was no telephone there, and a telegram announcing their arrival for luncheon came as 'we were sitting, as was our wont after breakfast, in the small glass vestibule in front of the large hall'. It was the butler's day off, but Gian hastily remarshalled her forces and when the visitors arrived all, including Frances, were at their

[1] RA GV CC44/224.   [2] RA GV CC44/225.

appropriate stations except the host, who was not to be seen. Some minutes after the Prince and Princess had been shown into the drawingroom by Gian, and Frances had made her curtsey there, the door 'gently opened and he smilingly advanced, greeting the royal visitors with warmth, but in exactly the same kindly, homely way with which ordinary mortals would have been welcomed by him'. Gian was to write to Queen Mary on 4 December 1921:

... His one thought throughout that terrible war was the sorrow it brought to your Majesties & his joy & pride in all that you did of unselfish devotion for the country was unbounded, his one regret that he was past being of any active use to the King. I know that he had never had your Majesties out of his thoughts during that terrible time ...[1]

While the close link between the British monarchy and the armed forces was of long standing, the identification of the royal family with the special interests of the general population in time of war was a more recent phenomenon. It was in tune with the spirit of the time, interpreted until now in this narrative mainly by a member of a privileged class. But war, like death, had become a great leveller: the simple privations of civilians, if relative, were suffered in common; the fighting men went forth from all classes and communities (the women with them) and failed to return, to castle or cottage, with the same regularity. Old men forget: but old men also remember, with a clarity that defies reason, the distant past. Lord Mount Stephen, too old, so he thought, to do more than recklessly turn in his carefully garnered securities, and take a vicarious pride in his young Canadian relatives and English friends 'at the Front', was probably fully aware that from the familiar places of his boyhood, too, the young were pouring forth in numbers never hitherto approached in the professional, imperial wars of the past. Mary Symon, daughter of his old friend the Provost of Dufftown, was one of three poets of the north-east of Scotland, writing in the Doric, who conveyed with very much the same sentiments albeit differences of style, the going forth, the war experience, the coming—or not coming—back; the others were Charles Murray ('Hamewith') whose native Alford touched Symon country at the Cabrach (one of the Mount Stephen Trust parishes, the Cabrach had since 1815 had a library boasting the motto: 'Add to virtue knowledge'); and thirdly John Mitchell, born under Ben Rinnes, brought up in the

[1] RA GV CC47/694.

Cabrach and latterly proprietor of the Royal Athenaeum restaurant in Aberdeen.[1] Some of this verse was probably first published in the local Press; it would find its way to exiles the world over. It would lose something in translation, but the old fisherman at Brocket would have appreciated in the original Mary Symon's glimpse of the boy's fishing-rod left hooked-up in a willow high over the Dullan water, and of the alder tree where he had whittled his name:

> Doon, laich doon the Dullan sings—
> An' I ken o' an aul' sauch tree,
> Where a wee loon's wahnie's hingin' yet
> That's dead in Picardy;
> An' ilka win' fae the Conval's broo
> Bends aye the buss o' ern,
> Where aince he futtled a name that noo
> I'll read on the Soldier's Cairn.

George Stephen had come from Gordon country. Dame Nellie Melba in her memoirs recalled that in 'one of his rare moments of expansion' he had told her how as a boy he would earn a shilling by carrying a letter twelve miles for the old Duke of Richmond, heir to the extinct Dukedom of Gordon.[2] 'Running barefoot over the stubble is the first memory I have, and in a way it is one of the sweetest memories of all' he had told her; '. . . Those shillings I earned were the best earned money I ever made, because as you may know yourself, if you want to get over stubble with bare feet, the only way of doing it is to run. It's when you drop into a walk that you start to feel it . . .' Mount Stephen reminded her of her father, and one thing she recalled about her father was no doubt equally true of Mount Stephen: '. . . she had watched his face light when she sang a Scottish ballad and memories of his homeland crowded in on him . . .' That she sang to Mount Stephen one of the Robert Burns ballads in her popular repertoire is indicated by the mention in her memoirs of *Comin' thro' the Rye*. It was Mount Stephen who pointed out to her (as indeed he had once told Sir

[1] Mary Symon and John Mitchell were both born in 1863, Charles Murray in 1864. Mary Symon's poems are collected in *Deveron Days*, Aberdeen, 1933; John Mitchell's were privately printed; there is a copy in Aberdeen University Library; Charles Murray's collection: 'A Sough o' War' (London, 1917) is contained in *Hamewith and other poems*, first published London, 1927, many times reprinted. Murray was writing from South Africa, where he had seen war service.
[2] In 1876 he obtained the patent of Duke of Gordon, becoming Duke of Richmond and Gordon.

Mountstuart Grant Duff over lunch at a friend's house) that the
Rye was an Ayrshire stream—not the cereal—so that 'coming
through' meant crossing by a well-known ford. Again comparing
Mount Stephen with her father Melba wrote: 'He had the same
shrewd humour, the same absolute directness . . .' When she
thought of how 'this great man was largely instrumental in building
the Canadian Pacific Railway and bringing untold prosperity to
lands which would otherwise have remained desolate' this notable
Australian singer, Nellie Mitchell, 'felt proud indeed of being a
Scotchwoman'.[1]

Mary Symon's *A Recruit for the Gordons*—like Murray's *Bundle
and Go*—contains this shrewd humour: the ploughman, halfway up
the farm hierarchy, was off with the morning ('leavin' to 'list'
as 'Hamewith' puts it) the Gordon motto 'Bydand' on his cap—
somewhat ineptly, as at the feeing market a farmer would ask a
'likely lad': 'Are ye bidin'?' meaning: 'Are you staying put where
you are at present?' The worse the news from the Front, the
keener they were to go—most of them: both Mary Symon and
Murray are scathing about those who were not; 'total exemption'
was a suspect phrase. In the former's *After Neuve Chapelle*, there
are implications of local losses, and lines which now call to mind
the rows of headstones at that place carved with eastern symbols,
set at an angle to those with the 'Bydand' crest:

. . . . . .

Oh glens that gave the Gordons, is't you will give as well
The cohorts of the damned and done that heed nae Neuve Chapelle?

God! Will they ever wauken, the loons that sit at hame?
While din-faced Sikhs an' Ghurkas fecht to keep oor shores frae shame.
Oor kin fae a' the Seven Seas are tummelin' to the fray,
But there's laggards yet on lown hillsides 'neath skies that span the Spey,
On braes where Charlie's banner flew, an' Jean sae kindly kissed,
Where the very peweet's yammer is a wistfu' "Loon, gang 'list"—[2]

. . . . . .

[1] Melba, *Melodies and Memories*, pp. 267–71; John Hetherington, *Melba*, London,
1967, p. 188. David Mitchell, an exact contemporary of Mount Stephen, had set out
from Angus for Australia on a sailing ship in 1852. Hetherington writes (p. 81): '(Melba)
never cheapened her professional standing by singing for her supper; she would sing to
guests in her own house or at a party given by some intimate friend . . .'

[2] 'Jean' is Jean Maxwell, Duchess of Gordon, who helped to raise a regiment of
Gordon Highlanders during the Napoleonic War by passing to recruits their shilling
in a kiss from her mouth. (The battle of Neuve Chapelle was in 1915; conscription was
introduced in 1916.)

The shrewd humour is everywhere in *The Glen's Muster-Roll* (Symon again) as the schoolmaster takes us back to the scene of George Stephen's early education, listing with identifying phrases the boys now scattered overseas: Davie, in the German prison-camp Sennelager, post-cards cheerfully: 'I'm already owre the Rhine'. Gaspard Farrer's surprise at Frank Meighen's apparently sudden assumption of the rank of Colonel was as nothing to the 'Dominie's': '. . . Dick Macleod, his sanshach sel' (Guidsake, a bombardier!)' But the 'Dominie'

never crawed sae crouse

As the day they gaed the V.C. to my *filius nullius*.

But he winna sit "Receptions" nor keep on his aureole,
A' he says is "Dinna haiver, jest rax owre the Bogie Roll".
An' the Duke an' 's dother shook his han' an' speirt aboot his kin.
"Old family, yes; here sin' the Flood," I smairtly chippit in.
(Fiech! Noah's? Na—we'd ane wirsels ye ken, in '29.)
I'm nae the man tae stan' an' hear them lichtlie Loon o' Mine.

The laird's young brother is 'stan'in' owre his middle in the Flanders clort an' dub, Him 'at eese't to scent his hanky, an' speak o's mornin' "tub" '. But the humour wavers as the 'Dominie' contemplates Robbie, 'Front bench, a curly pow, A chappit hannie grippin' ticht a Homer men't wi' tow—' his potential scholarship winner, ('nae the first fun' fowin' peats') visualized once as a 'blythe young Bajan' [first year University student at Aberdeen]:

An' noo, an' noo I'm waitin' till a puir thing hirples hame—
Ay, 't's the Valley o' the Shadow, nae the mountain heichts o' Fame.
An' where's the nimble nostrum, the dogma fair and fine,
To still the ruggin' heart I hae for you, oh, Loon o' Mine?

Some indication of what the Scottish recruits thought of their adversaries was given in the reply of a Gordon home on leave to his parish minister's question: 'And what do you think of the Germans, Sammy?' Glancing hastily round, lest he be overheard speaking treason, the kilted Highlander admitted: 'They're just folk like ourselves'.

John Mitchell's *Tibbie Tamson o' the Buck* or *A Cabrach Wife's Views on Things in General* in 1917 was to have echoes in Gaspard Farrer's letter to John Sterling of 22 March of that year; Farrer's efforts to keep within the war diet were comparatively successful;

there was no difficulty with either meat or sugar but it was rather a trial to go short of wheaten bread: 'During my many trips over the St.P.M. & M. and C.P.R. it certainly never occurred to me that the day would ever come when one would be short of that product in which we were so much interested and which at that time no one would buy at a price remunerative to the poor farmer. You would be interested to see our substitutes, oatmeal bread, maize bread, barley bread . . .' Tibbie felt rather more strongly about the sugar, especially since the traditional Scottish confectionery still seemed plentiful; as to the bread: 'The fite bread—weel, it's dirty fite, like water fae the Dee, It palls upon the palate, an' it disna' please the e'e . . .' Even in the Cabrach, the local produce, from potatoes to whisky, were under restriction:

They've commandeer't the tatties, an' they've commandeer't the hay,
They've commandeer't the corn an' meal, forbyes the neeps an' strae,
They've commandeer't the fusky that keeps oot the caul' an' weet,
If they'd commandeer some common-sense, we'd get tae Berlin yet . . .

There were, however, local compensations, a hare or two, fish from the stream, a leg of 'braxy mutton', the odd pig or cattle-beast shared out in the Glen. And best of all, her daughter's Gordon Highlander husband home after the battle of the Aisne, although with an empty sleeve and covered in mud: Jean 'scraupit aff the dubs an' dirt until she cam' tae Jock'.

> An' aifterhin' he tauls aboot the Battle o' the Aisne,
> An' hoo *he* focht a hale platoon an' kill't them ane b' ane,
> Till deil a German Hun wis left tae cairry on the fray,
> So, pickin' up his ither airm, he stoppit for the day . . .

Wrote Miss Louey Lawrence to Frances Wolseley on 12 April 1917: '. . . We rejoice to know of your appointment to the Board of Agriculture where your help will be most useful—the right person in the right place . . . By the way, is there anywhere near you where we could get a few potatoes—here they are difficult to come by . . .'[1] Queen Mary's Diary for April 1917—the Court was at Windsor—records: 'We again went to Frogmore to finish planting our potato plot & worked from 3 to 5. Got very hot and tired'.[2]

The main factor behind these shortages, leaving aside the submarine warfare, was the proposal by the new Chancellor of the Exchequer, Bonar Law, accepted by the British Cabinet, to restrict

---

[1] PVW 140.   [2] Pope-Hennessy, *Queen Mary*, p. 508.

purchases from the United States.[1] Towards the end of 1916, following President Wilson's re-election, the American Federal Reserve Board had issued a warning to U.S. banks against giving further borrowing facilities to Allied Governments. Writing of this to Tuck on 1 December 1916, Farrer had used a phrase of Mount Stephen's: ' "What maun be, maun be", and if the people of the US shut down upon us, we must resign ourselves to get on as best we can without them . . .' Gaspard admitted to Sterling in his letter of 22 March 1917 that at least the wartime diet meant that his waistcoat buttons were less on duty. After his frugal meal, however, it is clear from his correspondence that he and his brothers could still enjoy not only coffee sent by a business acquaintance in Brazil but brandy supplied direct from his merchant in Cognac. But he was getting slightly impatient with America; possibly the reflection that but for the railroad pioneers there might have been no golden prairies influenced his sharp reaction on 6 February 1917 to a Press cutting sent to him by a friend of Mount Stephen, a former A.D.C. to the Governor-General of Canada, Lieut. General the Earl of Cavan, now serving with the B.E.F.:

I would not worry . . . I should sit tight and do nothing. If later we find—I say we, for I am in exactly the same boat as you—that we are mulcted for American Income Tax as well as British, it will be time enough to consider selling our holdings of Americans at present on loan to the Government. I have no intention of making any return to the US Government and do not advise you to either.

The American declaration of war on Germany on 9 April 1917 did not solve this particular problem, since special war taxes were then introduced. On 11 May Gaspard was writing to James Stillman, back in France after going through London in February ('more friendly than he has ever been before', Gaspard told Sterling):

. . . Lady Mount Stephen is busily engaged in expounding the intricacies of the US Income Tax Laws, and how Congress in its wisdom has decreed that a husband is bound to provide the funds for the payment of his wife's Income and Super Tax. But alas you know how deaf he is—or can be if he chooses! The form which Washington has sent us here to fill in is a triumph of obscurity, and leaves our own Income Tax Officials green with jealousy. And then to make confusion worse, the tax rate seems to be changed about every 24 hours, so that the rate of today is

[1] See Devlin, *Too Proud to Fight*, pp. 554 and 585-8.

never the rate of yesterday, nor again the rate for tomorrow. When your Government and ours have done there won't be much for us, and—horrible thought—it would seem that there would be no resource left to us but to enlist among the bureaucrats! ...

Gaspard had regretfully declined Sterling's invitation to Metis which in April he had seriously considered: there was too much work in hand at Bishopsgate and elsewhere. 'I have talked the matter over with the Boss and he quite concurs', he wrote on 24 April. Even with the advent of the U.S. on their side every ounce of service was needed if they were to prevail. On 26 May 1917 he wrote to Arthur Villiers, serving with the Oxfordshire Yeomanry in the B.E.F., who had written of the death at Gillemont of young Valentine Fleming. Gaspard had forwarded the letter to Robert Fleming and enclosed his reply with his letter: 'He came in to see me later in the day. Poor fellow, he could hardly speak, but it will be a satisfaction to you to know that your letter was greatly appreciated. I have seen a good deal of Fleming during the last two years, and his anxiety about his sons has always seemed to me to be almost beyond his control ...' Patrick Shaw-Stewart was home from Salonica and off to France. Gaspard's friend of the searchlights was on a fast ship in the North Sea. His brother Frank was working hard at the Red Cross, and at the Sandwich house (where again the Commanding Officer and his Brigade Major were guests), his other brother, Harry, had dug up some of the garden for vegetables, the gardener having gone to serve. (Wrote John Mitchell:

An' noo they're fichrin' wi' some fads 'boot plooin' parks an' plots,
An' ilka ane's a gair'ner fae Lan's En' tae John o'Groats;
Balgownie's goufin' links they'd saw wi' cabbages an' beans,
An' plant pitaties, leeks, an' kail on Murcar's bonnie greens ...

Gaspard was to write to James Norman Hill on 8 November 1922 of the re-seeding of the Sandwich golf course.) Now he continued his letter to Villiers: 'Lord Mount Stephen has gone down to Brocket for the summer. I heard from him this morning; he sends you his love ...'

THE BROCKET BOMB

On 22 June 1917, following a Sunday at Brocket, Gaspard wrote to Sterling whose message from Metis to the Boss had been a welcome surprise: he had feared Sterling had been unable to secure canoemen and had abandoned the trip altogether. Winter in England had lasted until the end of April, since when they had had the most continuously glorious weather Gaspard could ever remember there, day after day of bright sun 'with a clearness in the atmosphere that reminds one of Metis'. At Brocket it was 'a piping hot day' and Mount Stephen hardly left the house although Gian and Gaspard 'walked round the farm, and inspected the woods which German prisoners are cutting up'. He fancied there were few visitors at Brocket in these days; motoring had become impossible for lack of petrol and the train service was execrable. Most friends were busy on war work 'while most hosts and hostesses, however hospitable their instincts, find it almost impossible to entertain on account of lack of servants'. The Great Northern Report had arrived, the figures to 31 December satisfactory enough but Louis Hill's forecast of the probable increase in expenditure was anything but encouraging. There were rumours of a new ore lease but Gaspard could not make out exactly what the terms were. He wished James Norman would give as much attention to the property as he did to the Texas Oil Company and to golf. Again on 18 July 1917 Gaspard wrote of having been to Brocket where Sterling's recent cables to Mount Stephen had indicated a triumphant end to his fishing season 'though perhaps not equalling Mrs. Reford's performances'. There was also, however, news of the sudden death of Mrs. Meighen: her son-in-law Robert Reford had been trying to persuade her to Metis a few days earlier. 'She is the last of the Boss's sisters and the one about whom he cared the most. I expect he will feel her death a good deal, though outwardly he takes his troubles philosophically enough'. Elsie Meighen had been the youngest sister; Eleonora, Mrs. James A. Cantlie, had died in Montreal the previous December, a week after the death of her daughter, Mary Adami.

Mrs. Hill had sent them Joseph G. Pyle's life of James J. Hill, published that year in two volumes. Gaspard had 'just dipped into it; it looks to me as if it might be accurate enough in its facts, but a regular newspaper man's writing. Not a life that could possibly live or be of interest to any but those most immediately concerned; nine-tenths of it could have been cut out with advantage—at least that is my first impression'.

To Robert Winsor, whose two elder sons, Bob and Phil, had

joined up, Gaspard wrote on 11 July 1917 of air raids on London, Zeppelins coming in over Essex where Mrs. Cecil Baring's children were indignant at being ruthlessly despatched to the cellar. Despite air raid drill at Bishopsgate, 'I have not yet been told where my own funk hole is, but I intend to get there—at the double—when the time arrives'. Young Phil, now with the American Red Cross, was welcome, he repeated, at No. 7. He wrote again on the 26th that bombs had twice narrowly missed Barings. On 7 September he told Sterling:

> Yes, I see your letters to the Boss, and often too reading between the lines see the difficulties you are in in writing them. I usually try to write to him every other day at least; . . . I was at Brocket a fortnight ago and found them both in excellent spirits. He was looking better than I had seen him for some time, but they are both very deaf, and it requires all my exertions to make them both hear at the same time. It is rather melancholy to see the garden and grounds all going to the deuce, but it is of course inevitable and is the case with every place in England . . .

The weather in August and September had been deplorable 'disastrous to harvest and to progress on the Western Front'. He hoped to go away for a week or two but it was not easy: one committee sat daily and another weekly and he did not care to be absent from them. Travelling to Sandwich, moreover, was difficult, the road closed and the train service bad. He fancied he would have to invite the C.O. and his Brigade Major as guests again that winter if the house were not to be entirely commandeered. 'You talk in your letter of my motor car; did you not know that I have never possessed one and now do not suppose I ever shall. Those who are today the happy possessors of cars find themselves without chauffeurs and without petrol'. Turning to a more congenial subject:

> Your fishing record this year was particularly interesting. Do you not think that we in former years have gone too early and come away too soon? Looking at your catch and Mrs Reford's, and your results this year, that is the conclusion to which I have come. The Boss says tut, tut, it all depends on the season, but I have my doubts in this case whether he is right. My own belief is that to get there about the 21st June is early enough . . .

After two weeks at Sandwich—the longest holiday he had had since war broke out—Gaspard wrote to Sterling on 22 October 1917: 'I never enjoyed a holiday more, even the days when I did nothing but loaf went all too fast, and I rejoiced to find how easily I shall be able to be content in retirement and idleness'. There had been air-raids almost every night, and in London a bomb that week had just missed his house in St. James's Square. He continued:

On Saturday I went down to see the Boss for the Sunday rather congratulating myself that at any rate there I should be free from these disturbances. I did not get down till after dark, but on reaching the house found that the previous night a bomb had been dropped on their lawn about 120 yards from the house. Every window on that side was blown in and many of the window frames as well, besides many windows elsewhere. But happily this was the extent of the damage. It occurred at 9.30 at night and our poor friends had difficulty in finding a weather-tight room to sleep in. I am afraid she is a good deal upset, though she would not admit it; but it is quite plain that her nerves are all on edge. He, you will be amused to hear, went quietly to bed and never had a better night. Next morning I went out to see the hole—about three feet deep and 8 to 10 yards in diameter. The trees all round are scored with gashes made presumably by pieces of the bomb or flints thrown up. Many bits of steel, presumably parts of the bomb, have been found all round, so far as 200 yards from the scene of the explosion. In one of the trees there is a steel bolt about an inch in diameter, which has penetrated so deeply into the stem that no effort of mine could move it. If any one of those pieces had gone through the windows of the house, the results might have been serious for those inside. I cannot tell you how thankful I am that they have escaped. I had gone down partly in the hopes of persuading them not to come up to London at all this winter, and so escape the risks of bombs. It was certainly not a propitious moment to urge my suit.

Blossy will remember that after crossing the bridge over the water on the way to the house one mounts a hill, and as one gets on the level there is a white gate, inside the gate being the lawn until one gets up to the house, that is where the bomb fell between the gate and the house, and as I say about 120 yards from the latter ... We rather expect a tiresome time for the rest of this month while the moon is bright. How much I have made of all this, and yet what a trifle it is to what our poor fellows are undergoing at the Front. Not once or twice a month but most continuously day and night. Bombs and shells and every other kind of horror. I wonder how they stand it or how anyone lives through it ...

He had dined the previous week to meet the American Red Cross Contingent and listed the guests, American and British: 'I never saw such magnificent pearls and should judge they must have been worth at least twice the amount of the splendid subscription which the American Red Cross presented to our Red Cross ... Tell

Blossy the American Y.M.C.A. have asked permission to put up dormitories in the garden of St. James's Square . . . 100 beds with sittingrooms and offices . . . They have promised to do their building without cutting down the trees . . .' This became known as the Washington Inn.

That summer Canada had launched its first 'Victory Loan' campaign. Lord Shaughnessy immediately promised a large subscription on behalf of the Canadian Pacific (which had already lent considerable sums in cash and securities to both British and Canadian Governments) to be doubled if the Canadian public subscribed a certain sum. He received a cable:

Hearty congratulations on your speech on Monday and on what the C.P.R. has done and promise to do to help win this brutal war. Am proud of the Company when I think of the change in its position since the day when its application for a quotation on the London Stock Exchange was curtly refused.

Mount Stephen.

In the event, all three of Canada's Victory Loans (1917, 1918 and 1919) were substantially over-subscribed.[1]

STILLMAN, STERLING AND BLOSS

To Winsor on 17 November 1917 Gaspard conjectured on the various methods by which the wealthy were likely to be denuded of the greater part of their incomes: '. . . I look forward to a great increase in the death duties. To me the very big individual incomes have always seemed a danger in the community and a very moderate blessing to the possessor, and the inheritance of big fortunes an unmixed evil for the inheritors . . .' On this subject he wrote one of his teasing letters to Sterling on 15 January 1918. He had not heard from him direct since 25 October: 'But for your letters to the Boss I should have begun to doubt your continued existence; happily, however, from a recent letter to him I learn that you "cannot afford to die", and inferentially that present and prospective burdens of the State make it almost too expensive for you to live. As you know, on the subject of Death Duties I have never been quite sound according to your view, though I have never before seen reason to bless them with enthusiasm. Your letter however

[1] See Brown and Cook, *Canada 1896–1921*, chapter 12 'The War Economy'.

has again modified my views, and if Death Duties ensure your continued life they will have my approval without reserve . . .'

Stillman was back in New York but not at all well: Gaspard feared he would never be fit for work again. Writing on 2 February 1918 to James Stillman Junior—now practically head of the City Bank, which Gaspard said must be a great satisfaction to his father, he went on 'I hate to think of the weakness and suffering that has fallen upon this strong and self-reliant man . . .' He quoted Sterling 'his courage never forsakes him'. Stillman died that year at the age of 68. Burr writes that his reticence: 'so marked an idiosyncrasy and which he made use of with the skill of a trained psychologist—heightened and deepened for strangers or mere acquaintances the impression of power. That power was real . . . When a man says nothing, nothing whatever, but instead of answering sits there fixing on you a penetrating, immovable gaze, and all the while you know he has illimitable power either to make or mar, you grow afraid . . .'[1] The other side of his life—his friendship with the American woman painter, the impressionist Mary Cassatt, sister of Alexander Cassatt of the Pennsylvania Railroad, who had settled in France, and his passion for collecting women's dresses— hardly served to clarify the character of this mysterious man who 'Had he not been a banker . . . would no doubt have been a fashion designer'.[2]

A member of a recent United States mission to London was shocked to see how tired their people all looked, Gaspard had told Winsor on 17 November 1917. (Earlier he had himself written: 'the last three years has made us all old men'.) 'Of course that is inevitable', he went on, 'but I am confident there is plenty of fight in us left . . .' His reaction to Lord Lansdowne's 'peace offensive' made public in the latter's letter to the *Daily Telegraph* that month (it had been turned down by *The Times*), was conveyed to Winsor on 6 December: President Wilson might be far off from reality, but Lord Lansdowne was equally so in his appreciation of the German mentality of the moment. With parts of the letter Gaspard disagreed *in toto*; with parts, while he agreed in principle, he saw no evidence of the Germans viewing the matter from a like standpoint 'so that even where one agrees, one regards his pronouncement as unfortun-

[1] Burr on *Stillman*, p. 197.
[2] Frederick A. Sweet, *Miss Mary Cassatt, Impressionist from Pennsylvania*, Norman 1966, p. 182.

ately inopportune, and this is the general feeling here'. He and his brothers were living in one corner of the house in St. James's Square, he told both Winsor and Sterling that winter, partly for lack of servants, partly in the hope of making the coal allowance last out. A trip to their bedrooms was like a passage to the North Pole. The house next door had just been taken over by the Government and they were in dread of being the next victims. But they weren't grumbling: a nephew who had transferred from the Cavalry to the Royal Flying Corps had just been shot down and was dead. Patrick Shaw-Stewart 'our partner that was to be' was killed in Flanders on 30 December.

The Mount Stephens spent Christmas at Brocket but on 15 January 1918 Gaspard told Sterling: 'The Boss is in town and glad to be up. He is very well and sensibly acquiescent in the inevitable discomforts of life under present conditions'. Reporting to Tuck on the 24th that the Mount Stephens were 'very glad to be up with a chance of seeing something of their fellow creatures', he added 'Cavan has been home on leave and very nearly lost the sight of his eye cutting rhododendrons, a branch sweeping back and hitting him in the face . . .' His 'friends in New York' wrote that the confusion at Washington 'passed all understanding'. Answering Sterling's last letter he wrote: 'Your pious wish to have our War Office made me laugh'. To Beverley MacInnes in Toronto, Mount Stephen's former secretary, Gaspard wrote on 28 January: 'If you were to see him sitting in his chair talking I doubt whether you would consider him older than when you left, but locomotion is now a serious difficulty to him, and a walk up and down Carlton House Terrace, or at Brocket as far as the kitchen garden and back, is more than he can attempt on many days . . .' The head of the Brocket bomb had been found in the hole, 'a pretty solid piece of metal which I could not lift without taking two hands to it . . .' Herrings in the west end were sevenpence and smelts as high as a shilling a piece.

John Sterling died at Grand Metis on 5 July 1918 at the age of seventy-four. There is again a gap in the Farrer letter-books for most of that year; although Sterling had tended latterly to write direct to Mount Stephen, Gaspard would certainly have commented on this event to one of his diminishing circle of correspondents. One is left wondering to what extent Sterling's preoccupation with death duties at the turn of the year, followed by

Stillman's death in March, contributed to his own demise at an age which it almost seems he must have reached many years before. Stillman's biographer Burr writes of a 'certain strain of mysticism and intense emotion, which lay at the bottom of both natures. These feelings, probably the very last of which the world around them would have suspected as dominant in a shrewd lawyer and successful banker, were, one suspects, in both men the outcome of an imaginative and intense loneliness. They were real, however. Mr. Stillman told more than one friend of being awakened in his house in Paris by a strong awareness of John Sterling's need and finding, by cable, that his friend's mother had died that night . . .'[1] It is doubtful if, even suffering the repercussions of wartime conditions, Sterling's groove-bound daily routine had altered one iota. Farrer, coping simultaneously in August 1913 with an American and an Argentinian issue, had boasted to him: 'My hours of attendance in the morning have almost equalled yours, and I have stayed much later at night than you ever do, and I don't intend in future to submit to your posing to me as an example in the matter of business attendance'. One can only hazard a guess that to someone Gaspard penned a sadly triumphant postscript to the effect that at last John Sterling had passed over, and that without doubt all the trumpets had sounded for him on the other side.

On 11 December 1918 Farrer acknowledged letters from J. O. Bloss, one enclosing 'the Gas Company's Resolution about J. W. with his photograph'. (Sterling had been on the board of several such companies.) 'It would probably be difficult in any photograph to reproduce the bright spirit of the man, but this particular photograph, to my mind, represents him neither in spirit nor in attitude. But we who cared for him so much are no doubt difficult to satisfy . . .' It is even possible that Gaspard had been at Metis that year; Bloss had found a fishing rod and box which he thought might have been left by him. Bloss had given up the house which latterly he had shared with Sterling and was established at the Metropolitan Club, where they had both been accustomed to spend a good deal of their leisure time. Seven days later Gaspard was writing to George H. Church, of Sterling's firm, Shearman and Sterling:

I very much appreciated your cabling me the news of poor Blossie's

---

[1] Burr, op. cit. pp. 190-1.

death. I confess it was a shock, but on second thoughts I am inclined to think it is as well that he has followed his great friend . . . he had no one to look after him.

But what a tragedy it is with these two men who started the year apparently in the best of health and no reason why they should not have many years to live before them, and both have gone. You must have known him well and I know will regret him as I do. To me personally he was always charming, absolutely unselfish and only anxious to find some way in which he could serve me, both in New York and at Metis . . . Particularly at Metis as part host with Sterling he was always first to try and get me the best pools, the best canoe-man etc, etc. I shall miss him much with his cheery, hearty laugh and unfailing good temper . . . Stillman, Sterling and Blossie were the three men whom I knew best in New York and all have gone this year. He had written to me several times recently and was obviously feeling poor Sterling's death more and more as time went on. Probably he hardly knew himself how much he leaned on Sterling's stronger character . . .

QUEEN MARY'S JOY-RIDE

On 10 August 1918, in a long letter from Queen Mary to the King about various activities (they were often separated as each made their exhausting tours of centres of military or civilian activity) one comes across the unexpected confession:

Then this afternoon I actually took a "joy ride"—went to Brocket for two hours—Such a lovely warm day at last. We found dear old Ld. Mount Stephen wonderfully well considering he is in his 90th year. He went in a little pony chaise with us to the garden which looked very pretty just with some roses & ordinary flowers, no bedding out or anything of that kind, as they have no gardeners, only 1. or 2. old crocks & some women . . .[1]

Years later, Frances Wolseley was to write of the Brocket garden she remembered:

. . . the little formal garden, with its bay trees in the big pots, and the red brick house behind them. Then the great beech trees that overshadowed, in the heat of summer, the sloping path that led down to the great lake. In winter one had the outline of these high trees and their branches, and in between one caught peeps of the water below, where the moorhens swam gaily about; there was always variety and something new to look for. Then in summer the path led one to those ancient yews which

[1] RA GV CC8/219.

Gian, with her skill in garden lay-out, had rescued from the undergrowth
of laurels that had been allowed to conceal their beauty. In between the
rich green yews she and her practical gardener would plan out square
beds filled with massed pink verbena, hyacinth candicans and many
other plants, and one joined, as a guest, in that planning . . .

Gian wrote to Queen Mary the day after the joy-ride:

> We feel we must send our heartfelt thanks to Your Majesty for the
> "Perfect Afternoon" which we had yesterday, every minute of which was
> a delight to us.
> I cannot tell Your Majesty how much good it did "dear George". Your
> Majesty seemed to revive him, & he was so happy & so well all the evening
> & we sat out by the Front door till dinner time, talking over our happy
> afternoon and Your Majesty's goodness & kindness to us & of the
> kindness it was to make an afternoon to come down here.
> It is always such a joy & delight to have Your Majesty in our house
> and Princess Mary & Prince George were an additional joy. George says
> that Prince George reminds him so much of the King, especially when he
> smiles. Prince George is most attractive. I think Your Majesty knows how
> much we think of Princess Mary. She grows more like Your Majesty
> every day. Again dearest Madam please accept our heartfelt gratitude
> for so perfect an afternoon & with our respectful love . . .[1]

THE ARMISTICE: MANIFOLD CHANGES

After the Armistice on 11 November 1918 it was to Robert
Winsor in Boston that Gaspard first attempted to communicate
his feelings. 'No words that I know in their most exaggerated
superlative can fit the situation', he wrote on 14 November, '. . . In
this country where everything has been under Government control
it will be difficult to get back into the habits of thought that ruled
our lives before the war, and perhaps still more difficult to adopt
those new habits of thought and new ways of business which the
changed conditions of affairs will demand . . .' To J. J. Hill's
son-in-law Michael Gavin in New York he wrote on the same
day: '. . . On the whole people in this country have taken the end
of the war as soberly as one could wish; a few of the very young,
boys and girls, have been making merry, but the great majority of
people have lost too many members of their families to do more
than be thankful that the fighting is over . . .' He thanked him for

[1] RA GV CC47/589.

news of the Hill family, especially of Mrs. Hill, and hoped to pay her a visit when he could cross the Atlantic. Describing how at No. 7 they stumbled about the passages by the light of a tallow dip: 'I can hardly believe that we shall ever return to our former extravagant ease of life, and I for one shall not much regret that. Some of the Spartan simplicity of life which Lord Mount Stephen used to preach but not practise, will be none the worse for any of us ...' To John Pillsbury, who for some time had miraculously been restoring the fortunes of the Pillsbury Washburn Flour Mills in Minneapolis (another of those properties which Farrer had believed would come out right in the end: it possessed, besides, the valuable asset, in days of increased use of electricity, of the St. Anthony Falls, and as Farrer was to write to Pillsbury on 17 March 1919: 'Men may come and men may go, but presumably the Mississippi will flow on for ever, and in these days of electricity the power be of a value which was not dreamed of in former times ...') he wrote on 15 November 1918: '... Anything so dramatically sudden as the collapse of Germany could hardly be conceived. If we here in Europe have had to bear the burden and heat of the day, it was without doubt your country's assistance that proved the deciding factor in victory ...' He added: 'I sent (the 1918 figures) on to Lord Mount Stephen, who with Mr. Hill was one of the original owners of the water power now belonging to the Company. He has always taken the keenest interest in your North West country and follows its affairs today. He writes me this morning: "Messrs. Pillsbury and Loring have done well and deserve all the credit you give them ..." ' To J. O. Bloss, the letter he would never receive, he wrote on 12 December: '... The Demobilisation of crowned heads seems the only demobilisation that is easy in practice. We have been trying to get back members of our staff and members of our household in London and Sandwich, but so far without success ... I feel all the better for ... eating about half of what one used to. We have not in our house touched butcher's meat for more than a year, and certainly do not miss it ... The greatest scarcity is fuel and light ... At Sandwich we are happy to get the military out of our house by the New Year ... We are looking forward to spending a week there at Christmas. Lord and Lady Mount Stephen will be at Brocket, but will probably return to town immediately after'.

Even the Armistice did not automatically bring an end to anxiety and sorrow. Young Phil Winsor had not been heard of for some time, and it was only after 'everyone moving heaven and earth to get news' that Gaspard discovered that he had died alone in a French hospital on 24 October, and arranged for his brother to collect his effects. Writing early in 1919 to one of the younger generation in New York, Gaspard was glad to see him signing himself 'still as Junior. During these last five years, we in this country have never dared to ask our friends after sons and brothers for it was impossible to follow the losses or know who was alive and who was dead, and it is now almost the same with my friends in America . . .'

The death of John Sterling posed the question of who was to be responsible in the United States for Mount Stephen's securities and balances; this was happily settled by George Church taking these over. Writing about this on 28 February 1919 to John Turnbull in Montreal, Gaspard added:

You will be glad to hear that Lord Mount Stephen has so far escaped cold and influenza. We have been having a very trying winter, cold weather with a great deal of rain and week after week passing without a glimpse of the sun. It is a most trying time for old people, and with all the influenza about we have been in terror lest he should have it. Lord Mount Stephen is hoping any day to hear from, or better still to see, Frank Meighen; he is at Cologne in command of his battalion and had hoped to get away before now, but we understand that his demobilization is unlikely for the present.

On 26 April 1919 Farrer wrote a long letter to James Norman Hill, acknowledging one of October 1918 with photograph of the latter's Long Island house, and bringing him up to date with the news in general. He would defer a visit to the ample pile until Atlantic shipping conditions had improved—he was 'too old for the four in a berth business'. Released from the censor's grip he described the wartime desecration of Sandwich—the little river had been developed as a port through which latterly all munitions had been shipped by barge, or by train ferry to Calais; nearly 20,000 men had been at work there, and hundreds of miles of railway track covered what had once been grass meadows. At No 7 St. James's Square he hoped soon to reopen his library. Most of the surviving Bishopsgate staff were back (in another letter to a cousin he talked of 'returned warriors and accumulated ladies'): 'I at least am certainly not fit to cope with the new conditions in business . . .' He continued:

The Boss is in town and in great form, better than I have seen him for some time past. He will be 90 on the 5th June next. She also is well and in great form. She has just been buying herself a Queen Anne coffee pot, much to her delight, and has got it home safely without his discovering it. The question now is, if she has it out on the table to use and enjoy, whether he will discover it or not—if he does there will be Hail Columbia. And then there is not only the danger of his discovering it, but the greater danger of the indiscretions of still more observant friends and guests! So you can see, poor lady, no sooner are the troubles of war over than others come along . . .

'The Captain' had let his ancestral home and was living in the dower-house. '. . . He says he is broke . . .' His son got through the war unscathed but had rebelled against the family plan for him to go into the Farrer law office and had taken up forestry . . . he had missed some lectures at Cambridge on demobilization but sent his wife to them instead and passed with great success. He went on: 'Your forecast of Ore Certificates has proved correct, and recent dividends, or rather such small part of them as our Government now allows us to retain, have been most acceptable: they stand between me and the workhouse. How pleased your father would have been had they come in his time'. What, he asked, had happened to E. T. Nichols? He hadn't written for several years and Gaspard never saw his signature on Great Northern matters. Farrer had written to Nichols on 8 February 1917 congratulating him on his election as a director of the Chase Bank (the letter quoted above p. 50).

Drought followed the winter's rains and in June 1919 Farrer was writing to Lord Cunliffe, on whose New Issues Committee he had been sitting for five years—and which he was now anxious should be disbanded—'. . . I tremble for my walnut trees, in which I am much more interested than in the Peace Conference . . .' By the end of July he had resigned from this last committee and was thinking again in terms of a trip to America by 1920 . . . even a passage by aeroplane, he thought, might be available.

MOUNT STEPHEN AT NINETY

Frances Wolseley's work in Sussex had brought her into contact with a new friend with whom in 1918 she had taken Massetts Place, an Elizabethan manor house, where they offered training for women in small-holding. Mount Stephen wrote on 16 December 1918: 'Many thanks for your interesting letter which I received this morning. I am so glad to hear you are well and happy in your quarters . . .' Again he returned a cheque repaying a loan 'which I hope you will accept as a Christmas present from your old God-father'.[1] This was followed on New Year's Day 1919 by a gift of pheasants from Brocket. In June Frances yielded to Lady Mount Stephen's insistence that she attend a Buckingham Palace garden party, etiquette demanding that she be 'presented' anew on assuming her title. Any reluctance was chiefly associated with the cost of dressing for the occasion—eighteen guineas, as it turned out. Her diary records:

> The King was the first to come our way, and quickly perceived Lady Mount Stephen. He asked about my Godfather, and said that although he was 90 years of age, he ought to come to the garden party in a bath chair.

Frances was presented and was much gratified at being congratulated on her 'splendid work for women'. Then Queen Mary approached . . . 'she came directly to Lady Mount Stephen and had a little talk with her, also about my dear Godfather'. Her Majesty also had an apt remark for Frances. 'I felt sure that my Godfather, sitting comfortably at Brocket in the little entrance hall, feeding his tame pheasants and ducks, as was his wont, would be pleased to hear upon (Gian's) return that his goddaughter had been satisfactorily presented'.[2]

Frances records her anxiety that year about her mother's health. During the autumn she made repeated requests to be allowed to visit her at Hampton Court Palace, but was put off. Then one Sunday during a rail strike Louisa telegraphed asking her daughter to come that day if possible, and Frances set off by car.

> She chanced to be well that day, and we had a touching little reconciliation, when amidst bitter tears on my part, I craved her pardon for anything that I might unwittingly have done to hurt or pain her, whereby I might have given her the impression that I had not revered both my parents. Seeing her lying there, so strangely active-minded and yet bodily helpless, so girlish looking, for this was the impression that remained for always after, I felt what a wonderful charm she had. Then too, her repeated assurances, that I was to believe that any faults in our understanding had been on her side, made me feel the fineness of her

---

[1] PVW 140.   [2] PVW 121/1104 ff.

character, which though sometimes concealed must in the end assert
itself, and I left her room feeling a greater admiration for her fine qualities
than I had ever done before . . .[1]

Louisa died on 10 April 1920. Driving away after the funeral
service at St. Paul's which Gian had attended Frances learned the
terms of her mother's Will. At first she obviously thought it would
be easy to prove that her father's intentions for her had been clearly
stated in his original memorandum and would stand. It gradually
came home to her that this was revoked by the later one and that
litigation was neither practical nor wise.[2] Gian had written on 18 April
with a cordial invitation to Brocket. Frances' memoirs record:

Some weeks passed, and I paid a visit to my Godfather, who was full of
interest in my mother's Will, and begged me the first evening to draw
my chair well near his, so that I might relate to him clearly the conditions
. . . Having ascertained what they were and that a small annuity was mine
together with the marriage settlement money, he made a pretext of having
left his notebook under his pillow upstairs, in order to send his wife
away in search of it. Then it was that he asked me "How will you manage?"
Had I said that I was going to be badly off, he would, I am confident,
have offered to help me, but knowing that I could just manage, and particularly so, with the shared country house, I said "I can manage alright".
He beamed on me with pride and a degree of satisfaction, that rewarded
me well for my answer.[3]

   On 18 February 1920 the Prince of Wales had paid a visit to
Brocket on his return from a very successful tour of Canada and the
United States. Frank Meighen had given a dance in his honour at
the Drummond Street house in Montreal. The following day Gian
wrote to Queen Mary: '. . . we enjoyed it so much that dear George
was very anxious I should write Your Majesty how much the Prince
impressed him. HRH's charming simplicity struck him very much
and HRH's wonderful sense and thoughtfulness about all he has
seen . . . it is no wonder the Prince captivated Canada and America
. . .'[4] Frances Wolseley records: 'It was not merely because he was
Prince of Wales and likely to become King in future years that my
Godfather invariably had beside his bed the youthful likeness of
King Edward VIII. He used often to say: "That young man has
a great future before him; I admire his character" '.

[1] PVW 121/1117.   [2] PVW 121/1124 ff.
[3] PVW 121/1126.   [4] RA GV CC47/642.

From Balmoral Castle Queen Mary wrote to Gian on 29 September 1920:

It was such a pleasure getting your letter & hearing a good account of you & "dear George" from Brocket. I am sorry it has been such a wretched summer for him & that he has in consequence not been able to be out as much as usual. That the sight is beginning to fail grieves me much but I suppose this is to be expected at his wonderful age ...

The Queen agreed about the difficulty of picking up 'anything of historical interest except by paying huge sums & then the things are not worth it which is annoying to my businesslike mind, a sentiment which "dear George" will highly approve of!!!'.[1]

END OF TRACK

Sometime in 1921 Frances Wolseley went up to London to see Mount Stephen, recording merely: 'The years are going on, and I felt compelled to do so, as it might be the last time, and I wanted to see him, still vigorous enough to enjoy life'. Certainly it appears that by the middle of that year Mount Stephen was neither vigorous nor enjoying life. First the impact of the war, then the momentary satisfaction of the peace had roused him; now all was anticlimax. Shielded, presumably, from a consciousness of the post-war residues of changing labour relations, social demoralization, attitudes of 'eat, drink and be merry for tomorrow the deluge', he still felt he had lived for long enough. One cannot imagine that he would have entered with any enthusiasm into Gaspard's preoccupation with the mystery of why high-quality coal which cost 32–33s at the pithead should cost 63s a ton at his door, or why attendances at cricket matches and race meetings, and dashing about in char-à-bancs should suddenly be on the increase, far less with the problem of how Britain was to pay her debts to America, or whether the Allies would pay theirs to her, or whether the day would ever come when the people of the United States would be inclined to treat the railroads fairly. (As to Britain's debts to America, even Gaspard's statistical flair failed him when it occurred to him to assess the notional value of flesh and blood and set it against the cost of armaments.) Past even worrying about the disinclination of the sons and grandsons of the old railroaders

[1] RA GV CC44/233.

to continue on the treadmill—a 'disquieting feature of the situation today' which Gaspard had noted on a post-war trans-atlantic visit—Mount Stephen had arranged his affairs to his satisfaction and felt no further responsibility towards anyone. Gaspard wrote to Tuck on 30 July 1921: 'He has felt the heat a good deal and it is difficult to keep up his interest in life and all that is going on, but his physical health is good considering his age. They are at Brocket and likely to be there until the autumn'. On 22 August he was writing to Frank Meighen, who was planning to come over in October: '. . . Your uncle has, alas, failed very much this year and it is increasingly difficult to rouse him to interest in anything that is passing. He is at Brocket and living the quietest possible life . . .'

Queen Mary had written from Buckingham Palace on 10 August:

Dearest Gian

The King & I are deeply distressed to hear that our dear old friend is ill & at his great age I must confess it makes us feel very anxious. We feel deeply for you knowing how unhappy you must be at seeing his distress & discomfort. It was too kind of you writing to tell us about the illness & of course we will not mention it to anyone. Thank God dear Sir James is with you for a few days as he is a great comfort & support. I hope dearest you will not overdo yourself with the nursing but will be good & cheer "dear George" up during the day time. I shall rely on you to keep me informed how matters go & I hope the next report may be a better one. You know how much I am thinking of you. Perhaps you will give our love to "dear George" if it will not make him suspicious.

Ever yr. most affect: old friend
Mary R.
Mary is *much* grieved.[1]

Perhaps for the first time Gian disregarded a royal command: from this time onwards she rarely left her husband. The engagement of the Princess Mary to Henry, Viscount Lascelles, eldest son of the Earl of Harewood, was announced on 24 November 1921. Gian was to write to Queen Mary on 4 December:

. . . I was just able on that Friday afternoon [25th November] to show him his gift to her, for he was very ill that day, but he was able to look at it & smile, he was just semi conscious . . . From Saturday morning till *Tuesday* at 11.45 he was quite unconscious, and throughout those days we

[1] RA GV CC44/236.

thought every breath would be the last; it was a particular agony to me all that Sunday 27th & yet to feel that after 24 years I was still with him holding his dear hands was I felt much to be thankful for indeed & that during these four months I had never had to leave him for 5 minutes day or night through being ill or knocked up. I am so grateful but Your Majesty will know what an agony those last days were—he died just as he had lived, just simply, breathing less & less—until it stopped, and life was ended. Col. Meighen, who had come over on purpose to see him has been everything to me, he sat up all those nights with me & during the day too. I cannot say what care & tenderness he has given to me & his great love & devotion to his Uncle was such a comfort, his Uncle was to him the great figure in his life. I do not know what I should have done without him, my sister, and George's devoted friend Gaspard Farrer, who wrote the little appreciation in the Times. I have had all this love & care, as also that of dear Sir James, who has never left him since he returned from Scotland . . .

Yesterday we laid him to rest as simply as we could, knowing that he wished this; his own Canadian wagon carried him to Church, his own horses & coachmen drove it & his own men carried him to his grave, so tenderly & carefully, & we have laid him beside the grave of his first wife, & there is room for me when the time comes. I have only one thought how can I be sensible & as he would wish me to be, & after all these years his influence will help me, for I only lived for him, & the rest of my life will be filled with the pride of having been the wife of such a truly great & simple man. Your Majesty will forgive this long letter, but I can't help writing to tell you all that is in my heart before I think of writing to anyone . . .

Your Majesties' & Princess Mary's dear message came to me just before starting yesterday & I had it (in) my pocket to help me through & just thinking of Your Majesty's courage on all occasions it gave me courage.

My most respectful duty & gratitude to the King & my love and gratitude to Your Majesty for the friendship to us both through all these years, it was our greatest & most valued possession . . .[1]

In her reply Queen Mary wrote: '. . . You know well what we felt about your "dear George" and how truly we looked on him as an old and devoted friend, ever ready to help at all times & in all kinds of ways. We do indeed mourn a dear friend & shall ever miss his genial presence . . .'[2]

Gaspard Farrer in turn wrote to Edward Tuck on 7 December 1921:

[1] RA GV CC47/694.   [2] RA GV CC44/237, 7 December 1921.

You and Mrs Tuck will like to hear something of your old friend's last days. He was really never ill in the sense of having a specific illness but was just worn out with length of years. He had been failing most visibly throughout this year, but it was not till the beginning of August that we saw any reason for serious alarm. He then had a fit of dizziness, took to his bed & never left it. From time to time we had very anxious moments, but he always rallied and was often able to sit up in bed, smoke his cigar and tell his wife with a chuckle to clear out & let him have a quiet hoose [*sic*]. As a matter of fact he could not abide her being out of his sight, and she practically never was during all those four months. You know something of her devotion to him; she had absolutely given up her life to him, abandoning all her former interests and pleasures to minister to his wishes & comforts. She has been quite splendid all through, and I could not have believed myself that anyone, man or woman, could have stood the strain, mental and physical, which she has been under. Lord Mount Stephen was unconscious for the last 4 days of his life, and the doctors assure us that he was throughout free from suffering. He himself was longing to go and for his sake we cannot regret that the end has come; he could have got no more pleasure out of life. He is buried by the side of his first wife in the churchyard at Lemsford, which you may remember, just outside the park gates.

The Press have rendered a wonderful tribute to his character and work, and the sympathy of his many friends has been most touching. Among the messages was that from you and Mrs. Tuck, which Lady Mount Stephen greatly appreciated for she knows the real affection which you both had for him. She had been talking to me shortly before his death of how she was wishing to write to Mrs. Tuck; I do not suppose she had time; she really had time for nothing but nursing him. I am going down to Brocket tomorrow to try and help her with all the business that now falls upon her. My impression is that she will stay on at Brocket for some weeks and then give it up for good. It will be too large a house and place for her only, but I hope she will find some other smaller home in the country where she can amuse herself with her garden, her cows, and other country interests.

He added: 'We had had cabled intelligence of Mrs. Hill's death a few days previous to Lord Mount Stephen's, but we thought it better not to tell him . . .' He wrote to Louis Hill on 12 January 1922: '. . . We did not dare tell him about your mother's death; indeed when the news arrived he was barely conscious and the news could only have distressed him. He always had the greatest admiration for her and her character, as I know she had for him and his. The simplicity and truth of their natures must especially have appealed the one to the other . . .' Louis had sent a copy of the resolutions passed in tribute to Mount Stephen at a recent Great Northern meeting, and Gaspard commented: 'I always thought your father and Lord Mount Stephen were an ideal combination and together personified imagination controlled by judgment to perfection, while their entire confidence in each other gave them a strength which surmounted all obstacles and all difficulties'. Time was when he might have put it differently, but the germ of truth was there.

Writing to George Church in New York on 20 December 1921 to thank him and his wife for a message of sympathy in which ladies of the Sterling connection had joined, Gaspard said: 'Lord Mount Stephen's death certainly will mean a great break in my life; I have known him for 41 years, and for over 30 have either met or corresponded almost daily . . . You will probably have seen from the papers that he has left his estate, or at least what remains of it, to the King Edward's Hospital Fund; he had already provided for everyone who had a vestige of claim upon him in his life. Needless to tell you the legacy falls to the hospitals at a very auspicious moment, as they are sadly in need of funds. My endeavour will be to keep the fund together as a fund and prevent the capital being dissipated in operating costs. Poor Sterling, the very thought of its disappearance would have been enough to horrify him through and through; he had taken such infinite pains with its accumulation and the selection of its investments'. One of the first tasks, however, was to provide a sum of £710,000 for death duties, and the King's Fund was consulted as to which securities they would prefer to have sold, and which they would rather keep. The lists which appear in the records show that the bulk of Mount Stephen's money was still in American Railways, with large sums also invested in Argentina and Uruguay. Farrer remarked to Tuck on 30 August 1922 on a recent rise in the price of Great Northern and Northern Pacific, adding: 'There are still a good many holders in this country and some of considerable amounts. Many of them women, and most of them friends of Lord Mount Stephen; people whom I should never have put into an ordinary share. Can't you see him with his cheery optimism brushing aside with some impatience my timid banker's caution, and declaring that GN and NP Shares were as good an investment as he knew, as indeed for many years they were, and would have been still but for Government interference . . .'

Gaspard had been fond of referring to Mount Stephen as 'our breezy Brocket friend'. In the appreciation which he had written some months earlier for *The Times*—insisting that when the time came it should be published anonymously—he stressed this characteristic:

... What was the secret of Lord Mount Stephen's success? The broad, massive brow, the finely-shaped head and hands, the voice ringing with a burr racy of his native land, all told of tenacity and power; in mind simple and direct, in spirit extraordinarily buoyant, he had the gift of instantaneously inspiring confidence and arousing enthusiasm and devotion; but his optimism was always tempered with caution and sagacity. This buoyancy of spirit was perhaps his most striking characteristic, permeating his life and all he did and all who came in contact with him; in his presence doubt and difficulties vanished and hope and confidence revived ...

... Business happened to be his line, business in which there played the spirit of New-World adventure, which his own nature gladly met half-way. Nearly all his ventures were brought to success, and success was dear to his soul—not for the money which success brings, for that he cared little, and gave with quixotic generosity to all who had claims upon him, and to any cause which he thought deserving; but he believed in hard work, and loved to see the results of creative effort and the prosperity and happiness they brought to others.

Naturally shy, he was rarely persuaded to pay visits, but under his own roof in Montreal, on the Matapedia and at Metis, and later at Brocket, it was his great happiness to gather his friends together; his contemporaries have passed away, but he loved the young, and many still remember, and will miss, his cheery welcome, the simplicity of his ways and thoughts, his ready sympathy, and his wise counsel.[1]

Gaspard wrote to Frank Meighen on 26 January 1922: '. . . The tributes of which you write are very satisfactory and I only wish we could rub them in the faces of those pernicious Grits who 40 years ago for their own base political purposes attacked your uncle and the CPR so savagely . . .' Of Gian he said: 'She has heard from your sister about coming to Canada; at present she says, no, impossible, but I do not think this is necessarily a final no . . .' On 7 April he told Frank: '. . . Mrs. Reford is spending this weekend with Gian at Brocket and I hope may finally persuade her to take the trip to Canada this year'. By 30 May he was telling him: 'Lady Mount Stephen is much looking forward to your visit and subsequent escort to Canada . . .' and on 4 July he wrote to Arthur Villiers:

[1] *The Times*, 1 December 1921.

'. . . Lady Mount Stephen sails for Canada on the 13th'. To Tuck he wrote on 30 August:

. . . Lady Mount Stephen was very much touched at the telegram she received from (Mrs. Tuck) just as she left for Canada. Lady Mount Stephen has written to me several times and is obviously enjoying herself enormously. She loved Metis, killed several salmon . . . She is now on her way to the Pacific Coast and I fancy should be at Banff today. The Company have given her a car, and Mrs. Reford and Frank Meighen have gone with her, so I expect she will have a royal time . . .

Wrote Queen Mary to Gian from Balmoral on 1 September 1922: '. . . I like to think of you at this moment travelling across Canada in the *C.P.R.*, the creation of your own dear one, such a marvellous construction which required so much courage and perseverance to carry through . . .'[1]

The parish of Mortlach in Banffshire has a religious history which goes back to pre-Christian times. In the sixth century A.D. came the foundation of St. Moluag; after the victory of Malcolm II over the Danes in 1010, of which the Battle Stone in the churchyard is a relic, the King, as a thankoffering, ordered that Mortlach Church should be extended by three spears' length, and that the parish should become a bishopric. (A century later King David I—a 'sair saint for the crown'—removed the bishopric to Aberdeen). The building has undergone other changes since, but still boasts three thirteenth century lancet windows. It has another, placed there by Gian Mount Stephen in memory of her husband, and containing possibly the only ecclesiastical manifestation in stained glass of a steam locomotive emerging from a tunnel. Facing it is a tablet commemorating 'the old warrior', Sir Donald Stewart. Here in this ancient place of worship, with its relics of both war and peace, Gian had asked that a memorial service should be held, simultaneously with the private funeral at Lemsford and with the memorial service at the Chapel Royal, St. James's in London, at noon on Saturday 3 December 1921.

Taking as his text the words in *Genesis*: 'Then Abraham gave up the ghost, and died in a good old age, an old man, and full of years, and was gathered to his people', the Rev. John Barr Cumming said:

The life we commemorate today is fitly described in words which were written of a brother man 37 centuries ago—so close is the tie that binds men together through the long years. When the child George Stephen first opened his eyes on that life he was to see so much of, the world was vastly different from what it is now. The successive decades as they came and went opened up new vistas and were the spoil of great minds who planned and grasped the opportunity. The Old World and the New World were both alike to such as he—the latter gave greater scope for the vision the former called into being, and the powers he possessed— resolution, courage, industry, integrity, concentration of mind and purpose, all of the highest order—were like the varied rays of the prism uniting and combining in the clear shining of stainless light. He was not hindered or handicapped in his upward climb to fame and fortune. What he touched, he grasped and mastered and made his own . . .

Speaking of the Canadian Pacific, he continued:

. . . Think of what it has done conveying our Scottish men and women to homes in the West, . . . As they went on, so they came back again in the day when the Motherland in peril called to her children—these sternfaced children of old Scotland came back to fight and to conquer and to die . . .

Now in days to come it may chance that some wise mind will rewrite the history of the nations, not making wars the milestones of progress, nor the warrior chief and brave soldier the sole hero, but rather marking the stages of man's upward ascent by the triumphs of invention and discovery and science, and noting the names of the men who planned them. When that is done, high on the role of fame will stand the names of those who sent great ships across the seas for food, who bound continents together by swift railways, and did these things to unite men, not to divide them. In that day, when that is done, shining afar as a bright particular star, will be the name of George Stephen . . .

This upland parish, resting on the shoulders of the everlasting hills, the boy with his books, his early dreams and ambitions, his farsightedness, his hard woık, his singlemindedness,—these were his till all that men covet was also his—wealth, position, honour, comfort, love—unspoiled through it all, loving the old home of his humbler days, and never refusing help, counsel, and sympathy to those who like him had dwelt here. That is his record. God rest him. He helped those in need for the Lord had helped him. He was a man, take him for all in all, we shall not look upon his like again . . .[1]

[1] *Dufftown News*, 10 December 1921.

Index

26

Hill, James Jerome—*contd.*
1897, discusses with Mount Stephen
and Farrer Eastern Minnesota issue,
q.v., 122; Farrer suggests applying for
G.N. share quotation in London before
announcing new distribution; G.N.
outlook promising: Farrer hopes Hill
can come to Metis, sees him there,
123; Farrer cables, writes urgently
on Eastern Minnesota issue, quotes
Mount Stephen's approval G.N. capital
increase scheme, rejects idea Deutsche
Bank act for them in London, 123–5;
Farrer quotes favourable Press comment on G.N. annual report and
Mount Stephen's approval, adds plea
Louis Hill be given more responsibility,
125–6; cables Farrer on Eastern issue,
hint of New York offer, 126; Farrer
recapitulates Eastern discussions to
Louis, presses Hill for action: answer,
127; sends Farrer G.N. figures, 127–8;
Farrer sends comments on Eastern
Minnesota Mortgage: recommends
issue mid-January; cable exchanges:
New York offers, 128–9; Kootenay
railway connection, 129; cables Mount
Stephen has sold Eastern issue in
New York, 129; appoints Louis assistant; imminent London visit, 130;
quoted by Farrer on co-operative
management G.N. and N.P., 130–1;
less influence than expected with N.P.,
131; Farrer supplies G.N. information
to *Economist* for article, commending
Hill's management, tells Hill Mount
Stephen thinks article worth circulating
to shareholders, 132; plans G.N.
rights issue Spring 1898: war with
Spain intervenes, 132–3; in London:
G.N. discussions, 134; his G.N. plans,
London visit, 135–6; Farrer writes,
136, 136*n*; to Mount Stephen on
Spokane Falls and Northern purchase,
137; London friends' response to
rights issue, 137–8; Farrer to Northcote
on Hill's high reputation, to Hill
declining railroad trip, hopes Hill to
visit in Spring, 138–9; London visit
Spring 1899, 139
  part in rescue of Baltimore and
Ohio, 146–9; accompanies Farrer to
England, 147; operation of G.N. praised
by Farrer, 149–51; gives Farrer and
Mount Stephen latest statistics, 150–1;
Farrer on Strathcona, 163–4; disappointed by results of his and
friends' participation in N.P. reorganization, 167–8; to Farrer on N.P.
annual report, 168; satisfactory reply

to Farrer's queries on recent developments to be sent to Mount Stephen,
169; disposal of N.P. holdings reported:
rumours unfounded, 170–1; Schiff
seeks approval of Oregon plans,
171–2; relations with Harriman emer-
gent factor; voyage with Schiff, 172;
Schiff on attempt to buy his Oregon
stock; Farrer optimistic on N.P., 173;
to Harriman on plan for harmony of
interests, 174–5, 176*n*; presses plan on
N.P., 175–6; Schiff comments on letter
to Harriman, 176–7; his Oregon plan:
Schiff writes of his and Harriman's
reactions; plans European visit; writes
Farrer, 178; in London and Paris;
Farrer briefs Mount Stephen on G.N.–
N.P. allegations: suggests present
degree of control of N.P., 179–80; in
Paris, corresponds with Farrer and
Mount Stephen on N.P. Bonds and
G.N. results and market; discussion
with Gwinner on N.P. control: Farrer
fears market reaction to dissolution of
voting trust, 181; visit from Farrer; N.P.
purchases; hints to Schiff will soon control N.P.; cryptic cable to Mount
Stephen, dissolution of voting trust;
allots N.P. shares to London friends,
182; family entertain Farrer at Christmas; non-committal call on Schiff in
New York; joins board of Erie Railroad,
183; Farrer offers further help on N.P.
voting control, 183–4; something else
on his mind: to Farrer on basic soundness of G.N., 184; Press campaign in
advance of new G.N. issue, 184–6; lack
of liaison with London, 186–7; question
of Chicago connection: Milwaukee
considered; appears to be going after
Burlington: Sterling confirms to Farrer,
187–8; cables Mount Stephen on
Burlington purchase-Farrer's measured
response, 188
  early discussion on possible purchase
of 'Q', 190; abortive attempt at 'Milwaukee'; reconsiders 'Q': Perkins
prepared to deal, but price high;
rejects Harriman overture; purchase
concluded, 191; writes Mount Stephen
justifying deal, 191–2; receives protest
from Schiff, 192–3; to Pacific coast;
earlier confidence in N.P. control;
return to New York: Union Pacific
buying N.P.; gets Morgan's to go
after N.P. Common, 193, 193*n*; conflicting evidence, 194*n*; compromise
solution: stands by Morgan: confidence
in friends, 195, 195*n*; cables London

428 *Index*

Mount Stephen, Lord—*contd.*
writes of visit to Windsor, of Hill in London, 232; Farrer writes on broadening financial base of N.S., 234; anxious to see James Norman Hill; Farrer sends latest list of N.S. shareholders, 235; Farrer writes of need for Revelstoke to see Hill about U.P. relations, 235*n*; involved in advance to G.N., 235–6; lends Brocket for honeymoon of Princess Alice, 236; gives another large donation to King's Fund, 236–9; reference to Queen Victoria's letter, 236*n*; reveals that Kennedy given fifth interest in St. P. M. & M., 237–8; King's Fund donation based on Argentine securities, 239; Sterling describes reactions in New York to Supreme Court's dismissal of N.S. appeal, 240–1; and reports Hill's plan as presented to meeting: Hill to write when free; Mount Stephen passes (?) Hill's criticism of Supreme Court judges to Prince of Wales; Sterling reports more details after Hill's second meeting, 241, 242; Clough asks Sterling for Mount Stephen's proxy; Mount Stephen keeps Prince of Wales informed, 242–3; confident about N.S. shares; cables Hill about St. Paul cable in *Times* (Harriman's petition to prevent *pro rata* distribution), 243; forwards Hill's reply for Prince of Wales, 243–4; hopes for dismissal of Harriman's petition; forwards confident cable from Farrer; bases confidence on value of property, 244; to Bigge on dividend delay (see 'Northern Securities Company'); advances King's Fund dividends, 245; interviews with Harriman in London, 246, 247–50; compares notes with Farrer; concludes Harriman far from confident of victory, 248–9; associated with Farrer in appeal to Hill for harmonious relationship with Harriman, 249–50; discussions at Barings on American railroad propositions, 252; his opinion on Hill–Harriman relations quoted by Farrer to J. N. Hill, 253; Farrer on importance of J. N. Hill seeing him, 253–4; Farrer thanks Harriman for explaining point of view to, 255; Hill's dividend plan adds to frustration of: Farrer asks opinion, 255–6; Farrer sends him Hill's cables; Tuck writes opinion of Hill plan; 'becomes daily more savage', 256; advance of dividends to King's Fund, 257; shows Farrer Sterling's letter on Harriman, 257–8; wife's illness, 258–9;

Farrer reports Hill's anxiety about unexplained buying of N.S.: implies Hill must expect trouble if no settlement with Harriman, 261; Farrer raises question of N.S. case being tried on its merits, 261–2; trusts favourable judgement be followed by Hill–Harriman agreement; satisfied friction could have been avoided, 262; incurs Farrer's disapproval by assuring Hill no need to fear N.P. sales on favourable N.S. decision: Farrer cables Hill united revised opinion, 264–5; on Hill replying stressing N.P. control as decisive factor both cable feared consequences of continued litigation and fighting; cable copied to Sterling, 265; message from Hill mentions large cash balance: confirmed by Sterling, 266; Farrer to Hill affirms co-operation of Mount Stephen, Strathcona and himself in 'any reasonable policy' but repeats argument for peace with neighbours, 266–7; Farrer associates him in opinion to Hill on N.S., 267–8, repeats their personal liking for Harriman but assures Hill of their loyalty, 268; sees Farrer: they agree their plain message has done Hill no harm; Hill writes on iron ore prospects, 269; writes ten page letter to Hill; Farrer explains to Sterling need to counter combative advice Hill gets: they would be content if he consulted Sterling, 269–70; Farrer to J. N. Hill on his and Mount Stephen's exchanges with Hill, 270; to Wolseleys on N.S., 271; Farrer and Ellis facetious over gift to King's Fund of Argentine Securities, 272–3; Farrer's similar comment to Hosmer on award of G.C.V.O.; at Windsor with King Edward VII: earlier refusal of award, 233; to Bigge on choice of Argentine bonds, 273–4; indignation at switching of Argentines: wants Finance Committee for King's Fund, 274; suggests names: anxious Fleming should be member; promises further donation when N.S. case settled, 274–5; Bigge to Prince of Wales on Mount Stephen's views on Fund; Finance Committee appointed; promised donation in form of G.N. shares: hopes Strathcona may follow suit, 275; to Bigge enclosing cutting for Prince and Princess of Wales on rise in G.N. shares and prospects for N.S., 275–6; advises Wolseleys on investments; tells Sterling Farrer free for Metis (contradicted); following Supreme

Index

442 *Index*

Wolseley, Sir Garnet—*contd.*

contacts with Sidney Glyns; attitude to Gian Mount Stephen, 145; Mount Stephen's management of investments; writes wife news of Mount Stephen baby, 152; stays with Alice Northcote, 152–3; early years of decline, 154–62; tuberculous gland: Frances' account, 154–5; relations with Lansdowne, 155, 155*n*; post-operative weakness, lunch with Mount Stephen, invited to Brocket, 155–6; social engagements: the clubs, 156–7; Hebridean cruise: memory failing, neck not healed, 157; at Brocket, 157–8; looks forward to retirement; dines with Mount Stephens; resignation offer not accepted; daughter's concern, 158; attitude to Frances, 158–9; attend's Stewart's funeral; dependence on Mount Stephen; distrust of Lansdowne, 159; enjoys Brocket visit; retirement postponed: dreads future, 160; retirement; 'Army Night' in House of Lords: confrontation with Lansdowne; Mount Stephen advises but chary of discussing debts, 161–2; Mount Stephen writes on investment of Frances' christening present, 161*n*

dedicates memoirs to Mount Stephen, 230; directorship with Union Castle Line; further neck trouble, failing memory, 231; writes on Frances' gardeners, 233; wife writes of Mount Stephen's letter on Northern Securities, *q.v.*, 271; wife on Mount Stephen's advice about N.S., 277; wife writes quoting Mount Stephen on N.S. dividends, 282; at Brocket: to Louisa on house-party and on Mount Stephen's gift to Frances, 287; loss of memory, 287–8; family estrangement: relations with Mount Stephen, 288; unhappy over Frances, 289; wife and daughter disagree over where Garnet ought to live, 289–90; relations with Frances deteriorate, 290–1; daughter criticises his doctor, 291; Mount Stephen writes Frances of parents' self-sufficiency, 292; cruising in Hebrides, confused about John McNeill and his island, 305–6; fantasy about Shah of Persia; Mount Stephen tells Frances parents prefer own company; discourages Frances, 306; Frances writes, is again rebuffed: Mount Stephen advises writing only to mother: latter excited over Garnet; Louisa scathing about Frances, 307; to Louisa: never wishes to see

Frances again, hopes she is not mentioned in Will, prefers Louisa makes any bequest, 307–8; Louisa on visit to Brocket and cordial reception: Mount Stephen reveals Frances' income; disapproves of Frances receiving dress from Lawrences; he and Louisa try to make Frances help former governess financially: Mount Stephen advises against: thinks Frances should stop writing to either parent, 308; lodges memorandum with new solicitor recording Frances' 'desertion' of parents; Mount Stephen reports parents well; Frances' birthday gift to him returned, 309; at Mentone, missing Louisa who is at Vichy, 335–6; last visit to Mount Stephens, 336; death at Mentone, 336–7; daughter's honours; Mount Stephen's depression at death of, 338

Wolseley, George, 337

Wolseley, Louisa (Lady Wolseley, Viscountess Wolseley), 1, 2, 3, 4, 7, 8, 9, 96, 97, 98, 99, 100, 102, 103, 104–5, 106, 107, 108, 109, 110, 112, 114, 115, 116, 139, 140, 143, 145, 152, 153, 155, 157, 159, 160, 161.
230, 231, 232–3, 271, 277, 282, 287–8, 289–92, 305–10, 335–8, 353, 390–1

Wolseley Papers (Hove, Sussex: *notes* prefixed W/P, LW/P), 1*n*, 3*n*, 4*n*, 5*n*, 6*n*, 7*n*, 8*n*, 9*n*, 96*n*, 97*n*, 98*n*, 99*n*, 101*n*, 102*n*, 103*n*, 104*n*, 105*n*, 106*n*, 107*n*, 108*n*, 109*n*, 110*n*, 112*n*, 114*n*, 115*n*, 116*n*, 140*n*, 152*n*, 153*n*, 155, 155*n*, 156*n*, 157*n*, 158*n*, 159*n*, 160*n*, 162*n*, 230*n*, 231*n*, 233*n*, 271*n*, 277*n*, 282*n*, 287*n*, 288*n*, 289*n*, 290*n*, 291*n*, 306*n*, 307*n*, 308*n*, 336*n*

Wolseley 'Ring', 2, 8, 97, 106, 110

Wolverton, Lady, 141

Wood, Sir Evelyn (General, Field Marshal), 106, 106*n*, 108

Woodlock, Thomas Francis, journalist (railroad editor *Wall Street Journal* 1895–1904; editor 1904–5), 216

Woodstock, Ontario, 30

Worcester Cathedral, 141

Wright and Davis railroad. See 'Duluth Mississippi and Northern Railroad'

Yale University, 43

Yankton, South Dakota, 53

York, Duchess of. See 'Queen Mary'

York, Duke of. See 'King George V'

York Cottage, Sandringham, 140, 298

Yorke, Henry F. R., 143, 293

Yorke, Lady Lilian, 293